Empire of Labor

Empire of Labor

HOW THE EAST INDIA COMPANY
COLONIZED HIRED WORK

Titas Chakraborty

UNIVERSITY OF CALIFORNIA PRESS

University of California Press
Oakland, California

© 2025 by Titas Chakraborty

All rights reserved.

Library of Congress Cataloging-in-Publication Data

Names: Chakraborty, Titas, author.
Title: Empire of labor : how the East India Company colonized hired work / Titas Chakraborty.
Description: Oakland, California : University of California Press, [2025] | Includes bibliographical references and index.
Identifiers: LCCN 2024030515 (print) | LCCN 2024030516 (ebook) | ISBN 9780520399631 (cloth) | ISBN 9780520399648 (paperback) | ISBN 9780520399662 (ebook)
Subjects: LCSH: East India Company. | Labor—India—Bengal—History—18th century.
Classification: LCC HD8684 .C43 2025 (print) | LCC HD8684 (ebook) | DDC 331.0954/1409033—dc23/eng/20241125
LC record available at https://lccn.loc.gov/2024030515
LC ebook record available at https://lccn.loc.gov/2024030516

34 33 32 31 30 29 28 27 26 25
10 9 8 7 6 5 4 3 2 1

*In memory of Binapani Chakraborty and
Shyama Chakraborty*

CONTENTS

List of Illustrations viii
Preface xi

Introduction 1

1 · *Beruniyās* of Bengal: Mobile Hired Work and the State in Seventeenth- and Early Eighteenth-Century Bengal 20

2 · "Quarrelsome Workers": Boatmen in the Early Eighteenth-Century Company State 64

3 · "I Would Rather Be the Foremost Prince of Any Lower Court": European Sailors and Soldiers in the Early Eighteenth-Century Company State 107

4 · "Less Than the Lowest Class of Laborers": Silk Reelers and the Company State, 1650–1779 148

5 · "Prisoner" of the Magistrate: Boatmen, European Sailors, and the Colonial Police, 1790–1817 186

Conclusion: A Colonial Rule over Labor 231

Glossary 241
Notes 245
Bibliography of Primary Sources 299
Index 305

ILLUSTRATIONS

FIGURES

1. Painting of Dutch trading headquarters at Hugli *36*
2. Detail from painting *37*
3. Lease document, 1733 *39*
4. Terracotta plaque of galley boat, Jor Bangla Temple *75*
5. Watercolor of large boat (*bajra*), 1799 *75*
6. Watercolor of large cargo boat (*ulak*), 1799 *76*
7. Watercolor of flat-bottomed cargo boat (*patella*), 1799 *77*
8. Watercolor of a small boat (*polwar*), 1799 *77*
9. Detail from terracotta plaque of *naukā vilās* motif, Dadhimadhav Temple *89*
10. Pencil sketch of Hugli *114*
11. Terracotta plaque of large European ship, Dadhimadhav Temple *116*
12. Graph of indebted deserters versus those with company credit *123*
13. Graph of average number of deserters for the years 1680–1760 *132*
14. Statue of the Jagadhātrī idol, with attendants, at the Amritalal Daw estate *138*
15. Close-up of statue of mounted European sentry guarding Jagadhātrī idol *138*
16. Handwritten template for boatmen's contract, 1805 *209*
17. Continuation of boatmen's contract, with *majhi*'s statement *210*
18. Contract of indenture, EIC army, 1770 *218*

MAPS

1. Seventeenth-century riverine route of the Patna fleet *68*
2. Eighteenth-century routes for riverine and coastal travel between Patna and Calcutta *69*

TABLE

1. Production in VOC's silk re-reeling unit at Kalikapur *157*

PREFACE

In the summer of 2012 shortly after I had started working on this book, the largest labor unrest in India's recent history shook the Manesar plant of Maruti Suzuki, the largest transnational automobile corporation in India. The violent confrontation between workers and supervisors on July 18, 2012, which led to the death of a human resources manager, was the culmination of the management's retaliation against the independent union workers had created earlier that year. Even though contract workers (labeled as "temporary") make up 75 percent of the workforce, earning a wage half that of permanent workers, substantial sections of both groups would consolidate their grievances to form a single union, a feat achieved only through years of difficult organizing. The contract workers, who are never considered "skilled," form the backbone of the workforce for manufacture-driven growth in Haryana state. In fact, such an overwhelming number of working-age men and women are funneled into temporary contract work that the state is now facing manpower shortages for even the few existing "skilled" jobs. In the meantime, these "unskilled" workers, along with their permanent colleagues at the Manesar plant, churn out a car every 50 seconds, 1,200 a day. Both permanent and contract workers reel under the crushing pressure of this work speed. After the 2012 altercation, the state government, under both the Congress Party and then the Bharatiya Janata Party, resolutely intervened on behalf of the transnational corporation—overnight the case ceased to one of labor dispute and instead became a case of murder, wherein the state bore all the charges for the legal proceedings and prosecuted the workers. In August 2012, the Manesar plant reopened in the presence of 1,500 policemen, who monitored work in the factory. The deputy commissioner of police, Maheswar Dayal, asserted that "the Maruti management has decided to stay on because of police presence." In 2017 a district court convicted thirty-one workers in the July 2012 incident, of which thirteen received life imprisonment. This judgment was the harbinger of the Indian government's labor codes issued in 2020, which raised the bar for forming unions, reduced legal access to aggrieved workers, and increased government control over unions, among other things.

The aftermath of the Manesar plant conflict, with its enormous significance in terms of the defeat suffered by the Indian labor movement, unfolded in Indian public life right at a time when I was putting together a story of how the English East India Company transformed a world of work in eighteenth-century Bengal. Much of the architecture of the labor discipline—police terror, deliberate de-skilling, and low wages—that the Manesar incident laid bare was reminiscent of EIC's many-faceted strategies for imposing control over a very unruly world of work in the early eighteenth-century Indian Ocean world. While these parallels became clear, what struck me most was the Haryana state-appointed special prosecutor's denunciation of the workers at the Manesar plant as traitors who had conspired against Prime Minister Narendra Modi's "Make in India, Make for World" initiative. The special prosecutor was not content with the district court's 2017 ruling and demanded death sentences for intractable "anti-national" workers. The irony of this righteous rage is twofold. First, and this might be obvious to many readers, is that "Make in India" facilitates conditions that allow transnational capital to thrive and tether Indian workers to the global supply chain. The second, and much less known and appreciated irony, is that Modi's hypernationalist slogan shrouds the colonial or "alien" roots of this much-touted nationalist culture of work. This book gets to the bottom of these roots.

This book was conceived as a doctoral dissertation at the University of Pittsburgh. I would like to first and foremost thank my advisor, Marcus Rediker, for putting trust in me. His enthusiasm and encouragement allowed me to carry on with my research across continents, even though I continually heard from multiple quarters that there is not enough material to be found for executing such a project. I also thank him for all the intellectual support for my researching a history from below in a non-European, colonial context. Patrick Manning remains an enormous source of support and I thank him for continually pointing out to me the many gains of this book. Michael Fisher's pithy comments were extremely useful during the initial revisions.

I have been extremely lucky to receive the advice and support of scholars from across the world. My teachers in Kolkata, especially Professors

Suchetana Chattopadhyay and Ratnabali Chatterjee, were very helpful at crucial moments in the design and research of this project. Their works have always been an inspiration. At Jadavpur University I was fortunate to get guidance from Saswata Bhattacharya and Satyabati Giri for sifting through middle Bengali literature of the fifteenth to nineteenth centuries. I also want to thank Nilanjana Patra and Sarmistha De for all their help at West Bengal State Archives. Mathias van Rossum has been an amazing friend and collaborator for all these years. Many conversations with him have helped me understand better the VOC world of work. Many thanks to Hugo S'Jacob for his generosity in teaching me the art of reading seventeenth-century Dutch manuscripts. Professors Jan Lucassen, Sanjay Subrahmanyam, Subho Basu, Cynthia Talbot, and Amiya Bagchi generously took time out of their busy schedules to read the manuscript. The work is much improved for their valuable comments. I would especially like to thank my not-so-anonymous readers, Professor Clare Anderson and Professor Indrani Chatterjee, for meticulously reading the manuscript and pushing me hard to bring out the best in the book. I also thank my other anonymous readers for their extremely helpful comments.

The research and writing of this book would not have been possible without the support of multiple institutions. Fellowships from the University of Pittsburgh and American Institute of Indian Studies allowed years of valuable archival research. My postdoctoral stint at the Institute for Historical Studies, University of Texas at Austin, provided valuable time and support for reconfiguring an otherwise very messy dissertation into a book. I am extremely grateful to Professors Madeleine Hsu and Sumit Guha for their support during my time there. I also thank Courtney Meador at IHS for every kind of help she provided.

At University of California Press I am extremely grateful for the support of Niels Hooper and Nora Becker. I especially thank Niels for believing in the significance of the story that this book tells. Niels and Nora have accommodated my many demands and queries and deftly shepherded this project to conclusion. I am also extremely thankful to Kathleen MacDougall for her meticulous copyediting.

At Duke Kunshan University I have been extremely lucky to receive unstinting support from my colleagues while I combined my work on completing this manuscript with my teaching and service responsibilities in an impossible situation of living across three countries and two continents throughout the pandemic years. I cherish most the encouraging comments on my work from James Miller, Sumathi Ramaswamy, Prasenjit Duara, Jay Winter, and Kolleen Guy.

My parents, Utpal and Gouri Chakraborty, have been my biggest source of strength. They have continually put their trust in a daughter who hardly ever did anything "normal." My father has always planned out the logistics for my impossible travel plans for research. My mother read too many *maṅgalkābyas* with me and spent nights laughing with me at all the nuggets of lewd asides in these eighteenth-century poetries. They took unusual joy in traveling with me to terracotta temples in various districts and silk reeling manufactories in Berhampore, Murshidabad. My grandmother, Binapani Chakraborty, and my aunt, my *piya*, Shyama Chakraborty, to both of whom this book is dedicated, have been proud of everything I did since I started elementary school. It is my misfortune that they did not live to see this book's publication. Jackie and Joseph Olsavsky have always offered a warm home in the US years after I left the country for work. I owe my greatest gratitude and thanks to Jesse Olsavsky. It is hard to describe in words the countless ways in which he has assisted me. While I am alert to the poet's caution, "Death will not correct a single line of verse, she is no proofreader, she is no sympathetic lady editor," Jesse has offered me and this book all the sympathy, patience, and diligence of a stellar lady editor.

Introduction

ON SEPTEMBER 20, 1921, labor leader N.M. Joshi introduced in the Legislative Assembly of British India a resolution to repeal the Workman's Breach of Contract Act (1859), as well as sections of the Indian Penal Code which made breach of contract a criminal offense. In that resolution, Joshi, later to become general secretary of the first trade union federation in India, the All India Trade Union Congress (AITUC), averred: "This kind of legislation namely, criminal liability for a breach of contract is, in my opinion, an inheritance from England. In England from time of Queen Elizabeth, there have been legislations putting all sorts of liabilities upon the poorer classes. And, when the English government and European merchants came there they brought that inheritance into India. I believe this kind of legislation, is *alien to the Indian sentiment.*"[1] The 1920s were a momentous period in organized labor politics in India, when a "working class" emerged as a political force in a nationalist, anticolonial struggle.[2] A sign of these turbulent times, Joshi's 1921 statement laid bare the colonial roots of India's modern labor relations. The earliest labor laws issued by the British empire in India were English or "alien" in provenance and ensured that "the employers should have a hold upon the workmen, that the workers should not be able to leave their masters." Joshi explicated the modernity of these laws: "it is a class legislation discriminating between class and class; it is an indentured system; it is slavery." Through these laws the English mercantile forces introduced an alien regime of work which, while breeding novel forms of servility peculiar to their Indian colony, also became the incubator of India's modern class relations. Over the years colonial labor legislation strengthened the arms of European and Indian employers and enabled the colonial magistracy to enforce "moral effect" (i.e., labor discipline) upon the Indian coolie.[3] By the early twentieth century these laws had defined the culture of work on Indian soil.

Historians of Indian labor have only partially addressed Joshi's observation about the historical relationship between colonialism and the Indian worker. There is now a significant body of scholarship which shows that the judicial construction of labor under colonial rule created various relations of servility.[4] This literature however does not probe Joshi's statement far enough to enquire about the circumstances under which the first colonial labor laws were introduced in India. How "alien" was colonial labor discipline to the Indian context?[5] What was the prior world of work? Histories of labor, as Dipesh Chakrabarty rightly alleges, often deploy the modern category of "labor" to generalize about "a whole host of words and practices with divergent and different associations." "Labor" subordinates divergent "life worlds" of work to the globalizing urges of capital. In Chakrabarty's schema, a "life world" dissociated from the universalizing impulse of capital can be reconstructed.[6] Joshi's insight sharpens as well as rectifies Chakrabarty's critique. In the first place, Joshi posits the British empire's intervention in shaping labor well before the late nineteenth-century Factory Laws. Second, Joshi signals the existence of a prior Indian world of work and intimates at a historical conjuncture when the Indian work experience was subjected to colonial labor legislation. While Chakrabarty apprises us of the "autonomy" of "life worlds," Joshi alerts us to the historical process which compromised this autonomy.

In picking up Joshi's trail, *Empire of Labor* examines the transitions in the experience of hired work and its relation to state-building under the English East India Company (EIC) in Bengal between 1651 and 1817. The company had to rely on unruly indigenous and European workers, who persistently and constantly ran away from employers when their demands were not met. Workers' demands, which drew upon noncapitalist perceptions of time and wages, rhythms of work, and customary privileges that animated the "life worlds" of both indigenous and European workers, often clashed with the interests of the European companies. Moreover, the EIC in Bengal confronted a world of fragmented political jurisdictions by rival indigenous and European employers, which further facilitated the ability of workers to voluntarily move between or away from employers and make their own demands. Focusing on indigenous boatmen and silk reelers as well as European sailors and soldiers, this book tells the story of how the EIC rose to power as the supreme political force in Bengal by controlling and curtailing the mobility of its workers—and how in the process, the EIC fundamentally transformed the experience of work. The story begins with the earliest accounts, from 1651, of the EIC's dealings with hired labor in the region. That was the year Bengal became an important node in the EIC's Asian trade following an order from the governor of Bengal, Shah Shuja, to relieve the EIC from payment of customs duty, substituting instead an annual, fixed payment of 3,000 rupees. The story ends by unraveling a long, arduous process between 1753 and 1817—involving extreme intercompany competition, restructuring of the silk industry, imposition of military and police power, and the introduction of draconian regulations—through which the EIC finally undermined the older customs of work. As a result, the power workers once had possessed to successfully make demands on their terms and conditions of work declined.

This long unraveling of "life worlds," *Empire of Labor* argues, ultimately reveals the genesis of the colonial modernity of India's labor relations. Partha Chatterjee characterizes colonial rule as a "rule of difference" premised on "the alienness of the ruling group" to the ruled.[7] Such a premise, over the course of two centuries, established legal racism and abetted European violence on a native population. Disciplining labor was part of this intricate "rule of difference." Such a rule for silk reelers was premised on what Edmund Burke described as "a system sacrificing the being of that country [Bengal] to the advantage of this [England]."[8] Bengal's peculiar subordinate position in the political economy of the British empire—a place for levying land revenues to finance England's accumulation and producing trade goods to augment British manufacturing interests—shaped the fate of the silk reeling industry. Reelers, as one of the lowest-paid workers, thus were products of the "colonial rule of difference." In contrast, the globalization or universalization of the home-bred Master and Servants Acts and Mutiny Acts determined the EIC state's relationship to boatmen and European sailors and soldiers. The metropolitan English police and magistracy provided the model for the surveillance system that was necessary to make these regulations effective in Bengal. England's working poor at home faced increasing police control of labor under the Master and Servants Act at the same time that boatmen and European sailors faced the EIC state's police and judicial system as an unprecedented form of discipline.[9] Yet, special statutes and not just regurgitation of old ones from England were needed in responses to local needs. After all, the EIC state in Bengal oversaw a world of work radically different from that in England. These new laws embedded boatmen within an expanding, militarized EIC state. For European sailors, new statutes instituted the Calcutta police as the scourge of wayward European workers, severing them from a past when they could easily slip into, and out of, an Asian world of work.

THE WORKERS

Empire of Labor focuses on hired workers—in particular indigenous boatmen, silk reelers, and European sailors and soldiers—whose changing relationship with the state reveals in hitherto unexplored ways what was specifically "colonial" about regimes of work under the EIC state. These workers labored to link the EIC's overseas commerce with the agrarian society of Bengal. The value of the EIC's annual Asian imports averaged between 1.25 and 2 million pounds sterling in the eighteenth century, of which trade in Bengal represented as much as half of the EIC's total trade in Asia, where a predominantly European crew moved commodities and bullion on intercontinental vessels between Bengal and Europe. While many of these sailors signed their contracts with the company in England, the EIC recruited a large number of them from among the runaways of their foremost rival in Bengal, the Dutch East India Company (VOC). Just like the EIC, the VOC had witnessed the value of its trade in Bengal soar from 150,534 florins in 1648–49 to more than 4.6 million florins in 1720–21. Much of this value was built on trade in raw silk. In the 1710s raw silk formed as much as 19 percent of the value of the total exports of the EIC from Bengal. During the same decade, raw silk formed almost 30 percent of the VOC's total exports from Bengal and 83 percent of total Asian silk sold in the Amsterdam market between 1697 and 1718.[10] Silk reelers from Kassimbazar, many of whom worked directly for the European companies—sometimes in the thousands—prepared the silk. They are the first documented contract workers in the Indian subcontinent working for commercial concerns. From the seventeenth century on, they worked from their homes or in European or indigenous manufactories to re-reel silk yarns bought from peasant producers, cleaning and standardizing them to fit them for sale in overseas markets. Commercial success went hand in glove with military gains. Since 1698, the VOC and the EIC maintained standing armies in their respective headquarters. These predominantly European-manned armies never exceeded 2,000 men in size and often utilized off-duty European sailors resting in anchored ships. The EIC also regularly hired deserters from rival European companies to keep its army going. With these armies both the VOC and EIC organized highly militarized inland fleets that moved people and commodities from their various settlements in the Bengal hinterland to their respective headquarters. Hundreds of boats with sometimes over a thousand boatmen moved these fleets. They performed a whole host of tasks from pilotage, rowing, and towing. Boatmen were of different kinds—sailing different kinds of vessels which at times they owned—and companies hired them for varying periods of time. Boatmen, silk reelers, and European sailors and soldiers worked for wages within the interstices of the eighteenth-century peasant economy and global commerce, domains that remain unstudied in labor histories.

Apart from these workers, who form the principal focus of this study, the book takes into account many other forms of hired work. As chapter 1 demonstrates, forms of hired work in Bengal were myriad. Consequently, the companies regularly hired from among the indigenous population porters, cartmen, peons, smiths, and carpenters as well as other hired workers contracted from Europe or other parts of Asia. These workers are discussed throughout this book. Moreover, a substantial number of women came from neighboring villages, often with their children, to work on construction sites where they received three-fourths the wage of a male construction worker, and their children half. However, unlike the boatmen, silk reelers, and European sailors and soldiers, none of these workers left behind a steady archival paper trail spanning centuries, which would provide the opportunity of tracing transformations and continuities in their respective realms of work.

Waged work as an evolving form of social relations is probably the least explored subject in Indian history. Such neglect renders inadequate the otherwise robust critique of the Asiatic Mode of Production (AMP), a model Karl Marx formulated in the 1850s and 1860s for understanding Indian society. While such a formulation allowed for the study of Indian society outside the paradigm of religion, it also conjured an idea of a "village community" bound by servile caste relations impervious to change and external to market-based commodity production.[11] Much of what we know of Indian society prior to the onset of colonial rule comes from putting the historical veracity of AMP under scrutiny.[12] Subsequent scholarship has also brought to the fore a new understanding of institutions considered central to Indian village society, such as caste.[13] For example, new studies on slavery have destabilized our long-standing assumptions about equating caste with slavery—slavery as an institution was not bound by caste and in fact could enable caste mobility.[14] Likewise, meticulous scholarship uncovering high levels of commercialization of precolonial Indian society has presented a very dynamic picture of village India.[15] One might wonder why, with the focus on high levels of commercialization, historians have not turned their attention more specifically to waged work. While there is widespread recognition that waged work emerged in the early first millennium C.E. within the stratified "village community," unlike the scholarship on slavery, research on precolonial forms of hired work is very limited and often couched in assumptions about caste servility.[16] Except for David Washbrook's important article, even those scholars who challenge these assumptions explain work within the framework of caste relations.[17] This book offers the first comprehensive analysis of hired work from the precolonial into the colonial periods in one region. It demonstrates that certain indigenous occupations involved the participation of multiple castes, and hence, collective action relied minimally on caste identities. Caste relations only partially ordained waged work. In the last instance, hired workers in the precolonial period were anything but servile.

Such conclusions with respect to hired work situate this book within a second important tryst of Indian historiography with Marx's AMP analysis. Though new findings against the grain of AMP have altered the premise of Indian historiography, historians have not come to any consensus regarding the essence of the AMP, specifically, that the historical trajectory of precolonial India was distinct from that of premodern or precapitalist Europe's. While affirming that high levels of commercialization indeed fortified hired work as a particularly important form of social relationship, *Empire of Labor* also asks, even if the *form* of waged or hired work was prevalent in both India and Europe for over a millennium, how did the *nature* of hired work differ in each place? In other words, commercialization in different parts of the world did not give rise necessarily to the same experience. The precinct of the Mughal province of Bengal played an important role in a differential appreciation of waged work for the EIC and its workers. Instead of locating difference in "caste servility," this book situates difference in the relative lack of servility in hired work in precolonial India when compared to contemporary Europe—a divergence that was later impounded by colonial state building.

In order to document this divergence, the study of European workers as part of the global workforce in company settlements and the larger workforce of hired workers in Bengal becomes imperative to this book. Studies on the Portuguese empire in India have shown the various trajectories of lower-class Portuguese in India, occupying a unique liminal identity between Europeanness and indigeneity.[18] Yet, rarely have historians studied European workers of the European companies alongside workers indigenous to the

Indian subcontinent.[19] Much has been written on the European sailors and soldiers in Europe and in the Americas and on Indian soldiers and sailors in India and the wider British empire.[20] Those relatively few studies which have considered the subjecthood of European sailors and soldiers in the British empire in India have explicated the role race and class played in institutionalizing imperial identities of difference.[21] Even though this scholarship has revealed the presence of a vast number of "poor Europeans," it stops short of comprehending them as "workers." In not doing so, this otherwise rich scholarship unwittingly accepts the rule of difference of the British empire as a naturalized order beyond inquiry.[22] Workers of European origins too participated in the world of waged work in Bengal and, contrary to being different, their experiences at least until the early nineteenth century bear striking resonances with those of other hired workers in the region. Alessandro Stanziani rightly intuited that the coercive and unfree nature of work in the Indian Ocean world was built on the British state's long history of employing wage earners, especially sailors, as patently unfree workers. Yet, Stanziani could not conceive of the English or European sailors as part of Asian world of work.[23] The lacuna in perceiving European workers as part of the Asian labor market precludes any examination of how the same set of workers experienced waged work differently in Europe and in Bengal. That these workers, unlike in Europe, could re-evaluate their worth in Bengal and could determine terms and conditions of their hire like other workers in the region is of enormous significance to drawing a comparison of "servility" or lack of it in Bengal and in Europe for much of the eighteenth century. Additionally, this erasure fails to notice that in its struggle to discipline the infractions of European soldiers and sailors, the EIC anticipated the methods later used to extend control over indigenous hired workers, such as boatmen. As workers rooted in both Europe and Asia, the experiences of European sailors and soldiers lend comprehension to the divergence of hired work as a social relation between Europe and Bengal.

Acknowledgement of this divergence is necessary to launch a trenchant critique of "free" waged work as a uniquely European experience—a claim that labor historians have strongly debunked by showing that waged work was a "fiction of free labor" in all parts of the world including Europe and colonial India.[24] Yet, the critique remains incomplete especially when scholarly synthesis of labor in the Indian Ocean world solely emphasizes servility with dual roots in European imperial designs as well as in "Asian forms of slavery."[25] Without reckoning with the unique world of work in precolonial

India, wherein hired workers, including European rank-and-file workers of the East India companies, enjoyed the relative "freedom" of determining their terms of hire as opposed to customary practices in Europe, shibboleths of Asian servility are continually resurrected. Aside from this iconoclasm, *Empire of Labor* sets out to retrain our focus on colonial governance as the technology of power that tore down "life worlds" of work globally and erected in their ruins a specific culture of work built on the "fiction of free labor."

In order to maintain focus, the book discusses only those sectors of work which were based purely on wage relations. Weavers, who seldom worked for a hired wage, especially in the early eighteenth century, have attracted the most attention from historians. The centrality of textiles (both silk and cotton) in the value of Bengal's long-distance trade and the decline of textile production is at the heart of the longest standing debate in Indian economic history, dating back to the nineteenth century—that is, de-industrialization.[26] Yet weavers were only one small albeit significant segment of the workforce engaged in Bengal's commercial activities. Much more numerous were the hired workers who labored in urban or peri-urban settings in the seventeenth and eighteenth centuries. Beside hired work and semi-independent artisanal work, the settlements of the VOC and EIC became crucibles of a peculiar form of household slavery that linked Bengal with other nodes of European company settlements in the Indian Ocean world where company servants bought many of their slaves from. Women formed a substantial majority of this workforce. As I have shown elsewhere, until the mid-eighteenth century, household workers, unlike other workers, even a substantial majority of those who worked for a hired wage, had their roots in slavery. The major change in household work during the period covered in this book is demographic: for the period before 1770, most of these workers came from various outposts of the Indian Ocean world as slaves and when manumitted entered the Free Christian and Portuguese population of the settlement. For the period beginning after 1770 the Indian subcontinent became the hinterland for slaves.[27] While large numbers of local women took up household work for hire in the second half of the eighteenth century, slavery remained an important source of workers for care work. Histories of neither household workers nor weavers can lend clarity to the changing nature of hired work from the eighteenth century into the early nineteenth century.

Despite their enormous relevance to the single most important debate on India's trajectory from premodernity to modernity, why haven't historians studied these workers or waged labor generally over the eighteenth century? While conceptual blinders as discussed above provide some answers, others might be found in the difficulty of recounting experiences of workers who navigated a plural, polyglot world. Thus, though new histories of labor have increasingly brought to light workers and workplaces outside of industrial shop floors and agrarian production, they rarely venture outside the realm of the nineteenth-century EIC state and its archives to find illuminating examples of the changing world of work.[28] Dependence on English language sources has created a two-fold problem. First, inordinate focus on the colonial archives of the EIC hinders comprehension of an indigenous world of work. The use of indigenous sources alongside multiple European sources is necessary to reconstruct the world of work in the eighteenth century going beyond colonial historicity. Second, sole use of English language sources precludes the possibility of excavating the multiple political and economic jurisdictions that for the much of the eighteenth century crisscrossed Bengal. Just as workers did, it behooves the researcher to navigate this complex political and socioeconomic milieu with its variegated repositories of knowledge.

This study has explored a few of these repositories in three languages, including the archives of two rival companies, the EIC and VOC, and middle Bengali literary sources. Company archives of the EIC and VOC are extremely heterogenous. They include better-known sources such as the *Overgekomen Brieven en Papieren* (OBP) series of the VOC, the letters sent from Asian settlements of the VOC to the Dutch Republic, and various proceedings of the EIC and its ever-burgeoning institutions especially after the 1770s. Of the OBP series the most overlooked parts are the various attachments that the Hugli council sent to Batavia. This book utilizes a plethora of such attachments. Among lesser-used sources are the various Factory Records of EIC factories located within Bengal and the almost unused judicial records of the Mayor's Court and the Court of Oyer and Terminer and Gaol Delivery in Calcutta. Judicial records of both the VOC and EIC—including papers of their various courts through the eighteenth into the nineteenth century—form an important base of sources for this book. Of these, some, such as the judicial records of the VOC directorate in Bengal, have never been used before. Other completely unused archives include private and family papers of various lesser-known company officials such as Samuel Radermacher, George Lodewijk Vernet, and George Vansittart. All details of archival collections including private collections are given in the bibliography of primary sources and cited in the notes. Various company officials published accounts of their time in Bengal and the East; some are well known such as the accounts of Captain Alexander Hamilton, and others are strangers to historians such as the accounts of the seasoned English common seaman Edward Barlow or the shipmates of the capsized VOC ship *Ter Schelling*, who participated in the Mughal expedition of Assam in 1662–63. Thus, company archives encompass disparate repositories kept by institutions, officials, and plebian servants of the companies. Vernacular literary and oral sources—didactic religious poems (*maṅgalkābyas*) and Eastern Bengali ballads (*Pūrbabaṅga Gītikā*)—have been especially necessary for comprehending state functions within the multiple layers of societal hierarchy and dependency typical of seventeenth- and eighteenth-century South Asia that workers navigated. These sources and how they allow us to refine our understanding of company archives are further detailed in chapter 1.

STATES AND WORKERS

The workers discussed in this book moved within the Mughal provinces of Bengal and Bihar, a political geography enmeshed in multiple jurisdictions. The borders between these provinces were never very firm, and in 1733, the Mughal emperor Muhammad Shāh placed the rule of Bihar under the *subahdari* (governorship) of Shujauddin Khan, then governor of Bengal. Regional power politics, instead of creating politically hermetic entities, enabled larger cultural or economic formations.[29] One hallmark of this fluid regional power politics was the assertiveness and relative autonomy of *zamīndārs*, lower-level bureaucrats of Mughal imperial government with hereditary rights of revenue collection and governance. As the Mughal and later, the Mughal Nawabi state, shared governance with *zamīndārs*, demarcations of legal jurisdictions often remained hazy and contested. Such contestation was heightened because Mughal imperial power was predicated on the allegiance of the *zamīndārs* and hence the imperial state was always suspicious of betrayal. Since the social origins of *zamīndārs* were varied and numerous, European companies including the VOC and EIC could enter this political fray as *zamīndārs* themselves. The EIC secured *zamīndāri* rights over three villages in lower Bengal from the Mughal emperor 'Alamgir in 1698. As *zamīndārs*, the companies governed the mobility practices of their hired workers, many of whom were their subjects. There was also a separate and significant source of their governance—the charter that the EIC received from the English crown which vested in the company all forms of state power in Asian lands. The conjoined state power derived from these separate provenances determined the nature of the EIC's sovereignty, including their power to discipline their workers. Even though in recent years Philip Stern has reminded us that the EIC was a "body politic" going beyond the pre- and post-Plassey divide, labor historians have not yet studied the implication of such statehood.[30] This book, for the first time, examines how the EIC's relationship with its hired workers was premised on its evolution as a state power in relation to the English crown and Parliament, the Mughal and Nawabi states, and the neighboring *zamīndāris* from the seventeenth century. Since the EIC became exclusively a state entity only in 1813, its evolution as an employer is also a story of its evolution as a state.

The physical movement of hired workers magnified the uncertainties of the EIC state's sovereignty. Within the porous political geography of Bengal, imperial Mughal and Nawabi authorities always held sway over the subject workers of the EIC. Moreover, as the Bengal hinterland of the EIC's operation was vast, the hired workers of the company moved through territories which were under the jurisdictions of other, rival *zamīndārs*. To complicate matters further, many hired workers came from other *zamīndāris* or imperial urban centers where the EIC state had little power. Such was the case with workers hired in the prominent cities of Patna, Kassimbazar, and Dhaka. These were major political and economic centers with a population of over 200,000 each. Long established as important nodes of the global textile trade, these cities harbored merchants from all parts of the world including the European companies. The conurbation of Maksudabad-Kassimbazar-Murshidabad is especially important for this study because from this extended urban area the companies regularly hired thousands of silk reelers to prepare raw silk for export. Maksudabad, named after the legendary merchant Maksus Khan, developed as an important merchant town by the middle of the seventeenth century. Later, Murshid Quli Khan, the Dīwān (chief revenue officer) of Bengal, set up the center for his Dīwāni at Maksudabad. When he became the governor of Bengal, he declared the place—now renamed Murshidabad—as his capital. Six miles away from Maksudabad, the European companies in the 1650s and 1660s set up their factories, centering them around Kassimbazar.[31] The region had long been known as the production center for high-quality silk yarns. Both the EIC and VOC built impressive silk reeling units which employed a large number of reelers to do the finishing work on silk yarns. The VOC's reeling unit was located in a village,

Kalikapur, adjacent to Kassimbazar. The strong presence of Mughal imperial officials in these cities eclipsed the power of governance by mercantile *zamīndārs* such as the VOC or EIC. Workers were hired or often moved to places where the EIC's jurisdictional reach remained weak or absent.

The substance of EIC's state power transformed greatly beginning in the 1750s; aggrandized state power offered unique means of governing hired workers. From being one of the many mercantile *zamīndārs* in the region, the EIC made steady inroads into Mughal imperial power, gaining revenue collecting rights over entire *parganas* and finally by 1765 over the provinces of Bengal, Bihar, and Orissa. For contemporaries in both England and Bengal the 1750s were revolutionary, witnessing worldwide crisis and the restructuring of empires—"global imperial revolutions."[32] Amid this tumult, as India became a theater for the global Austrian war of succession and then the Seven Years War, the EIC army saw major reforms under the guidance of the military officer and future EIC governor of Bengal, Robert Clive. One of the reforms was the subjection of the EIC army to the English Articles of War, which ruthlessly dealt with deserters, often through capital punishment. As the military reforms bore fruit, leading to the EIC army's serial victories against its European and Indian adversaries, the EIC could increasingly monopolize military labor by restricting European common soldiers from switching allegiances and finding employ in the armies of rivals, a practice to which they had long been accustomed. Such monopolistic control over labor also extended to the silk reeling industry. In the 1750s and 1760s the EIC expanded its commercial production of raw silk by first combining terror and better wages to induce reelers to desert other merchants and work exclusively for the EIC, and then by introducing new technology. As the EIC introduced new Piedmontese filature technology in reeling, their reliance on the techniques of local reelers rapidly waned. For both European soldiers and silk reelers the EIC's expanded rule came as a decisive rupture from their long-standing culture of independently finding employers and negotiating conditions of work including time and wages.

This rupture allows us to rethink the EIC state's intervention in modes of governance in the Indian subcontinent. Historians have long debated the impact of Clive's tremendous victories at Plassey and Buxar on Bengal's society and politics.[33] EIC officials and their interlocutor in the British parliament debated ways of resuscitating "a usable ancient constitution in Bengal," that is, appropriate forms of governance rooted in the culture of a foreign milieu.[34] As the mantle of the Dīwanī fell into the hands of the EIC, the EIC state continually recalibrated the institution according to its unique ideas of governance and needs in order to make the most of this windfall. Faced with this riddle of transfer of power, certain historians have claimed that the EIC state was a complete handiwork of sub-imperialist forces learning from and building upon the tendencies of eighteenth-century subcontinental statecraft in the aftermath of the decline of the Mughal state.[35] Others have demurred, pointing instead to the metropolitan and ideological origins of EIC's governance in Bengal.[36] Introduction of the Mutiny Acts is one such clear instance of the metropolitan root of governance creating a major breach in the culture of military labor in Bengal. These acts put European rank and file in Bengal through the gauntlet of a regulated, sharply hierarchical, and unsparing military discipline long before the EIC subjected the Indian *sipahi* to a new regime of discipline.[37] Reelers encountered the weight of EIC governance both in the realms of market and production as the EIC restructured the industry, its workers, and their relationship to the state. The silk reelers' occupation and position in Bengali society was intimately related to high levels of commercialization in early eighteenth-century Bengal—much like the process of commercialization in the upper Gangetic plains—which affected various segments of society and economy, as all recent histories of EIC's intervention in eighteenth-century commerce of Bengal show.[38] Yet scholars are at variance regarding the transformative role of the EIC state's violence on Bengal's commerce, state-market relations, and mercantile behavior as a socially embedded practice.[39] Force, as this book shows, hamstrung reelers' access to the market while new technology made them dispensable to EIC state's plan of expansion of the silk reeling industry. Additionally, like other manufacturers such as weavers they found themselves in a situation unprecedented in the region or elsewhere in the world—with their wages wedded to the revenue needs of the state.[40] The increase and then collapse in their wages testifies to their experience of the discipline imposed on them as both a worker and a revenue-paying subject.

Even more hired workers lost their practice of mobility as a negotiating tool when the EIC instituted a novel and singular rule of law beginning in the 1790s. After 1784, the British Parliament, with its increased supervisory power over company rule in Bengal, sent Governor General Lord Cornwallis to Bengal with the express intent of introducing "a new order of things, which should have for its foundation a security of individual property, and administration of justice, civil and criminal."[41] The reforms entailed, first, *zamīndārs* becoming absolute proprietors of their land holdings, but second, the implementation of a new "impersonal law system" which stripped *zamīndārs* of their judicial and law enforcement powers, instituting in each district a judge and a magistrate. Cornwallis thus inaugurated a uniform, centralized rule, removing all the competing and overlapping jurisdictions that had been the distinctive feature of state formation in the region.[42] A centralized police force under the magistrates emerged as the chief recruiter of workers for the state, especially boatmen and European sailors. A series of regulations issued in 1806, 1816, and 1817 criminalized breach of contract, the practice of desertion, and strengthened magistrates' power to surveil all movements of European sailors and boatmen. These regulations were modeled after statutes that the English state had been issuing for four centuries to discipline, among other things, the mobility practices of their artisans, laborers, servants, sailors, and soldiers. These "grotesquely terroristic laws," as Marx characterized them, aimed at imposing "the discipline necessary for the system of wage labor" under the aegis of capital.[43] New studies of labor have shown that the EIC state issued these labor regulations at a frenzied pace from the 1750s onwards, first centering on the presidency towns and then the provinces. Nonetheless, following the rich historiography on labor regulations in the early nineteenth century, these studies treat regulations as the harbingers of new forms of discipline.[44] This book shows, on the contrary, that regulations followed or only formalized state practices in controlling workers that had emerged well before the regulations were drafted. Police violence was already a standard practice in the recruitment of boatmen, European sailors, and soldiers by the 1790s, decades before the regulations of 1806, 1816, and 1817 were passed. Thus, it was not just the men in the upper echelons of the EIC, such as the parliamentarian and head of the Law Commission Thomas Babbington Macaulay, who were responsible for creating a rule of law but also lesser police administrators like James Wintle, the magistrate of Bhagalpur—with a reputation as a ruthless but efficient recruiter of boatmen for the state—who were responsible for designing the regulation that criminalized boatmen's desertion.

Centralized governance cemented hired work within a very narrow continuum of free and unfree labor. Generations of historians have shown that the age of British imperial abolition of slavery of the early nineteenth century saw an efflorescence of new forms of labor such as indentured servitude and convict labor, which not only ensured a larger share of British access to labor markets in Asia but also in more ways than one blurred the distinction between slavery and freedom. Thus in the 1810s, imperial projects such as the citadel of St. Louis in Mauritius had government- and privately owned slaves, liberated Africans, Indian convicts, locally convicted prisoners, as well as corvee laborers working next to each other, thereby displaying the variegated conglomeration of unfree labor forms that the British imperial project could command from all corners of the world. Waged work in early nineteenth-century colonial Bengal, as this book demonstrates, does not contrast with this conglomeration of unfreedom but rather exemplifies its similarity as an apotheosis of colonial rule's continuum of free and unfree labor. Hired work within the European empire-building process was always tethered to convict labor. From the very inception of its empire in Asia, the VOC utilized convict labor to discipline the segment of its workforce who were working for a wage, as was the practice throughout the early nineteenth-century British empire. For sure, the concerns of labor were not the only basis for penal transportation and labor. Nonetheless, resolutions for the labor needs of an expanding empire seamlessly fit into other concerns of imperial governance such as implementation of what was perceived as a civilized form of punishment, the weakening of political networks that threatened imperial stability, not to mention curation of the racial character of colonial possessions on a global scale. Similarly, this grand scheme of imperial governance necessitated state intervention through the use of convict labor and criminalization of desertion, often on pain of penal labor, to define the contours of hired work. Unsurprisingly, the magistrate and the police force were the key institutions of the colonial state in allocating and governing both convict and hired workers. The hand of the state in defining hired labor is most visible in public works projects where the state via its police force directly pressurized the revenue-yielding landed proprietors, *zamīndārs*, into supplying all forms of formally unfree labor, such as convicts and corvee workers, alongside a large number of impressed hired workers. including boatmen working below the market rate.[45] Thus, working under the threat of penal labor as well as alongside penal laborers, the meaning of hired work as a form of "free" labor readily diminished.

FLIGHT AND THE CULTURE OF WORK

This book examines hired workers' practice of running away from work in the long term. Historians of South Asia have studied flight among peasants and artisans, exploring to what extent flight constituted a form of protest. This book moves away from the framework of "resistance" and instead reveals flight to be an integral part of the political culture of precolonial South Asia.[46] Indeed, flight mirrors the divergence of the culture of hired work in Bengal from the European experience. As an agrarian frontier, Bengal witnessed a rapid demographic shift through the extension of settled peasant cultivation.[47] All Mughal and Nawabi political forces, especially the revenue-collecting officials—the *zamīndārs* and *ta'alluqdārs*—were involved in this process of settling in migrant peasants or forest populations, as indigenous Bengali sources make amply clear. The constant flight of peasants was an outgrowth of this process. Hired workers, just like the peasants, had "a thousand countries to go to," and hence their employers, including European companies, had to accommodate their customary practice.[48] Through flight, workers articulated their sense of the "just" and the "right"—the "just" wage, the "right" technique, the "just" demeanor, and the "right" time. Flight in early eighteenth-century Bengal was akin to "disobedience," a form of political practice which emerged in modern Europe, in Raffaele Laudani's words, as a "second level obedience" as well as a form of legitimate dissent but one which necessarily did not have any revolutionary potential.[49] Moreover, flight could challenge state power but also alternatively bolster it, as the silk reelers' mass desertion from the VOC to the EIC did for the EIC state in the 1750s.

Yet, by the early decades of the nineteenth century the EIC state had declared all forms of flight from work to be unlawful, a measure which served to impose a new culture of work. Flight constituted the crux of criminal breach of contract. European sailors and soldiers were the first to bear the brunt, an experience that became generalized as the "culture of work" by 1860, as the Workman's Breach of Contract Act (1859) and sections 490–493 of the Indian Penal Code of 1860 show. When he was designing the "symmetrical" penal code, the greatest gift of the British empire to India, Thomas Babington Macaulay as the head of the Law Commission hesitated to make breach of contract a criminal offense, because the shadow of slavery loomed large in such provisions in an era of abolitionism.[50] Yet, the Law Commission decided to make "exceptions," targeting this exceptional law at those contract breakers "from whom it is exceedingly improbable that any damages can be obtained," thus making clear that the intent of the law was to discipline the laboring poor.[51] Even in the post-1870s' climate, when the followers of legal theorist Henry Maine made much noise about restoring and preserving "Indian customs," these laws never came under scrutiny.[52] So ingrained was the discipline enshrined in these laws that three years after their repeal, workers leaving the premises of tea plantations still feared they would be labeled "absconders."[53] In 1921, on the floor of the Indian Legislative Assembly, N.M. Joshi reminded lawmakers of the "alien nature" of this imposed culture of labor.

Attentive to divergences in the experiences of hired work in Europe and Bengal, and under Mughal/Nawabi rule and the centralized EIC state, discussion of customs of hired work is central to this book. In South Asian historiography the term "custom" emerges as a discursive category that the British colonial state deployed in shaping the contours of the episteme of Indian indigeneity.[54] As Nicholas Dirks notes, both Governor General Warren Hastings and British member of the House of Commons Edmund Burke, even though antagonists, "introduced the notion that tradition could be useful for rule."[55] Thus, "conservation of Indian customs" became imperial rhetoric at various phases of British colonial rule in India. Even Utilitarians, who otherwise believed in reforming Indian society, paid lip service to this ideal.[56] Scholarly works on hired and/or waged labor in India too have discussed the role of custom—specifically, the colonial and postcolonial state's reluctance to remove older and often oppressive precolonial customs from the economic sphere.[57] Critics of this approach have laid emphasis on the dependence of modern capitalist accumulation on "archaic" relations not specific to capitalism, without putting to the test the historical veracity of the "archaic" nature of these customs or relations.[58] These histories are not adequately sensitive to the potency of the ideological construct of "tradition" in sustaining colonial rule in India. As Dirks correctly observes, "The British displaced their own politics into such domains as custom and tradition, simultaneously endowing them with new meanings and applications, and absolving themselves from the recognition that power was being deployed by them rather than by the fixity of the hold of the past, seen as custom or tradition rather than history."[59]

Empire of Labor historicizes colonial semantics of custom by tracing the shifting registers of hired workers' customary practices that the EIC state consciously reckoned with, beginning from the mid-seventeenth century.[60] It unearths those customs of work, which were completely erased from the late eighteenth-century official discussions on Indian customs. Thus, while both the EIC and VOC recorded the "custom" of paying "honorarium" to boatmen in the early eighteenth century, any understanding of the "nature" of boatmen or their customary labor practices in India had disappeared by the later half of that century. While some customary labor practices were completely forgotten, others were reformulated. For instance, the boatmen's custom of carrying salt on board figured only in the discourse on the legality/illegality of salt trading. By the late nineteenth century all discussions of customs of labor emphasized the servile nature of the Indian worker stooping to the "traditional" authority of the *sirdar* and *kangani*. EIC records from the early eighteenth century on hard negotiations with workers without the presence of any intermediary confirm the amnesia of late nineteenth-century colonial officials in constructing this discourse on native servility. Juxtaposed with this obliviousness to past reckonings was the denial of certain practices as customs. The common practice among European sailors and soldiers to switch employers once they reached Bengal, or even the propensity among indigenous armies to hire European common soldiers or sailors as artillery men for much higher wages, never constituted "custom" in the language of EIC officials. These elisions not only reflect the discursive blinders of the colonial state's understanding of custom and the worker, but also its total foreclosure on any practice that amounted to encroachment by the worker on the state's power to regulate labor.

The book follows a chronological order. Chapter 1 provides a detailed picture of many forms of the relationship between hired work and the state as extant in seventeenth- and early eighteenth-century Bengal. The primacy of mobile hired labor and *zamīndāri* jurisdictions were the defining elements of the social, political, and cultural life of seventeenth- and eighteenth-century Bengal. The EIC, like its major counterpart the VOC, entered this world as *zamīndārs*. Even as *zamīndārs* and merchants engaged in organizing multiple forms of hired work, they faced many problems in controlling their workforce. The problems in controlling the mobility of their workers stemmed from the limited and contested jurisdiction of *zamīndārs* over their workers. The culture of hired work in Bengal that emerged in this milieu was one where the employer and the employee were bound in a reciprocal patron-client relationship. Chapter 2 elaborates on the work of boatmen in the massive fleets of the East India companies. It explains the place of the boatmen in the sociocultural world of eighteenth-century Bengal and how that shaped the various terms and conditions of hire. Manifold customs of the boatmen and the weak and limited jurisdiction of the EIC state over them prevented the EIC from introducing a cohesive order of cooperation. Chapter 3 examines the lives of European sailors and soldiers in Bengal from the seventeenth century well into the 1760s. Through desertion these workers created a second recruitment ground in Bengal where all the East India companies as well as the various landed elites and the Mughal/Nawabi forces competed to hire them. Though the EIC struggled for much of the eighteenth century to take advantage of the situation, they succeeded in making significant changes only in the 1750s. In 1759–60, they routed their chief competitor, the VOC, forcing them to reduce drastically the size of their military. Simultaneously the EIC introduced stringent discipline in its armies, heavily cracking down on desertion of its rank-and-file European soldiers. Chapter 4 turns to silk reelers. As workers silk reelers were unique because they worked in manufactories for commercial purposes from the seventeenth century on. Despite their resemblance to modern factory workers, reelers obstinately held onto their choice over mobility and work hours. This obstinacy prevented the European companies from expanding silk production in Asia. As the EIC in 1750s subdued one after another all its competitors, they used force as well as lucrative wages to monopolize the labor of the reelers. A decade later when the EIC introduced new technology from Europe to expand its silk production in Bengal they no longer relied on the skills of the indigenous reelers for the expansion of raw silk production. The wages of the reelers collapsed and their practices, especially mobility, were of very little consequence to the EIC's raw silk production. Chapter 5 discusses how the EIC state between the 1790s and 1810s drastically transformed the recruitment of boatmen and European sailors and soldiers with a centralized law and order administration. The centralized police administration of the EIC conjoined the local police force to the needs of the EIC's military and ship captains as well as independent travelers and private ship captains. This unified, centralized rule was unprecedented in the region. The police force as successful recruiter shaped regulations as well as enforced regulations. The rule of the police and the regulations of the EIC state effectively circumvented the autonomous mobility of boatmen and European sailors and soldiers. Their ability to shape the wages and customs of work, including labor time through desertion, were reduced drastically.

ONE

Beruniyās of Bengal

MOBILE HIRED WORK AND THE STATE IN
SEVENTEENTH- AND EARLY EIGHTEENTH-CENTURY
BENGAL

ACCORDING TO LEGEND, BIR HAMBIR (1565–1620), the greatest of the Malla kings, the *zamīndār* of Bishnupur, and an ardent patron of Gaudiya Vaishnavism, raised the deity Madan Mohan out of poverty. The deity had visited Bir Hambir in dreams and recounted the misery of his situation in the house of an impoverished Brahmin who could not provide for him. The next day, Bir Hambir searched for Madan Mohan high and low and found him in a house of a destitute Brahmin in the neighboring *zamīndāri* of Birbhum. He draped the idol of Madan Mohan in a shawl, and brought it to Bishnupur.[1] The ambulatory practices of the indigent migrant deity Madan Mohan can be seen in the spatial and ritual practices of the Vaishnava temples of Bishnupur, built primarily in the seventeenth century. There is no fixed sanctum for the deity in these temples. Consequently, temple priests carry the resident idol from the sanctum in the lower level of the temple to the upper level or to the edge of a plinth so that it can actively participate in the festivities of the devotees. Physical movement was central to the history and modes of worship in Bengal Vaishnavism—a widespread religious movement which defined much of the popular culture of medieval Bengal. An important event in the biographies of Chaitanya, the central figure of the movement, is his procession in the town of Nadia, an urban settlement on the banks of Bhagirathi. On this journey, Chaitanya and his devotees broke caste taboos and ridiculed the intellectual rigors of Brahmins; the procession continued even when the state-appointed judge of the town, the *qāzī*, ruled that the marchers should stay away from the streets of Nadia.[2] It was in their very mobility—and their defying of the state—that devotees experienced divine love for Kṛiṣṇa. Among other things, these idols, the legend of Madan Mohan, and the procession episode from Chaitanya's biography are a memorial to the itinerant poor and their relationship to the *zamīndār* in late medieval Bengal.

The representations of mobility in the rituals, legends, histories, and iconography of Madan Mohan and Chaitanya also capture a paradox inherent in the socioeconomic and political life of late medieval Bengal. On the one hand, a *zamīndār* was expected to welcome a migrant. Indeed, his merit could be measured by his ability to provide shelter to migrants from other *zamīndāris*. On the other hand, movement was a transgressive act against the state. Hence, mobility could be both useful and detrimental to the interests of the state. This dualism of mobility marked the relations of work in eighteenth-century indigenous Bengali society, as much as it did religious consciousness.

Labor historians have by and large bypassed any examination of precolonial Indian society. Yet, the specter of precolonial formations continually haunt labor historians in their efforts to excavate the colonial and postcolonial axes of exploitation. Much of this problem stems from an overreliance on colonial archives. Alternatively, excellent works such as Nandita Prasad Sahai's state-artisanal relationship in eighteenth-century Marwar, drawing on a completely noncolonial indigenous archive, remain silent on the British colonial interface with state-artisanal relations.[3] In a very few instances historians have successfully reconstructed precolonial society from colonial archives, going against the grain of colonial historical narratives and hence demonstrating the colonial provenance of conditions of work in India. Prasannan Parthasarathi's use of English colonial sources to demonstrate the higher living standards of eighteenth-century South Indian artisans and laborers in comparison to English workers is a good example.[4] Yet, the productive possibilities of such excursus is limited for regions such as Bengal. More generally in using colonial archives alone one sees a reprise of the fundamental pitfall of history from below—that is, an inability to address imperial formation—that generations of historians have rightly pointed out.[5] Here, a decolonizing of labor history is necessary to excavate the precolonial state-worker relationship as the crucial step to establishing how such relations were supplanted by a colonial rule over labor. Such efforts entail first, the utilization of precolonial indigenous corpus alongside multiple company archives—especially the English and Dutch East India companies—from the seventeenth and early eighteenth centuries. Second, an alternative methodological approach is in order—to read both VOC and EIC archives *in light of indigenous sources*. In doing so, one begins to comprehend that the companies were not functioning just as overseas commercial entities but were one of the crucial political agents in the region—specifically, *zamīndārs*. As the shared features of company governmentality with precolonial governmentality along with their differences become legible, the limits of company statehood and the contours of subalternity of their workers, too, become visible. Key to this early eighteenth-century statehood and subaltern subjectivity was the mobility practices of the workers.

This chapter investigates the physical mobility of hired workers and its centrality to the state-subaltern relationship in early eighteenth-century Bengal. It follows the first three lines of enquiry suggested by Antonio Gramsci for a history of the subaltern—namely, (1) the formation of these workers from within the social, economic, and political structures; (2) their active attempts to both affiliate themselves with as well as influence the political formation that dominated them; and (3) the responses of ruling groups to subaltern actions.[6] In Bengal wealth inequality and steady commercialization had resulted in a very mobile working population, especially among hired workers.[7] The expansion of agrarian and urban horizons depended upon the ability of land settlers, especially *zamīndārs* including the EIC, to make good use of this workforce—in employing them, settling them, and governing them. Nonetheless, in employing such a mobile workforce the European companies, as *zamīndārs*, were acutely aware of their limited ability to control the mobility of their worker-subjects, even after they had acquired some judicial power over them. There was no one political authority managing movements of the laboring population, since the law-and-order and administrative powers of the local *zamīndārs* and the supra-local Mughal/Nawabi authorities often overlapped and clashed. Lack of clear jurisdictions, very emblematic of the fluid unified politics of the region, prevented state entities from developing a totalizing, "pastoral" power such as that in England, where the Master and Servant Acts had for centuries given enormous power to a centralized state to assign employment to the working poor while severely restricting their mobility.[8] Within Bengal's de-centered political milieu, caste structured hired work only to a limited extent, and any form of slavery to "the unity of community" was absent.[9] Even though relatively unmoored from caste relations, hired work as facilitated by this political milieu was not an abstract economic relationship between employers and workers congealed in wages, but rather a patron and client relationship with reciprocal obligations and customs surrounding the wage payment.

WORK IN MIDDLE BENGALI LITERATURE

To reconstruct the social relations of work in the seventeenth and eighteenth centuries, I have relied heavily on two different kinds of Bengali literary sources—*maṅgalkābyas* and the Eastern Bengali ballads. These large corpuses of premodern Bengali literature provide a rich window into local, indigenous mentalities towards work, in particular, labor mobility, hired work, and its relationship to social and political hierarchy. In recovering premodern ways of life from literary sources, Jacques Le Goff remarked, "the history of mentalities is based on a) a certain type of interpretation, or reading, which can be made of any document and b) special types of documents which provide fairly direct access to collective psychologies."[10] Le Goff relied on the first method, finding the literature from the early Middle Ages in Europe to be "stunted, abstract and aristocratic." However, unlike medieval European literary productions, premodern Bengali literature is suffused with images of everyday life. These sources provide rich descriptions of the mobility and social relations of hired work of many different kinds—itinerant blacksmiths, woodcutters, agricultural workers, cowherds, forest clearers, and artisans. Notwithstanding this advantage, it is important to explain how a historian of labor can read these texts in new ways that have not been done by other scholars.

In Bengali, *maṅgal* means auspicious or beneficent and *kābya* means poetry. *Maṅgalkābya* is one of the most important forms of medieval Bengali literature. These were didactic religious poems written under the patronage of local *zamīndārs*. The poets came from a wide variety of backgrounds—from indigent migrants to court poets—though they almost all belonged either to Brahmin or Kayastha caste groups. Linguists and historians of medieval Bengali literature argue that *maṅgalkābyas* emerged in the fifteenth century as a Brahmanic response to the emergence of Islam in the region.[11] Muslim dynasties ruled over Bengal from the fourteenth to eighteenth centuries, seizing power from the staunch Brahmanic Sena rulers. Under the Bengal sultans and then the Mughals, Bengal saw the spread of Islam through various Sufic saints, and the devotional movement of Bengal Vaishnavism from the sixteenth century which then led to the formation of various heterodox sects at the crossroads of Vaishnavism, Sahajiya, and Sufic beliefs. In such a situation, espousers of orthodox Brahminical belief, fearing the loss of their social base, composed religious poetry targeting marginalized groups, especially tribal communities. This has resulted in what Kumkum Chatterjee calls "vernacularization of Sanskrit Puranic corpus,"[12] whereby sometimes, non-Brahmanic and anti-Brahmanical deities are incorporated into the regional Brahminical pantheon.[13] The most common deities evoked in this genre are thus a heady mix of Puranic goddesses such as Chandi and Shib with gods and goddesses of very local origins such as Manasā, Sītala, and Dharma.

Maṅgalkābyas are simultaneously both an oral and written tradition. As narrative religious poetry the *maṅgalkābya* is performative in nature and its recitation brings the blessings of the deity it eulogizes onto the listener as well as the reciter. Apart from being recited as a part of worship, *maṅgalkābyas* exist in several manuscript forms dating back to the fifteenth century. The bulk of the manuscripts, however, come from the eighteenth century. Their authorship is ambiguous; multiple manuscripts, penned by different scribes, attribute authorship to one particular name. Dates of composition by scribes or attributed authors of the *maṅgalkābyas* are often conveyed in chronograms or riddles alluding to a year.[14] In the absence of the dates of composition, scholars often take into account those references to people or incidents in the narrative that can be found in other historical records. Linguists agree that the existence of *maṅgalkābyas* predates their manuscript forms. While parts of the legends as oral songs or *bratageet* are much older, the poets of the *maṅgalkābyas* lived between the late fifteenth and late eighteenth centuries.[15] For my purposes, I have used various critical editions of each *maṅgalkābya*. In almost all cases, editors not only mention the various manuscripts they have consulted for each poem, but also chart the different versions in related manuscripts. In my references, I have tried to make clear the exact version used.

The *maṅgalkābyas* use blunt, vivid images based on ordinary things and happenings, a trait which is absent from Sanskrit poetic traditions.[16] Except for Bhāratcandra's *Annadāmaṅgal*, which is highly stylized court poetry, almost all *maṅgalkābyas* glorified the gods in the language of the people.[17] The gods of the *maṅgalkābyas* are far more human than gods of the Sanskrit tradition. For example, Shiva (Shib) of the *maṅgalkābyas* is an impoverished farmer, always engaged in squabbles with his wife. Such gods riveted the devotee-audience of the *maṅgalkābyas*. Kriṣnaram Das's *Rāimaṅgal*, a seventeenth-century *maṅgalkābya*, gives a glimpse of the audience. In the introduction to the text, Kriṣnaram claims that the deity Dakṣin Rai exhorted him to:

> Write a *maṅgal* poem in my name
> My name will thus spread in the deltas
> ....
> Not knowing my song the minstrels sing
> Other songs all night long
> Honey collectors and salt makers watch with pleasure
> Their manifold histrionics.[18]

Performance was central to *maṅgalkābya*, bridging any dichotomy of oral and literary cultural forms. Performance was geared towards men and women of the lowest order of society, the prospective proselyte to the worship of a deity fiercely competing with other such deities to win over a similar populace.[19]

These poems have been used by in several ways to explore the social and political milieu of medieval Bengal. Some scholars, such as David Curley, question the descriptive precision of the texts. Emphasizing the didactic nature of the *maṅgalkābyas* in his analysis of the sixteenth-century poet Mukundaram Chakraborty's *Chaṇḍīmaṅgal*, Curley argues that the *maṅgal* poems offer a paradigm of medieval Bengali moral dilemmas and their resolutions; representation of reality is secondary in these texts and hence should not be used to understand actual events.[20] In contrast, Tapan Raychaudhuri and Aniruddha Ray have used these poems to corroborate specific events and historical developments in medieval Bengal.[21] The evolution of the genre itself, Kumkum Chatterjee notes, displayed conscious efforts on the part of certain eighteenth-century poets of *maṅgal* poems to incorporate historical commentaries on subcontinental politics, appropriating the Persianate *tarikh* tradition of history writing.[22] My use of the texts is more in line with Dimock and Inden's; according to their reading, the *maṅgal* poems offer a "realistic ideal" of Bengali society, because when poets constructed their vision of an ideal societal order, they borrowed heavily from the quotidian. The poems, as Dimock and Inden rightly point out, were "both physical and metaphysical, and sometimes it is difficult to tell the difference between the two."[23] Especially when the audience were illiterate working people like honey collectors and salt makers, the transcendent had to emerge from the immanent, or the material world. Hence, vivid descriptions of idealized yet mundane social relations impinged on the divine exploits of the deities.

In addition to the *maṅgalkābyas*, I also use a different kind of poetry, the Eastern Bengal ballads, collected as *Purbabaṅga Gītikā*. These ballads and songs, collected in the late nineteenth and early twentieth century, are primarily from the Eastern deltas. It is very difficult if not impossible to date the *Purbabaṅga Gītikā*. Since the ballads were at the time of their collection part of living oral traditions, some parts of them are much older than other, more recent additions by the performing artists.[24]

I have used the ballads in conjunction with other historical sources. Even though certain ballads narrate historical events, they do not make explicit any consciousness of historical transformation.[25] It is perhaps because of this limited concern with historicity that experiences associated with different historical periods, easily evident to students of history, sit next to each other seamlessly in any one ballad.[26] While this is a similar concern for *maṅgalkābyas* and also for company archives (much of the quotidian details of company activities were written down for their immediate relevance to governance, managerial, or business purposes, with no contemplation of their historical/anthropological value), the extant dateable manuscript versions and the unique practice of dating the compositions by authors or attributed authors of the *maṅgal* poems mitigate the problem to a certain extent. Accepting the difference between the ballads, the *maṅgalkābyas*, and company archives as narratives and historical sources, this study treats the ballads as coeval with *maṅgalkābyas* and company archives. Complementing the *maṅgalkābyas*, the ballads provide the "realistic ideal" of indigenous society, exceeding the limits of company archives. Most importantly, the notion of coevality allows for an examination of the convergences and divergences of experiences as discussed in the company archives and the ballads.[27]

MOBILE HIRED WORK

By no means was the "realistic ideal" society of the *maṅgal* poems a society of equals. One of the plot functions of the *maṅgalkābyas* is the loss of status of protagonists, due to circumstances or through direct intervention of jealous deities fiercely competing with other deities for fame—a conflict ultimately resolved through the right worship of the deity.[28] Depictions of extremely mobile, heterogenous groups of working poor conveyed these kinds of stories of loss and restoration of status. Wealth inequality within villages had given rise to various forms of mobility, and the depictions of itinerancy in these poems portray the many strategies for sustenance by the wandering poor. Poor men and women moved within and between settlements and made their living as agricultural laborers, forest clearers, peregrine artisans, and even as beggars. Hired work formed an integral part of these manifold mobile practices. Among their employers were *zamīndārs*, peasants of various means, and merchants. While hired work emerged as one of the markers of wealth and grandeur or the lack thereof, hierarchical specialization emerged within the domain of hired work. If read along with the company archives of the seventeenth and early eighteenth centuries, *mangalkābyas* reveal this vast variety of hired work and the mobility practices of hired workers across villages and *zamīndāris*—and rural and urban sectors.

From the very inception of settlements (i.e., forest clearance), land settlers employed large bodies of peripatetic workers. An early eighteenth-century history of the province of Bihar recounts that following Emperor Shah Jahan's (1628–1658) expedition in the province it was customary for wood cutters and plowmen to accompany the emperor's troops so that after the removal of hostile inhabitants, forests could be cleared and lands cultivated.[29] A similar picture of the deployment of large numbers of mobile workers for land clearance, from pre-Mughal times, appears in sixteenth-century poet Mukundaram Chakraborty's *Chandīmangal*. In his *mangal* poem Mukundaram describes how an indigent forest-dwelling hunter gatherer, Kālketu, an outcaste from Bengal's caste society, becomes a member of the small landed gentry, much like small *zamīndārs* or *ta'alluqdārs*, with the blessings of goddess Chandi. His bounty manifests in an imaginary rural and urban conglomeration called Gujarāt (not to be confused with the province in Western India) over which he rules. In laying the groundwork for Gujarāt, he employed huge numbers of migrant workers, sometimes organized by their leaders into gangs for forest clearance: "Hearing the news of forest clearance organized by Mahabir (Kālketu), hired laborers (*beruniÿājan*) poured in from different directions. *Bīr* (Kālketu) bought axes and drills and distributed them amongst the laborers. From the north came a hundred wild people. *Bīr* welcomed the day laborers with paan leaves and areca nuts. From the south came under their leader five hundred workers. Dafar Miñā, a day laborer from the west came with two thousand men."[30] These workers did not settle in the cleared lands. The settlers were people from the village of Kalinga, who migrated to Gujarāt after a devastating flood.[31]

While *zamīndārs* or *ta'alluqdārs* were land settlers and the primary arms of the Mughal fiscal apparatus tethering villages to the imperial revenue-collecting system, their presence was not the source of status distinction within village settlements, where individual farming created a vast chasm between wealthy and poor peasants all over Mughal India. Differential size of holdings, possession of cattle, seeds, plows, or wells were indices of wealth and distinguished the prosperous peasants from the indigent, small peasants.[32] Descriptions of wealth, expressed not just in terms of land but also in other property, can be found in the ballads. In *Dewāna Bhābnā*, a village headman's wealth included twenty-eight *bighās*[33] of land, ten milch cows, oxen for many plows, and a storehouse full of rice.[34] Wealthy peasants who were owners of multiple plows had "hāl" (plow) added to their official epithets of distinction. During Shah Jahan's expedition to the province of Bihar in the mid-seventeenth century, imperial officials singled out *hāl mir*, or wealthy peasants with four, five, or more plows and honored them with *dastar* (turban) to encourage them to bring more and more land under cultivation.[35] Similarly, seventeenth-century poet Dbija Bansidās's *maṅgalkābya*, *Padmapurān*, gives a detailed description of a flourishing peasant, Bachai Adhikarī, who is known to all as Hālua Bachai; "hālua" being derived from *hāl* or plow. An owner of five hundred plows and a "wealth" of cows, Bachai resided in his pleasure house in the middle of his crop fields. His agrarian wealth gave him such power that no one could walk the streets against his orders.[36]

Also, the employment of servants itself became an index of wealth. Fifteenth-century poet Bipradās Pipilai's *Manasāmaṅgal*, a short description of two wealthy peasants (*pradhān kisan*), Gora and Mina, included a reference to their command over a servant (*golām*).[37] Ability to marshal resources for cultivation, including servants, distinguished rich peasants from the poorer ones. Yet, all peasants whether rich or poor employed agrarian hired workers.

Here it is important to keep in mind that a significant section of small landholders were also migrant peasants. It was common for peasants with small holdings in one village to go work on lands in other villages. Each village thus had peasants with their own holdings (*khudkāstha*) and migrant peasants (*pāhikāstha*). While *khudkāstha* peasants were secure in their holdings, *pāhikāstha* peasants were keen on getting leases, given their precarious link to the village.[38] They received leases from the land-settling imperial bureaucrats operating under the Mughal fiscal structure, such as the *zamīndārs* or *ta'alluqdārs*. The distrust between the small peasants and rural gentry is seen in the eighteenth-century poet Rameśwar Bhattacharya's *Shibāyan*. The poet stressed the formalization of leases between the rural gentry and the small peasants because:

> Never have faith in the words of a man of wealth
> With a lease, consequences are for the better.³⁹

In *Shibāyan*, the small peasant indicates that agreements over land use between the peasants and *ta'alluqdārs/zamīndārs* were a major issue of contention. Small peasants' links to agriculture were often precarious, which the poet explains in poignant words: "the crop tells the peasant, I will eat you first."⁴⁰ Crop failure intensified contentious hierarchical relationships as such events often entailed chronic indebtedness by small peasants to wealthier members of the village, which were carried over through generations.

Despite their differences all landholders, big or small, hired itinerant agricultural workers. The *Manasāmaṅgalkābyas* of multiple poets repeatedly describe migrant agricultural workers hiring themselves out to various members of landed peasantry. In her war against the Shib-worshipping merchant and *zamīndār* Chāṅd the deity Manasa inflicted severe blows on the merchant, causing him to lose his entire fleet. In a state of complete destitution, Chāṅd went from door to door to eke out a living. In the fifteenth-century poet Bipradās Pipilai's *Manasāmaṅgal*, the seventeenth-century poet Ketakadās Kṣhemananda's *Manasāmaṅgal*, and the eighteenth-century poet Visnupala's *Manasāmaṅgal*, a Brahmin hired Chāṅd as a cultivator (*kriṣan*).⁴¹ Manu's injunction prevented Brahmins from touching the plow and thus it was imperative that a Brahmin landholder look out for hired agricultural workers. Alternatively, in the fifteenth-century poet Bijay Gupta's rendition of this story, Chāṅd went to a village headman, or *maṅdal*, named Jagāi, who hired him to weed the rice fields.⁴² As village headmen, *maṅdals* were influential members of the village community, as well as revenue-collecting officials directly responsible to *zamīndārs*. *Zamīndārs* had to reckon with the power of the *maṅdals* because of their independent roots in the villages, which is evident from the various contributions *maṅdals* received from the villagers during festivals.⁴³ Even humble peasant cultivators such as Shib, in eighteenth-century poet Rameśwar Bhattacharya's *Shibāyan*, were no strangers to employing servants on land. In a domestic argument between Shib and his wife Gouri regarding how to cultivate rice on his land, the latter suggested that cultivation should be left to hired servants.⁴⁴

Lack of trust in footloose hired agrarian laborers sometimes brought together small and wealthy peasants. With tenuous links to the land, hired laborers could move on from employer to employer if their wages dropped. This practice caused distress for small peasants as sixteenth-century poet

Mukundaram Chakraborty elaborates: "In times of scarcity, my agricultural labor hand (*hālyā*) sold out."[45] Distrust often added to the vulnerability of hired laborers, as small peasants could gang up with the wealthier peasants against agricultural laborers, setting aside their own differences. In fifteenth-century poet Bijay Gupta's *Padmapurān*, Chānd, as a perambulatory destitute, found employment as an agricultural worker with the task of weeding the lands of the village headman, Jagāi. Under the spell of Manasā, who misled him, Chānd snipped the rice plants instead of weeding. A livid Jagai took to hitting Chānd, while other small peasants assisted Jagāi in abusing the destitute laborer.[46] Here vernacular poetry functions as a conduit for instilling within a subaltern milieu the Brahmanical conduct as prescribed by the Apastambā Dharmasūtra, that masters should resort to corporal punishment if displeased with agricultural laborers.[47] Since it was risky to employ hired labor, when they could, small peasants used family members, who were susceptible to hyper-exploitation. Shib, the small peasant of *Shibāyan*, hired his nephew Bhīm rather than hiring unrelated labor hands. His reason: "Family members together do good agriculture—they remain akin in times of scarcity, whereas greedy agricultural labor hands (*hābhātyā hālyā*) would sell out fast."[48] The relationship at work between Shib and his nephew Bhīm was one of subordination, even though they were related by blood. Not only did Bhīm help out Shib with cultivation, but he also did the lion's share of the work. In exchange for carrying out these tasks, Bhīm received one square meal per day, though he irked Shib by consuming copious amounts of rice. The inconstant availability of migrant hired workers forced the use of family labor in agriculture despite the irritations.

Moving from one job to another was necessary for the destitute, cutting across gender and caste, because such mobility provided flexibility and control over their time. In Ketakadās's *Manasāmaṅgal*, a Dhībar (fisherman caste) family is a good example. While the brothers Jālu and Mālu maintained their caste profession, their widowed mother went to the merchants' colony to winnow and pound rice in exchange for broken bits of rice. The widow also spun cotton yarn and then sold it in the village market. Selling Jālu and Mālu's catch ensured that the family could buy rice, and the widow's earnings added salt and oil to their diet.[49] In his period of tribulation after his shipwreck, the formerly rich merchant Chānd in Bipradās's *Manasāmaṅgal* first took up the job of a woodcutter, then that of a hunter, then worked as an agricultural laborer, and finally as a cowherd.[50] The flexibility of moving from one job to another indicates that the poor made choices about how to use their time and diversify their incomes. Such examples can be seen in the ballads as well. In *Manik Tārā*, a young widow of a barber takes her only surviving son and goes to live with the fishermen. Though the work is beneath her caste status, she weaves fishing nets, along with pounding rice in the paddy and spinning yarn for sustenance.[51] Such diversification of income by the poor was also widespread in other regions of the subcontinent.[52] If not as hired workers, the poor moved from one village to another as beggars. In the story of Jālu and Mālu in the *Manasāmaṅgal* poems, the deity Manasā, disguised as an old woman, asked Jālu and Mālu to ferry her across the river. As a Brahmin widow, she moved from village to village, begging for a living.[53] The intra- and inter-village ambulatory practices among the indigent members of the villages show their strategies for making a living for themselves and their families, which often, though not always, included hired work.

Practices of physical mobility opened up possibilities of social mobility for cultivators who lived by hire. In sixteenth-century poet Mukundaram's *Chaṇḍīmaṅgal*, Kālketu, after settling Gujarāt with the goddess Chandi's benediction, appointed a man named Bulan as the headman. However, Bharu Datta, a Kayastha and the headman in Bulan's previous dwelling place, Kaliṅga, resented this appointment. Bharu, like Bulan, had been compelled to leave Kaliṅga following a devastating flood and had resettled in Gujarāt. The new headman of Gujarāt, Bulan, had been his old servant. Thus, Bharu Datta warned Kālketu: "Think well before you act lest you are later ashamed of your own deeds. Bulan wore old clothes, pounded my paddy. The cultivator will now become headman (*deśmukh*). The staff in the hands of servants (*nafar*) and wealth in the hands of young women is the source of great sorrow."[54] Bharu's class resentment (and misogyny) points at the fluidity of status, thanks to the expanding agrarian frontier. It is difficult to ascertain Bulan's caste status. In some manuscripts he is the son of a Kayastha but in others his caste status is obscure.[55] Bharu did not resort to any aspersions against Bulan about his caste status. Even when he made clear his own caste status, the word Bharu used for Bulan was *nafar* or servant—an Arabic word which makes no reference to Indic caste distinctions. In a text which portrays Kālketu as a ruler keen on upholding the caste order of Bengali society despite his low birth, it is remarkable that agrarian hired work was not signified by caste. Apart from removing Brahmins from agricultural labor, caste rules did not regulate agrarian hired work, hence opening possibilities for both downward or upward social mobility for the mobile working poor.

Artisans, like agrarian hired workers, moved within and outside villages in rendering their services for wages. *Zamīndārs* were keen on settling artisans. For example, the *zamīndār* of Mahiṣadal over the eighteenth century gave out various lands to leather workers, blacksmiths, and book binders who in turn provided their services to the *zamīndār* along with a host of other employers.[56] *Padmapurān*, fifteenth-century poet Bijay Gupta's *maṅgalkābya*, provides a detailed literary profile of itinerant blacksmiths providing service to a *zamīndār*. In order to manufacture a foolproof iron room, the merchant-*zamīndār* Chāṅd summoned 1,400 blacksmiths. After getting the specifications for the desired iron room from Chāṅd, the smiths set up their workshops in a field adjacent to his residence. Work had taken a toll on their bodies—the smiths looked "terrible" (*bikat*) with "crooked backs" (*bheṅgur kakali*) and "ash-covered faces" (*nāke mukhe pariyachey aguner chāli*). As for their comportment, the poet could only compare it to "hammer blows" (*kamarer bol cāl haturer baṛi*).[57] Though the artisans portrayed here are very similar to recently destitute Chāṅd, largely because of their mobility, there were important differences.[58] Unlike Chāṅd, they owned their own tools—they all came with a hammer in one hand and weighing scales in the other. After setting up their workshops, they gathered the other necessary material such as coal.

Artisans did not only move within the village of their residence, fulfilling the demand of the corporate body of village community or what Max Weber called "demiurgic" labor, but also to other villages or urban settlements.[59] The influx of artisans in the thirteenth century from Central Asia into North India, which brought in its wake massive urbanization, is well documented.[60] Artisans from Central Asia started coming to Bengal in the same period, continuing a migration that endured into the sixteenth century. An interesting religious inscription from the Sylhet district from 1588 mentions the name of an artist, Abdallah Khan Bukhari, who was a new immigrant. His crude style of inscription makes it clear that he was a recent initiate to his trade. Not only was he not aware of the well-developed *tughra* style of inscriptions from the Bengal Sultanate period, but he was also evidently very ill-versed in the *nastaliq* style of the Mughal period. His unsure hand tells us that the engravers' profession remained porous even in the sixteenth century, absorbing newcomers from distant lands such as Bukhara.[61] As described in all *Dharmamaṅgals*, the settlement of Dom families in Lausen's *zamīndārī* in Mainā is also a representation of migration of artisans. The Doms—a caste group—under their leader, Kalu, made a living through basket making among other trades, and they followed Lausen to Mainā, leaving their former settlement in Ramati.[62] In VOC records too, Doms come up as basket makers and bamboo carvers who frequently traveled from nearby villages to VOC construction sites. The 90 caulkers and 100 carpenters working for the VOC for 160 days at Falta, the anchoring place of EIC and VOC ships, in 1739, could only be explained by migration from neighboring villages, as Falta had a small population.[63] Thus artisans, even while reserving control over their tools and raw material, moved around seeking employment like hired agrarian workers. They served the demands of a market that exceeded the limits of the village community.

There were several parallels between the worksite of blacksmiths described in Bijay Gupta's text and company construction sites of the early eighteenth century, suggesting similar ways that artisans moved among villages, towns, and employers. Carpenters and masons poured into VOC work sites and set up their shops. Their shop units had at most three divisions. Since these divisions reflected differential wage rates, they were presumably hierarchical. The highest paid were the master masons and carpenters, below them were the general masons and sawyers, and at the bottom were coolies.[64] This three-tiered division on the artisanal shop floor is also seen in Bijay Gupta's *Padmapurān*. In Bijay Gupta's poem, the fourteen hundred blacksmiths had one master smith, Tārāpati, whose good judgment they praised:

> Tārāpati was the clever one
> He hand picked one hundred smiths for the work.[65]

The master smith was assisted by smiths who worked under him. Then there were porters who helped carry the coal.[66] In fact, at VOC sites coolies who worked as assistants were usually better paid than general coolies doing porterage work for the companies.[67] It is quite likely that these coolies, as carpenters' or smiths' assistants, must have performed some skilled work in addition to carrying coal. Tārāpati is further praised because

> Tārāpati is most talented of them all.
> He made the measurements and laid the foundations.[68]

According to this description, Tārāpati was also an architect. This is very similar to the role played by master masons in making recommendations for repair of VOC-owned houses in Chinsurah in 1739. The unnamed master mason, along with the Dutch master carpenter Jan Janszen van der Huis, supervised a report based on their inspection detailing the specific renovations that were to be done for VOC houses and warehouses.[69] Hired artisans and their assistants moved between villages and company settlements performing in work settings with similar hierarchy and specializations.

By the eighteenth century, hired work was widespread in both agricultural and manufacturing sectors in villages and urban centers. Employers of hired workers were wealthy peasants, *zamīndārs*, and merchants. Given the widespread mobility practices of the village poor, hired artisans and laborers not only sustained village or *zamīndāri* needs at their places of origin, but also moved about to cater to other *zamīndāris* and commercial interests in the region. As important bureaucrats within the Mughal fiscal system, *zamīndārs*, settled and governed hired workers; they also hired workers from other *zamīndāris* for commercial purposes or for their own needs. Sometimes the *zamīndāri* authorities and commercial entities were one and the same, as was the case for the European companies.

THE VOC AND EIC AS *ZAMĪNDĀRS*

The European companies—specifically, the EIC and the VOC—who hired workers in Bengal functioned as both commercial and state entities. By the end of the seventeenth century, Bengal provided 40 percent of the EIC and VOC's combined trade from Asia to Europe.[70] The commercial fortune was sustained by these two companies through their unique state power, derived in part from European states granting them charters and in part from Mughal imperial government allowing them legitimately to take root within its territory. Within Mughal Bengal, by the early eighteenth century the EIC and VOC—the two most significant European East India companies operating in Bengal—had rooted themselves as *zamīndārs*. By definition, a *zamīndār* was both a state entity and an employer of hired labor.

Within the early modern European context both the VOC and the EIC were state entities at their very inception. The formation of the VOC to expand Dutch mercantile activities in Asia was the Dutch Republic's political solution in the face of a harsh economic embargo imposed by Iberian empires on Dutch merchants in 1598 as retaliation for the Dutch war of independence. The States General quickly bestowed on this new organization powers "to maintain troops and garrisons, fit out warships, impose governors upon Asian populations, and conduct diplomacy with eastern potentates, as well as sign treaties and make alliances." Not only did the VOC carve out a substantial empire in Asia by the mid-seventeenth century, the "merchant warriors" took over full responsibility for the Dutch state's warfare in Asia.[71] As Bengal grew in importance economically in the VOC empire, its administrative position rose from just a branch of the Coromandel *gouvernament* into a separate directorate in 1655. Similarly, the EIC was a unique political body—a corporation with governing rights endowed by the English monarchy and underscored by a permanent joint stock since 1657 with exclusive rights to all English commerce in the vast Asian and Pacific region between the Cape of Good Hope and the Magellan Strait. By 1700 the EIC was a well established state entity whose charter established the company's political rights "to appoint governors and officers abroad, to make law, erect courts, judge and sentence offenders, erect fortifications, declare martial law, coin money, make war on non-Christians, conduct diplomacy, and, in the words of Charles II, to '"chastise correct & punish such of Our Subjects as are or shall bee by the said Govern' & Company imployed or under their Comand.'"[72]

The modality of the EIC and VOC's political authority as "true lords" in Bengal, however, was rooted in the local system of Mughal *zamīndāris*. While the EIC might have created a "political system in itself and on its own terms" as Philip Stern argues, much of its provenance, salience, and limitations can be understood, at least in Bengal, within the parameters of *zamīndāri* power.[73] The *zamīndār* stood at the apex of a pyramidal revenue-collecting structure whereby land revenue and customs duties were gathered for distribution among the imperial household and various officials of the Mughal and its successor Nizamat/Nawabi state and the important officials at subordinate levels of government.[74] Origins of the *zamīndārs* were many and often tied to the course of Mughal conquest and Nawabi control over Bengal. While some had roots in the region as rulers predating the Mughal conquest and had demonstrated allegiance to the new imperial rule, others were officials of the Mughal imperial overlords themselves who received their *zamīndāri* as a matter of mutual loyalty and convenience.[75] By the time the EIC purchased its *zamīndāri*, it was not uncommon for merchants to secure *zamīndāri* rights. The Burdwan *zamīndārs* were successful Khatri merchants closely associated with the Mughal military operations in the province in the seventeenth century.[76] Indeed, the paradigmatic *zamīndār* of the *Manasāmaṅgal* poems was a merchant. Along with revenue collection *zamīndārs* shared with imperial officers governing powers for the state, including civil administration and criminal justice. Most *zamīndārs*,

FIGURE 1. Hendrik van Schuylenburgh, "A picture of the VOC's trading post or the headquarters in Bengal in the city Hugli." Source: Wikimedia Commons.

excluding the very big ones, were land settlers, responsible for extending both rural and urban frontiers. Much like other *zamīndārs*, the EIC and VOC both extracted revenues, settled vast numbers of workers, and maintained armies, bolstering their political power in the region.

By 1700, both the EIC and VOC secured landholding rights from the Mughal government. In 1656 the VOC leased the villages of Chinsurah, Bazar Mirzapore, and Baranagar from the Mughal state for an annual ground rent of 1,574 rupees.[77] A century later, in 1755, Louis Taillefert, the outgoing director of Bengal, wrote in his memorandum to his successor, Adriaan Bisdom, that at least part of this legal right (i.e., the VOC right over Baranagar) was definitely a *zamīndāri*.[78] At any rate, for the lease-holders in Chinsurah, Bazar Mirzapore, and Baranagar, including workers such as boatmen, the VOC was the *zamīndār-fiscaal*—an allusion to the VOC's legal power as a landholding entity at the intersection of Mughal governance and VOC governance in Asia.[79] The *zamīndār*-like pomp and grandeur of the Dutch director is evident in the well-known Hendrik van Schuylenburgh painting of the Dutch settlement at Chinsurah and Bazar Mirzapore (also known as Hugli). The VOC director is seen reclining in his palanquin in a leisurely manner amidst two long files of native soldiers, with guards bearing a trumpet and flags in the front (see figures 1 and 2).[80]

FIGURE 2. Detail from Schuylenburgh's painting.

The VOC settlement in Hugli was part of a larger port town, comprised of several European settlements. It had its origins as a Portuguese settlement in the late sixteenth century. Mughal emperor Shah Jahan had conquered it in 1633, and then allowed Europeans to build their settlements in the region for trading purposes. The EIC too made their beginnings in Hugli, but eventually gained their *zamīndāri* further away from other foreign settlements. The Anglo-Mughal war of 1684–90 interrupted the EIC's operations in Hugli. Despite their loss, the EIC was fortunate enough to be reinstated in Bengal after 1690. Even though the EIC restored their operations in Hugli, they shifted their headquarters to a location further south, down the river Bhagirathi, where in 1698 the company purchased *zamīndāri* rights over three villages—Sutanuti, Gobindapur, and Kalikata—for 1,300 rupees from the descendants of the *zamīndār* Lakshmikanta Mazumdar under close supervision of the Mughal governor of the province, 'Aẓīm-ush-shān.[81] These villages became the nucleus for Calcutta.

Revenue collection was their primary duty as *zamīndārs* for both companies in their main settlements. Evidence for VOC's revenue-collecting activities are hard to come by. At the time of leasing, the VOC agreed to collect an annual revenue of 582 rupees from Chinsurah, 199 rupees from Bazar Mirzapore, and 793 rupees from Baranagar. The French traveler Sieur de L'Estra, who visited Hugli in early 1670s, noted that the VOC director levied taxes for the use of the river and forest around Chinsurah.[82] The EIC, similarly, made handsome profits from revenue collection. When the EIC purchased their *zamīndāri* in 1698, the land revenue was assessed at 1,194 rupees and 14 annas. In 1717 the total collection was 40,013 rupees and in 1747 it rose to 70,525 rupees.[83] As revenue collectors, the companies fulfilled their political obligations as Mughal *zamīndārs*, while extracting considerable sums of revenue for their own profit.

Increased profits from land not only meant higher tax rates but also rapid increase of the settlement size. Settlers came from the Bengal hinterland, Europe, and across the Indian Ocean world. Both the VOC and EIC gave out numerous leases and oversaw the buying and selling of houses in these places. House-sale documents surviving from early eighteenth-century Chinsurah and Bazar Mirzapur show that merchants of various Indian Ocean origins bought into the VOC settlements. Dutch employees of the VOC and Dutch free burghers lived right next door to native Christians, as well as Muslim, Hindu and Armenian merchants, and even other European merchants such as Greeks.[84] Apart from the market, one distinct neighborhood of Bazar Mirzapur was the "Muslim" ground. Even though the Portapur neighborhood was called Muslim, Dutch men lived alongside Muslim and Armenian merchants.[85] The important landmarks of Chinsurah were the company garden, the church, along with the square facing it, the Armenian quarter, and the Straw bazaar. While only Christians lived around the church square, in all other neighborhoods the population was extremely diverse. In the Armenian quarter, Dutch employees of the VOC had both Armenian and Greek neighbors.[86] Many of the houses were owned by Portuguese and "Free Christian" or manumitted enslaved women who ran taverns or lodges where European sailors and soldiers rented rooms during their stay in Bengal.

Finally, the most ubiquitous structures in Chinsurah, Bazar Mirzapur, and larger Hugli were the small thatched huts in which resided the poor working people whom the VOC regularly hired. Among these hovel-dwelling settlers were boatmen. Bilingual lease documents (*pāṭṭās*) in Bengali and Dutch for the entire eighteenth century demonstrate the VOC's enduring efforts at settling various working people (see figure 3). The *zamīndār-fiscaal* leased out small pieces of land—often a few *cāṭhāhs*—to weavers, guardsmen, and carpenters. Boatmen too received these meager pieces of land. As leaseholders they paid rent, often a few annas or a rupee annually.

Similarly, the EIC too took an active interest in giving out leases and settling people. Calcutta, before the arrival of the EIC, was a moderately sized trading center. A number of wealthy weaver families (Bysacks) and merchant families (Seths) had relocated from Saptagram, the port town close to Hugli,

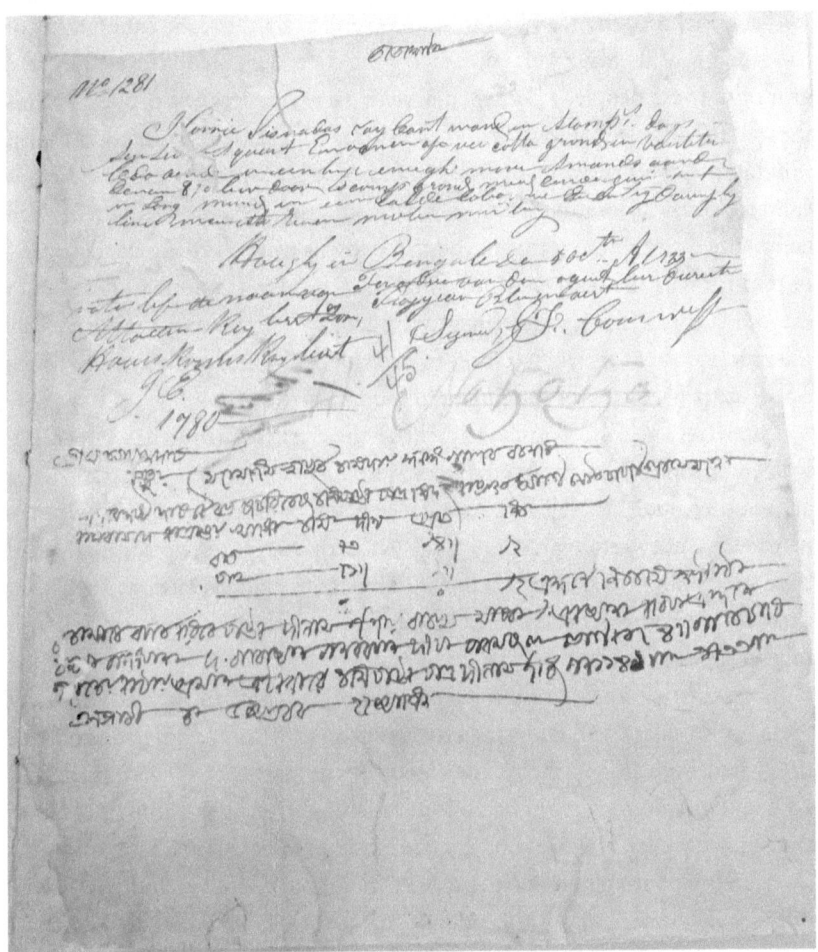

FIGURE 3. Lease (or *pāttā*) document issued by the VOC in October 1733 to Hare Kriṣna Das Kaibarta, most likely a boatman. Source: West Bengal State Archives, Kolkata.

when it declined in the early 1600s, and settled in Govindapore.[87] In addition to the Seths and the Bysacks, Armenians and Portuguese were present in the area throughout the seventeenth century. In fact, from the sixteenth century, the Portuguese used Bettore, on the other side of the river from Govindapore, as a satellite market for their primary riverine port, Saptagram. The first settlers whom the EIC brought in were the owners of four "victualling houses," which provisioned the company ships. As in Chinsurah and Bazar Mirzapore many of these establishments were run by Portuguese and "Free Christian women." Victualling houses rented out rooms to European sailors and soldiers, each occupying a bed in shared rooms. By 1703, the inhabitants of the EIC grounds, who were already paying rent, demanded leases for these grounds. These people, whether they were native settlers or Europeans, thus showed their desire for long-term habitation. That same year, several English inhabitants, who had already built "handsome buildings," were given leases valid for thirty-one years.[88] Two years later, in 1705, the Fort William council complained that inhabitants of the three towns were cheating the company of rent for half the land they possessed. In response, the council devised an elaborate lease system, requiring ground rent to be renewed every year.[89] By the first decade of the eighteenth century the EIC was already systematizing elaborate procedures for settling their *zamīndāri*.

Likewise, the EIC consciously chose their preferred settlers, especially working people. Even though weavers were early settlers of Calcutta, having arrived there long before EIC's advent, the EIC arranged to settle new weavers in the city between 1731 and 1732.[90] As early as 1706, the company had appointed one of the native merchant-settlers, Nityananda Datta, as the liaison between the company and the Calcutta weavers.[91] The total number of dwellings in 1706 were eight brick houses, and 8,000 thatched huts. By 1756, the number of brick houses rose to 498 and thatched huts to 14,450.[92] Most of these hut dwellers worked in the city for hire. A section of boatmen that the EIC hired were among them. The emerging city demanded a variety of jobs. First and foremost, construction of buildings required huge numbers of laborers. Masonry work included not just the construction of brick houses, in which the wealthier inhabitants of the city resided, but also civic and communal buildings. Apart from the old fort, the first church of Calcutta, St. Anne's church, was built in 1704.[93] The first hospital of Calcutta was built in 1709.[94] Wealthier sections of the indigenous population also needed such workers. Wealthy native families in Calcutta often boastfully claimed to be "jungle-clearing inhabitants" of the city, or settlers who cleared forested lands. However, the actual backbreaking work of land clearing was carried out by migrant workers, much like the migrant forest clearers of Mukundaram Chakraborty's poem. The opulent houses of self-proclaimed "jungle-clearing" families were thus surrounded by the thatched huts of people who not only paid rent but also did various kinds of work for these families, including land clearance.[95] Construction work also included reclaiming land by draining water, desilting the largest body of water in the city, Lāl Dighī, and building numerous roads and bridges. A large number of inhabitants of the huts were personal servants of the European servicemen of the EIC and wealthy native families. Many low-income indigenous people worked as guards of the city. Guards were in demand because, by the middle of the eighteenth century, the settlement around the fort had become a commercial, administrative, and military center. Residential complexes with sprawling gardens belonging to the Europeans had also grown within this area. The area around the fort was fenced in. Native guards or "peons" were hired to safeguard these boundaries. In 1706, for example, the EIC paid for the service of thirty "paiks or black peons" following several incidents of robberies committed by "country robbers."[96] In 1726, an additional eighty men were employed as security guards following incidents of robbery.[97] Even though hut dwellers were an eyesore to EIC officials because they did many "offensive" things, including "easing themselves under the wharfs, along the riverside," these "black people" were absolutely essential for the maintenance of the settlement.[98]

As an urban trading settlement, the Calcutta *zamīndāri* provided many avenues of revenue collection absent in agrarian landholdings. A large part of the revenue came from rent or duty collection in the markets. Between 1743 and 1747, 28 percent of the revenue came from duties collected at markets.[99] Native merchants sometimes directly built infrastructure for the EIC headquarters. The Seths of Calcutta—Jonardan, Gopal, Jadu, Banarasi, and Jay Kriṣna—took it upon themselves to develop the long road connecting the Old Fort with the northern parts of Sutanuti. The Seths owned their gardens north of the fort long before the EIC gained the *zamīndāri* rights to the region. In return for their service, the EIC gave them a discount of 8 annas per *bigha* for the assessed ground rent.[100] Poor people too made cash contributions towards the city's civic structures. In June 1704, the Fort William council mentioned that "petty fines from the black inhabitants" would be used in repairing the highways and filling up the holes in the city.[101] Small-time criminals drawn from the lower rungs of Calcutta society predominantly paid these fines. Moreover, just like the VOC, the EIC as *zamīndārs* enjoyed certain levies exclusively paid by poor people. Boatmen in both Chinsurah and Calcutta paid a special tax to the companies for carrying out their profession. As more people settled in the city, they contributed towards the city's infrastructure, thus both defraying the EIC's costs and adding to the income from revenue collection.

Much of the subaltern European population residing in the provisioning houses and socializing in the inns of Calcutta or Chinsurah, were part of the military. Both the EIC and VOC achieved the privilege of fortifying their headquarters following the *zamīndār* Sobha Singh's rebellion in 1695. Unsure of his own military strength in the face of this serious rebellion, comparable to the unrest in the early days of Mughal conquest of the region, the provincial Mughal governor of Bengal, hopeful of the companies' military cooperation, had allowed the VOC and the EIC to fortify their settlements and keep their own militaries.[102] Providing military assistance to Mughal imperial forces was a longstanding practice. During Mir Jumla's Assam expedition (1662–63) and during Shaista Khan's war against Arakan (1665–66), the Nawabs requested aid from both the VOC and EIC, especially boats and men.[103] Dutch naval assistance was key to the Mughal victory against the rebel Sobha Singh. The rebellion ended in 1698, but the companies' right to maintain their military continued.[104] Even up to 1701, the muster rolls of the VOC in Bengal recorded military personnel under a special category—"military sent out by the headquarters at Batavia because of the ongoing rebellion of the Raja, kept here extraordinarily."[105] After 1701, the category of "military" crept into the muster rolls of the VOC.[106] In 1697, the VOC had over two hundred armed men in Hugli.[107] It reached its zenith in 1725–26, with 321 soldiers, though ordinarily the strength of the army fluctuated from fifty to three hundred soldiers.[108] The muster rolls of the EIC army are available only from 1714, when it had 258 men, which then steadily grew throughout the first half of the eighteenth century.[109] At the peak of the Anglo-Dutch war of 1759 in Bengal, the VOC was able to muster an army of only 1,000 men, whereas the EIC was heading an army of 2,100 men.[110] With standing armies at their disposal the VOC and EIC, like *zamīndārs*, became the key political powers to reckon with in Bengal.

Both the VOC and EIC, thus, acquired political power in the region as *zamīndārs* through settling their revenue-paying subjects and maintaining armies. In doing so they also entered an indigenous world of work. Their settlements were receptacles for many forms of labor. Many of their hired workers were also settler subjects of their *zamīndāris*. While their *zamīndāri* control was limited to their headquarters, their mercantile activities extended their presence to various places in Bengal, including Patna and Kassimbazar, places that are crucial to this study. As is discussed in the Introduction, these were important Mughal administrative centers with considerable commercial activities. Here not only did both companies rely on workers who were also their *zamīndāri* subjects but also hired large numbers of workers, including boatmen and silk reelers, who were not their subjects. In employing these workers the companies engaged with the larger world of work in Bengal.

Control over workers in places beyond their primary settlements was tricky because even though the companies maintained their armies at Patna and Kassimbazar and also hosted armed convoys sent to or from Chinsurah and Calcutta, their law enforcement power as *zamīndārs* was heavily circumscribed by the direct authority of the Nawab and the imperial military and police officials or *faujdārs* in these places.

STATES AND MOBILE WORKERS

In a rapidly expanding agrarian frontier, state authorities, starting from the Mughals down to the *zamīndārs*, played a dual and contradictory role of facilitating while simultaneously controlling peasant mobility. This contradiction can be seen in the official directives of two successive Mughal emperors, Shah Jahan and Aurangzeb, in the province of Bihar. Through his imperial orders regarding extension of agriculture in Bihar, Shah Jahan hoped that "the people and the *riaya* (peasants) would be attracted by good treatment to come from other regions and *subahs* (provinces) to bring under cultivation wasteland and land under forests."[111] While Shah Jahan wanted people to move out of their original homes to settle newly cleared lands, some thirty years later, an imperial circular issued by Aurangzeb to a revenue administrator of imperial lands (*dīwān-i khāliṣa*) of the same province hoped to stall people from deserting their homes. The second clause of the circular mentioned: "If anyone amongst the cultivators (*karindas*) has fled, they [*'āmils*, or imperial revenue officials] should find out the reason thereof and try hard in the matter of his return to his native place."[112] The emperor advised persuasive methods to curb mobility. The paradox of both encouraging and curtailing mobility was further complicated as *zamīndārs/ ta'alluqdārs* competed with each other to settle peasants. By performing various benevolent acts such as giving out loans to peasants, maintaining irrigation, and building embankments, they tried to attract peasants from neighboring *zamīndāris/ta'alluqdāris* to migrate into their own land.[113] Due to excess land in proportion to human beings and more importantly, the uncertainties of the imperial state regarding the jurisdictions of local *zamīndārs*, such mobility could not be regulated and hence was feared.[114] The multiple jurisdictions and law enforcement systems of the Mughal, Nawabi, and *zamīndāri* authorities facilitated the mobility of their subjects but failed to control it.

In contrast, a centralized state-initiated strategy to control the mobility of peasant populations emerged in late medieval England. The state reserved the power to coerce anyone to work, which the 1349 Ordinance of Laborers (the earliest labor legislation in Britain) makes clear: "That each man and woman (homo et femina) of our realm of England—of whatever condition, free or bond; able in body; under 60 years of age; not living by trade; nor exercising a particular craft; nor having assets with which to live or land to cultivate; nor serving another—shall be bound to serve anyone who requires his/her services, as long as the service is appropriate to his/her estate."[115] A special kind of hired labor, "service," had mainly put to work young men and women as laboring dependents in rural households, typically contracted for a year with a remuneration consisting of room and board and often a small cash hire. The presence of the English state in coercing people to work was conspicuous in several aspects—the centralized state and not village-level government officials forcefully put to work unoccupied men and women, fixed wage rates, and safeguarded contracts against any forms of breach, especially flight. Justices of the Peace, the central government's institution, became particularly important in enforcing compulsory service and defending contracts. At the level of villages, parish constables were the local officials dealing with complaints against breach of contract. Justices of the Peace held sessions each quarter where the cases that the parish constable could not resolve were tried. Moreover, their annual session became "hiring fairs" when the state ensured that no men or women remained "masterless" but instead were assigned to households as laboring hands. Justices of the Peace also insured that contracts made between employers and servants abided by the stipulations of the statutes.[116] While in the fourteenth century these acts were informed by the need to capture labor in the post-Black Death era when the land-man ratio was skewed, from the sixteenth century onwards, these acts aimed to bring down labor costs in the interests of the commercial classes.[117] By Elizabethan times the centralized state's design for poor relief further supplemented such acts. The church and state worked in tandem to strengthen the state's "pastoral power" over charity, assuring subjects that they would be relieved of helping out individually any vagabonds and idle beggars or "undeserving poor."[118] Instead the state would exert its "pastoral power" by criminalizing vagrancy and putting roaming beggars and even children born to poor parents to forced labor in workhouses or apprenticeships. As one scholar states, "the leitmotiv of Elizabethan poor relief was work."[119] This uniquely harsh nature of the English state's paternal benevolence did not go unnoticed by Indian observers in the early twentieth century, as the introductory quote from N.M. Joshi demonstrates.

Similarly, throughout the seventeenth and the eighteenth centuries the States General, the central government of the VOC in Amsterdam and Batavia, devised laws to carefully demarcate and weed out illegitimate mobility of its subjects in Asia. Unlike the EIC the VOC had carved out a substantial empire in Asia by the mid-seventeenth century with an intricate hierarchical structure of settlements. Within this structure, power was distributed along different nodes—especially between the Dutch Republic and Batavia. Just like matters of succession of governor generals or recruitment of personnel in Asia and Europe, provenance of laws regarding mobility of subjects display similar diffusion and/or parceling of power between these nodes.[120] Such law making and implementation involved arduous debates and disagreements not only between power centers in the Dutch Republic and Batavia, but also between lesser settlements and Batavia, as will be discussed in chapter 3. However, all nodes in this power structure heavily proscribed the movements of soldiers and sailors: "vagabonding company servants who have been searched for over a month and by their own officers, the servants of the commissar of the native affairs, the commandants of the foreign posts and all other people, apart from judicial servants, were apprehended, shall, being soldiers, without trial be sent to island Edam and being seamen to (island) Onrust with an ordinance that there, after chastisement, will work in the rope factory without payment for twice the amount of time of their absence."[121]

In Batavia, VOC's headquarters in Asia, from its founding days in 1622 through at least 1752, the VOC government monitored all forms of movements of its non-European dwellers: "No Chinese or native of any nation, free or enslaved, should go out in the city or outside the city on moonless nights after 9 on main roads or alleys without a torch on pain that if that person is caught after 10 without the light will be put in chains and in violation of this ordinance will be arbitrarily punished." [122]

The VOC created an elaborate pass system with assistance of neighboring kingdoms which clearly defined vagabondage. All subjects of the VOC government in Batavia and the adjacent principalities could move in and out of the jurisdictions of their governments only with valid letters of permission. In absence of such letters all these governments agreed to arrest and hand over wandering people to the state authorities of the government under whose jurisdiction such people resided. In Batavia, the VOC government endowed the commissioner of inland affairs with power to punish errant wanderers however he chose, after the first offense. In the case of a second infraction, with prior notice to the governor general, the *commisaris* could put the defector in chains and make him work in his designated district for six months.[123] Here, the state not only persevered to fix its subjects within a certain spatial boundary but also laid claim on their labor. Most importantly, a 1718 VOC statute passed in Amsterdam earmarked the act of absconding to rival employers as treason:

> No one, irrespective of the time he or they have served for the company, shall take up service with foreign nation or on other ships than that of the company, in addition to the punishment of giving up all their wages as a deserter according to the statute of the all powerful Lord states general against desertion framed on 30th May 1625 such person will be punished to death after investigation; if anyone, especially seamen, shall be captured who has given himself up in the service of foreign East India company, either in Europe or in Indies, he will be punished with death alongside confiscation of his goods.[124]

The VOC state thus identified desertion as the highest form of criminal offense. In defining these licit/illicit mobilities, the state laid claim to the life, property, and labor (hence wages) of its subjects.

In Mughal Bengal, the closest we can come to any imperial directive regarding itinerancy are two 1665 circulars from the Mughal emperor Aurangzeb. In the first circular, sent to revenue officials in Bihar. the measures suggested by the emperor were ameliorative and far from punitive. In another imperial order issued the same year to Muhammad Hashim, the recommendation to *'amils* was the following: "If after inquiry it is found that, in spite of their (peasants) being able to till and having had rainfall, they are abstaining from cultivation, you should urge and threaten them and employ force and beating."[125] The state was extremely concerned about peasants not working the land, and they were ready to use coercive force. But, both of these imperial circulars (*farmān*) reveal that, unlike the English statutes, desertion was not formally criminalized. Members of the upper echelons of the imperial bureaucracy could issue similar orders (*parwāna*) and unsurprisingly these orders too display the same ambivalence about the criminalizing of flight. One such order from 1635 in the Mughal province of Gujarat narrates the flight of a peasant, Ashaq, across three villages and two *sarkārs*; Ashaq returned to his original village of birth only after the "consolation and assurance for sympathetic consideration" by the imperial official (*desāi*) of the *pargana* wherein his native village was located. The *parwāna* went on to prohibit imperial officials responsible for the other villages to make any claims on Ashaq.[126] The lack of criminalization becomes clearer if one reads these *farmāns* and *parwānas* in light of the *Fatawa-i-'Alamgiri*, a massive collection of legal opinions and judgments compiled in a similar time period at the behest of Aurangzeb. The Fatawa recommends using only generous, persuasive methods to encourage peasants to cultivate, not forcible methods.[127] What is articulated in the orders can be termed as a jurisdictional control over labor, or restricting the producer to a piece of land.[128] These laws were aimed at errant peasant taxpayers and not at hired workers, agricultural or otherwise. Even though the Mughal emperor, alongside other rank-holding nobility, revenue officials, and wealthy peasants, laid claim to the revenue from land, the Mughal imperial state did not claim any exclusive control over the *labor power* of the peasantry.

For hired workers, especially military labor, the centralized Mughal state issued orders to redress flight but only to the extent of imposing fines on reinstated workers. Though contracts solidified such state-worker relationship even in wartime, absconding entailed only payment of fines deducted from salary.[129] Likewise, elsewhere in the Indian subcontinent, where centralized governance took root, notably in the Maratha territories, desertion was a civil offence—the state punished desertion by placing a fine collectively on the village from where the deserter came.[130] Similarly, Brahmanical conduct prescribed fines as punishment for hired workers who deserted.[131] Why did the Mughal and the Nawabi states not issue laws similar to the English statutes governing workers? One answer is that the moral tenor of multiple legal texts and rulings which do not consider flight as a criminal offense. One may seek other answers, at least in the case of Bengal, in the enormous layers of *zamīndāri* autonomy. Village-level police and judicial administration were left primarily in the hands of *zamīndārs*.

For the Mughals, and then the Bengal Nawabs, the official heads of the police and criminal administration were the military governors, or *faujdārs*. Bengal was divided into nine *faujdāri* divisions and Bihar into eight, with an extensive area under their control.[132] The *faujdār*'s chief task was to prevent *zamīndāri* rebellion and to provide military support to revenue-collecting agents. He was posted in prominent cities within the division under his control. In these cities, the *faujdār* received assistance from the town prefect (*kotwāl*), who carried out the chief policing activity with the assistance of the prominent people of the city. *Faujdārs* also carried out the criminal justice of his division with the help of a judge (*qāzī*), and an assistant judge (*nāibqāzī*). However, this judicial and police setup hardly had any presence outside of the cities.[133]

While the *faujdārs* had their own strongholds in some urban areas, a collaboration between *zamīndārs* and *faujdārs* maintained law and order in most parts of the province, where the reach of the *faujdār* remained weak. *Faujdāri* presence in much of the countryside was felt through the *thānas*, or toll points, which also acted as police outposts, many of which lined the rivers, the primary highways of transport. Small numbers of employees in the *thānas* were directly responsible to the *faujdār*, and they were paid by a small grant of land in the *zamīndāris* where they were posted. The *thānas* were understaffed and had to rely on *zamīndāri* assistance in their expeditions against robbers. By the early eighteenth century, *thanas* fell under almost complete control of their respective *zamīndāris*. In addition, *zamīndārs* maintained their own countervailing police system outside of Mughal or Nawabi supervision.[134] This pluralistic, collaborative governance had serious limitations. It is ironic that the chief task of the *faujdār* was to quell *zamīndāri* revolts, when he was heavily dependent on the *zamīndārs* for police and military personnel. An early eighteenth-century Persian text commented upon the unreliable character of the *zamīndārs*: "It is the way with most of the zamindars of India to abandon the path of straightforwardness and to watch every side and join whoever is the stronger and is being victorious."[135] *Zamīndāri* revolts were frequent occurrences in Bengal beginning in the seventeenth century. Much of Eastern Bengal remained in rebel hands throughout the seventeenth century, and the focal point of rebellion in the late seventeenth and early eighteenth centuries shifted to the western parts of Bengal and in Bihar.[136]

Like *zamīndārs* in the region, the companies were law enforcers and justice givers, sometimes in cooperation with and oftentimes in contravention to the authority of the *faujdār* or the *qāzī*. With the military force at their command, both the EIC and VOC enforced the law—especially the law that they themselves had minted, either in Batavia, or in London, or in Chinsurah/Calcutta.[137] As a directorate, the Hugli council of the VOC had one law enforcement official, the *fiscaal*, formally an official under the Council of Justice in Batavia, who dispensed justice in consultation with the council in Bengal as well as in Batavia. In general, the Hugli council followed the statutes designed in Batavia with active guidance of the States General in Amsterdam. However, from time to time through heated debates with the governor general in Batavia, the lower-level Bengal government made significant modifications in enforcing the statutes. The EIC originally set up a *zamīndāri* court in Calcutta to try natives in criminal and civil matters. Later, in 1726, they received a royal charter from London to set up a Mayor's Court and a Court of Oyer and Terminer and Gaol Delivery to try English subjects. The aldermen and mayor were sent from England, while the president and five men of the Fort William council acted as justices of the peace and commissioners of the Court of Oyer and Terminer and Gaol Delivery.[138] As records indicate, jurisdictional division between the *zamīndāri* courts and the mayor's court was not always maintained; indigenous litigants too came to the mayor's court.[139] These law courts or judicial officials sometimes even issued death sentences. As Shirin Akhtar shows, *zamīndārs* in Bengal often carried out death penalties, even though it was a violation of their judicial powers.[140] Both the VOC and EIC gave out death sentences to their European servants and slaves with de facto impunity. While discussing the death sentence of a slave of a junior merchant, the VOC director Jan Sichterman said, "in this land (Bengal) everyone knows that one has as much law as he has courage and power to execute something." Sichterman boasted being "infamous" in his endeavors to mete out harsh punishments to anyone he deemed an offender of VOC interests, which he claimed "restored the awe and respect for the company." He also added that both the French and English carried out capital punishments in their settlements, "in full view of the world," and no one objected to it.[141] Later, Louis Taillefert, director of the VOC (1755, 1760–63), explained that the legal jurisdiction of the VOC only excluded capital punishment for natives of Bengal, Bihar, and Orissa. As for the rest, the "local government seldom or never meddled even in criminal matters."[142]

Impediments to effective policing also stemmed from the limited jurisdictions of the *zamīndāri* forces. The authority of *zamīndārs* was limited strictly within the bounds of their *zamīndāris*. Robbers who committed theft in one *zamīndāri* and took shelter in another were difficult to apprehend. Inter-*zamīndāri* rivalry and competition facilitated crime, as extradition and punishment depended upon good will between two *zamīndārs*. Such good will was rare in eighteenth-century Bengal as a few *zamīndāris* attempted expansion at the cost of smaller *zamīndārs*, thereby heightening inter-*zamīndāri* competition and mistrust. For example, the Dinajpur *zamīndārs* were well-known warrior rajas who between 1682 and 1780 brought under their administration over four thousand square miles of land through sheer use of force. Raja Prannanth alone defeated and usurped twelve neighboring *zamīndārīs* between 1682 and 1720.¹⁴³ The fragmentation of *zamīndārī* jurisdiction was heightened in cases where the *zamīndārī* spread out over noncontiguous areas, making it difficult to determine the jurisdiction where the crime was committed. Moreover, many *zamīndārīs* were internally fragmented as a result of too many descendants. Nine shareholders of Muhammad Aminpur *zamīndārī* were responsible for the maintenance of the Cātoā *thana*. The weak police control as a result of divided authorities over the *thana* ultimately ended in Cātoā becoming the headquarters of Maratha invaders of Bengal throughout the 1740s.¹⁴⁴

The European companies exerted their jurisdictional authority by either clashing with other *zamīndārs* or entering into diplomatic relations with them. The companies utilized their military to guard their inland shipping. The instruction given out to Captain Pielat, commander of the VOC Patna fleet in 1723, specifically mentioned every *zamīndār* and his military strength along the way—the goal of these instructions was to prepare the fleet commanders for combat with these local lords whenever the need arose.¹⁴⁵ A few years later, when Commander van der Helling learned from his spies that a *zamīndār*, engaged in a dispute with a *faujdār*, was crossing Sitakund with an army of two thousand mounted men, he immediately gave orders to set up an impromptu army camp located in the shadow of a mountain which provided a "good chest shield."¹⁴⁶ The cannon was put in place, the sentinels circled the camp—the company was ready for a fight, if it came their way. The EIC, too, launched military offensives against demanding *zamīndārs* without mincing words. In July 1719, the Chakwar, a rebellious clan of an autonomous chiefdom around Patna, raided EIC possessions. The Fort William council sent a squadron under Captain Richard Hunt and two ensigns.¹⁴⁷ Two years later, not far from Chakwar land, at Bīrpur, Richard Hunt led a retribution campaign in which he took prisoners of war and "were oblig'd to burn part of the town."¹⁴⁸ Sometimes, the dealings between the *zamīndārs* took the form of diplomatic relations. The VOC records provide a rare and overlooked window into this extremely important aspect of intra-*zamīndārī* relations and the relations between the European companies and lower-level political powers in the region. For example, in 1733 the VOC entered into a formal contract with Mohammad Adraseer, the *zamīndār* of Kharagpur, in the *sarkār* Mongeer, whereby the *zamīndār* stated that he would ensure safe passage of the VOC fleet through his territory and provide all help to salvage VOC boats which met with accident within his territory.¹⁴⁹ Such multilateral relationships of conflict or negotiation made policing extremely difficult, for apart from respecting the limitations of their jurisdictional powers, the companies had to rely on the goodwill of other *zamīndārs*.

An overarching, strong political force above the *zamīndārs* might have solved the policing problem stemming from limited and competing jurisdictions, but the reach of the Mughal (and after 1717, the Nawabi) forces remained very weak. In 1699, when the governor of Bengal decided to post a *qāzī* in Calcutta, who would be responsible to the *faujdār* of Hugli, the EIC settled the situation by giving a hefty bribe to 'Azīm-ush-shān, the governor.[150] The limited interference of imperial forces was not fully reversed in the Nawabi period. Historians do not agree to what extent *zamīndāri* powers were attenuated in the Nawabi period, with Murshid Quli Khan's and subsequent Nawabs' attempts at regional centralization.[151] As later chapters in this book demonstrate, from time to time companies approached the Nawab and/or other imperial officials requesting *parwānās* to seek redress against their workers. Sometimes such requests were fruitful and at other times not, leaving companies to their own devices. Similarly the Nawab's offices did sometimes emerge as a refuge for workers seeking redress for their grievances or leverage for their demands vis-à-vis the EIC. But that was not necessarily the chosen path for these workers. Most importantly, the companies, like other *zamīndārs*, continued to exercise their judicial powers with the military forces at their disposal. One estimate shows that only a small force of 200 cavalry and 4,000 infantry represented the military power of Murshid Quli Khan.[152] In such circumstances, *zamīndārs* were expected to help out central forces with a fixed quota of cavalry and boats as well as victuals and other daily necessaries.[153] As a result, the military power of the *zamīndārs* grew rapidly. For instance, the Raja of Birbhum had 2,000 cavalry and 1,200 shield-bearing soldiers.[154] Militarily formidable *zamīndāris* ultimately meant no resolution to the divisive nature of police jurisdictions.

Moreover, even though the Nawab interfered with the *zamīndār*'s legal jurisdiction from time to time, he scarcely interfered into the bilateral/multilateral relations among *zamīndārs*. In 1721 when Kanta babu, an important broker of the EIC, was accused of murdering his wife, the Nawab Murshid Quli Khan promptly arrested him. Kanta babu was later told that the Nawab's jurisdiction included the *zamīndāri* of the English.[155] In another instance, in 1739, the Nawab's forces arrested a party of EIC soldiers when they went "too far into Muxadavad" pursuing four deserters. The soldiers had violated the jurisdictional boundaries of the Nawab's authority.[156] Such deliberate interventions in the activities of the EIC were many, especially as the Nawabi forces in Bengal, contrary to the designs of Mughal imperial forces in Delhi, wanted to rein in the powers of the EIC and counterbalance the EIC's importance in the region by promoting other trading groups, chiefly the Armenians.[157] Yet, the Nawab's authority over the EIC *zamīndāri* had its limits. In 1740, when the EIC approached Nawab Ali Vardi Khan with a complaint against the *zamīndār* of Sultanpur, who had stopped one of the EIC boats and robbed a peon on it, the Nawab advised the EIC "to take their own satisfaction." Accordingly, the EIC sent the army under the commandership of Captain Sourbuts to Sultanpur.[158] In matters where two *zamīndārs* fought each other, the Nawab remained neutral.

The Nawab's neutrality made extradition of convicts impossible, as did the European companies' inability to make firm arrangements with either the Nawabi government or the indigenous *zamīndārs* on such matters. Even though occasionally European companies signed treaties for mutually returning deserters (see chapter 3), the imperial government in Bengal never concluded such agreements with the companies even though they continued to lay jurisdictional claim on subjects of the European companies. Moreover, the companies' negotiations with adjacent *zamīndārs* precluded such arrangements. The 1733 contract between the VOC and Mohammad Adraseer made no mention of convict or vagabond exchange, even though the VOC had achieved this privilege in and around their headquarters in Batavia. If convicts deserted to territories of other *zamīndārs*, the companies had to fight the *zamīndārs*, without any help from the Nawab, for retrieving the accused. Rupram Kolu, an oil presser, who rented a shop in a Calcutta bazar, was indebted to the EIC for rent arrears in 1718. To avoid paying up rent, the next year, he ran away seven miles to the north of Calcutta, to the adjacent *zamīndāri* of Ram Bhadra, from whom the EIC had purchased its own *zamīndāri*. The EIC sent out a party of their native gunmen to apprehend Rupram. While the gunmen were escorting Rupram back, Ram Bhadra's army attacked. Rupram got away and there were two or three casualties on the English side. The EIC retaliated by kidnapping Ram Bhadra's uncle along with a relative and a servant. The furious Ram Bhadra plundered an EIC *gomastah* and nine other Calcutta merchants who had gone over to Ram Bhadra's territory to do business. This time the company sent fifty European soldiers and thirty *burkundāzes* (native gunmen) under the commandership of Captain Nicholas Rowe and Ensign Gulielmus to Ram Bhadra's territory in order to "peremptorily demand the immediate delivery of all our people with their goods and money, or that we will burn his whole country and destroy all before us." The next year the same querulous *zamīndār* attacked Baranagar, a Dutch *zamīndārī* adjacent to Calcutta, and several displaced tenants of the VOC came to Calcutta "to request our [the EIC's] protection." The EIC allowed these people along with their families to settle.[159] All these activities continued without any involvement of the Nawab. Such incidents give us a sense of how the EIC's and for that matter all European companies' law enforcement mechanism was enmeshed in conflicts with other political equals in the region. Conflict with the Nawab or the neighboring *zamīndārs* severely curtailed the companies' ability to monitor the mobility of their subjects, especially the recalcitrant ones.

In Bihar the distinction between local and supra-local political jurisdictions was even more complicated due to the presence of *jāgīrdārs*. Unlike in Bengal, from where Murshid Quli Khan removed all *jāgīrdārī* claims to Orissa, Bihar did not see any restructuring of the *jāgīr* system. In fact, the Bengal Nawabs continued to grant *jāgīr* lands in Bihar until the middle of the eighteenth century. That compounded the problem of maintaining law and order or dispensing justice for both the *jāgīrdārs* and the *zamīndārs*. Often their interests clashed, leading to anarchic situations within a locality. VOC officials at Hugli noted such clashes during and after the 1725 rebellion of *zamīndār* Bir Shah in the *sarkār* of Purnea. Eighteenth-century historian Salimullah tells us that Seif Khan, the *faujdār*, and a trusted friend of Murshid Quli Khan, successfully crushed the rebellion, driving Bir Shah's son from the region. In order to stifle such rebellions in the future, the *zamīndār*'s land was given as a *jāgīr* to the head of the Nawab's artillery, as one VOC report observed.[160] The VOC report also noted that the tensions between the *jāgīrdār* and the *zamīndār* were still brewing a year later, even though such information is lacking in Salimullah's account.[161] Similarly, in several places close to Patna, the Subahdar of Bihar and the rebellious autonomous chiefs of the Chakwar clan maintained equal number of armed forces. The Chakwars commanded 2,000 cavalry and 2,500 gunmen. Another eighteenth-century historian of Bengal, Ghulam Husain Tabatabai, who came from a *jāgīrdārī* family in Bihar, was candid in his misgivings about *zamīndārs*: "They are a set of men faithless to a high degree, short sighted, impatient of control, ever ready, on the least appearance of revolution, to turn their backs on their masters, and to forget the most important favours received at their hands."[162] This mistrust was one of the many signs of a lack of any centralized rule in early eighteenth-century Eastern India.

With such overlapping and competing jurisdictions, what was the power of the state in coercing labor? In eighteenth-century Bengal there clearly was not one state. For the most part, imperial and Nawabi forces could successfully coerce labor only in and around some of the urban centers. One comes across such city-based forced labor in the seventeenth-century poet Rupram's *Dharmamaṅgal*, which describes how the vizier of the King of Gaur ordered his *kotwāl* to levy forced labor (*begār*) from the city dwellers in order to build a temple for Dharmathākur.[163] Each house had to send two people with a shovel to work at the construction site. People started deserting, and so every evening after work, the laborers were tethered. Despite this use of force, these workers received 5 gandā,[164] cowries, and a half seer[165] of rice a day for hire. Force was counterbalanced with wages, as the captive labor pool was small and could be maintained only temporarily. An account by Dutch participants in Mir Jumla's Assam expedition in 1662–63 noted that outside of Dhaka, along the way through which the imperial military had passed, only one in twenty houses were occupied. People had deserted with their belongings for fear that "the army of the Mogols could carry away with them whatever came their way."[166] It is not clear whether the army tried raiding the villages for provisions and money or for manpower. One needs to consider such impressions with a grain of salt, as the Mughal emperor and imperial officials issued multiple orders banning *begār*.[167] It is likely that the imperial state depended upon their officials and *zamīndārs* for such coercion. For military labor, the Mughal state often held their officers personally liable for errant soldiers; officers could expect deductions from their salaries in cases where soldiers for whom they had provided security fled without return. Labor governance including recruitment thus devolved on the personal capacities of these officers.[168] Besides, *zamīndārs*, after all, were an important source for military labor to the imperial government, as were East India companies. Certain *dharmasūtras* vouch for rulers' claims on labor; rulers could call for labor in lieu of taxes.[169] Even so, the ability of the *zamīndārs* to coerce labor within their jurisdiction was further constrained by the fact that intermediary land settlers retained their own rights to coerce labor.[170] Effective coercion thus depended upon time-consuming and arduous negotiations and arrangements among discrete competing sovereign authorities—Mughal, Nawabi officials, *zamīndārs*, *ta'alluqdārs*, or smaller holders of rent-free land.[171]

The most common form of bonded labor discussed in the *maṅgalkābyas* or ballads was not coerced labor (*begār*) for the state, but debt bondage. In Mukundaram Chakraborty's *Chandīmaṅgal*, Murāri Śīl, the village moneylender, personified the relationship between the village community and Kālketu's forest-dwelling (Byadh) family. As a creditor, Kālketu was bound by debt to bring to Śīl's house the meat of animals that he hunted from time to time. He was also obligated to perform certain chores for the Seal household, such as bringing wood from the forest. His debt to Murari Śīl tied the forest-dwelling untouchable Byadh's ambulatory practices to the economic life of the village. Many like Kālketu were indebted to the "crooked" Murari Śīl, who went door to door collecting interest. Debts often passed on through the generations.[172] Multiple *dharmasūtras* mention intergenerational norms of repaying debt through manual labor.[173] Through Dingādhar, the protagonist of the ballad *Mahiṣāl bandhu*, one finds a moving depiction of debt bondage over generations. Though born into a small landholder family, Dingādhar was reduced to being a servant of Balarām, the village moneylender, because he was unable to repay the one hundred rupees that his father had borrowed. Dingādhar was bound to Balarām as his cowherd for six years. He pondered upon the weight of his debt slavery: "The sin of debt is never to be pardoned in this birth or the next."[174] Even so, in the absence of state intervention, it is only to a limited extent that debt bound workers. Debt bondage of silk reelers and its effects is discussed in chapter 4.

The state authorities—Mughal, Nawabi, and *zamīndāri*—created a tension between efforts to mobilize a laboring population to settle the expanding horizons of both agrarian and urban land, on the one hand and to prevent them from deserting their settlements, on the other. This state-generated "tensional force," underpinning mobility was further accentuated by the overlapping and contested jurisdictions of the local and the supra-local authority of the land settlers, *zamīndārs*, and the Mughal emperors/Bengal Nawabs. In such a situation, the capacity of any one state authority to coerce labor through the prevention of illicit movement was limited.[175] Workers in such a scenario faced coercion primarily through debt bondage and occasionally through the state use of forced labor (*begār*). Both the VOC and EIC realized that even when they achieved their political place in eighteenth-century Bengal, they were beset with a number of jurisdictional problems typical of the powerful *zamīndāri* system. The problems were further accentuated by their lack of political power in most places outside their headquarters, where they were obligated to act strictly in their capacity as merchants. All these circumstances made it impossible for them to control the mobility of hired workers the way they did in Europe and their other Asian possessions.

THE MEANING OF HIRE

In a region marked by high levels of commercialization through global trade and politically by strong *zamīndāri* control and lack of centralized state authority, hired work, though ubiquitous, nevertheless stopped short of becoming a purely market relation. As Om Prakash has claimed, Bengal was the gateway for bullion imports into Mughal India.[176] Chāṅd's head pilot in the seventeenth-century poet Jagajjiban Ghoṣal's *Manasāmaṅgal* says, "Money is the unparalleled enchanter of the world," seducing paramours of other men, swaying their fidelity and blinding them to caste restrictions, and "without money a man loses the respect of his sons and the pleasure of his wife's embrace."[177] Given the widespread use of money and hired labor in the region, as early as the sixteenth century a specialized term for hired labor emerged in Bengali literature. Sixteenth-century poet Mukundaram Chakraborty's *Chandīmaṅgal* refers to forest clearers as *beruniÿajan*, a term derived from the Persian word *beruniÿā*, meaning "the outsider." However, in Bengali, unlike in Persian, *berun* means hired work. Thus, both forest clearers and tailors in the same text refer to their work as *berun*.[178] In Bengal, mobile work was synonymous with hired labor. While monetization and unequal peasant holdings led to mobile hired work, almost all social relations of hired workers and employers bore the mark of patron-client relationships. A host of studies now show that the political and economic spheres in premodern Bengal were intricately intertwined.[179] Markets themselves, as Sudipta Sen explains, were extensions of the patrimonies of *zamīndārs*. Almost all forms of wage relations were practiced in a society where the domain of the political was not separated neatly from the economic. One can notice the inseparable nature of political and economic realms in Brahmanical jurisprudence which, while centering around the ethical/holy life of the *gṛhastha* (married householder), was "also a socio-political blueprint of proper management of society by the king."[180] For workers, entering into wage relations meant entering into this politico-economic relationship of a client to a patron, even though they were aware that there were several other such potential relationships and both retained the option for exit. This polysemy of wage relationship, or what David Washbrook calls "lack of sociological 'differentiation' in Indian labour relations," was best manifest in the hire, as "'wage' might comprise many different things."[181] Several *maṅgalkābyas*, such as the *Manasāmaṅgalkābyas* and the *Chandīmaṅgalkābyas*, which presented the societal ideal of hierarchical order, represent hired work as a relationship bearing the mark of dual and sometimes contradictory notions of (economic) exchange and (political) obligation, often expressed in wage payment.

Poets of *mangalkābyas* depict several explicit, monetized examples of hired labor. In Pipilāi's text, in exchange for his work, the destitute Chānd demanded a meal a day, four pieces of clothing, and one rupee per month. Chānd was given the task of weeding, and was provided with tools—a pair of scissors, a basket, and a straw hat.[182] In Jagajjiban Ghoṣal's story, Chānd as a porter was offered a hire of five annas.[183] However, Jagai, the headman in Bijay Gupta's text, commandeered Chānd's labor in return for a square meal of rice. In such cases where wages were fully paid in kind, the distinction between pure exchange and relations of obligations became blurred.

Some transactions of hire thrust on the employer the obligation of sustaining the worker. In seventeenth-century poet Ketakadās Kṣhemananda's *Manasāmangalkābya* the destitute Chānd bargained with the Brahmin landholder, his employer: "I will stay at your place; Give me enough food and water to fill my belly; And I will do any work that you will ask me to do."[184] As conditions of his hire the worker demanded entry into the household of the Brahmin. Chānd's hire was his subsistence. However, the arrangement soon came to an end when the Brahmin kicked Chānd out of his household due to his poor work. Conditions of exchange determined the limits of obligation of the employer to his hired worker.

The paternalism of the Brahmin householder towards his hired worker, Chānd, while similar to paternalism of householders of seventeenth-century England, differed in important ways. The English translation of Xenophon's *Oeconomicus* is instructive. By the late seventeenth century, the rising middle class in England saw in this text a manual for designing and disciplining the household, including patriarchal control over servants. In the English translation, "slaves" in the original Greek text is transformed into "servants"—the condition of servants on English estates, even while not being the property of their masters, approximated the conditions of slaves in ancient Greece in as much as they were part of the *oikos* (estates) as servile dependents, without being part of the master's family. The normative nature of this servility stands in stark contrast to Chānd's position in his employer's household. In Gentian Hervet's widely popular translation of *Oeconomicus*, Ischomachus prescribed appropriate measures to discipline absconding servants who stole from their masters: "I take here a pece of Dracons lawes, and here a pece af Solons, and so endeuour my selfe to bringe my seruantes to folowe iustice. For me thinketh that these men haue made many lawes to teche men iustice. For they haue wrytten, that he muste be punysshed that steleth, and he that robbeth muste be put in prison and put to dethe."¹⁸⁵

While masters of hired workers in the *maṅgalkābyas* often resorted to corporal punishment, paternal discipline, vide Brahmanical conduct, could not claim the hired worker's life. Nor was there any direct recourse to the state, unlike in sixteenth-century England, where patriarchal control over servants could always call on the help of the state to instill a sense of "justice and rightfulnes." In the eighteenth century Daniel Defoe echoed such symbiotic relationship between masters and the state in governing servants when he suggested that a master who was unwilling to send his errant servants before justices of the peace should be heavily fined.¹⁸⁶ If the Greek *oikos* constituted the foundation of the seventeenth-century English polis, the polis strongly and explicitly structured the moral order of the *oikos*. Such a relationship between discrete entities of the *oikos* and the polis is absent in the *maṅgalkābyas*.¹⁸⁷

Limits of state control also made way for a plural means of sustenance beyond hired work. For instance, access to forested lands mitigated to some extent the dependence of the landless poor on hired labor. Eighteenth-century historian Ghulam Hussain Salim described the human landscape of Bengal: "And the wilderness and habitation of this country are similar [to other parts of Mughal India] in that the people erect huts of thatch made up of bamboos and straw.... Whenever quitting one place they migrate to another straightaway. They erect a thatched hut similar to their former one.... Most of their habitations are in jungles and forests. So their huts are surrounded with trees."¹⁸⁸ Indeed, the forest hut of the hunter-gatherer family of Fullarā and Kālketu, hut embodied Salim's historical description. Forest land was abundant despite the forest clearance activities of the Mughal state. Forests were occasionally taxed under the Mughal state—but only that part of the forest cover which was used as pasture land near a densely populated village. In thinly populated villages pasture lands were not assessed for revenue.¹⁸⁹ In Eastern India, large parts of forested lands came under the control of autonomous chiefs (*peshkashi zamīndārs*), who paid a fixed tribute to the Mughal state. Since these chiefs came from tribal societies in the forests, they maintained the communal rights over forests even while extending agrarian land.¹⁹⁰ Moreover, given that only 1.5 percent of the land was measured, wooden tracts of land would be least likely to be taxed even in *khālsa* (imperial) lands. As late as 1798, the EIC civil servant and doctor Francis Buchanan Hamilton in Bengal noted, "The woods are not considered property for every ryot may go into them and cut whatever timber they want."[191] The destitute could thus live off the forest. The image of the forest as autonomous territory is recurrent in texts from the fifteenth through the eighteenth centuries. The Dom families of the *Dharmamaṅgals* and the Byadh family of Kālketu and Fullarā in Mukundaram Chakraborty's *Chaṇḍīmaṅgal* utilized the forest as a resource for sustenance. Their status as untouchables meant that their huts were located in the midst of forests. The forest's wood, foliage, and meat provided them with marketable commodities as well as essential material for everyday use, such as food and clothing. However, forest dwellers did not maintain complete economic autonomy.[192] Members of settled communities were constantly in contact with forest dwellers for essential commodities of everyday life.[193] Even though the forest provided them with resources which connected them to the moneyed economy of the village—Kālketu and Fullarā through bringing meat and food to their creditor's family and the village market, and the Dom families through bamboo and reed mats which they sold in the village market—it also provided them with shelter and resources outside the realm of a market economy.

Access to forest resources was open to all—caste barriers had no sway outside of settled lands. In the fifteenth-century poet Bipradas Pipilai's *Manasāmaṅgal*, the once-rich Chāṅd after his shipwreck found refuge in one such forest. There he collected a load of branches and sold it to a village potter for 4 pons or 5 annas.[194] Two centuries later, the depiction of the destitute Chāṅd in Ketakadās Kṣhemananda's text painted a similar picture. Chāṅd's perambulations led him to meet a group of woodcutters. A day's work of chopping wood in the forest fetched them 10 annas in the village market. Woodcutting, they declared, was the "practice of their *jāti*."[195] It is unlikely that *jāti* here means caste, precisely because woodcutting historically was never a caste occupation—every member of the village society had access to the wood.[196] Rather, *jāti* here refers to a collective existence dependent on cutting, collecting, and selling wood. The porosity of this collectivity is evident from the woodcutters' ready acceptance of Chāṅd into their group. Since the rights over the forest's bounty belonged to no one there was no anxiety about sharing resources.

Mobility, collective rights such as access to forest resources, and availability of seasonal work ensured that the poor in Bengal were not wholly transformed into a large pool of dispossessed and readily available unskilled labor for hire. By the early eighteenth century, a steady source of menial workers or "coolies" settled in villages around urban settlements—especially company settlements. However, this was by no means a pan-Bengal phenomenon. In fact, the VOC officials found it difficult to recruit coolies once they moved outside their regular territory of work. In 1719, the VOC's Hugli council sent the merchant Pieter Hoofmeester to Kanthi to oversee the unlading work of a ship near Kanthi. Hoofmeester was a fish out of water in an unknown hostile place. He wrote a letter to the director of the Hugli council requesting a long list of necessities. The list included "200 coolies from Hugli," as "a coolie from Hugli can do more work than 10–12 coolies here who are merely salt makers." Hoofmeester further complained that he could "get not even 10 men together" as it was already salt-making season.[197] Kanthi's poor chose to work at the salt pans in preference to the onerous work of porterage. Similarly in 1734, the company had to hire four coolies with boats carrying saltpeter at Bakarganj on the journey through the delta, for the pay of 1.6 anna per day or 0.6 anna more than the usual rate of coolie hire around Kassimbazar as coolies were hard to come by.[198] Dispossessions in Kanthi or Bakarganj did not automatically lead to a supply of coolies, as could be easily found around company settlements such as Hugli.

Artisanal work, too, was hired work and hence came to be marked by the dualism of exchange and obligations. From 'Ain-i-Akbari, we know that artisans received piece wages for their manufactured items in the Mughal workshops.[199] The *maṅgal* poems also hint at distribution of wages paid by patrons to the artisan after receiving the finished article.[200] Certain texts explicitly mention artisan's remuneration in cash.[201] Yet, the voluntary nature of this transactional relationship was subtly qualified. In eighteenth-century poet Narayan Deb's text, the ironsmiths declare that they have "eaten the salt" provided by Chāṅd.[202] The eating of salt was an act of fealty, a practice common in the military culture of South Asia. Indeed, salt constituted a part of the wages of rank-and-file soldiers. Once a common soldier voluntarily accepted salt from his military superior, loyalty was expected from the soldier on the condition that the superior paid the soldier his hire.[203] Thus, Narayan Deb positioned the ironsmith explicitly as the loyal subject of Chāṅd, bound by a reciprocal bond of exchange. Hire for artisans implied both voluntary work as well as a sense of duty, fealty, and obligation.

Limits to commodification of labor were evident in the various customs of payment to all categories of hired workers with limited implication involving caste. In the *maṅgalkābyas*, wages alone—paid in cash or kind—do not fully convey relationships between the employer and his hired worker. For instance, in *Chandīmaṅgal*, Kālketu welcomed the day laborers with *pān* leaves and areca nuts. Even though the wage is inscribed in the very Bengali name of their profession—*beruniyājan*—Mukundaram does not mention any wage payment as the primary medium binding employer to employee. Instead, bestowal of *pān* leaves and areca nuts mediate the relationship between Kālketu and the workers. *Pān* leaves and areca nuts had a symbolic meaning in premodern Bengal and South Asia. Like the gifting of ceremonial silk robes (*khil'at*) in the Mughal imperial circle, people in positions of political power gifted *pān* to their subordinates, thereby sealing a bond in an asymmetrical relationship.[204] Gifting of *pān* was specifically limited to lower gentry, especially small *zamīndārs* and *ta'alluqdārs*.[205] Moreover, caste did not ordain the *pān*-gifting ceremony. As an untouchable, fortified by the benediction of Chandi, Kālketu gifted *pān* to the *beruniyājan*, a collectivity defined by their migrant hired work with no reference to caste. Mukundaram's text is unique in that the ruler is here seen giving *pān* to all his subjects, including hired workers of all kinds. In other *maṅgal* poems, there are several instances of *pān* being offered to artisans, just as Chāṅd does to the ironsmiths in the seventeenth-century poet Narayan Deb's *Padmapurān*.[206] These artisans are often ascribed lower caste status, such as *karmakār* and *kāmār*. In some instances there is no reference to caste, such as in the eighteenth-century poet Mukunda Kabichandra's *Biśallocanīr Gīt*, where Chāṅd gifts *pān* to the two artisan brothers, simply referring to them as *kārikar* (artisans) when commanding them to manufacture the seven ships needed for his overseas trading voyage. Even a ship captain in the seventeenth-century poet Kṛṣṇarām Dās's poem *Rāimaṅgal*, initiates the relationship of employer with his two shipwrights by gifting them *pān*.[207] It is significant that men who are not explicitly part of landholding political positions engage in an explicitly political practice as it signals the conjoined nature of the political and economic domains in the perceptions of the poets, patrons, and listeners of *maṅgal* poems. The artisan, even while receiving his hire, was bound in a political relationship of trust with his employer/patron through the ceremonial practice of gift giving.

If hire symbolized political relationship over and above exchange, then the *oikos* in the *maṅgalkābyas* became an analogy for the polis. Employers *honored* services of their artisans; modes of payment mirrored court ceremonies wherein political elites sealed various relationships of dependence. David

Curley argues that in regional courts of Bengal through the seventeenth century, the gifting of *pān*, native to the region, gradually gave way to the Mughal court etiquette of presenting a silk robe (*khil'at*).²⁰⁸ While anyone with the status of a king would offer a robe to people of high importance (ministers or vassals), *pān* came to be associated with people of lower orders. *Maṅgalkābyas*, however, portray patrons offering both forms of honor to their artisans. In Bipradās Pipilāi's fifteenth-century tale, the still-rich Chāṅd, pleased with his work, rewarded the ironsmith with silk garments.²⁰⁹ The practice continued into the seventeenth century. As *Biśallocanīr Gīt* shows, in return for building him ships, Chāṅd "honors" the artisan shipbuilders with "gift clothes" (*prasād basan*). Chāṅd also offered the artisans *pān* and money.²¹⁰ Mukunda Kabicandra thus described the two prevalent practices of courtly culture to establish the relationship between the artisan and his merchant-*zamīndār* employer. Though artisans in other *maṅgal* poems, often portrayed as impecunious and powerless subjects, were never given the robes of honor, there are several instances where they were offered gold jewelry, a practice associated with the robe-gifting ceremony.²¹¹ In Jagajjiban Ghoṣal's text, Biswakarma, who is commissioned to build an iron room, was sent away with jewelry after the completion of his task.²¹² Poets of *maṅgalkābyas* chose elements of the Mughal culture of robe-gifting alongside representations of *pān*-gifting, to portray the customary bond of reciprocity between the employer and the employed. Just as the Mughal emperor and the Nāẓim of Bengal rewarded the revenue-collecting services of their employees, the employers in *maṅgalkābyas*, who were usually various forms of local gentry, bestowed rewards on their artisans. Hire was a customary bond—not just a disembodied and abstract economic practice—which contributed to the constitution of the entire polity.

Despite their wages, workers shared a patron-client relationship with their employers.²¹³ In such relationships, the fulfillment of customary bonds was important. The social act of wage payment exceeded economic transaction; it encompassed both the political allegiance of the worker in return for the honorific acknowledgement of his work and the paternalistic concern of the employer for the subsistence of the worker. As Nandita Sahai argues, customs were articulations of legitimacy, necessary for rulers and elites to exact revenue and labor from a subaltern population. As workers carried over their notion of customary relationships to company grounds, the companies as *zamīndārs* and merchants—much to their consternation—were compelled to negotiate wages as "customs" or social exchanges with enormous political significance.

This chapter has described the widespread availability of hired work as well as the nature of the employer and state in seventeenth- and early eighteenth-century Bengal from the vantagepoint of hired workers. Mobile hired work was ubiquitous to both rural and urban life. From *zamīndārs* down to settlers, peasants or merchants, big or small, all employed large numbers of hired workers. As a region connected to vast overland and overseas networks of trade, hired work was part and parcel of Bengal's commercial life. The presence of any centralized political control was thin throughout this period. Supra-local political forces—the Mughal imperial state and the Bengal Nizamat/Nawabi—heavily depended on *zamīndārs* for the day-to-day administrative affairs of the province. The *zamīndārs*, with their substantial legal and judicial powers and law enforcement armies, became the primary force for settling and regulating, mobilizing and immobilizing, workers' lives. In this scenario, rights and obligations which constituted the dominant form of political relation—the *zamīndār*-settler relationship—made their mark on hired work. Payments of "rewards" and "honors," which were sometimes extra-monetary and always adjacent to wages, cemented relations of trust, obligation, and reciprocity between hired workers and their masters.

In Bengal, European companies operated both as merchants and as states. With flourishing trade, the companies created and maintained their primary trading settlements as *zamīndārs*. On the one hand, the companies as *zamīndārs* settled people, collected tax, maintained armies, framed laws, and dispensed justice. On the other hand, they faced the limits of their powers just like other *zamīndārs*, as their jurisdictions jostled with the jurisdictions of other neighboring or rival *zamīndārs*, the imperial *faujdārs*, and the Nawab. Because of their position as *zamīndārs* in a complex, decentralized political landscape, the companies from the late seventeenth century onward had to engage in arduous negotiations with hired workers, especially boatmen and silk reelers as well as with their European sailors and soldiers. Articulating themselves as *zamīndārs* with limited power in a foreign culture of work, the companies were impelled to accommodate the forms of mobility and ideas about wages which formed the bedrock of that culture.

TWO

"Quarrelsome Workers"

BOATMEN IN THE EARLY EIGHTEENTH-CENTURY
COMPANY STATE

AN ARMY OF ABOUT ONE HUNDRED VOC soldiers under the command of Captain Jan Geldzak set sail for Patna from Chinsurah in Hugli on the morning of September 16, 1736. September was not a good season for sailing, given the rains and strong countercurrents in the river Hugli. Geldzak's fleet crawled past crumbling banks of the river on both sides. It took them six days to reach Nadia, double the time required in summer months. With the constant help of native pilots, for the next fifteen days, the fleet meandered through various streams moving towards the confluence of the Jalangi and Ganga rivers. Entry into the Ganga was no mean feat. The only passage was a narrow sliver of water. Oarsmen had to pull all the vessels one by one with ropes against the current, requiring nine hours of continuous work. The fleet crossed the Ganga and reached Pintij, in the former province of Bihar. Upon arrival at Pintij, Geldzak had to pay his pilots 10 rupees as was the "custom" for rewarding boatmen to cross over to Bihar.

The next ordeal awaited the fleet at Sitakund, just north of the reefs of Jahangira. The pilots brought bad news—the river at Sitakund was dry and unhospitable to sailing due to a swathe of shallows. After much deliberation, the head pilot reported that a narrow riverbed sandwiched between the bank of the river and the sandbanks was still navigable. However, the narrow passage was only fit for small vessels. Geldzak sent out peons at Kondecatta, a mile below Sitakund, to muster as many small (and light) vessels as possible. For the next two days, the oarsmen performed the backbreaking task of unlading goods from the merchant vessels onto the small vessels and subsequently pulling all the vessels, including the empty merchant vessels, with ropes through the narrow river bed. The head pilot got a reward of 6 rupees for getting through Sitakund. After crossing Sitakund, it became clear to the boatmen that the vessels would have to be hauled up until Mungeer. The oarsmen accomplished the task by building a tow path and dragging the vessels until Mungeer in an astonishingly short time of only two days. From Mungeer the fleet moved on towards Patna with little trouble.

After two months of sailing, the fleet arrived at Patna on November 27, 1736. At Patna with no work at hand the captain and members of the fleet rested. The English Patna fleet had arrived much earlier and thus were finished with their preparations for departure sooner than the VOC fleet. As soon as the English fleet left for Calcutta in mid-December, Captain Geldzak started preparations for the return journey. Luckily, he could hire eighteen *ulak* boats for carrying saltpeter at a reasonable rate to sail down the Sunderbans and then to Chinsurah. Usually, upcountry boatmen avoided the journey through the Sunderbans. After receiving the memorandum of goods laden on the merchant vessels from the chief of the Patna factory, Aukema, the Patna fleet under Captain Geldzak commenced its return journey to Chinsurah on January 31, 1737. Without much trouble, the fleet arrived at Badderpourgola where a VOC cashier from Kassimbazar waited with freshly hired *ulak* boats, carts, and porters. Opium, a lightweight commodity, was placed on the newly hired small *ulaks* and oxcarts and sent to Chinsurah under the escort of Geldzak and a few other soldiers through the river Jalangi. The rest of the fleet, carrying saltpeter, traveled through the Sunderbans to Chinsurah under the command of Ensign Scheurs. Geldzak reached Chinsurah on February 20 and the saltpeter fleet under Ensign Scheurs arrived a month later.[1]

This journey, revealed in Jan Geldzak's journal, was representative of the "Patna fleets." The Dutch and the English East India companies both organized these fleets, from 1701 onwards, to move military personnel from their respective headquarters to Patna, in order to then escort commodities down to Kassimbazar and finally on to Calcutta/Chinsurah. Only recently have historians turned their attention to this intricate world of transportation in eighteenth-century Bengal, focusing on routes, means, and modes of transport.[2] However, the backbone of this intricate world—transport workers, especially boatmen—find almost no place in their narratives of the EIC state's increasing management of transport. While scholarship on work and workers on deep-sea vessels in the eighteenth century across Asia has grown over the last twenty years, histories of boats and boatmen are woefully lacking.[3] Boatmen were an important group of workers in eighteenth-century Bengal. James Rennell, the first geographer of the EIC to map Bengal, estimated that in 1781 that there were 30,000 boatmen making a livelihood out of managing the river Ganga's traffic.[4] Another estimate from 1815 reveals that the number rose to 50,000 boatmen annually, plying some 5,000 boats of various capacities.[5] Boats, too, were a mainstay for the European companies' inland transportation network and the companies had been directly hiring boatmen since the seventeenth century. In the early eighteenth century, companies employed as many as three hundred boats in one fleet, hiring over a thousand boatmen. Manning inland waterborne transportation was no less intricate than manning a large East Indiaman requiring a great deal of rowing, fathoming, fording, heaving, towpath making, lading, and unlading. The deep-sea vessels in the Age of Sail have been compared to factory-like workspaces, and so too did the fleets of the VOC and EIC, with their synchronized and specialized workers, resemble one large complex machine.

Nevertheless, through their mobility practices, boatmen constantly undermined the synchronized operation of this complex machine. This chapter charts the contentious boatmen-company relationship in the early eighteenth century. Company officials, especially the army, orchestrated the fleet as an amalgamation of the distinct skills of various boatmen and other transport workers who moved through a tortuous route and performed an elaborate task over months. On the principle of what the seventeenth-century polymath and father of political economy William Petty called increasing "convenience" or creation of situations that would lead to constant cost reduction, the companies struggled to create an order in recruitment and supervision of boatmen.[6] In other words, their goal was to achieve what Marx called "cooperation," or "when numerous workers work side by side in accordance with a plan."[7] Yet, no such "plan" of the companies could ever take off as the boatmen's notions of state, authority, customs, time, and wages were at odds with the "value of conveniency." Moreover, the companies had to vie with one another as well as with other indigenous merchants such as the salt merchants in implementing their plan for their hired boatmen. Using information from the archives of both the VOC and EIC, the *maṅgalkābyas*, and boatmen's songs, this chapter explores the route, structure, and work process of the Patna fleets and the integral function of boatmen in it. Several recruitment zones and processes along the route indicate that there was no streamlined market for boatmen's labor ready with recruitment agents and intermediaries. Boatmen's perceptions of work and life, which shaped the hiring process significantly, had their moorings in the sociocultural world of the eighteenth century. Often boatmen articulated their "customs" in advancing their demands on hire and time in their wranglings with the companies. They augmented their bargaining chips by deserting. The companies, unable to control their mobility, had very little choice but to acquiesce to their demands.

MOVING THE FLEET

Beginning in 1701 the transport sector of the VOC and EIC witnessed major transformations as a result of the militarization of company settlements. Following the rebellion by *zamīndār* Sobha Singh in 1695, the Bengal Nawab allowed the companies to keep their own military forces.[8] The ability to militarize meant deploying large numbers of boats in "fleets" which carried company troops to escort the movement of commodities among all outposts, particularly between Patna and Chinsurah (VOC's headquarters) and Calcutta (EIC's headquarters). Noting the effectiveness of the militarization of inland transport, the first EIC geographer of Bengal, James Rennell, stated: "In a military view, it [the Ganga] opens a communication between the different posts, and serves in the capacity of a military way through the country; renders unnecessary the forming of magazines; and infinitely surpasses the celebrated inland navigation of North America."[9] Even though European companies hardly dominated the traffic on the Ganga, which was the subcontinent's major highway of inland trade, their large, heavily militarized fleets stood out. For instance, one VOC fleet, travelling to Patna in 1724, consisted of more than 300 European soldiers and 156 boats.[10] Of those 156 boats, only 10 carried goods; 75 vessels carried common soldiers, and the rest carried officials and their belongings.[11]

Larger convoys, in turn, brought about a change in the route for inland shipping. Throughout the seventeenth century, the companies used the Bhagirathi and Hugli rivers as the prime waterway to outposts north of Hugli. Hence, boats coming from Patna first made a stop at Kassimbazar and then sailed for Hugli.[12] For smaller consignments the route was suitable but not for large, militarized fleets. To ensure the smooth movement of a large number of medium-weight vessels, the companies chose a new riverine route whose water level allowed for year-round navigation. Thus, the river Jalangi was preferred to the Bhagirathi/Hugli. Rennell noted that neither the Kassimbazar stream of the Ganga nor the Hugli was fit for navigation

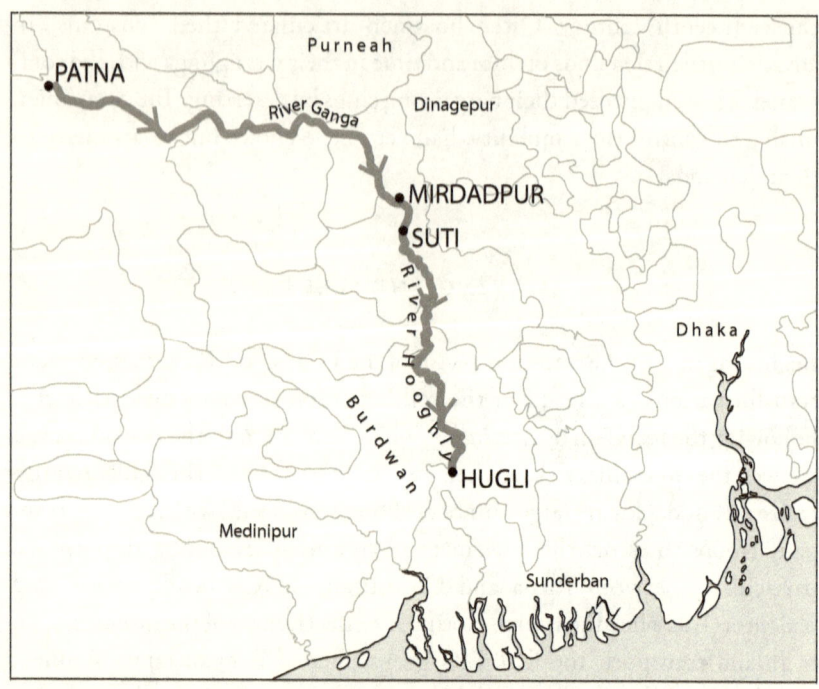

MAP 1. Seventeenth-century riverine route from Patna to Hugli.

between October and May because of alluvial deposit. The Jalangi, which suffered only two to three months of low water, was the preferred route (see maps 1 and 2).[13]

There was no particular time of the year for the movement of the fleets. The VOC sent out their vessels anytime between July and September from Chinsurah, and the vessels arrived from Patna anytime between December and April of the next year. The EIC's departure or arrival time of the fleet showed even less of a pattern. Vessels from Calcutta were sent as early as June or as late as September. Departure of laden boats from Patna followed a similar time frame. This sets inland shipping in stark contrast to Indian Ocean maritime travel where the rhythm of monsoon winds determined the seasons for sailing.[14] The reasons for this flexibility were many—first, year-long navigability of the Jalangi; second, use of a wide variety of boats with both oars and sails allowed less dependence on favorable winds; and finally, reliance of the companies on boatmen with distinct skills. Ecological factors structured how discrete groups of boatmen, depending upon their regions of operation, showed preference for one route over other. The distinctions among boatmen

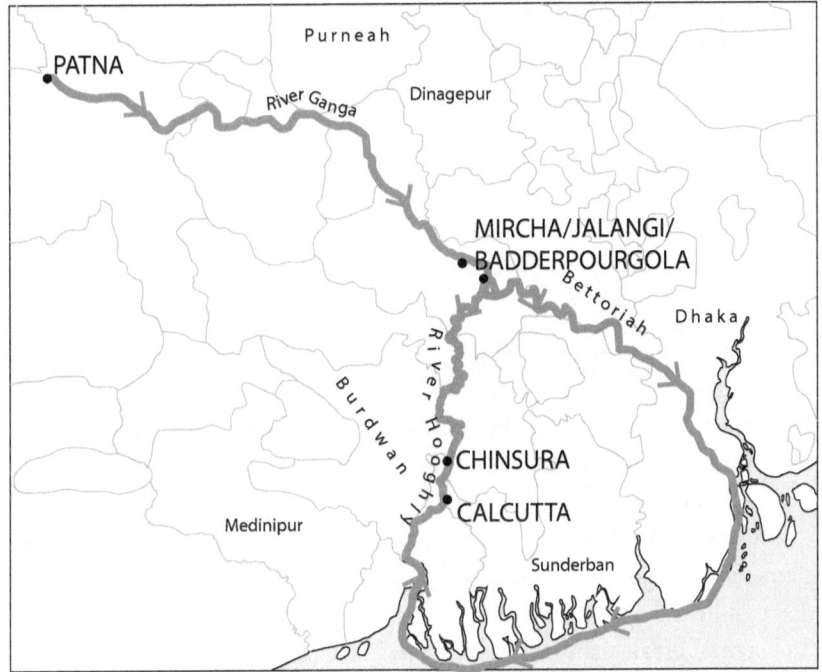

MAP 2. Eighteenth-century routes for riverine and coastal travel between Patna and Calcutta.

are discussed in detail later in this chapter. With increased flexibility, fleets could often be dispatched according to various needs of the companies such as the schedule for overseas voyage and the procurement of commodities upstream, rather than being dependent on seasonal navigability.

Irrespective of the seasons, the daily schedule for fleet boatmen on the move remained the same. Their usual workday lasted from sunup to sundown. With cannon shot or bugle call at daybreak, the entire fleet set sail, and half an hour before sunset, the fleet camped at an empty site by the riverbank chosen by the *darogah*, or principal native supervisor of the fleet.[15] However, in times of emergency, boatmen would work for the entire twenty-four hours, with two- to four-hour breaks. Such workdays (and nights) could last a week or more at a stretch.[16]

The strenuous—not to mention tedious—work of rowing was tempered with work songs called *sāri*. Rhythm—either fast-paced or slow, depending on the nature of work at hand—was central to these songs. Boatmen at work singing *sāri* are mentioned in Bijay Gupta's fifteenth-century text, *Padmapurān*:

> Boatmen in all vessels sing sāri
> As they come down the stream.[17]

These songs were sung in unison, where the song helped the rowers unify and ultimately increase their pace:

> Row, row say the rowers singing sāri
> ....
> Their song made a huge noise
> As the boats moved
> Muddying the water of the river.[18]

The thrashing oars turned the color of the river water brown as the boats moved forward. These songs were rooted in the social and cultural world of late medieval Bengal.

It was the custom of the boatmen of Bengal not to make any stops in the course of their journey throughout the day. Even though the boats passed through densely populated villages lining the banks of the river, they never took a meal break at any of these places. Each evening, boats halted at uninhabited places. Except for the army officers, everyone got together to set up enormous makeshift camps. After dusk, the campsite was dotted with several burning ovens carved out of the ground by the pick axes and trowels that all boats carried. The crew of each boat huddled around its own oven, cooking and eating their communal meal of boiled rice.

Even though the boatmen could withstand the physical exertion of rowing for over twelve hours on one meager meal a day, company officials and their soldiers on the other hand had no desire to stave off hunger for that long. Hence, the companies always included in their fleets special medium-sized vessels called "oven boats." These boats were company creations with brick ovens built into them. This was a departure from the practices of indigenous travelers, for whom eating a hot meal during a journey was unthinkable. In the 1770s, the narrative of inland travel by a native doctor, Bijayrām Sen, shows that indigenous travelers were accustomed to eating their daily meal only after the boats had anchored in the evening.[19] In contrast, every top army official had an oven boat assigned to his service, and there were also oven boats preparing food for the rank and file of the army. These boats were constructed by the companies in their headquarters and obviated the need to stock up on provisions prior to the journey, given that for most of the journey, the fleet would move through densely populated regions.[20]

The *dandies*, or rowers, of the fleet, performed several essential tasks in addition to rowing. Often, where the river was too shallow or the countercurrents too strong, they had to lay down their oars, get off their boats, and drag them with ropes, wading knee-deep through the water. The upriver journey against the current was especially backbreaking. Hauling could last for several days. When VOC Captain Pielat's fleet reached the reefs of Oeriab on September 29, 1727, he had to patiently wait for three days as boatmen from the English fleet, ahead of the Dutch fleet, dragged their vessels one by one through a narrow pass amid the reefs. Pielat was preparing his own men to do the same.[21] And the oarsmen of Captain Geldzak's fleet in 1736 performed the miraculous task of pulling all of the vessels past the city of Bhagalpur against a strong current while both banks of the river were caving in.[22] If the boatmen were lucky, the water by the banks of the river would be deep enough for them to drag the boats while walking on the banks. But walking on land meant that they had to make their own towpaths by leveling out thick bushes of reed. The oarsmen of Captain Geldzak's fleet in 1736 made such a towpath spanning several kilometers between Sitakund and the fort of Mungeer. A French traveler in 1735 marveled at the hard labor of the *dandies*: "Isn't it surprising, I say, that these men can withstand such hard work and that for earning the equivalent of three sols per day? Hence, these are in my opinion the most miserable of all the people of the world."[23]

Majhis were the chief steersmen of the boats.[24] All forms of river-craft employed a *majhi* as the head boatman for his superior experience in navigation and his intimate knowledge of the terrain and contours of the riverbed. Certain *majhis* were solely employed for pilotage work. Sailing on lightweight vessels (*polwars*) accompanied by a few peons or a soldier, these *majhis* sailed ahead of the fleet, signaling to the commander of the fleet whether the path ahead was free of dangerous shallows or contrary currents.[25] Sometimes, a head *majhi* handled the pilotage work for the whole fleet. During his voyage of 1736, Captain Geldzak left the movement of the entire fleet from Sitakund and Mungeer to the decision of his pilot.

Since frequent accidents were among the ordeals of river movement, the fleets included mechanics. Maintenance of the boats was a major concern of the commander of the fleet. Carpenters, caulkers, and smiths were the maintenance crew on the move. They performed tasks such as mending damaged boats. In 1728, during Captain Hogerwerf's fleet's journey to Patna, a vessel carrying soldiers crashed against the shore near Mircha. A carpenter was immediately put to work. By noon, the vessel rejoined the fleet.[26] Two such incidents happened the next year with the fleet of Commander van der Helling. Not far from Kriṣnanagar, a plank in the garrison writer's boat came loose. A carpenter was dispatched, and by early afternoon, the vessel again joined the fleet.[27] Later in the journey, a little above Bhagalpur, oars of five vessels carrying soldiers broke. By the next day the carpenter and smiths of the fleet had repaired the oars.[28] Carpenters and smiths were essential for making the anchors for Ensign Scheurs's journey through the Sunderbans in 1736.

After reaching Patna, the fleet dispersed and the soldiers rested for a month or two at the barracks in Patna, Railly, and Fettua. Once the head of the Patna factory handed over the completed memorandum of goods on merchant vessels to the commander of the fleet, they embarked on the return journey. The fleet commander also oversaw the recruitment of new boats to join the return fleet.[29] The downriver journey had many challenges. The heavy-bottomed *patellas* contracted at Patna could not travel down the Bhagirathi as the water level of this tributary was exceedingly shallow. Moreover, boatmen from Patna were averse to traveling through the tidal waters of the deltas, which required different ecological knowledge and skills. The companies thus had to arrange for an elaborate transshipment.

In the seventeenth century, Mirdadpur in Malda was the transfer point of goods from large vessels to smaller vessels. A special official from the EIC Kassimbazar factory was sent out to Mirdadpur to oversee this work.[30] In the eighteenth century, the transshipment point moved near the confluence of the Ganga and Jalangi, at any of the three villages of Mircha, Badderpourgola, or Jalangi. These smaller ports were located around Bhagwangola, the principal riverport of the region. Both Europeans and indigenous observers noted the importance of commercial activities at Bhagwangola. In the eighteenth century, a fleet in the service of the Nawab was posted at Bhagwangola. Due to the economic importance of Bhagwangola, the Marathas raided the place multiple times starting in 1743 and then one last time in 1750 when they were successful. Boatmen in this region thus hired themselves out to merchants from all corners of the subcontinent and beyond, as well as to important political figures, including the Nawab.[31]

The transshipment zone of Mircha, Badderpourgola, and Jalangi was an area of intense activity. Work included the unloading of vessels coming from Patna, storage in makeshift sheds, and finally, porterage of goods and luggage from the unloading point to the loading point on the river. Low-bulk commodities such as opium and textiles were placed on lightweight *polwars*, which then made their way to Chinsurah or Calcutta. Ox carts were hired to carry to Kassimbazar the soaps needed for washing raw silk. In years when vessels were hard to come by, companies hired ox carts to carry opium and textiles to Kassimbazar, from where they were shipped to Chinsurah/Calcutta via the Hugli. The companies sent part of the saltpeter consignment via the Jalangi, but the bulk of it made a long haul on hired *ulaks* and the company sloop through the Sunderbans. Even though the lower course of the Ganga through the Sunderbans was deep enough for the *patellas*, the upcountry *majhis* refused to sail through the unknown forested deltaic lands, especially fearful of the roving bands of infamous Arakanese pirates who would round up anybody they could find and enslave them. Their geographical familiarity ended at Bhagwangola.

The companies sent out their overseers to organize work at the transshipment point. The VOC's Kassimbazar factory sent out a cashier who was responsible for all arrangements. The VOC rented a house not far from Mircha, along with servants, for the lodging of the cashier for a few months as he made all arrangements for the fleet coming from Hugli and Patna.[32] Every day, the cashier was ferried from his residence to Mircha on a palanquin, where throughout the day he oversaw all transport activities. The principal task of the overseer (i.e., the cashier) was to hire boats, which would sail through the deltas or go down the Bhagirathi. Competitors were many, as not only rival European companies were hiring boats, but also indigenous and Armenian merchants. The overseer had to haggle with the boatmen, offer them food money, and pray that the fleet arrived soon, because the boatmen could go over to other competitors at any moment. The overseer's expectation that he would be ready with the necessary boats so that the fleet "did not lie still for a long time" once it arrived further heightened his anxiety.[33]

Several other forms of synchronized work were needed for the movement of the fleet. At the transshipment points the fleet hired large number of cartmen and coolies. Eight to ten palanquin bearers (*kahars*) looked after the traveling comfort of higher officials. Each fleet included a Persian writer, a head peon, ten to twenty common peons, two to four *qasids* (couriers), and one or two rounders. Since the companies frequently had to send letters to the local *zamīndāri* courts or received letters from them, they maintained a Persian writer on the journey who could perform the tasks of translator and letter writer. On certain voyages, they even employed a second translator.[34] Throughout the journey of the fleet, the exchange of letters and information meant an intricate network of courier service. The couriers moved back and forth between different segments of the fleet, also known as "companies," conveying news from the commander and captains to officials at different settlements and vice versa. A few of the couriers received a monthly wage of 4 rupees, but along the way the fleet captain hired several such couriers, who were paid according to the distance that they travelled. They were often sent out with hired dinghies. All the couriers, irrespective of the nature of the wage contract, were also paid food money for their journey. A fleet of over 150 boats needed its own communication service—one or more persons who could connect the commander's boat at the helm with the soldiers' boats at the end of the fleet. Rounders performed the task of carrying the orders of the captain of the fleet to the head boatmen of all the vessels of the fleet. Each segment of the fleet had its own rounder; hence, multiple rounders were employed in a fleet. For this task, the rounder was assigned a small boat with a *majhi*.

In their conscious, methodical, and systematic cooperation among various forms of otherwise disparate labor, the fleets resembled modern manufacturing. In order to create this cooperation, the company officials persevered to bring together indigenous workers with various skills to move their military forces and the commodities of trade. Never a smooth process, in bringing together this conglomerate of skilled work, the companies had to constantly face the obstacles of local payment practices, recruitment methods, and rigidities of customs.

RECRUITING BOATS

Boats were the mainstays of the Patna fleet. Even though the companies hired a wide variety of boats, they had standardized the hire to some extent.[35] A sizeable number were hired on a monthly basis. Boats in Bengal were rowing boats which came in several different varieties (see figure 4).[36] Of the larger boats, the *bajra*, or "pleasure boat," carried covenanted servants of the companies.[37] *Bajras* of varying sizes were reserved for the top army officials of the fleet (see figure 5). The largest *bajras*, which often the commander of the Patna fleet used, needed three *majhis* and twenty other rowers. The smallest *bajra*, reserved for the ensign, needed one *majhi* and eight rowers. Boat hire for *bajras* varied according to size. A *bajra* with twenty oars and three *majhis* could be hired monthly for 54 rupees and 8 annas, and the hire of a *bajra* with eight rowers and one *majhi* was 24 or 25 rupees.[38] The most common boats were the *ulak* (see figure 6). The *ulak* was a medium-sized vessel, usually weighing around 60 tons. These mainly carried soldiers and their baggage.

FIGURE 4. Detail of terracotta plaque, showing armed soldiers on a galley boat, at the Jor Bangla Temple, Bishnupur. Source: Wikimedia Commons, photo by Susmita Santra.

FIGURE 5. Pleasure boat (or *bajra*), from Frans Balthazar Solvyns, *A Collection of Two Hundred and Fifty Coloured Etchings: Descriptive of the Manners, Customs and Dresses of the Hindoos* (Calcutta, 1799). Source: Wikimedia Commons.

FIGURE 6. Utilitarian boat (or *ulak*), from Frans Balthazar Solvyns, *A Collection of Two Hundred and Fifty Coloured Etchings: Descriptive of the Manners, Customs and Dresses of the Hindoos* (Calcutta, 1799). Source: Wikimedia Commons.

A surgeon attended to the sick soldiers or "impotents" of the VOC/EIC army in special *ulaks* earmarked as "dispensary" boats. Most *ulaks* had either eight or twelve oars. *Ulaks* with eight rowers were hired for 25 rupees per month, and *ulaks* with ten rowers for 29 rupees.[39]

However, such hiring practices were never fully standardized. The companies hired some boats according to cargo weight. Large flat-bottomed, unwieldy cargo boats such as *patellas*[40] (see figure 7) and *bangela/bangelaars*[41] were often hired on cargo weight terms. The length of a boat hire depended upon the boatmen's preference for the amount of time they were willing to expend and the destinations they chose. Thus boatmen coming from Patna refused to sail through the deltas. Boatmen also fixed their hire according to distance. The EIC in particular practiced hiring boats by distance. Boats could be hired for travel of less than fifty kilometers (between Badderpourgola and Rajapur), or for as long a distance as between Rajmahal and Calcutta (over 300 kilometers) or Mircha and Calcutta (over 250 kilometers).[42] Boatmen operating lightweight vessels at the transshipment point usually followed this practice. The VOC too complied with such practices. They most often made such arrangements with *polwars*, lightweight pilot vessels of 15–20 tons (see figure 8).[43] Boats could also be hired on a daily basis. At transshipment points, *majhis* of *polwars* often demanded their pay in a similar fashion.[44] Small dugout canoes called dinghies (*dingelaar*), manned by a lone boatman, were constantly hired throughout the journey for couriers. These boats too fixed their hire on a daily basis.[45] Despite the uniformity of the workday, the length, both spatial and temporal, of hire for boats varied widely.

Hiring practices were further complicated by numerous forms of boat ownership. The *majhi*, or head boatman/steersman of the boat, was usually the

FIGURE 7. Cargo boat (or *patella*), from Frans Balthazar Solvyns, *A Collection of Two Hundred and Fifty Coloured Etchings: Descriptive of the Manners, Customs and Dresses of the Hindoos* (Calcutta, 1799). Source: Wikimedia Commons.

FIGURE 8. Pilot boat (or *polwar*), from Frans Balthazar Solvyns, *A Collection of Two Hundred and Fifty Coloured Etchings: Descriptive of the Manners, Customs and Dresses of the Hindoos* (Calcutta, 1799). Source: Wikimedia Commons.

owner. Large boats could cost around 300 arcot rupees, while small dinghies could cost around 5 sicca rupees. Some *majhis* had in their possession more than one boat. A *majhi* named Draub, for example, sailed his own boat in the EIC fleet in 1741. The following year, Draub employed Balaram as the head boatman of the same boat while Draub himself headed a new boat that he had bought.[46] The companies owned a few boats and hired boatmen to row them.[47]

In certain instances, boats were hired out by local merchants. These merchants sometimes had long-standing relationships with the head boatmen.[48] Thus, even head boatmen in many cases could be a hired worker without any possession of boats. Oarsmen, in almost all cases, were hired workers.

Little is known about the wages of *majhis* and oarsmen, for the account books often subsumed wages within boat hire. From the few instances when VOC records mention the wages of boatmen, it seems the *majhi* wages ranged from 2.8 rupees per month and 6 rupees per month and oarsmen's wages ranged between 4 rupees per month and 1 rupee and 2 annas per month.[49] It was in the 1740s that the *majhis* and *dandies* received the low wages of 2.8 rupees per month and 1 rupee and 2 anna per month. Displacement caused by Maratha invasions likely brought down their wages.

This wide variety of hiring practices highlights the lack of a streamlined labor market for boatmen.[50] To man the fleet, the companies had to enter into negotiations with indigenous workers, and thus they were forced to accommodate several local practices. The very nature of the work, which demanded recruitment of mobile workers over a large geographical space, made a controlled, single market for boatmen's labor impossible.[51] That the fleet was not built on a steady, smoothly functioning labor market, is most evident from the various recruitment strategies of the companies.

The early eighteenth century provides examples of the companies' adoption of multiple methods of labor recruitment, where use of an intermediary labor recruiter was rare. Labor historians of South Asia often project backwards the recruitment practices in the colonial period onto the precolonial period, thus accepting as timeless *sardar*-coolie, *lascar-ghat serang*, and *ghat majhi-majhi* relationships of recruitment.[52] New scholarship focusing on non-EIC sources challenges such assumptions.[53] My evidence on recruitment of boatmen affirms this newer research. As early as September 1679, the EIC in Kassimbazar had two *majhis*, Harish and Gopal, who acted as their "press masters."[54] In 1684, in Patna, a *majhi* named Khidu recruited fifteen *patellas*. The next year, the same person was solicited for recruitment of saltpeter boats, including several *patellas* and *muteas*. Khidu, Harish, and Gopal disappear from the records in the subsequent years. The figure of the *ghat majhi*—as labor recruiter—appears only in November 1730, when Sergeant De Loffernun, heading a delayed fleet from Patna, reported that he needed lightweight vessels to proceed any further. The EIC council at Kassimbazar sent out a *ghat majhi* and a peon with 200 sicca rupees to Mircha to recruit light boats.[55] In August 1732, a *ghat majhi* was someone responsible for recruitment of *polwars* at Hugli.⁵⁶ The *ghat majhi* as recruiting agent then becomes a common figure only from the 1740s onwards.⁵⁷ In 1745 the Fort William council mentioned a *ghat majhi* "who provides boats for the company on all occasions." Even then this *ghat majhi* did not recruit boats all on his own. In the midst of the Maratha attacks, he was accompanied by the company *banian* (native accounts keeper for the EIC).⁵⁸ A head boatman as a recruitment agent in the first half of the eighteenth century was still a nascent figure co-existing with other avenues of recruitment.

Due to lack of any recruitment agent, company guards or peons played an important role in the recruitment procedure in the early eighteenth century, especially for the VOC. Recruitment procedures at the point of transshipment, Mircha, are the most well documented. In 1732, the VOC officials at Kassimbazar delegated the task of recruitment of light vessels to a "Company Majhi" named Binod and a peon; they toiled for forty-four days gathering around eighty vessels to travel down to Hugli.⁵⁹ In the next two years, Binod, the same *majhi*, along with two peons again recruited *polwars* and pilots. They sailed as far as Ratanganj, a couple of miles from Mircha, on two dinghies to hire ten *polwars*.⁶⁰ But there were occasions when the peons were left alone with the task of recruitment. In 1734, the rowers of all vessels going down to Chinsurah from Mircha were recruited by the peons. For five days the peons "hauled" these rowers "from different places."⁶¹ As late as 1743, eighteen peons at Mircha were assigned the task of recruiting boats and coolies. Significantly, they had to be vigilant "to make sure that they (the boatmen and the coolies) were not impressed by others."⁶² Peons were especially resourceful recruiters in the midst of the Maratha attacks in the 1740s, when there was a labor shortage as people fled their villages by the hundreds. In such a situation, peons impressed workers and kept the other competing companies, merchants, or local potentates at bay. Even though the peons played a critical role in recruiting workers and securing them against the competitors of the VOC, they were paid a meager wage of 1 anna per day.⁶³ In 1753, the peons continued to perform the same job for the slightly better wage of 2 annas a day.⁶⁴

There were several occasions when the company officials had to directly negotiate with the owners of the boats. All the officials the VOC employed at the transshipment point of Mircha-Badderpourgola-Jalangi—Abraham Ormea, equipage officer Christoffel de Wind, cashier Christiaan van Bevenage, and cashier Ewout de Leeuw—had some form of direct dealings with the boatmen.⁶⁵ A letter from Kassimbazar dated May 22, 1738 reported that the EIC cashier Mr. Kemp went to the toll point at Jalangi to recruit boats with the help of the superintendent of the toll point for the fleet coming from Patna.[66] In October 1735, the Patna chief of the EIC had to directly persuade the boat owners to sail as far down as Calcutta.[67] The same year, boatmen at Dhaka signed bonds (*muchlekhas*) with the factory chief to reach Calcutta within six days.[68] Such direct dealings not only affirm the lack of a standardized practice of hiring, but also attest to the *sardar*-coolie or a *ghat majhi*-boatmen relationship as a later colonial invention for organizing work. These changes in recruitment patterns of boatmen under the EIC state are discussed in detail in chapter 5.

Recruitment practices were extremely varied in nature, as were the boats employed and their terms of hire. The primary recruitment grounds were Calcutta/Chinsurah, Patna, and the transshipment zone of Mircha-Badderpourgola-Jalangi. While recruiting boatmen in this early period, companies encountered no existing recruitment practices involving middlemen recruiters. Both the VOC and EIC used a variety of their native servants—*banians* and peons—to recruitment boatmen. Sometimes, these indigenous servants of the companies worked on their own to gather boatmen and at other times they accompanied European officials of the companies in recruitment ventures. European officials also approached boatmen *directly* in all three recruitment zones to hire them for the fleet. But from the 1740s on the EIC, especially, tried to build up a system of recruitment based on middlemen recruiters in their *zamīndāri*, Calcutta.

BOATMEN IN THE SOCIAL WORLD OF EIGHTEENTH-CENTURY BENGAL

Like any other worker in early eighteenth-century Bengal, most boatmen experienced the indigenous state through the presence of the *zamīndārs*. In Ketakadās Kṣhemananda's text, *Manasāmaṅgal*, Jālu and Mālu, both coming from the Dhibar, or fishermen's caste community, to which a number of boatmen belonged, had to pay a water tax (*jalkar*) to the *zamīndār* Chāṅd.[69] The EIC enforced similar duties on the people residing within their *zamīndāri* in Calcutta. *Majhis* in Calcutta thus had to pay a *dustoree*, or duty, on their income, collected annually. Each boat had to pay a sum of 2 rupees. In certain years, when the demand went as high as 5 rupees, the *majhis* complained en masse to company authorities, threatening to go to the

Nawab's court if the rates of duties did not come down.⁷⁰ Even as subjects of *zamīndārs*, boatmen were aware of the authority of the *faujdār* and the Nawab above the *zamīndārs*. They were also aware that though the *zamīndārs* were relatively autonomous, the *faujdār* or the Nawab could nevertheless intervene to rein in their authority.

All state officials, including *zamīndārs*, *faujdārs*, and the Nawabs, could forcibly demand the services of boatmen, but only with limited success. The *zamīndār* could collect tax in kind, as Chānd did by demanding services of the fishermen at his will. Texts describing Brahminical conduct, such as *Gautama Dharmasūtra*, too mention that the ruler could demand one day's worth of work from boatmen in lieu of taxes.⁷¹ Given the fragmented and overlapping nature of jurisdiction by the various state officials, conscription alternated with other uses of force. This is very evident in the naval warfare (1659–60) between Mir Jumla, leading the imperial army of Aurangzeb, and Shuja, his recalcitrant brother, the governor of Bengal and aspirant to the imperial throne. In this warfare, there was no clear imperial force—while Mir Jumla represented the official imperial army, Shuja was the head of a rebellious "imperial" army. Shuja had an edge over Mir Jumla because of his long-standing familiarity with the region, which enabled him to recruit a good number of boats. Yet, Shuja was aware of the untrustworthy nature of the *zamīndārs*, who could have helped Mir Jumla with boats. In order to hinder the process, Shuja engaged in what Jadunath Sarkar calls a "scorched earth policy"—he burnt all boats on his way to the eastern coast of the Ganga. Mir Jumla, too, unsure of the political tendencies among various *zamīndārs*, sent his own imperial army officials to solicit boats directly from mercantile quarters, especially from the EIC and VOC at Kassimbazar and Hugli.⁷² In important urban settings such as Patna, Murshidabad, Rajmahal, and Hugli, the Mughal *faujdārs*, even with the presence of *zamīndārs*, retained the capacity of forced recruitment of boats. The instability of the state, however, enabled the boatmen to evade its reach. In 1744, when the Marathas attacked Bengal and came as far down as Rajmahal and Burdwan, a panic descended over Murshidabad, even though the Nawab Nazim Alivardi Khan's army was camped very close. The boatmen and cartmen operating under their nose demanded an exorbitant hiring rate of 40 to 50 rupees for every 8 kos (approximately 25 kilometers).⁷³ The imperial state officials' constant participation in the competitive market for hiring boatmen is discussed in the final section of this chapter. For boatmen, the indigenous state made its presence felt through taxation and sometimes forced recruitment, but also as outsiders paying a handsome hire.

Just as boatmen encountered the state in various ways, they experienced their social identities, including caste, in multifaceted forms. When groups of workers are referred to by their caste names (e.g., *kāhārs* or *doms*), their place in indigenous society or links with land are readily explained. The social place of boatmen in indigenous society, however, is often elided in company accounts. Nevertheless, this omission is not necessarily a handicap in revealing boatmen's social position; it only underscores the intricacies of the social world that very mobile workers such as boatmen traversed. One can only explain the silence on caste affiliations by acknowledging that professions like rowing or pilotage were not monopolized by any one particular caste. Not only did the boatmen—the most important group of transport workers—belong to different castes, in performing this work, they often transgressed the norms of prescribed caste occupations. Such a phenomenon was not new in eighteenth-century Bengal. As both Hiteshranjan Sanyal and Gautam Bhadra show, there are ample examples of horizontal caste mobility in terms of occupation in middle Bengali texts.[74] The relatively low status of all these castes vis-à-vis the so-called clean castes, however, implies that the propensity for mobility was prevalent among lower-caste men and was linked to their status as either landless or owners of very small plots.

All information on boatmen's caste affiliations comes from demographic surveys made in the nineteenth century. Two different surveys at the provincial level show that boatmen of Bengal came from the castes of Chaṅḍāla, Patuni, Jāliya Kaivarta, Mālo, Turāhā, and Tiyār.[75] In Bihar, the boatmen generally belonged to the Māllā caste, even though there were at least seven different Māllā castes.[76] Surveys at the district level made the list even longer. In Bhagalpur, the majority of boatmen came from the Kewat caste in addition to Dhunar, Kalāwat, and Sarhiya castes.[77] According to an account on Patna written in 1838, boatmen came from Chaiṅg and Bindu castes. Many of the caste brethren of the Chaiṅgs were mostly to be found by the banks of Padma in the Natore district of the Rajshahi region in Eastern Bengal.[78] Given the mobile nature of their profession, it is not surprising that intraregional migration was common among these boatmen. In Hugli, an important hub for company activities in Bengal, boatmen were predominantly Bāgdis. Tentulias, Majhis, and Dandamajhis—among the Bāgdis of Hugli—were all boatmen.[79] The Bāgdis of Bengal, who came to be listed as a "criminal tribe" after 1871, were considered occupational woodcutters and navvies. The Bāgdi boatmen of Hugli disrupts this stereotypical picture.[80] Similarly, the Chaṅḍāla boatmen transgressed their caste occupation: Chaṅḍālas were generally associated with making their living from cremation grounds. For most boatmen caste groups, rowing boats was one of the many means of eking out a living. Thus, their caste status was not indicative of any one occupational group they belonged to.

Large sections of the so-called Muslim population in Bengal worked as boatmen. Caste divisions were always prominent within Bengal Islam.[81] By the end of the nineteenth century, colonial surveys noted that Muslim boatmen belonged to certain caste groups. Large sections of Nikāris, a Muslim Bengali caste group, and Mājhis, another Muslim caste group in Bogra, were boatmen.[82] In Bogra, the Baramāsias, a Muslim caste, were all boatmen. Their caste name was directly related to their profession: twelve (*bara*) months (*māsa*) referred to their year-round stay on boats.[83]

The ritual purity of the castes is difficult to determine. By the end of nineteenth century, most of them were considered unclean, meaning that Brahmins could not accept water from their hands. Chaṇḍālas, Mālos, and Bāgdis were traditionally considered untouchables. However, in Hugli, the untouchability of Bāgdi boatmen was qualified by the early twentieth century. Though Brahmins could not drink water touched by them, their touch would not defile the water of the Ganga or dry foods and oil, making it convenient for the Brahmins to avail themselves of the Bāgdi boatmen's services.[84] Kaivartas were a large caste group with several internal divisions. One large section, the Hāliya Kaivartas, had taken to agriculture by the late nineteenth century.[85] While certain sections of Hāliya Kaivartas were considered clean, most of the boatmen who belonged to the Jāliya Kaivarta subcaste were considered unclean.

Boatmen recruited for company fleets did not come from a specific caste. Hence, caste-based fraternity, in terms of monopolizing the occupation and collective action against the companies, played little role in the hiring process. Caste affiliation was further complicated by boat ownership. While many *majhi*s owned boats, they also worked for merchants with boats. These merchants, often referred to as *mahājans*, clearly did not share caste affiliations with the boatmen. The lack of caste-based recruitment might also explain how even a small crew could include men from different castes and/or different villages or cities of residence. Thus, of the two *majhis* and seven oarsmen of the boat that Michael Macnamara, a private European traveler, hired in 1789 for a month, in the Sonargaon *pargāna* of Dhaka, the *majhis* and three oarsmen came from one village, Jairampur, while the rest of the oarsmen came from another, Noahbad. Macnamara hired these four oarsmen directly to work on the boat that the two *majhis* and the three oarsmen had brought with them. As a result, the crew included people with names as different as Anādi and Imānnuddin.[86] Similarly, of the eight boatmen of the vessel carrying an EIC official from the city of Chhapra in the Saran district of Bihar province to Calcutta in 1794, six were from Chhapra while one was from the nearby village of Ratanpura and another from a different *pargana*, Azimganj in the Saran district.[87]

Even as the companies hired boatmen and negotiated their demands, cutting across multiple castes, caste did shape the lives of boatmen even at work. The commensal practices of boatmen are indicative of their caste belonging. Their refusal to eat during the workday and then cooking and eating in small groups likely with kinsfolk at the end of the workday are indicative of caste practices. Evidence from 1790s indicate that some boatmen brought their children to work, indicative of hereditary transmission of boat rowing or steering skills. Thus Kurmoo, a boatman from the city of Chhapra in the Saran district of Bihar brought along with him his eight-year-old son on his journey to Calcutta and back. Boatmen married within their respective caste and were highly sensitive to their social standing among their kinsfolk within villages. Thus, when the women of Premnarain *majhi*'s family suffered molestation during his absence in 1794 at the hands of a EIC police official, his "relations and connections ... threw a slur upon his character" and Premnarain faced "ejection" from his society. Despite their caste belongings there is no evidence of caste councils or caste headmen mediating between boatmen and village and supra-village state authorities. EIC revenue or police officials extorted money from boatmen individually and in such cases only a select few close relations of the boatmen were held as security and never an entire caste population of the village. Sometimes boatmen stood security for other villagers who were not boatmen. Extortion of collective fines or levies (*cesses*) from villages were common and in these instances boatmen paid their dues along with other villagers of different castes and occupations and petitioned against such extortions collectively with other villagers of multiple caste affiliations.[88]

Similar to their caste identities, the religious affiliations of the boatmen hint at a very eclectic mix of spiritual practices. In discussing boatmen, the VOC referred to their internal social differentiation only when it interfered with the movement of the Patna fleet. One of the many reasons for the difficulties of transshipment at the confluence of the Ganga and Jalangi was the stubborn refusal of the *majhis* from Bihar to sail through the mangroves. In VOC official perception this stubbornness was symptomatic of the religious affiliations of the *majhis*: "Hindu" *majhis* from Patna were most reluctant to move any further south of the village Jalangi while "Muslim" rowers at Jalangi had no trouble traveling through the deltas. Though much of this observation is shrouded in inaccurate understandings of indigenous society, the assumption is significant. Even though ecological determinants did not affect much the schedule of the fleet, they oriented the boatmen's disposition to different landscapes and routes. In a way, the distinctions among boatmen made by the VOC were pointing at two different sets of boatmen conditioned by different geographical and hence spiritual settings.

Bihar and the western deltaic region in Bengal had come under the Indo-Aryan civilizational orbit from the fifth century BC, whereas the eastern deltas remained more or less remote to this cultural world. Especially from the tenth century CE, state formation in the western Bengal and Bihar region was predicated on the patronizing Brahmanical religion. Peasantization in this belt was linked to land donations to Buddhist and Brahmanical orders. In contrast, various Sufic preachers, who were often called *pīrs*, brought the eastern deltas under the plow in a comprehensive manner only from the seventeenth century. They were responsible not only for the mass Islamization of the region, but also, through their connection with the Mughal imperial system, the extension of the Mughal state's authority over major parts of Bengal.[89]

Islamization as a popular practice in the Bengal deltas took the form of *pīr* worship.[90] This was an extremely heterodox practice. The Islamic content of such worship was often questionable not only because *pīr* worship and the ballads surrounding them involved the participation of both the Islamized and non-Islamized rural crowd, but also because legends of the *pīrs* often proudly declared the *pīr* to be a prophet who came after Muhammad.[91] One of the most popular *pīrs* of the eastern Bengal deltas was Pīr Badar, the guardian spirit of waters. His origins are veiled in mystery. Some of Badar's legends tell of mind-boggling heterodoxy, as the one wherein Badar was a Portuguese sailor. In Jayaraddi's account of Manik Pīr, Pīr Badar wielded power over the river goddess Ganga by forcing her to acknowledge Badar as "her elder brother." Shrines of Badar (*badarmokām*) dotted the entire eastern Bengal delta lands. Worship of Pāṅch Pīr (five saints) also assured safe passage for the boatmen. But the origin of this *pīr* is unknown. The shrines, which were often a small tomb with five bumps or a mound at the foot of a banyan tree, are scattered all across the deltas. Rivaling the popularity of Pīr Badar and Pāñch Pīr was Gājī Saheb, who guarded his followers from the tigers of the Sunderbans. Unique to Bakarganj, where the company fleets always made a stop and recruited boatmen, was the shrine of Bara Auliyā (twelve saints) whose origins were similarly inscrutable. Khwaja Khizr, well-known in the larger Muslim world as a patron of the seas and waters, was worshipped all along the rivers. Finally, in the western deltas was the abode (*makām*) of Shah Machhandali, a very popular *pīr* amongst sailors. Machhandali's legend boasts of his heroic acts rescuing many capsizing boats.[92] These *pīrs* of uncertain provenance permeated the religiosity of the deltaic boatmen.

Followers of these cults of *pīrs* were recognized by company officials as Muslims. However, just as caste was widespread irrespective of religion, so was the worship of *pīrs*. It is no surprise that even today, songs about *pīrs* include passages such as this:

> The *shirni* [food offering] of Gajī is over:
> Let the Muslims invoke Allah
> And the Hindus Hari.[93]

Lower-caste men and women in the deltas were especially attracted to such practices. As worshippers of deltaic *pīrs*, boatmen contracted at Mircha, Jalangi, and Badderpourgola belonged to the composite cultural and spiritual world of the lower reaches of the Ganga. Boatmen from Patna or the upper reaches of the Ganga were strangers to both the geographical as well as spiritual maze of the deltas.

The lower reaches of Ganga resounded with the songs, ballads, and rituals that boatmen composed to assuage their *pīrs*, so that the *pīrs* would attend to everyday trials and tribulations. On January 21, 1734, one rower in Captain Geldzak's return fleet met his end in the Sunderbans in the clutches of a tiger.[94] The knowledge of such dreadful consequences was creatively dealt with by the rowers of the delta through their prayers to multiple figures such as Gājī Saheb for protection from the dangers of the forest. Seventeenth-century poet Kṛiṣnarām Dās provides a detailed profile of one such Gājī, Baḍakhān Gājī, who much like Gājī Sāheb was a pioneering figure in the deltas and lorded over an army of tigers. Even though Baḍakhān Gājī was an adversary of Dakṣin Rāi, the principal deity of Rāimaṅgal, Kṛiṣnarām resolves the conflict between the two, resulting in the worship of both by the inhabitants of the deltas.[95]

Similarly, before starting their journeys, boatmen would invoke the name of Pīr Badar in a chorus:

In the name of Allah, the prophet, Pāṅch Pir, Badar, we do[96]

Or sometimes:

My good men
Gājī keeps his eyes on us
Cross the Ganga! Pāṅch Pīr! Badar! Badar! Badar![97]

Or:

Lift the anchor, sail the boat
Chanting the name of Badar
Sail the boat.[98]

Such invocations merged the world of work with the spiritual and cultural world. The boatmen's knowledge and experience of their work, refracted through the deification of the *pīrs*, was also a source of cultural production in the region.

Finally, boatmen belonged to the heterogeneous world of Bengal mysticism. In Eastern India between the ninth and eighteenth centuries, a plethora of devotional sects emerged which can be categorized under the ritual-theological complexes of Vajrayana Buddhism, Vaishnavism, Shaivism, Shaktaism, and Sufism. This produced a multilayered literary world marked by numerous genres, which were discrete yet connected in their form and content.[99] On one extreme are the theologies of orthodox Gauṛiya Vaishnavism written in Sanskrit and on the other, the songs of extremely heterodox sects composed in the everyday language of people. Boatmen contributed to the latter through their work songs called *sāri*. The icons, motifs, and even language of these songs were rooted in the multidimensional world of Bengali mysticism, but the form of these songs was the innovation of boatmen. As composers and performers of *sāri*, boatmen were also agents in the making of the heterodox devotional movement in Bengal.

In order to understand the boatmen's popular eclectic world of esoterism, it is necessary to depend on undated songs.[100] Most of these songs were collected beginning in the late nineteenth and throughout the twentieth century. Thus, using them as historical evidence can be problematic even when their locale remains the same. Space, after all, is not natural; by the twentieth century, these lands had been tremendously altered by advances in technology and the political and social consequences of colonialism and postcolonialism and hence the performing arts.[101] Notwithstanding these caveats, in this purely historical work, I use the songs primarily to situate their oft-used literary tropes and theological content within the history of religious and cultural thought and language of premodern Bengal.

There is consensus among various collectors of *sāri* songs that the predominant theme of these songs is the various exploits of Kṛṣṇa.[102] Kṛṣṇa's dalliances with the milkmaids (*gopīs*) and the divine love of Radha and Kṛṣṇa (*rasalīlā*) come up repeatedly in the *sāri* songs. One of the earliest extant *sāri*, collected in 1813–14, describes the scene of Kṛṣṇa's love sports (*līlā*) with the milkmaids on a boat:

> The young Kṛṣṇa is the head pilot
> The whole world is at play in the waters
> His magic turns water creatures into boats
> Kṛṣṇa is the *majhi* and the milkmaids the rowers
> As they row, their bangles and anklets rattle to the rhythm
> On the highest note, the women of pleasure sing.[103]

The following song, collected in early twentieth century, dwells on the same theme of Kṛṣṇa's love sports with Radha, the chief playmate of Kṛṣṇa amongst the milkmaids:

> O Kānāi [Kṛṣṇa], ferry me across the river
> I will pay you the money I make in the bajār of Mathura.
> You beautiful Kānāi, and your broken boat.
> Where shall I keep the pots of curd, and where shall I put my feet
> Kānāi replied, listen O, embodiment of *rasa* [savoring/pleasure]
> Why did you come to the brimming river in full monsoon
> First, put your pots of curd in the boat and then sit in the middle.
> Why do you drift in shame in the rain drops
> I will ferry all sakhis [Radha's friends/*gopīs*] for an anna each.
> But for Rādhikā I will charge her gold earrings.[104]

Both songs borrow heavily from a Vaishnava *pada* (lyric) on the episode of Kṛṣṇa's love-making with Radha on a boat (*naukā vilās*). Radha, a milkmaid on her way to the village market, met a boatman, Kṛṣṇa. Radha repeatedly begs Kṛṣṇa to tell her the price of the ferry ride. Kṛṣṇa playfully avoids answering until they reach mid-river, where they engage in divine union (*rasalīlā*). *Padas* (lyrics) on this theme were first composed in Bengali by

FIGURE 9. Detail of terracotta plaque, depicting the *nauka vilās* motif, at the Dadhimadhav Temple, Howrah, West Bengal, 1764. Source: Wikimedia Commons, photo by Biswarup Ganguly.

Bodu Chandidāsa in his Sri Kriṣna Kirtan, which dates back to the fifteenth century,[105] but the heyday for the Vaishnava lyrics was the seventeenth and early eighteenth centuries.[106] Lyrics inspired other fields of cultural production such as the terracotta motifs on primarily Vaishnavite brick temples (see figure 9). Similarly, by repeatedly invoking these lyrics in their own words over centuries, the boatmen placed themselves in the religious realm of Bengal Vaishnavism, while the rhythm (*tāl*) of rowing that made up the tempo of the *sāri* songs was these boatmen's original contribution to the Vaishnava literary world.[107]

Even the love songs involving a village damsel, which some collectors have categorized as "folk love," borrowed heavily from the religio-literary trove of Vaishnava lyrics.[108] The word for love in these songs is often *piriti*—the same word used so often in love songs by the Vaishnava poet Dīna Chandīdāsa.[109] The object of love/desire in these songs is *bandhu* (literally, friend), most evident in the Vaishnava lyrics, adulating the highest state of union between Kriṣna and Radha. In this state Kriṣna and Radha make love; Radha, the lover, refers to Kriṣna as *bandhuā*. In several *sāris* Kriṣna is the *rasik* (connoisseur or recipient of love), just as in the Vaishnava lyrics. But, of course, these songs did not belong to the ritual-theological routine of Gauṛiya Vaishnavism, which stipulated that the devotee could not participate or project himself/herself into the union of Radha and Kriṣna.¹¹⁰

Though the divine love of Radha and Kriṣna forms a popular theme, Ashutosh Bhattacharya, linguist and historian of Bengali language and collector of Bengali performing arts, notes: "One must remember that in Eastern Bengal the singers (of *sāri* songs) are all Muslims. Very rarely are a few singers of lower-caste Hindu origin. Hence, the songs have been composed and performed by Muslims. But, the themes in all instances are that of Radha-Kriṣna and Nimāi."¹¹¹ Research on religious beliefs and practices of Bengal Vaishnavism since the days of Bhattacharya shows that based on the Vaishnava lyrics, it is very difficult to determine the religious affiliations of the poets, especially when they bear Islamicate names.¹¹² Anthropological works, moreover, have affirmed the strong parallels between Islamic and Vaishnavite practices in rural Bengal.¹¹³

The uncertainty of religious identity then leads us to the heterodox devotional sects. Ramakanta Chakravarti mentions that fifty-six heterodox, devotional sects had emerged in Bengal by the middle of the eighteenth century.¹¹⁴ For these sects, Chaitanya, the fifteenth-century popular figure of the Vaishnava devotional movement in Bengal, and the icons of Radha and Kriṣna remained central, even when members of only a few of these sects would consciously identify their orders as Vaishnavas. These sects were truly eclectic and syncretic in nature. For example, Fakir Aulchānd, founder of the Kartābhajā sect, was himself a Sufi. One legend surrounding Aulchānd mentions that he was Chaitanya in disguise. Disgusted with orthodox Vaishnavism (Gauṛiya Vaishnavism), Chaitanya took up the garb of a fakir.¹¹⁵ Gauṛiya Vaishnavas reciprocated by maintaining their distance from these sects. These sects incorporated yogic practices of disciplining the body on the lines of *sahajiyā* beliefs, the earliest traces of which can be found in the cults of Vajrayānā Buddhism.¹¹⁶ In the tradition of all the major devotional sects coming down to the Sufis, these new sects emphasized the centrality of the guru (teacher) in their orders, but they rejected rituals of any kind.

All of these sects rejected caste, hence attracting a massive following among the lower orders of society. Instead of meeting in temples, mosques, or *dargā*, leaders of these sects had far more intimate contact with their following. For instance, the elders of the Kartabhaja sect organized all-night congregations (*baithaks*) in the house of a follower on any chosen evening. Different grades of disciples ensured wide participation.¹¹⁷ Bauls, on the other hand, were roaming troubadours who reached out to a wide audience, even though entry into their orders was difficult.[118]

Some of the *sāri* songs are extremely similar to the songs of these sects. For example, we find the use of allegory both in the songs of the Bauls and the *sāris*. The allegorical device had powerful popular appeal since even when the religious meanings were not clear, as depictions of the plight of mundane life in the everyday language of the people the songs struck a chord with many. In the songs of several sects, the figure of a boat's pilot was an important allegory for the guru. The human body was a frail craft in which the traveler set forth on the stormy river of life, and the senses are drunken boatmen who would invariably crash the boat on the rocky riverbed of life. One's only hope was the pilot-*majhi* or guru who, with a steady hand, would lead the boat to its final destination.[119] Similar imagery, which seems to have hidden meaning, is present in several *sāri* songs. For example:

> I fear going alone
> Come guru, let us cross the river together.
> ....
> First discard the habits of the body
> ....
> Follow the lead of Sujan, the majhi
> He will take you on the boat.[120]

The guru in the song is interchangeable with Sujan, the pilot. Disciplining the body is resonant with the *sahajīyā* practice of controlling the body and the senses, important to the practices of many of these sects.

The rustic language these heterodox sects used was also the language of the boatmen. Composed in very localized dialects, these songs were devoid of the embellishments found in the compositions of the great Vaishnava poet-theologian Kṛṣṇadās Kabirāj or the greatest poet of eighteenth-century Bengal, Bharatchandra. The notoriety of *sāri* songs was proverbial: "Any amount of praise will not make the corrupt honest, just as any amount of sāri will not pollute the waters of Ganga."[121] In this sense, the boatmen's songs aesthetically shared much with the songs of the sects, as in this excerpt from a Baul song:

> As the storm rampages
> In your crumbling hut,
> The water rises to your bed.
> Your tattered quilt
> Floats away from your shelter.[122]

In order to explain the futility of attachment, the song uses the metaphor of a crumbling hut in the monsoons—a lived experience of millions in the Bengal countryside. Given the fact that boatmen created and still create their songs while at work, the language is a conscious aesthetic choice, as quotidian as work itself.[123] The rough and ready form can have a far-reaching impact on the content of the songs. In order to explain how love causes pain, one *sāri* laments:

> Love is a jewel, love is care
> Love is a big headache
> No matter how hard you try
> You can't get rid of it
> Just as the bones of tyangrā fish
> Cleave unto human flesh.[124]

The aesthetic choice of the song is identical to that of the songs that the subaltern milieu of heterodox Bengal mysticism produced, while the theme of "love as jewel" makes it part and parcel of larger world of mysticism. Yet, the earthy sensuality of this song with no reference to God or guru places it in an ambivalent relationship with mysticism.

The similarity of the idioms of expression between *sāri* and Vaishnava lyrics or Baul songs puts the boatmen squarely in the cultural and spiritual world of mysticism that emerged in late medieval Bengal. The catholicity of the boatmen's reference to various spiritual icons points to the interconnected and intertextual world of Bengal mysticism and also that the boatmen were related to one or more devotional orders. It is all the more probable that they were lay followers of one or more sects as from a very early time the same pieces of land in Eastern India came under the moral and temporal jurisdiction of more than one sect.[125]

The socio-religious identities of the boatmen, thus, were many. Besides belonging to various caste groups, boatmen were also rooted in the heterodox world of devotionalism in Bengal. Since the lower-caste population in Bengal played a significant role in the iconography of *bhakti* traditions including temples, it is not surprising that boatmen from diverse caste backgrounds were part of that broader religious milieu.[126] Like the varied practices of recruitment and wage payment systems, the impossibility of pinning down the boatmen to one religious identity affirms the fluidity of their place within the social world of eighteenth-century Bengal. Boatmen drawn from multiple caste groups in one area was indicative of the mobile nature of their work—constant movement made it impossible for the occupation to remain the stronghold of any one group. In fact, if there is any unifying element cutting across the multiple identities of the boatmen—it is their work or occupation.

Everyday concerns, which the mobile nature of work elicited, shaped the spiritual, literary, and cultural world the boatmen inhabited. The eclecticism in the deification of the *pīrs* best reveals the influence of boatmen's spatial practice. From the *sāri* songs, we can demonstrate a reciprocal relationship between the cultural world of Bengal mysticism and the work world of the boatmen. Hemaṅga Biswās, collector and theoretician of Bengali music, argues that there is no purely mystical music in Bengal.[127] Even music performed at leisure and inward looking constantly mediates the mundane, everyday experiences of people. While it is hard to find any causal relationship between the work and the songs of the boatmen, it is clear that the one influenced the other. In making their work songs, boatmen borrowed heavily from the forms and imagery created by the various sects of Bengal mysticism. The work songs in turn made the boatmen cultural agents within this world. They composed *sāri* or rowing songs synchronized with the rhythms of rowing. This music, composed in the everyday language of the people and sung while they plied the Ganga, was the boatmen's original contribution to the composite world of heterodoxy in eighteenth-century Bengal.

BARGAINING WITH THE COMPANIES

Evidence from Patna and Mircha show that from the 1720s on, boatmen bargained directly and astutely with the European company officials, refusing to passively accept their worker "status."[128] The problem with explaining precolonial Indian social relations in terms of "status" is that it does not explain the practice of conscious exchange. For instance, in discussing how Murshidabad court artists received patronage, Ratnabali Chatterjee argues that exchange relations were built into the system of patronage. The ability of artists to move from one noble household to another indicated the existence of "social relations of conscious exchange," which were manifested in their mobility and availability for hire.[129] Even more so than the Murshidabad artists or other artisans in the region (see chapter 1), the transport workers—who were a disparate group of peripatetic hirelings drawn from various caste backgrounds, steeped in a climate of religious eclecticism, and habituated to a plethora of hiring practices—consciously entered into exchange relations with the companies and worked hard to safeguard their own perceptions of work. Significantly, such negotiations reveal the extent to which boatmen retained control over their mobility, by deciding the terms and conditions for their movement and their time, by demanding "customary" wages and other benefits, and finally by withdrawing their labor. These negotiations, which encapsulated the will of the workers, mirrored a company-worker relationship that differed greatly from the later contractual relationships of worker-employer in colonial India.

The advantage that the workers had over the companies in deciding their wages is evident from their "quarrelsome" settlements. The very competitive labor market, which the companies could not regulate, continued to rankle in the first few decades of the eighteenth century. On August 1723, the Hugli council of the VOC triumphantly announced that Patna officials had managed to recruit seven *patellas* and two *bangelas* for the "very civil prices" of 4 rupees and 3.5 rupees per 100 maunds, respectively.[130] However, incidents that September left a dent in the confidence of the Patna officials. Rumors about the imminent arrival of Mughal imperial soldiers in Patna and their need to hire boats spread like wildfire. With the imperial army hiring workers, the VOC had to depend on the boatmen's willingness and ability to remain available for hire. The best they could do as employers was to offer more money. Given the "extraordinary wavering nature" of the owners of the boats, the VOC consequently feared delayed departures and attempts by owners "to break their contract under one veil or the other." The Hugli council exhorted the Patna officials "as a precaution" that if that occasion arose, "they should not make the least changes to their (the boat owners') advantage."[131] Available documents do not show whether the Patna officials stood their ground. It seemed unlikely from the events of 1734, for Patna officials were only able to hire boats at the expensive rate of 15.5 rupees per 100 maunds. The English, whose fleet left earlier in the season, could manage a relatively better deal of 14.5 rupees per 100 maunds.

Only by agreeing to hire boats at such high prices could the companies feel competent to stall "the greedy intentions of the boatmen," as one VOC official put it.[132] The presence of a vibrant illegal trade in salt further added to the boatmen's bargaining power. In Mircha in 1734, VOC officials noted that the boatmen were asking for an "unheard-of hiring rate" of 20 rupees per 100 maund. Any amount of persuasion did not work because the boatmen threatened to leave the VOC and go over to the native salt traders coming from

Patna, who were hiring in great numbers that year. The VOC council in Hugli ordered the Kassimbazar official to somewhat concede to the demands of the boatmen. They lamented that the boatmen "could not be prescribed *any law* for demanding a stipulated hiring rate, which would be most profitable for the company."[133] Evidently, the lament harked back at legal measures such as the Statute of Laborers and Artificers that the English state had implemented so widely at home and which were absent in Bengal. In 1739, the company again found themselves fishing in muddy waters when the journey of the Nawab Nazim Alivardi Khan's son-in-law to Murshidabad from Patna coincided with the Patna fleet's journey. Apart from going over to the Nawab's son-in-law's entourage, the boatmen complained about the coming monsoons, which would coincide with their return journey. Given these circumstances, boats could only be hired at the high rate of 22 rupees per 100 maunds. After a hard bargain, the company had to "give in to the desires of the (boat)men" by contracting them at the rate of 18 rupees per 100 maunds. They paid almost 25 percent higher than the previous year's freight charges. The same year at Mircha, the VOC failed to hire an adequate number of boats by the end the of trading season, when the river started to dry. Most boatmen had already been taken up by native merchants.[134] In 1745 company officials again complained that boatmen demanded exorbitant rates of hire. The EIC cashier, Mr. Kemp, intervened to resolve the matter. Unable to bring down the asking price, he took the critical decision of hiring fewer vessels.[135] Competition with other employers thus was stiff and even the Nawabi officials participated in this competitive market, driving up boat hire.

The boatmen were very territorial. Boatmen coming from Patna would not go any further down than the confluence of the Ganga and Jalangi.[136] The companies rarely found a way around this inflexibility. In 1735, "with the greatest difficulty," EIC officers at Patna persuaded boatmen to go as far down as Calcutta. They agreed reluctantly and insisted on being released as soon as they reached Calcutta. The Patna council warned Calcutta officers that if the boatmen's needs were not looked after, "they [Patna council] shall not be able to procure any boats that will go to Calcutta next year."[137] Such exceptions to traditional practice remained short lived at best. Events from 1745 confirm the resilience of the practices of upcountry boatmen. When the EIC asked the boatmen of large saltpeter boats coming from Patna to sail through the Sunderbans, they were extremely reluctant to do so as they were contracted at Patna to sail only as far down as Badderpourgola (around the confluence of the Ganga and Jalangi). When pressed by the EIC's *ghat majhi* and a native bookkeeper, they demanded the rate of 24 rupees per 100 maunds. No amount of cajoling could bring them down to the usual rate of 16 rupees per100 maund. Seven days of coaxing did not change the boatmen from "continuing unreasonable in demands." The Kassimbazar officials, therefore, decided on hiring smaller boats in the region and sending the saltpeter down the Jalangi.[138] The VOC had to recruit *majhis* and rowers at Jalangi who came from the deltaic Bengal and who, according to the company, had no trouble traveling through the deltas. The task was expensive for a number of reasons.

For a start, transshipment points were a zone of intense negotiations between company officials and boatmen. Such negotiations reveal the remarkable role of the workers in deciding their own terms of employment. In April 1709, when the *darogah* Ram Singh was in charge of the return fleet, he had to arrange the difficult task of transshipment of boats at Kherimarie. The boatmen from Patna refused to go beyond Kherimarie, so the *darogah* had to recruit new boats. As was the custom, he communicated with Kassimbazar officials regarding his movements. However, the Kassimbazar officials did not approve of the hire rates for boats and pressed him to bring down the rate. Nevertheless, "the boatmen could not be reconciled to the rate [as recommended by Kassimbazar]." Ram Singh thus wrote to the Hugli council for their permission to give higher wages because he found it increasingly impossible to restrain the upcountry boatmen, who were getting readily hired by salt merchants sending their ware to Patna.[139]

As evident from Ram Singh's correspondences, time was of essence in his negotiations. But he was not "saving" the VOC's time but was instead "buying time" to access the labor power of the boatmen at a price that the boatmen demanded. A rhythm of mercantile activities not dominated by the European companies made it difficult for company officials to synchronize the boatmen's time to the timing of the Patna fleet. Recruitment of deltaic boatmen at the transshipment zone did not neatly correspond to the arrival of the Patna fleet. Often company officials had to hire boats days ahead to avoid delays in the movement of the fleet once it arrived. In such circumstances, they could ensure cooperation of boatmen only through the promise of various perquisites such as food money. As is described in chapter 1, food was often an important component of the wage, even for the most destitute or the most "unskilled" agricultural laborers in Bengal. In 1734 the VOC paid a daily allowance of 0.5 anna as food money to the boatmen for their retention period while awaiting the fleet from Patna.[140] In certain years the demands for food money could be very high. In 1737, the Kassimbazar cashier Christiaan van Bevenage was posted at Jalangi to supervise the transshipment of vessels coming from Patna. Not knowing the amount of opium coming, he hired one hundred boats, guessing that they would be enough for the fleet to move forward. Boats were fast disappearing that year because many of them had been taken up by salt merchants and merchants of other heavy merchandise. Van Bevenage thought it prudent to hire vessels when they were available, lest they were all gone by the time the fleet appeared. "But this could happen not without much bickering with the boatmen," van Bevenage reported. The boatmen demanded 18 rupees for each vessel and food money of 10 annas per day. After much haggling, van Bevenage managed to strike a deal with the boatmen at the previous year's rate of 16 rupees per boat and 6 annas for food money for the days they had to wait for the arrival of the fleet.[141] Money in exchange for "empty days" of waiting was absolutely essential to retain the recruited boatmen. The VOC always looked for ways of cutting what they thought was an "extra" cost, but boatmen insisted on keeping it, as negotiations in 1739 demonstrate. Like Christiaan van Bevenage, cashier Ewout de Leeuw was sent from Kassimbazar to Jalangi in 1739 to recruit boatmen, cartmen, and coolies in advance for the loading and unloading work of the Patna fleet. As in 1737, the boatmen again demanded 18 rupees for each vessel. De Leeuw was happy to recruit at the previous year's rate of 16 rupees and managed to hire twenty-two boats at that rate. However, he could not convince them to let go of their food money for the days spent waiting for the arrival of the Patna fleet and thus promised to pay their "old wages of previous years of 6 annes per day" until the beginning of the journey, against the wishes of the Kassimbazar council. He tarried on this payment and soon lamented, "since I had not paid the food money (for the days they waited for the arrival of the fleet), eleven of them have left to be hired out by native merchants who are daily competing here." De Leeuw decided to give the food money out "sparsely" to the rest of the boatmen from the next day.[142] Food money secured the company's claims on boatmen's time.

Boatmen debated not just their wages but every aspect of their service in order to safeguard what Prasannan Parthasarathi calls "workers' security." In December 1733, the steersmen and pilots recruited at Mircha refused to enter into the service of the VOC before they knew the actual size of the fleet coming from Patna. Before risking the dangerous passage through the Sunderbans, they wanted to make sure that they would have sufficient military presence.[143] In 1734, the equipage officer Christoffel de Wind negotiated with boatmen at Patna to move through the Sunderbans. The boatmen were unsure of their security and threatened de Wind that for the following year, they would not rent out their boats to the Patna fleet. Their threat proved successful and the VOC council unanimously took a resolution to contract boats at the asking price of the boatmen. The Kassimbazar council justified the decision by explaining that "thus far as one can find the boatmen making a reasonable demand, a small cost can be paid for one's great comfort."[144]

The boatmen effectively mobilized their knowledge of the immediate geopolitical landscape in their negotiations. When dissatisfied with their wages, they appealed to the Nawab's court. Boatmen were aware of the peculiar law-and-order situation in Bengal. Although the companies at their headquarters could dispense justice, sometimes in contravention to the interests of other *faujdārs* and the Nawab, the court of the Nawab remained the highest source of authority, provided he chose to interfere in the affairs of the companies. In December, 1741 EIC officials at Kassimbazar stopped 156 *majhis* and *dandies* at Rajmahal. They were on their way to the Nawab's court in Murshidabad to "complain for want of wages and subsistence." To calm them down, the EIC officials gave them 50 rupees. That same year, all boatmen recruited at Jalangi received an advance of 260 rupees.[145] Since the boatmen knew that the companies sought to avoid the Nawab's attention at all costs, they went all the way from Rajmahal to the Murshidabad court, instead of going to the *faujdār* at Rajmahal.

Wages were a battleground for "customary" rights and privileges. In South Asian history, there is surprisingly little discussions about notions of customary rights and privileges among workers in the premodern or precolonial period. Parthasarathi and Sahai are the only historians who have discussed artisans' perceptions of customs in the eighteenth century, even though they do not discuss how customs constituted the wage.[146] Yet, as E.P. Thompson says of customary rights and privileges in England, "custom passes ... into areas altogether indistinct—into unwritten beliefs, sociological norms, and usages in practice."[147] But unlike in England where wages functioned to eliminate customary rights, in Bengal wages were a site of customary rights.[148] If customs are inscribed into "sociological norms and usages," wage relations become an important site for examining its presence. After all, as is discussed in chapter 1, wages in the medieval Bengali context signified a reciprocal relationship between the patron and the worker, and hence held both economic and extra-economic importance to all parties participating in the transaction.

"Customs" of wage payment did not stop at demands for food money. A special privilege that all boatmen clung to dearly was the salt trade. Despite all efforts of the companies to eradicate this "privilege," boatmen consistently insisted on carrying salt on board, to sell on their journey upriver. The Mughal state conferred monopoly trading rights in salt to certain traders of their choice, and it was of the utmost importance to the companies to respect such monopoly rights. However, from higher-level European company servants to their native rowers, employees of all stripes participated in the illegal salt trade. In early 1732, the Nawab of Bengal, Shuja Khan, issued an official order (*parwānā*) to the *faujdār* of Hugli, Pir Khan, forbidding "the hat wearers" from the salt trade.[149] The VOC authorities blamed the Armenian merchant Khwaja Mohammed Fazee—who carried the privilege of trading in salt—for such an "instigation." The next year, the *faujdār* Pir Khan held up Captain Geldzak's fleet for nearly a month near Hugli during the upriver journey. Salt had been found in the holds of the vessels in the fleet, which the *faujdār* staunchly forbade. The VOC had a dilemma because the rowers were unwilling to part with their "old privilege," which allowed them to carry in the holds of the boats two bags of salt for every *maund* of cargo that they carried. While claims of antiquity always strengthened one's entitlement to "privileges," it is impossible to deduce the verity of the claims.[150] What is clear though is that all boatmen rallied behind this claim, flexing their collective bargaining power. The VOC reported: "without the enjoyment of which right our rowers were unwilling to touch the oars." After twenty-two days of sinuous negotiations, two senior VOC merchants succeeded in persuading the *faujdār* to loosen his hold. Between the *faujdār* and the oarsmen, the *faujdār* had to relent.[151]

Customs surrounding wage payments always carried political significance. The Nawab's office asked the EIC to sign a bond in 1727 stating that the vessels of their Patna fleet would not carry salt.[152] However, in violation of this bond, *majhis* and oarsmen carried salt on the vessels as special "allowances" made to the boatmen by the EIC above their usual wage.[153] In 1732, after the Nawab Shuja Khan, alerted the *faujdār* of Hugli, the EIC discovered that several oarsmen had managed to carry salt exceeding their usual allowance and that it had become standard practice.[154] The same year, as the EIC found it impossible to stop the salt trade of their fleet members, Captain William Holcombe, somewhere near Mircha, tried his best to convince the fleet's *polwar* boatmen to reduce their cargo of salt. He was predictably unsuccessful: the *ghat majhi* of Calcutta reported that it was futile to ask the boatmen to reduce their freight of salt onboard the Patna fleet for "they insist on carrying salt as usual with the same pay."¹⁵⁵ If injunctions on the salt trade articulated the Nawabi authorities' ability to shape regional politics of overseas trade—that is, preference for Armenians to other merchants—and to extend centralized control over *zamīndārs*, boatmen from Calcutta saw in salt trade an allowance that the Calcutta *zamīndāri* and hence, the entire Nawabi polity, had conceded on condition of their settlement and service.

Two years later, EIC boatmen staged a strike, unhappy with their inability to carry salt on board. In August 1734, Captain Holcombe complained that the oarsmen were running away "hourly," and he had to stop continuously to recruit replacements. So effective was their labor withdrawal that he had to call off his expedition when the fleet reached Nadia, near Hugli. The *majhis* of the boats blamed the company's decision to not permit the oarsmen to carry salt for such an unusual rate of desertion: "when they were allowed salt it was a security as being on the boat, but now the money they receive they tye in a bag and march away with it."¹⁵⁶ Salt thus served not just as "security" for the oarsmen but also for the company. Without providing them with freight space, the company could not count on their cooperation.¹⁵⁷

The boatmen's sense of entitlement to such trading privileges can be traced back to a sixteenth-century text, Achyutānanda Dās's *Kaivartāgīta*. Achyutānanda was an important figure of a popular Vaishnavite movement in Orissa. Though Achyutānanda's background is shrouded in mystery, he always styled himself as the patron saint of the laboring or menial castes. Thus, in *Gopālanka Ogāla*, he claimed to be the saint of Goālā (cowherds) and Kāmāra (blacksmiths), and in *Kaivartagīta*, he was patron saint of the Kaivarta (fisherman/boatmen).¹⁵⁸ In *Kaivartagīta*, Achyutānanda narrated the life of the mythical king of the Kaivartas, Dasarājā, who was born through the ear of Vishnu. By declaring that Dasarājā belonged to the same body as Kṛiṣna, Achyutānanda bestowed on the untouchable caste a dignity that was denied by the Brahminical order. Dasarājā was then crowned the king of the Kaivartas. Vishnu gifted Dasarājā a boat and horse to make a livelihood through trade. Trade was thus the birthright of the boatmen—not only the Kaivartas but evidently all boatmen of Bengal—and any violation of that right was violation of their moral economy.

Apart from trading privileges, the companies had to reckon with the boatmen's entitlement to customary wages throughout the fleet's journey. These were primarily payments made for pilotage work. There were several scenarios for such payments. First and foremost, company archives recorded these costs as payments "according to custom of the country" (*naar usantie van de land / volgens gebruik / na gebruik / na oude gebruik / volgens oude gewoonte*) made at various points of the journey. It was a widespread custom in Bengal and Bihar to acknowledge the deft pilotage work of the *majhis* after they had led the fleet over a certain distance. In 1736 Captain Geldzak had to pay his pilots 10 rupees on reaching Pintij for crossing over to Bihar from Bengal.[159] Similar payments were due to the *majhis* on entering the mouth of river Hugli via the Sunderbans on the return journey.[160] But, given the prevalence of manifold emergency situations, *majhis* had to employ their piloting skills in various unforeseen circumstances. During Captain Geldzak's September 1736 voyage, a pilot vessel belonging to the *majhi* Laalkori ran aground while measuring the shallows of Ruwenella, and the boat was shattered to pieces, beyond repair. Captain Geldzak immediately wrote to Chinsurah: "Pilots always sail blindly so as to find the least dangerous passage for the company's fleet whereby they run into accidents many times from which it is impossible to save themselves. Therefore, I request your Honor to give this aforementioned man Rs. 25 as a custom followed by other nations to this man to somewhat compensate for his loss and also to encourage others to take up such a dangerous calling."[161] Similarly, on his way to Patna in 1734, Captain Holcombe reported that one of the vessels had run into a sandbank. Holcombe acknowledged that it was a major blow to the *majhi* as the boat was "most of what the poor man had in the world."[162] To these indigent men with skills the companies regularly paid compensatory money for accidents as a "custom."

The VOC also termed payments made for emergency pilotage work as "rewards" or "honorariums." Hence, Geldzak had to pay a "reward" (or *present*, in Dutch) to his head *majhi*, who had suggested the plan for moving past Sitakund. Similarly, two years later in 1738 pilots received an "honorarium" (*vereering*) of 8 rupees for passing the shoals of Candia, just south of Bhagalpur.[163] In 1734, a boat belonging to the fleet crashed against shoals near Gangaprasad. Two *majhis* had to stay back to assist in salvage work. They too were paid an honorarium of 15 rupees. In the same journey *majhis* received a sum of 19 rupees for deftly passing the heavy-bottomed *patellas* through the shoals of Kasdi and Dhariab close to Kahalgaon.[164] It is difficult to say what was the exact amount each *majhi* received, as the VOC paid a lump sum amount to one head *majhi* who then distributed the amount among the others. The lump sum amount varied between 6 and 28 rupees. Such payments are very similar to the wages of artisans in the *maṅgal* poems, whereby wages also functioned as the employers' social recognition of the artisans.

Poets of *maṅgalkābyas*, recognized even the oarsmen, the most humble of all artisans, in such acts of compensation. In the seventeenth-century poet Dwija Ramdev's *Abhayāmaṅgal*, an elaborate account of the merchant Dhanapati's turbulent journey to Siṅhala details the merchant's anxious exchanges with his pilot and oarsmen. When a deadly storm overwhelms Dhanapati's fleet near Magra, he pleads with his oarsmen:

> Row brother oarsmen latching on to your oars
> I will give you golden bracelets studded with precious stones
> There is not much I can say as I face the end
> But I will give you my precious clothes if we pass Magra.[165]

The promise of gold and luxury clothes is another example of the patron honoring the service and loyalty of their artisans. Dhanapati's earnest assurance places boatmen within the milieu of a myriad of artisans depicted in the *maṅgalkābyas* (see discussion in chapter 1). Gift giving was necessarily an extension of the exchange relationships that merchants, *zamīndārs*, and employers practiced with other artisans and workers. In making such payments to boatmen, the companies were repeating this normative practice.

The individual or collective actions by boatmen inevitably created a frictional interface with state authorities, thereby revealing the limits of their power. Such actions thus reflected what sociologist Asef Bayat calls "quiet encroachment" on the power of the state: "The notion of 'quiet encroachment' describes the silent, protracted but pervasive advancement of the ordinary people on the propertied, powerful or the public in order to survive and improve their lives."[166] The "old privilege" of the boatmen encroached upon the power and privilege of the Mughal and Nawabi states and their favored traders. Within the indigenous context, almost all forms of worker-employer relationship were predicated on a web of customs and privileges. The "illegal" salt trade, hence, can be understood as one set of local customary practices encroaching upon the rights of the privileged merchants of the Mughal/Nawabi domain and galvanizing a conflictual relationship between the companies and the indigenous state. Such conflicts revealed the fissures in both imperial and *zamīndāri* sovereignty of the early eighteenth-century state entities. The boatmen continued to carry salt illegally in the holds of their boats even into the early colonial period, in violation of the laws of the EIC state.

Boatmen were not alone in negotiating favorable settlements with the companies. In fact, this was a common practice among all groups of transport workers in Bengal. In 1732, at Mircha, the VOC cashier van Bevenage hired carts for sending opium and military equipment to Kassimbazar at the rate of 3 rupees per chest of opium and 1 rupee for each soldier's chest. He also hired oxen at the rate of 11 annas each to carry the soldiers' tents and other equipment. Considering "the trouble in which one finds oneself" at the transshipment point "whereupon the unreasonable cartmen are in the habit of making their bills," van Bevenage reported that the deal was made "on very civil terms."[167] The next year, though the twenty-four cartmen agreed to work for the previous year's wages, they demanded 8 annas for each ox while they waited for the fleet to arrive. The demands were very similar to those for food money for the boatmen. The Kassimbazar council advised van Bevenage to "persevere at frustrating" the demands of the cartmen in the hope that the Patna fleet would soon show up. Van Bevenage persevered while "waiting with eagle's eye" for the fleet to arrive.[168] It was no mean task, especially because carts were in heavy demand as a local noble was then recruiting them in droves to carry his luggage to Patna. On top of that, many more were being recruited to haul stones at the construction site of the palace of Sarfaraz Khan, son of Shujauddin, Nawab of Bengal. Captain Geldzak's fleet arrived soon thereafter, and van Bevenage was relieved to dispatch all the opium. Settlements with coolies were fraught with similar "altercations."[169] Competition was on the side of transport workers. Once more we see the Nawabi officials as competitive employers, whose participation in the market for transport workers drove wages up.

Boatmen repeatedly relied upon the method of desertion to leverage all their demands. Instructions to the VOC commander and subcommanders of companies of the Patna fleet in 1729 stated clearly that:

> your honor should strongly forbid the Europeans (soldiers) from doing the least harm to the native steersmen and the rowers—from beating them or disturbing them and from touching their cook ware as such an act will compel these people [the native boatmen], especially the Heathens who according to their religion cannot consume this food to throw away their food to their distress and damage. *Apart from that, by extension there is fear that not only will these people [as they have done with the English] flee from their boats and run away landwards but also that one would not be able to get any more boats in the future.*[170]

Such warnings were reiterated in the instructions given to various officers of the Patna fleet in the years 1725, 1732, 1733, 1734, 1739, and 1743.[171] The boatmen demanded a certain etiquette of travel, which, if broken, impelled their threats to flee. The manuals given out to the commanders of the fleet or to captains heading a company of the fleet stressed concern for both recruitment and retention of workers. Since the companies were not in a position to draft laws, there was no possibility of criminalizing desertion. In fact, they somewhat acknowledged the legitimacy of desertion when, in 1725, a VOC official opined that desertion was inevitable if one was to ponder on the acts of defilement of boatmen's food, which caused "great chagrin and no less damage" to the rowers, a "very poor people."[172] Repetitive manuals of caution indicated how the company dreaded disquiet among the native workforce. From 1729 on, all instructions referred to one incident where the EIC "substantially" experienced repercussions from their maltreatment of native workers. Sometime before the year 1729, after suffering "heavy desertion of their rowers," the EIC fleet officials had to make European members of the fleet drag the vessels upriver.[173]

The multitudinous causes of desertion indicate that boatmen had considerable control over their hire and their time. In 1727, the VOC complained that both the *majhi* and the rowers "very easily left their vessels" if they feared storms coming. The company detected that the "principal" reason for desertion was that "they have nothing to lose, having got the two months' payment in hand."[174] The advance payment system militated against any efforts by the companies to synchronize the boatmen's work to increase "convenience." Increasingly in eighteenth-century Europe workers and employers had a differential disposition towards work and time—while workers saw in work a task to be completed, employers saw in work not just mere completion of a task but optimal use of the worker's time they had paid for.[175] The custom of advance payment prevalent in the boatmen's conditions of hire in Bengal created a whole different beast, as the companies were robbed of even the security of the completion of a task as a result of advances. They recommended changes in the advance payment system, but such measures could not be introduced until the early nineteenth century, as is described in chapter 5. Only by then could the colonial state under the EIC introduce a series of regulations designed to break the advance payment and desertion cycle. Rowers most commonly deserted on the "dangerous" leg of the journey through the Sunderbans. Rattled by desertion, the company had to accept the high wages demanded by replacement workers. In 1734, within six days between January 6 and January 12, the Patna fleet of the VOC suffered the desertion of twenty-two rowers. The commander of the fleet had to replace the deserters with rowers who charged 4 rupees each for the two-and-a-half-month journey. Later, on March 1, 1734, three more oarsmen escaped. The VOC had to hire three men for 3 rupees each for just fifteen days' work.[176] The desertion of oarsmen thus caused enormous discomfiture to the companies, and the only way to get around it was to accede to demands for a higher wage for the replacements. Lack of regulating power forced the companies to use the preventive measures outlined in the instruction manuals, but not to any *punitive* measures. The advance payment system and threat of withdrawal of labor on the pretext of danger, entailing short-term expensive hire, indicated that boatmen decided autonomously the amount of time or labor they would commit to the companies' fleets.

The evidence on how the companies tried to hold boatmen accountable indicate the limited jurisdiction of the companies over their errant boatmen as well as the growing control of the EIC over its middle-men recruiters by the 1740s. The companies had only limited power to bring boatmen to task. In 1719, on arrival of the Patna fleet to Chinsurah, the VOC officials discovered sixty-eight bags of saltpeter missing. Narottam, the *majhi* of the boat from which the saltpeter bags went missing, had signed a bond stating that if he were found guilty, he would pay with his boat to replace the missing saltpeter bags. What the outcome of the investigation was is not known. However, the company had to allow him to sail to Patna, where the officials were informed of the bond.[177] The VOC could not circumscribe his mobility. In 1745, the EIC too experienced an incident of theft. Of the boxes of bullion sent to Kassimbazar, one box had a hole in it, and silver worth 620 rupees was missing. The *majhi* of the boat along with four oarsmen fled the scene. The company guards and soldiers then apprehended the other people on the boat—a sergeant, an Armenian passenger, and three other oarsmen—and sent them to Calcutta. Since there was no proof that those prisoners had anything to do with the robbery and since the chief suspects were still at large, it was decided that "the nya [owner] of the boat, the person who was security for the manjee [*majhi*] together with the Gaut Manjee [*Ghat majhi*] must make good the deficiency to the Hon'ble Company." The EIC, it seems, was already starting to devise a system of security to ensure some form of control over the worker. When the owner of the boat from which the *majhis* and *dandies* had stolen the silver was interrogated, the EIC learned that "she is so poor as to have nothing but her boats for her livelihood and one of them broke and the other not above twenty rupees." The EIC resolved that the *ghat majhi*, a recruitment agent for boats, who worked regularly for the EIC, was to "make good the loss to the Hon'ble Company" as he "ought to have taken better security" for the boat and boatmen he had recruited. The Calcutta *zamindar* received an order to keep the *ghat majhi* under confinement in the *zamindari* court's judicial capacity until the *ghat majhi* paid the money.[178] This incident is striking because it shows that the *ghat majhi*, a worker closely related to the EIC, was most vulnerable to company's labor discipline. This incident also indicates that by 1740s the EIC was already devising a system of recruitment based upon intermediary recruiters, who could be held responsible and penalized for damages the EIC suffered on account of the boatmen's misbehavior. Thus, the intermediary recruitment agent was slowly emerging as a potential solution to the companies' dire need of disciplining boatmen.

The movement of the fleet was a cumbersome work process where boatmen of various kinds of vessels played a key role. These boatmen were drawn from a variety of lower caste groups. They came from specific social and cultural milieus with special skills. Most prominent was the distinct difference between deltaic boatmen and the upcountry boatmen from Patna—upcountry boatmen refused to travel through the deltas. Other "customs" left their mark on the terms of hire, such as the customs of carrying salt on board and paying honorariums to boatmen, as well as maintaining rituals of cleanliness. Notably, many of these customs were not rooted in specific caste relations, but in wage payment to all boatmen and cut across a whole range of castes. This range of practices, along with the boatmen's control over their time, ensured that there was no standardized recruitment procedure. The absence of intermediary recruiters further accentuated the lack of standardization, leaving company officials to deal directly with boatmen. It was not until the 1740s that a boatmen-recruiter became a fixture of the EIC's hiring procedures in Calcutta. More than other boatmen, the recruiter was held fast to the disciplinary regime of the EIC. This transition in recruitment and discipline was a prelude to the changes that the EIC state brought about in the late eighteenth century (see chapter 5). For much of the early eighteenth century, the EIC along with the VOC struggled to maintain smooth cooperation with their boatmen.

THREE

"I Would Rather Be the Foremost Prince of Any Lower Court"

EUROPEAN SAILORS AND SOLDIERS IN THE EARLY EIGHTEENTH-CENTURY COMPANY STATE

IN HIS EXPOSITION ON POLITICAL ARITHMETICK, William Petty acknowledged that sailors and soldiers were the "pillars of any commonwealth" that harbored ambitions of flourishing through trade. In Petty's estimation the soldiers' profession was "of greatest turmoil and danger, and yet of least profit," and sailors, though more valuable, required the same "industry and ingenuity" as the soldier.[1] In Bengal, while the world of maritime-military work was deeply intertwined, there was not much distinction between the status or wages of soldiers and sailors. For much of the seventeenth and eighteenth centuries poor working Europeans filled these ranks to erect company "commonwealths" in Asian lands. Yet, despite Petty's observations, these low-ranking workers of the company have rarely caught the attention of historians of Bengal and the English East India Company. On one hand, the EIC's ship labor before the nineteenth century, especially their European sailors, remains almost an unresearched topic. On the other hand, military historians have brushed aside the history of the EIC's military labor before 1760 as a ragtag army of highly undisciplined (often Dutch) mercenaries, unworthy of further analysis.[2] Yet, recent scholarship reveals that the EIC in Indian lands expanded their military significantly in the early eighteenth century. As the EIC transitioned into a landholding power in the early eighteenth century, they became increasingly reliant upon European recruits in Bengal to bolster the numbers of their military personnel.[3] Moreover, the EIC's ambition to institute "a robust civic life" often hinged upon its ability to hold these low-ranking European sailors and soldiers within the bounds of company settlements and company allegiance, something these "subalterns" refused to do.[4] This chapter unearths the labor market for hiring European sailors and soldiers in early eighteenth-century

Bengal. All political forces in the region hired European workers. However, because European sailors and soldiers could desert to other employers with ease, the EIC, like other political forces, failed to exert any meaningful control over this market of sailors and soldiers during the early eighteenth century. Only in the 1760s did it succeed in partially instituting control over them.

Despite their international origins, European sailors and soldiers participated in Bengal's local labor market. The market here was not made up solely of European companies or indigenous elites. European sailors and soldiers, through their practice of running away from work, actively shaped the contours of that labor market. As Dirk Kolff's research demonstrates, a mobile work force for military labor existed in precolonial South Asia.[5] In many ways, it resembled the mobile military labor market of Central Europe in the late Middle Ages, especially in the various German states.[6] However, beginning in the mid-seventeenth century, force became the hallmark of recruitment in the European military labor market, a change which was absent from the military labor market of South Asia. As early modern European states enlarged their armies, they intruded into village life both in England and Central Europe. Massive numbers of soldiers came from artisanal backgrounds, which indicates that army ranks were filled with people who had experienced a process of de-skilling.[7] This trend is noticeable in the background of low-ranking European soldiers in the EIC army as late as the early nineteenth century. As more and more people thronged the military labor market in Europe, wages remained low and stagnant. In Bengal, though, European sailors and soldiers could *reverse* this trend. In various indigenous armies, European sailors and soldiers were coveted as expert artillery men. Additionally, rival European companies recruited Europeans regularly for their armies and ships in Bengal. In such a scenario, where companies were competing fiercely to recruit workers, European sailors and soldiers used the strategy of desertion to maintain a high wage rate.

In understanding European sailors and soldiers of the EIC and other companies in Bengal as workers, the following analysis explicates the class conflicts on company grounds, which the EIC among others struggled to resolve. It thus departs from the long-standing practice of framing low-ranking Europeans as hot-headed law breakers, renegades,[8] adventurers,[9] or the "third face of colonialism."[10] European sailors and soldiers were first and foremost workers, and as workers their interests were often at odds with the interests of the state. This dissonance is best revealed by the companies' extreme anxiety to control desertion and thus to control the labor market. By deserting from one employer to another, these workers played an important role in the EIC's mercantilist competition on foreign grounds. William Petty enviously noted that in Europe the "Hollanders" attracted soldiers from Scotland, England, and Germany whereby "they people the country and save their own persons from danger and misery, without any real expence."[11] The Dutch may have had an advantage in Europe's military labor market in the seventeenth century, but in Bengal, competition tipped slightly in favor of the EIC state. By the 1760s the tide had turned completely in favor of the EIC. Following the victory over VOC forces at Bedara, the EIC limited Dutch forces to only 125 soldiers. Having eradicated their primary European rivals, in the same decade the EIC succeeded in significant measure to stall desertion among its soldiers through restructuring its army and revamping military discipline with an iron hand.

WORK AND WAGES

The companies' mercantile successes in foreign lands depended on successful deployment of their European rank and file for military or shipping labor. The VOC sent 220,000 soldiers from Europe to Asia after 1700. In the period between 1745 and 1765, VOC sent 2,800 soldiers yearly to Asia.[12] An equally large number of European sailors—over 3,000 each year for the period between 1690 and 1790—came to Asia as part of VOC's intercontinental crew.[13] Even though more and more Asian sailors were employed, especially in intra-Asiatic shipping after the second half of the eighteenth century, European sailors still constituted the overall majority of the crew throughout the eighteenth century.[14] "European" is a heterogenous term—the share of employees coming from all over Europe outside the Dutch Republic rose from 25 percent of the workforce in 1694 to 45 percent in 1780.[15] From what little we do know about the EIC's crew composition in the eighteenth century, it is safe to infer that the EIC mostly employed European sailors for their crews on its intercontinental vessels.[16] In the early eighteenth century, they relied primarily on the European soldiers for their armies in Bengal. The EIC recruited a substantial segment of their European soldiers locally in Bengal.

The military strength of the EIC and VOC developed from the last years of the seventeenth century, affirming their positions as *zamīndārs* in the region. The expansion of the military was the primary reason behind the formation of the Patna fleet. The size of the military often ranged in the few hundreds. Within these armies, European soldiers formed the majority. Of the 259 soldiers of the VOC army stationed in Bengal in 1751, 144 soldiers were categorized as "Europeans," 53 were categorized as "mestizoes," and 65 were categorized as "Eastern Soldiers."[17] These Eastern soldiers came from various Southeast Asian islands and were recruited at Batavia, the VOC's headquarters. Sometimes they were referred to as Makassarese and Bugis soldiers and at other times just as "Native Soldiers."[18] Finally, there were mestizo soldiers, who were born in Batavia of Eurasian origin. These mestizo and Eastern soldiers were able to rise to the ranks of ensign, sergeant, or corporal. Although the Dutch recruited soldiers indigenous to Bengal from time to time, their names never made it into the muster rolls as the company only hired them temporarily. In times of internal turmoil, recruitment of indigenous soldiers was best avoided since their loyalty to the companies was always under question. In 1743, when Bengal awaited a second Maratha attack, VOC officials at Chinsurah contemplated ways of increasing military manpower, but they ruled out the option for recruiting armed indigenous soldiers at Kassimbazar due to "the worry that if one recruits them, they are going to rob us first."[19]

The EIC could not rely on a similar solution, chiefly because it, as yet, had no colonies in Asia from which it could source non-European soldiers if the need arose. The EIC therefore responded to the situation by creating a separate category of soldiers: the "Portuguese." In 1695, following a French expedition in the Bay of Bengal, the Court of Directors, concerned about the strength of the army in the region, ordered the enlistment of Armenians and "Caffres & Black" soldiers with the justification that every recruit sent from England cost the higher price of 30 pounds.[20] Thus, the "Portuguese" soldiers were recruited as a cheap source of armed labor. From the 1740s onwards, the VOC also employed "toepassen" or Indo-Portuguese soldiers in their fleet.[21] The origins and identity of the "Portuguese" in service of the companies has been long debated.[22] In the estimation of an early EIC historian of India, Robert Orme, "The Christians, who call themselves Portuguese, always forms part of a garrison: they are little superior in courage to the lower casts of Indians, and greatly inferior to the higher casts as well as to the northern Moors of Indostan; but because they learn the manual exercise and the duties of a parade with sufficient readiness, and are clad like Europeans, they are incorporated into the companies of European troops."[23] One can conclude from the very low wages for the Portuguese soldiers and occasional references to them as "Black Portuguese" that these locally recruited soldiers were by no means considered equal to the Europeans, though an underlying Christian unity was invoked. The military mastermind behind EIC's victory at Plassey, Robert Clive invoked this religious unity in his notice to Portuguese soldiers in 1756, urging them to join the EIC army in their war against Siraj ud-Daulah.[24] Overall, despite significant numbers of non-Europeans in the company armies, European soldiers formed the backbone of the armies in this period. It was only after 1757 that the number of Indian soldiers, or *sipahis*, rose in the EIC's Bengal army.[25]

European soldiers were thoroughly wage-dependent workers on EIC grounds. Payment of the EIC army took place in Bengal on a monthly basis. The captain, major, or lieutenant was at the apex of the hierarchical order of the army, enjoying a wage of 35 rupees. Below him was the ensign, with a wage of 25 rupees. At 20 rupees, the sergeant came next, and the corporal and drummer each were paid 13 rupees. Common European soldiers, who filled out the ranks of the army most prominently received a monthly wage of 10 rupees. At the bottom rung of the wage structure was the 5 or 6 rupees paid to the Portuguese/Black soldier. While the wages of the European common soldiers and the Portuguese soldiers remained static throughout the period, the wages of the higher officials rose significantly. By 1747, a captain was earning a wage of 45 rupees.[26] The VOC's wage distribution was less stable. The VOC muster rolls were maintained using the Dutch currency, florins. The highest military official was the captain lieutenant with a wage of 60 florins. Below him in descending order came the lieutenant, the ensign, the sergeant, and the corporal. The wages of these officials varied over the first half of the century. While the wages of mestizo and indigenous soldiers from East Asia remained fixed at 9 florins, common soldiers' wages varied between 9 and 14 florins. Reasons for this variation could be multiple. The experience and bargaining power of the soldier, especially those recruited in Asia (enhanced through the practice of desertion), may have contributed to this wide range of wages.

Not only the wage rates and distribution of wages but also the hiring practices of the VOC and EIC differed. Typically, the European soldiers of the VOC signed multi-year contracts in Amsterdam and received their wages partially where they were stationed in Asia and partially in the Dutch Republic. Payment in Asia or in Europe depended on the debt of the worker to the company or to other persons in the Dutch Republic to whom the sailors and soldiers sometimes committed almost half of their wages.[27] A large number of European soldiers were recruited in Asia, for whom payment took place in the various Asian quarters where they were recruited and where they were deployed.[28] While most were recruited in Batavia, some were also recruited at Chinsurah.[29] The VOC also maintained a large number of sailors on land. A sizeable number of these sailors were put into military service whenever the need arose for extra men. Finally, from time to time, the VOC gave deserters a reprieve and admitted them into service at the lowest end of the pay scale.

The EIC recruited a substantial number of their soldiers locally in Bengal. All common soldiers received a standard wage of 10 rupees each month paid locally throughout the first half of the eighteenth century. Though sources on EIC's recruitment practices are thin, detailed muster rolls from 1750 show that only a few of these soldiers had signed regular contracts of three or five years and all were contracted in England. For example, of the 123 men in Major John Holland's company only eleven were contracted. The rest were not contractual workers even though some had served the company for sixteen years. Countries of origins for a large number of these uncontracted workers were Holland, Prussia, "German, " Switzerland, and Holstein. It is very likely that these were deserters from the VOC. Given that the EIC paid their soldiers in rupees and that the VOC always complained of chronic desertion of their men to the English side, it can be safely concluded that desertion was the principal means of recruitment.[30]

By the early eighteenth century, much like the practice for soldiers, most European sailors within the Anglo-American world received a monthly wage. Within the VOC a common seaman's wage would vary between 7 and 12 florins.[31] Payment method was the same as for the soldiers. The transition of European sailors into wage-earning workers started in the sixteenth century. By the early eighteenth century, the medieval nonwage, share system of payment applied only to fishermen, whalemen, privateersmen, and pirates. The passage of an "Act for the Better Regulation and the Government of the Merchants Service" in 1729 formalized in written contracts the relationship between merchant shipowners and seamen as one strictly bound by the exchange of money wages.[32]

As one of the earliest waged workers, sailors bore the burden of the hardships of shipboard life in the Age of Sail.[33] When the German-Dutch poet Isaac Sunderman (1661–1723) returned to Enkhuizen after his first successful voyage to the Indies as a soldier, he declared that the idea of making a huge fortune in the East was a myth.[34] On the contrary, he emphasized that the experience of sailors and soldiers was one of intense poverty. Moreover, the legend of the carefree sailor was far from reality: "but sadly a sailor for one third of his life could not come to land."[35] Seventeenth-century English common seaman Edward Barlow's sketches in his journals—a rare pursuit for a man of his class at work—illustrate the common sailors' experiences in foreign lands. His halftone pencil drawing of the port of Hugli depicts the long-meandering, densely populated inland riverfront (see figure 10). It depicts river traffic with boats and ships and the banks dotted with the flags of various East India companies marking their settlements. Yet, the land beyond the riverfront was a void for Barlow. His impression of the interior is encapsulated in the sketch of a lone rhinoceros, which in 1684 he and his mates carried on board the *Kent* from Hugli to London. For the most part, the shores of the East remained off limits to the lower ranks of the crew. Life at sea was made even more unbearable by the work itself: "[the] very nature of the work corrupted the crew on voyages."[36] The ghoulish nature of work on board was underscored by the pitch and tar and the "clamour and bullies of the crew."[37] Even the best ship was "a prison for the poor sailor," with the ship's captain or commander taking the role of jailer.[38] As the despot of the sea, he could "earn the poor sailors both heaven and hell on earth."[39] The constant struggle of a seaman with the commander of the ship forms the most compelling thread in Barlow's journal: "[A]ll the men in the ship except the master being little more than slaves."[40] Even in his last voyage in 1703, Barlow was battling the insufferable "proud, imperious and malicious temper" of the ship's captain.[41] Fallouts with the captain and mates on ship were one of the major causes of desertion among sailors.[42] It was not just the ship's captain but also other higher-ranking officials on board who could mete out punishment to the sailors.[43] Thus, one VOC report on desertion from 1711, a year of unprecedented numbers of desertions, identified "the fear of discipline/chastisements for the misdeeds committed on board" as a cause of the very desertions which the punishments were meant to prevent.[44]

Seafaring was unceasing work, with death lurching around each turn. As Barlow noted in his journal, the seamen "were not to lie still above four hours,"[45] and he lamented that his occupation was "one of the hardest and dangerousest callings I could have entered upon."[46] Prolonged work in unhygienic conditions resulted in illnesses of all sorts. Thus, for certain years in the early eighteenth century, the VOC lost as much as 15 percent of their seamen within the first few months of their arrival in Asia.[47] For seamen confined to ships at rest, tropical diseases particularly during the monsoon

FIGURE 10. Edward Barlow's sketch of Hugli, from *Barlow's Journal of His Life at Sea in King's Ships, East and West Indiamen, and Other Merchant Men from 1659 to 1703*, vol. II, ed. Basil Lubbock (London: Hurst and Blackett, 1934).

season were quick to claim their lives. "Death and desertion" was almost always uttered in the same breath by ship captains complaining of the constant need for fresh recruits.[48] The perils of life at sea might thus explain the mass desertions that occurred immediately after ships' arrivals at Bengal ports.

The world of maritime work was conjoined to the world of military work. Both death and desertion among soldiers were perennial problems. Though the working conditions of the soldiers laboring within the Bengal directorate were much better than those of the sailors of deep-sea vessels, death was a constant occurrence among the Europeans working in inland shipping. In 1728, out of the 333 soldiers of the Patna fleet of the VOC, seven died within a space of only three months.[49] The next year, the fleet was manned by 307 soldiers. Of these, thirteen soldiers were so sick that they were unable to work, and out of the rest, eleven died.[50] Moreover, combat situations were always life-threatening. For instance, in one day in 1719, three EIC soldiers were killed in an armed conflict with the Chakwars.[51] Frequent deaths among soldiers allowed sailors to come on land, only to be put to military work. As Barlow noted that on his arrival in Bengal in 1693, he was promptly put on a military mission to hunt down an interloper.[52] This complex world of work was a spectacle in the eyes of inhabitants of Bengal, as can be seen in the terracotta panels on temples. Artists' impression of the large European vessels, weighing several hundred tons, though inaccurate when compared to the marine art from seventeenth- and eighteenth-century Europe, depict in detail the world of work on these ships. The hull, bow, stern, the row of protruding canons, and rigging of the ship are clear as are the sailors clambering up the rigging and armed soldiers on decks (see figure 11). Maritime and military work meld together to evoke the sense of a fortress.

Quotidian hardships of work were often inscribed on the flesh. As one list of VOC deserters from 1687 shows, otherwise unremarkable sailors and soldiers were often identified by scars running "from above his left until under his right breast" or "signs of injury on the left side of his head and one under his calf," and life at sea could leave men with "crooked posture" or "severely stammering." Experience of collective misery in turn gave rise to collective sociability. Thus, sailors' and soldiers' Christian names often gave way to endearing monikers: Piet Janszoon Stael was known to his mates as Piet the Pendulum, Dirck Reijers was nicknamed the Castle Durendael, the shy Guijljam van Beveren was the Housekeeper, Arent Arentzoon was the Baptist, Elias Corneliszoon was Man Elephant, and Johannes Abrahamzoon was

FIGURE 11. Terracotta panel of a European ship, from the Dadhimadhav Temple, Amoragari, Howrah, West Bengal, 1764. Wikimedia Commons, photo by Biswarup Ganguly.

known as Jan Ding Ding. This alternative sociability created through workers' interactions independent of their superiors, arising in the zones of cooperation during the work day, was critical to the acts of desertion.[53]

THE PROBLEM OF DESERTION

Among all the East India Companies operating in Bengal in the early eighteenth century, the VOC was the most important recruiter of sailors and soldiers *from* Europe. VOC service provided the vehicle for European sailors and soldiers to enter the labor market in Bengal. On reaching Bengal, more often than not these sailors and soldiers ran away to enter into the service of one of the VOC's many rivals. As the company that brought the maximum numbers of sailors and soldiers from Europe, the VOC bled the most through desertion. Consequently, they kept the best records on desertion of European sailors and soldiers. These accounts of desertion reveal the social life of European sailors and soldiers in Bengal and the legal efforts of the VOC and EIC to contain such life and their inadequacies.

Incidents of desertions often illuminated the collective life of sailors and soldiers. Only careful coordination could enable groups of twelve, thirteen, thirty-three, or even fifty-three workers to escape company grounds. Synchronized cooperation at workplaces that companies both carefully imposed and inculcated inadvertently allowed for such subversive socialization. On his journey to Bengal on the ship *Wendela*, the seasoned VOC sailor Leendert van den Burg convinced his "partners" (*mackers*), the eight sailors on the ship, to run away to Calcutta in November,1734. As a thirty-seven-year-old veteran sailor who had been to Bengal multiple times, van den Burg's experience came in handy as he led the group of young deserters, all under twenty-five years of age. Van den Burg individually spoke to all the deserters after they were physically abused by the first mate and convinced them that they could all find better work with the English in Calcutta. The entire group waited for Van den Burg to give them the signal to lower the boat, as he had knowledge of the movement of the VOC patrol at Falta. When arrested by a group of native guards of the VOC, Van den Burg, knowing that the guards did not understand Dutch, communicated to the rest, "we should stick to the same story." Except for Christiaan Houvle, everyone told the same story in the *fiscaal*'s office, down to the first mate's curse word.[54] Collegiality built into workplaces was key in passing information needed to carry out collective desertions. On August 13, 1724, while waiting on an *ulak* very close to Calcutta, a VOC soldier went ashore and made his way to the Surman's garden on the edge of Calcutta. Two hours later, he returned to get his chest of belongings with an army of native soldiers headed by a EIC servant who could speak Dutch. The soldier then asked his "companion," a fellow soldier, lying sick in the boat, "Will you join me? I have already been hired." The other soldier immediately joined in. He then asked one other sick sailor on board, "What will you ... do lying there?" The fever probably got the better of him, for the sailor did not join the deserting soldiers.[55]

Spaces of socialization outside of the workplace, especially the waterfront area, were the spawning grounds for deserters. Known as sites of drunken brawls and other forms of debauchery, taverns or punch houses on the company grounds were also notorious sites for desertion. These resting places, most likely to be found in Hugli and Calcutta, were often run by women of Portuguese origin.[56] Transiting sailors, soldiers, and even low-ranking company officials lodged in these establishments. People missing from the daily roll calls on the ships or in the army could often be found in the taverns. In 1686, in the midst of the Anglo-Mughal war, a ship captain sent Pieter Abrahamzoon, a VOC gunner, to bring back a few runaways employed in the EIC service. He failed in his mission and on his way back, Abrahamzoon tarried and settled in for a drink with his mate at a nearby tavern, where ironically he met twenty VOC deserters. One of them, Abrahamzoon's mate, worked for the EIC, enticing men from the Dutch side.[57] In 1733, in their desperate efforts to stop desertion from intercontinental ships, the EIC felt it necessary to involve punch house owners, and strictly ordered them to report to the officer of the guard if they "entertain in their house any stranger." If the punch house owners failed to notify the EIC, and if the guards apprehended deserters from these establishments, especially those belonging to the company's shipping, the owner of the house "[would] not be suffered to remain here but will be sent directly to Europe."[58] The VOC too issued similar statutes ordering tavern keepers to inform the company officials of any "foreigners" soliciting company servants for recruitment and desertion; if any failed to do so, the tavern keeper would earn a hefty fine of 100 ducatons for each deserter.[59]

Intimate coordination was necessary because incidents of desertion were daring acts often involving armed confrontation with company forces. Seizing arms before running away was of immense strategic importance. For instance, eleven soldiers and two boatswains who fled the VOC ship *'t Weroname*, stationed at Falta, in close proximity to Calcutta, captured arms before their escape. In the early hours of April 10, 1733, while the quartermaster, two sergeants, and two of the four corporals kept watch in the deckhouse, the renegades encircled them "with knives and bayonets in their hands." When the quartermaster tried to fight them, he was "given two stabs with a knife on his breast."[60] The mutineers lowered the ship's boat, and at the crack of dawn, the empty boat was seen lying on the shore in Calcutta. Twelve soldiers from Chinsurah employed a similar strategy a few years earlier on the night of April 3, 1727. The company guards and five indigenous residents of VOC grounds tried to stop twelve soldiers from scaling the fence of the Dutch village at night. After a short argument, one of the soldiers took out a pistol and opened fire on the guards, stalling them so that they could not follow the runaways beyond the company boundaries. Later, it was found that "one of them had stolen a few pistols and taken those with them."[61] Likewise, on May 3, 1730, a group of six VOC soldiers "weaponed with firearms" crossed the company fences and took shelter in the French headquarters at Chandernagore.[62] Sometimes rival companies, to whom the deserters ran, encouraged deserters to bring arms stolen from their previous employer. The Ostend Company, one of the competing employers of European sailors and soldiers, always encouraged deserters to run away with arms from the EIC and VOC grounds. Runaway sailors and soldiers were a means for them to acquire weapons and ammunition.[63] Desertion was thus an extremely carefully crafted, premeditated act that warranted utmost vigilance on part of the companies.

The VOC's first measure was to rigorously restrict the mobility of workers within their *zamīndāri*. As early as 1676, VOC authorities issued strong orders "to confine people on board ships."[64] The common sailors of deep-sea vessels were not allowed to go ashore during the long layovers, and if allowed to disembark, their perambulation was restricted to a very circumscribed area around the ships and only for a very few hours. A VOC statute of 1685 prevented sailors from moving off the ships during the night without permission of the captain nor beyond the boundaries of the Chinsurah settlement, marked by the VOC bazaar in the north and the VOC warehouse in the south. On violating this rule for the first time, the offender would be fined 6 rupees. On repeated violation, court proceedings would be initiated against the offender. Such transgressors, VOC statutes further stipulated, could be whipped and put in chains which were only to be removed during the day so that they could work. If boats had to go to the shore to buy supplies, they could do so only with the permission of the *fiscaal*; the steersman and/or other officers would ensure that the sailors of these ships moved out of the vessels with proper permission letters.[65] Beginning in the early eighteenth century, it became routine to read out a similar statute on all incoming ships which declared that movement outside a half-mile from Falta was a punishable offence.[66] Even for circumstances and in regions where the VOC had little control, the directorate issued orders regarding movement of their crews. In 1677 when the VOC offered the *faujdār* Malik Kasim a sloop and a boat to assist in the Mughal state's war against a rebellious *zamīndār*, the Hugli council gave instructions to the steersmen leading a crew of twenty sailors to "not listen to any order . . . that needs you to go on land."[67] Needless to say, the sailors defied such orders. The company lamented that given the close proximity to land while the ships were anchored in the river, the movement of the sailors could not be restricted. They swam to the shores at low tide, used local vessels in the night to move to and from the ships, and some "got drunk and got pulled into the service of the English."[68]

Companies tried in various ways to get the deserters back into service. The lists of the returnees (*wedergekeerdes*) give the names of people who wandered back to their service. During 1711–12, when the VOC faced massive desertions, the Bengal council first tried to organize bounty-hunting of deserting personnel. The company appointed native guards to patrol the banks of the river and "prevent desertion at their level best." As a reward, they were promised 5 rupees for each deserter they brought back.[69] When such arrangements did not work, the company instructed the military patrolling the boundaries of Chinsurah factory that "on meeting some of the vagabonds, assure them, if they well-meaningly surrendered they [would] be pardoned." Such a conciliatory measure did work to some extent, and the company recovered six men.[70] In fact, there were times when, as the VOC declared, they had no choice but to "treat the rabble with a soft hand," especially when deserters to indigenous armies organized raids on company merchants or property with the help of their new colleagues.[71] In 1732, Batavia issued an unprecedented statute that granted blanket clemency to all returning deserters, immunity from deportation to Batavia, and also promised them restitution to the same posts that the deserters had held when they left the company,[72] perhaps explaining a relatively high number of returnees (24) in Bengal in 1733. Nonetheless, the VOC was never very comfortable with these acts of clemency, because these "faithless vagabonds," the Hugli council alleged, never remained in service for long. The returnees were repeat offenders. They would "pinch not only the weapons but also money" from their "lawful masters," but more importantly, they "seduced others" to "run away with them."[73]

When preventive measures failed, the VOC resorted to punitive measures. Deportation was the most common form of punishment for apprehended deserters, although it was often accompanied with flogging and three to twenty-five years of hard labor in chains in any of the penal colonies of the VOC empire. Needless to say, apprehended deserters fought back with jail breaks. In 1677, three out of six VOC sailors who had deserted near Sadraspatam with a sloop were caught in Balasore and then sent to Hugli. Their legs were chained to a wooden block, and they put under the guard of five native peons. However, the prisoners managed "to corrupt the peons," got the keys from them, and at daybreak they escaped. One was immediately caught and the company hopelessly tried their best to capture the other two.[74] In 1705, of the six deserters who were kept in custody on the ship *Dieren* anchored near Calcutta and were to be sent on to Batavia, three bolted in the dead of night, "breaking chains and manacles."[75] In 1712, the VOC arrested two deserting sailors and planned to deport them to Batavia. One of them managed to flee from prison "in a subtle way."[76] Two imprisoned deserters, expecting deportation, escaped in a similar manner in the early hours of December 24, 1725.[77]

The ultimate punishment for desertion was death. According to the laws of the VOC, desertion to foreign rivals in Asian lands was an act of treason. Though used sparingly, the VOC directorate of Bengal did not shy away from implementing such laws. According to my calculation, the *fiscaal* in the Bengal directorate sentenced twenty-one deserters with capital punishment, of which seventeen were carried out in Chinsurah.[78] If not death, certain deserters were put to severe punishments including walking the gauntlet of as many as two hundred soldiers.[79] Such punishments made even the death penalty look benign. Within the VOC's administrative structure, even low-ranking settlements in the Bengal directorate reserved autonomy in interpreting and implementing statutes framed in Dutch Republic law or in the VOC headquarter in Asia, Batavia. In certain years, the Bengal council sentenced deserters to death, independent of the statutes issued in Batavia. On May 19, 1733, the Hugli council reversed Batavia's 1732 statute of indiscriminate pardon for all returning deserters, stating that it was "not of any consequence," and instead reinstated the discretionary power of the Hugli council to grant pardon to returning deserters.[80] Use of such discretionary power resulted in four death penalties the following year.

The EIC, in contrast, faced legal difficulties in penalizing their deserters in Bengal. In England and other parts of the British Empire, the Admiralty courts tried deserting sailors who were in violation of the 1729 Act for the Better Regulation and Government of Seamen in the Merchants Service, which made desertion from merchant shipping a criminal offense. However, in the absence of any Admiralty court in Bengal, the EIC could not try their deserters promptly. In 1686, the EIC hastily set up an Admiralty court in Fort St. George in Madras.[81] The main purpose of this court was to try interlopers who threatened the company's monopoly. This Admiralty court was very different from its Atlantic counterparts. The jurisdiction of this court was nebulous, with no mechanism for making appeals to higher Admiralty courts. The "oath appointed by the Act of the 11th and 12th of King William the third to be taken by the Judges of the Court of Admiralty plainly refers to Pyracy, Robbery and felony."[82] Apart from wartime desertion it was unlikely that desertion would be considered a felony. The EIC in Bengal thus had to either ship their deserters to Madras or more certainly to the High Court of the Admiralty in England for legal due process. Moreover, the mutiny acts that made desertion an offense punishable by capital punishment applied to the English Army but not to the EIC army. In absence of such legal powers, the EIC had to depend on the brutality of army and ship officers to impose discipline on their European rank and file.

Despite legal provisions, companies could not stem the tide of desertion among its European sailors and soldiers. Death penalties were only partially effective in stopping desertion. For example, deserter Michiel Gerrit de Groot, captured on May 23, 1714, was hanged onboard the ship *Wateringen* "as an example for the others." His execution "created such terror amongst common sailors" that no one deserted for some time.[83] But only for a short time. As the company reported in late 1714, the sailors had "resumed their old practice." The VOC sailors and soldiers were aware that even if the company took back "repenting" deserters, those deserters could expect to start at the lowest salary level. Beyond that, even if the company forces could be successfully dodged, "strong currents and crocodiles" presented sailors and soldiers with "many dangers of losing their lives" in the river and the deltaic lands around Falta when, in the dead of night, they surreptitiously swam towards the shore.[84] Despite such dangers, the European sailors and soldiers still deserted. In certain years, desertion rose to a staggering one third or even one half of the total number of European servants of the VOC in the Bengal directorate.[85]

While crime and indebtedness were important motives for desertion, they provide explanations for only a handful of cases. Some deserters had committed serious crimes and ran away from harsh penalties. In 1676 Jacob Vreem, a carpenter from Utrecht, had been accused of murdering Gerrit Jootsen van Kampen, a line turner.[86] After two witnesses confirmed his crime, Vreem managed to escape from the prison in Chinsurah. In the same year, another head carpenter who had murdered a baanmeester escaped from the company's prison.[87] Such instances of escape from prison by deserters continued intermittently. Two prisoners escaped from the Chinsurah prison in 1714. Some of these convicts were death-row prisoners. Jacob Jacobz, for example, after an unsuccessful attempt to escape the *fiscaal*'s men, was hanged on the ship *Sleewijk* on April 27, 1726, as soon as he was captured.[88] But convicts comprised only a small fraction of the deserters and do not explain the collective flights, which were all too common. Indebtedness was endemic to lower-level company servants, especially among sailors and soldiers. Some had debts of over 100 Dutch guilders, and with a wage of just 9 guilders these workers were condemned either to endless wage slavery for the company or to suffer in one of the early modern debtors' prisons in Europe. One possible

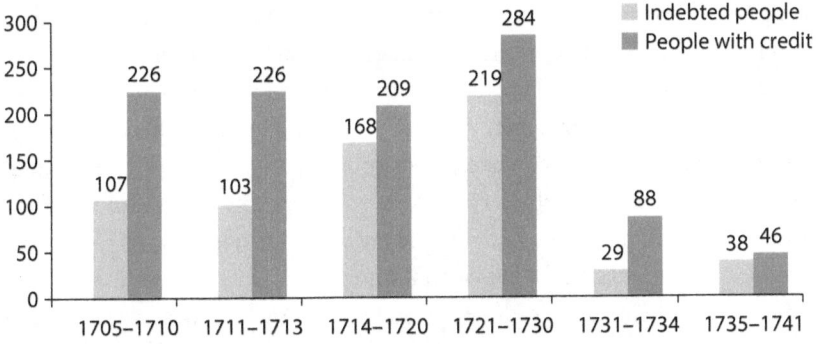

FIGURE 12. Graph of indebted deserters versus those with company credit.

way out of this quandary was desertion. Though indebtedness was a strong impulse for desertion, indebted workers were still a minority of the recorded number of deserters (see figure 12). In fact, the company owed even more than 50 Dutch guilders to quite a few deserters. What then spurred the workers who were not in any financial bondage with the company to escape? The answer must be sought in the unique employment opportunities that Bengal presented to European workers, indebted or otherwise.

DESERTION AND INTERCOMPANY RIVALRY

In the early eighteenth century, intercompany rivalry in Bengal reached new heights when the French East India Company and the Ostend Company established their own trading posts alongside those of the VOC and EIC. Intercompany rivalry extended to recruitment of European sailors and soldiers. Stiff competition drove up wages and European sailors and soldiers used the strategy of desertion to frustrate any efforts on the part of either the VOC or the EIC to stabilize the labor market or to bring down wages. The EIC quickly fathomed the severity of intercompany rivalry caused by the turmoil of desertion. The company tried to circumvent the problem by relying on desertion as a positive means for recruiting European sailors and especially soldiers from their rivals.

Since the seventeenth century, losing men to the EIC had been a constant source of concern for the VOC. In 1675, the VOC complained that men steadily deserted to the English side. In the midst of the Anglo-Mughal war of 1686–89, the two warring parties chose the VOC council at Chinsurah as mediator. Though ostensibly a neutral party, the VOC nevertheless had to combat the predicament of unbridled desertion and forced impressments of European sailors and soldiers. For runaways, wartime meant lucrative wages from the EIC. For example, the EIC offered Dutch sailmaker Marten Martenzoon a wage of 20 rupees, or 18 guilders, diet money of 5 rupees and also a young boy as his helper. He was expected to make a couple of sails for a confiscated Mughal vessel. The EIC presented similar enticements to a Dutch gunner, Abrahamzoon. When such allurements did not do their work the EIC resorted to the forcible press. We know of Martenzoon and Abrahamzoon's accounts because they were the rare workers who had turned down the EIC's offers; there were many more who did not.[89] The VOC had declared all runaway sailors and soldiers to the EIC as "enemies" and threatened them with the death sentence.[90] English ship captains took an active role in recruiting on VOC grounds. In 1676, when the VOC director pleaded with Walter Clavel. the chief of the English factory at Hugli, to return a few VOC deserters, Clavel replied that the company "ha[d] no command over" English captains directly recruiting men from among VOC sailors.[91] Faced with such aggressive and intrusive recruitment strategies by the English, the VOC directors passed a law to garner deserters from the English side, "a permission granted to the detriment and weakening of the competitors," especially the EIC in Bengal.[92] Nonetheless, the VOC seems to have sustained more damage. In 1706, a group of thirteen sailors ran away to the English.[93] In 1711, to the utter perplexity of the VOC, fifty-three sailors "to whom the company owes a good deal of money" ran away to the EIC.[94] Between 1706 and 1713, while the VOC experienced massive desertion of men to different indigenous armies, the EIC also actively recruited men from VOC grounds.

Apart from the steady loss of men from the VOC to the EIC, there were also instances when the VOC or the EIC complained about the French East India Company aggressively recruiting deserters. In February 1726, the VOC director wrote to French headquarters in Chandernagore informing them of the recent arrests of two French soldiers, sent from Chandernagore to clandestinely recruit men from the Dutch village. A few days before the incident, a VOC drummer had deserted to the French. The VOC used the captive soldiers to try to get back the deserter, but to no avail.[95] In 1743, a soldier from the EIC deserted to the French, where he was assigned the post of pilot.[96] However, the French company later returned the man.

Despite the few incidents of poaching European manpower from rival companies, the French were particularly cooperative in extraditing deserters who had taken shelter on their grounds. On two different occasions, the French helped the VOC in hunting down armed fugitives and convicts from within the precincts of Chandernagore. The French offered no living space to the runaways, and they even set up commando units to hunt down deserters from other companies hiding in or around the French factory. One French corporal of such unit was severely injured during an operation against six deserting VOC sailors.[97] Despite the cooperation of the French in returning deserters, fear of desertion to the French side always lurked in the minds of officers of the English company. In 1744, when soldiers and sailors posted at Kassimbazar expressed their discontent over wages, the EIC decided to increase their diet money and advance them half a month's wages rather than risk losing them to the French.[98]

During their short stint in Bengal (1722–45), the Ostend Company, often considered by both the EIC and VOC as "interlopers," recruited deserters from both the longer-established companies. Desertion to the Ostend Company remained a constant concern for the VOC and EIC between 1722 and 1727. By 1730, the Ostend Company had been formally abolished, but lived on as a motley group of renegade merchants under the commandership of Francois Schonamille. Desertion shot up in 1744, with the attack by Alivardi Khan, which eventually drove out the Ostend Company in 1745. Following an armed conflict regarding payment of customs during the Maratha attacks, Alivardi Khan routed the Bankibazar settlement in 1745.[99] During this time, despite the EIC's strict prohibitions on any "intercourse with the Ostenders or to furnish them with powder or any sort of ammunition," around three hundred sailors of the EIC deserted to Bankibazar.[100] The EIC council posted military guards at Perrins Garden in Calcutta and along the banks of the river in several boats, and notices in several languages prohibiting desertion were "affixed at the factory gates and other publick places about town."[101] But none of the measures could stanch the flow of deserters. Both the EIC and VOC directly appealed to the governor of the Ostend Company to return their deserters, but to no avail. The EIC even tried to personally plead with seamen to not run away to the Ostend grounds.[102] It was only when Schonamille escaped to Pegu in 1745 that desertion of EIC workers in epidemic proportions stalled. Schonamille left Bengal with a hundred European sailors and soldiers; even in his final flight from Pegu, he was accompanied by three French deserters and eight EIC runaways.[103]

Desertion in this period took European sailors and soldiers in all directions. Though the Ostend Company absorbed the bulk of deserters from the already-established East India companies, it also experienced desertion from among its own workforce. In 1726 three runaways from the Ostend grounds were employed as sailors on the VOC ship *Strikebolle* for 9 guldens and sent off to Batavia. The VOC made the decision to shelter such deserters at a "conference held with the English," where both parties came to the agreement to try their level best to "weaken the manpower of the Ostenders."[104] Fort William also sheltered runaway sailors from the Ostend Company. Like the EIC and the VOC, the Ostend Company sent senior officials to demand the return of their deserting men. When these demands failed, the Ostend Company warned that such actions would have "pernicious consequences" and that it would "give encouragement to sailors or soldiers belonging to the English to commit the same notorious offence."[105]

Large-scale desertion was sustained by competitive wages. In 1726, the Ostend Company offered common sailors and soldiers a wage of 14 guldens.[106] Compared to the 9 guldens for VOC service, this was definitely a much better deal. The EIC too had to admit that "extraordinary pay" led to desertion.[107] Wages in the eighteenth century also meant much more than money alone. The worker, who was not yet weaned from the patronage system of the precapitalist period, saw in wages an assurance of keeping his body and mind together.[108] Thus, a bottle of arak and extra food were very real earnings. When an agent of the Ostend Company informed sick sailors on a boat that he would "look after the costs and sleeping place" for them, it was a major incentive to defect, because during times of sickness, common soldiers and sailors of the EIC and VOC did not receive pay.[109]

The EIC offered the largesse of "ready money" to deserters, a much desired perk among common sailors and soldiers in the Age of the Sail.[110] The standard VOC wage for a common soldier was 9 florins. The EIC offered a similar amount. However, unlike the VOC, which only paid the wages of the sailors and soldiers partially during service and the rest at the end of their contracts of three to five years, the EIC paid the wages of their soldiers at the end of each month. The EIC thus depended on casual labor—often deserters from rival companies—for their army, turning Bengal into their recruitment grounds for soldiers. In certain years, there were several added incentives. In 1711, for example, the EIC induced large-scale desertion by paying 10 rupees cash to each deserter as a reward for deserting to Fort William.[111]

Besides, for many European workers desertion was the only means of retaining control over their time and wages. Among sailors and soldiers of the VOC it was long established practice to mortgage up to half of their wages via certificates of salary consignment (*transport brieven*) to multiple creditors in the Dutch Republic. Similar arrangement also existed in Asia, which the VOC sometimes permitted but outlawed at other times. The VOC issued these consignment certificates and paid the creditors of their sailors and soldiers directly. The reasons for such mortgages were many. ranging from cash flow for the splurges on alcohol at the waterfront to pressing needs of the family. The sailor would not get any salary in hand until such creditors were paid off.[112] Such practices explain further why sailors to whom the VOC owed large sums of their wages would flee to other companies. While the sailors had to surrender large chunks of their pay to the creditors in the Dutch Republic or in Asia, their earning from rival companies remained secure from such predatory practices. By running away sailors could reclaim time for earning their own income freed from the clutches of their creditors, if only temporarily, and the VOC. Moreover, given that the VOC from time to time pardoned their returning deserters, these runaways found avenues for reinstating their positions within the VOC and thus not completely ghosting their creditors. Especially for workers with familial ties back home the ability to return to VOC service was precious; for foreign recruits from Europe or uprooted single men such ties were thin.

Desertion thus turned Bengal into a second recruitment ground for European soldiers for all the competing East India companies. What were its mechanisms? The structure and institutions of the maritime and military labor markets in Europe have been studied in considerable detail. Thus, the figure of a "crimp" or "spirit" in the case of the English and "soul salesman" (*zielverkoper*) in the case of the Dutch are very well known. Embodying an extremely exploitative institution of recruitment, the crimp. the spirit, or the soul salesman all often resorted to extreme violence to recruit sailors.[113] The companies never shied away from using force in Bengal. In 1675, for example, an English sailor in VOC service was kidnapped and held hostage by an Englishman in EIC service on the grounds that being English, the sailor should serve the EIC.[114]

Though such coercive methods were in vogue, more benign methods of recruitment were more common in Bengal. The figure of a "debaucher" (*débouchant*) was key in alluring or seducing European subalterns to rival company grounds. As Marcus Rediker observes, less formal and exploitative ways of recruitment were favored in the New World, where labor was scarce and wages higher.[115] Debauching sailors and soldiers with money or most often with alcohol became a well-established practice in each and every East India company ground. The EIC took the most proactive role in this regard. As early as 1675, the VOC needed to recruit eight Black sailors for the *Schelvisch*, as quite a few of the European crew of the ship had gone "missing." They were "debauched by the English and taken into their service," a report by the VOC officials to Batavia noted.[116] The next year too, the VOC remarked that "yearly our sailors are debauched" to "strengthen" the manpower of EIC ships weakened by illness and death. In 1711, when the VOC lost one-third of their European workforce to desertion, they lamented that it was "an almost impossible task" to stop the "debauching of our men by the English and other nations." As a solution, they planned to adopt their adversaries' strategies to "dispose their men to desertion" to the VOC grounds "in a similar way."[117] Other companies too actively "debauched" new recruits. In 1726, when a few Ostend sailors came merrily drinking to the shores of Falta, they inevitably made the guards suspicious. When the sailors offered the guards half a rupee as a bribe to allow them to sit there, the guards took them for "recruiters from their (Ostend) community" and were thus ready to avert such "seducers."[118] Indeed, two years earlier, in 1724, the director and his council alleged that six VOC sailors had been taken away to the Ostend factory grounds "by way of debauching."[119] In the same year, two French soldiers, Thomas Chaelium and Philip Dubois, "debauched" a VOC soldier Louis Le Claire, but while escaping the Dutch village, all three were caught red-handed.[120] In 1727, the VOC decided to imprison "all foreign debauchers of our soldiers."[121]

Losing workers to any other state was a violation of sovereignty, which explains why desertion was considered treason. Asserting sovereignty to formulate laws and dispense justice in Asian lands was an important component of the statehood of the East India companies.[122] Control over deserters, like the war against interlopers, denoted an articulation of such state power.[123] Letter wars centering on retrieving and retaining deserters thus were an important element of intercompany diplomatic relations in Bengal. "Colours" and "flags" and the violation thereof marked the language of these letters. In 1724, for example, when the EIC impressed a few sailors and soldiers from VOC boats on the river near Calcutta, the VOC complained of "public violence done to our colours." They further warned the EIC that such violence "would certainly open the door to a great many larger misdemeanors, which may be a ground of misunderstanding between the two Nations."[124] In a letter to the EIC in May 1706 asking for the return of deserters in Calcutta, the VOC reminded the former of the "good harmony and concord" that existed between the Dutch Republic and the English crown.[125] The Ostend

Company would not return deserters to the Dutch, claiming that every single worker in the Ostend factory is "bound with oath in the service of the Kaiser."[126] VOC deserters had become new subjects of the Austrian crown.

The companies were not just mere extensions of the nation-states in Europe; they asserted their corporate statehood by an autonomous set of rules for their worker-subjects. While demanding the return of deserting second-mate Lubbert Lubbertzoon, in August 1724, the VOC reminded the EIC of "the articles of union peace and allies between the crown of England and the Republiek" reiterated in the years 1654, 1667, 1674, 1685, 1689, and 1699, which stated that deserters should be delivered whenever the notice of desertion was given by the aggrieved party. The EIC replied to this language of state and diplomacy with a legal scrutiny of the term "deserter." According to the EIC, "deserter" was a "military term" that applied to "the officers and soldiers of each nation deserting their colours and not to the indifferent subjects who are refugees of either nation or the servants of either of the East India companies."[127] Indeed, one company's "deserter" was another's "refugee." But what stands out is the assertion that the treaties sealed by warring nations in Europe need not be binding on company affairs in Asia; company servants were governed by a different set of rules abroad. The plethora of statutes regarding desertion, that Batavia issued—and sometimes Bengal, in contradistinction to Batavia—bear testimony to this assertion. Regulation of desertion and recruitment of workers—a problem specific to Asian waters—thus became a central medium for assertion of statehood by the corporate entities.

Treaties among competing companies for extraditing deserters were grounded in similar notions of sovereignty. The French East India Company was the most willing to try to resolve the desertion "problem" through diplomacy. In 1732, the VOC sealed a contract with the French for returning sailors, soldiers, sergeants, corporals, quartermasters, and young apprentices. According to the deal, the French could keep the deserter only if the nationality of the deserter was French, and the same applied for the Dutch. Furthermore, neither side could condemn the returnees to capital punishment. This contract was made effective in Chandernagore, Chinsurah, and Kassimbazar. In 1734, the same contract was extended to Patna.[128] The EIC had already entered into a similar contract with the French in 1728. In 1733, under the new director of the French East India Company, Joseph Francois Dupleix, the contract was extended to Kassimbazar.[129] The French wanted the bipartite treaty of 1732 with the VOC regarding return of deserters to be a tripartite one by pulling in the EIC. However, the VOC scoffed at the idea, as they knew that the EIC, who were "getting no or very few soldiers from Europe or Madras," had to build their military with the runaways from the VOC. Thus, they "[would] not be disposed to such conditions."[130] The VOC's doubts were not unfounded, and the ultimate failure of the French East India Company to bring together the VOC and the EIC was as much a diplomatic failure as an economic one.

The mobility of seamen and soldiers turned intercompany rivalry and the sovereignty of the "colours" on their head. These workers constantly trespassed the boundaries created by and for the corporate interest of the companies, sometimes with tragic consequences, as in the case of Jan Striker, a VOC soldier who had escaped to the EIC army stationed at the Kassimbazar factory in 1734. On hearing that his old friend Harmanus van Tomputten had come to Bengal as a soldier of the VOC, Striker visited him in the Dutch village in Chinsurah. Another soldier, Hendrik Tuske, joined them with alcohol. Soon Striker and Tomputten got drunk, "lost their senses," and "got into a fight with the natives." In a bid to save himself from the brawl, Striker started running, too drunk to realize that he was running onto VOC grounds. Striker was arrested and given the death penalty. On May 6, 1734, he was hanged to death on a sail ship anchored close to the VOC headquarters at Chinsurah, after which his corpse was "cut into pieces and fed to the fish." Meanwhile, his friend Tomputten had to walk the gauntlet.[131] Simple comradely conviviality had led Striker and Tomputten to fatally trespass the very complex sovereign borders of the East India companies in Bengal.

WORKING FOR INDIGENOUS ARMIES

The former governor of the EIC, Sir Josiah Child, a political theorist of mercantilism and the foremost champion of the EIC's monopoly rights, wrote a pamphlet in 1689, in which he prematurely and disingenuously declared the EIC's victory against the Mughals, with whom they were at war until 1691. Child claimed victory, citing a treaty secured by the EIC, wherein "an honourable article" stated, "No Englishman shall serve in the *Mogul*'s Dominions, and if any runs away from Ships or Factories, to be seized and delivered up to us." This "honourable article" along with the entire treaty were figments of Child's imagination. It is remarkable, nonetheless, that Child imagined such a clause on desertion in his fictitious treaty in order to valorize "the Eternal Honour of the *English* Nation, in those parts of the

World."[132] Indeed. losing men to native states was a major blow to the sovereignty of the EIC in foreign lands. Yet, such desertions were all too frequent as indigenous armies also competed to entice and hire European men.[133] In short, European soldiers were in high demand, not only among the European companies but throughout the entire military labor market in Bengal.

The VOC in Bengal suffered the highest number of desertions between 1711 and 1713 (see figure 13).[134] The reasons for the spike in desertion lay in the political turmoil that engulfed the entire subcontinent of India, including the province of Bengal, after the death of Aurangzeb in 1707. The emperor's son, Bahādur Shāh, ascended to power. The governor of Bengal—the grandson of Aurangzeb and the son of Bahādur Shāh, Prince 'Azīm (also called 'Azīm-ush-Shān)—began to quarrel with the Dīwān (provincial head of revenue collection) of Bengal, Murshid Quli Khan, who had long been a trusted imperial officer. In 1708, 'Azim successfully persuaded his father to transfer Murshid Quli from Bengal to Deccan. But the emperor Bahādur Shāh soon changed his mind and reappointed Murshid Quli as Dīwān of Bengal in 1710. In 1711, the emperor granted him the collectorship of customs at Hugli port and made him the *faujdār* of Midnapur district, a position occupied by Ẓiā-ud-dīn Khān, a trusted subordinate of 'Azīm. Ẓiā-ud-dīn refused to relinquish his post, which caused great strife between Ẓiā-ud-dīn on one hand and Murshid Quli Khan and his agent, Walī Beg, on the other, lasting for two years. In the meantime, Bahādur Shāh died and the Mughal throne passed to a different son of his, Jahāndār Shāh, in 1712. The same year, Farrukh Siyar ('Azīm's son and Jahāndār's nephew) launched another round of war for succession. When he sought support for a campaign in Delhi against Jahāndār from Murshid Quli, he was refused. Farrukh Siyar then sent troops against Murshid Quli. This strife finally ended when Farrukh Siyar became emperor in 1713. This dynastic and bureaucratic warfare provided extraordinary opportunities to European soldiers and sailors.[135]

In the thick of these political upheavals, the common seamen of the VOC, with "desertion in their head," began jumping overboard, sailing to shore in small boats in the dead of night, and joining the armies of the "Moors."[136] The political climate had "brought them [the deserters] the audacity" to attack the company village and also the factory in groups of ten or twelve or more armed people "to commit various insolences."[137] During this turmoil, the Dutch authorities were at their wit's end trying to halt the exodus of sailors and soldiers to the armies of Ẓiā-ud-dīn Khān, Walī Beg, and Farrukh

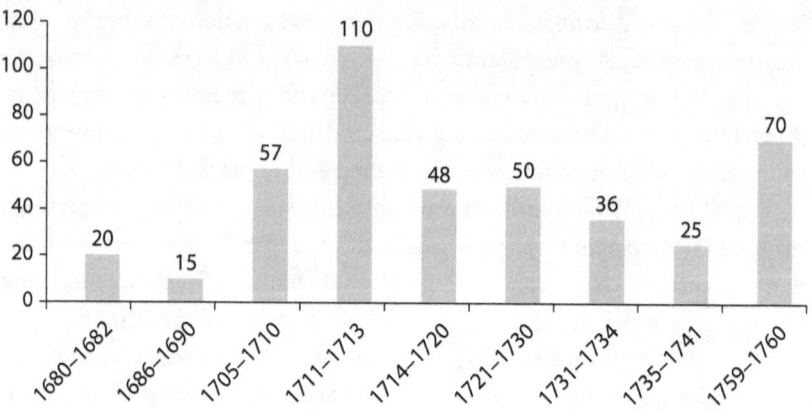

FIGURE 13. Graph of average number of deserters from 1680 to 1760.

Siyar. The VOC took extra care to ensure that ship captains supervised the reading out on the decks of incoming ships the statutes against desertion. They also made public readings of the statutes in the whole of Chinsurah, accompanied by drum roll. The situation was similar for other companies, including the EIC. Though "loitering" of common seamen was severely checked, no amount of extra military patrol succeeded in stanching the leakage. In fact, within less than a year, the VOC dismissed the twelve extra indigenous soldiers they had hired in July 1711 to guard the boundaries of the Dutch settlement, as "in Bengal they can always get away," despite "all serious means."[138]

Lucrative wages attracted European rank-and-file to indigenous armies. The European sailors and soldiers were prized as superior handlers of firearms. Thus, during military engagements, all sides aggressively recruited from among the soldiers and sailors in the East India company settlements. As incentive they offered the deserters an extremely lucrative wage of 40 rupees, or 36 guilders, per month.[139] This was an astronomical sum for even the most experienced common seaman or soldier.

Even though better pay was probably the most important factor inducing desertion, the VOC blamed the morally reprehensible nature of their lower orders for such desertions. They believed that "a short pleasurable life amongst the Moors" had great appeal for the plebeian members of the company.[140] This racialized rhetoric also masked the mercantilist disdain for the lack of discipline among the European rank and file. Reckless living with no concern for the future appeared to be the sailors' motto, as the accounts of the sinking of *Ter Schelling* demonstrate. Faced with a severe storm on the sand banks of the Bengal delta, the steersmen of the sinking ship "knew no calm" and with glasses of arak in their hands, they made sure that the rising waters could not touch their buoyant spirits. Confronting death, "their last escape being their drink," these sailors seemingly could not care less for their lives.[141] In a similar vein the VOC resented promise of the "lazy and unconstrained life," in the indigenous armies notwithstanding the very dangerous nature of the work. Though quite a few of the deserting soldiers and sailors did succumb to war or disease, there were many more, VOC officials believed, who died of their "drunkenness and foolhardiness," as their excesses "knew no measure."[142] The VOC's official resentment was very similar to the moral outrage among the mercantile elite in eighteenth-century Britain against the custom of "Saint Monday," which they alleged not only encouraged alcoholism among working people, but also militated against the ethic of a regular work week. Even though the VOC had little knowledge of discipline in indigenous armies, the VOC was convinced that its sailors and soldiers were always seeking out a life without discipline in those armies.[143]

Europeans running away to local courts in large numbers was a phenomenon the Portuguese Empire had already witnessed in the sixteenth century. In fact, such desertions gave rise to various Indo-Portuguese communities throughout South Asia.[144] G.V. Scammell shows that employment with the local rulers was also alluring for the "renegades."[145] As early as 1506, Ludovico di Varthema observed that Portuguese deserters at Calicut were manufacturing canons for the king.[146] In Bengal, between 1608 and 1624, Mirza Nathan, a participant in the Mughal imperial campaigns to subjugate rebel *zamīndārs* in Eastern Bengal, observed *firingī* (European) troops, most probably Portuguese, as part and parcel of all *faujdār* and imperial armies.[147] The Jesuit priest Padre Godinho, while traveling in the Mughal Empire in 1663, observed that most of the gunners in the Mughal army were Portuguese and Dutch. In Bengal, during Nawab Mir Jumla's Assam expedition in 1662–63, not only Dutch and English sailors and soldiers but also a VOC surgeon and VOC carpenters were part of the army. Among the recruits were fifteen survivors of the *Ter Schelling* wreckage. They observed that ships laden with canons moving against the current on the Ganga were singularly operated by English, Dutch, and Portuguese (both Black and white) sailors and soldiers. The VOC carpenters were "acknowledged as bosses" of an army of artisans engaged in making a ship "that corresponded with the Nawab's wishes and design." The wages, though varying widely, were far better than what the European sailors and soldiers could have earned in the service of the VOC or EIC: at the end of twenty-eight days, each member of the *Ter Schelling* got a wage of 20 rupees, or 18 guilders. The *Ter Schelling* sailors observed that Portuguese and English "volunteers" got even better wages.[148] "Volunteering" fetched the English 50 rupees, or 45 guilders per month, while the white Portuguese earned around 40 or 50 guilders. There were also other ways for European sailors and soldiers to make money. Two Dutch deserters along with three English deserters in the same expedition managed to pick up 575 rupees—a handsome fortune they stumbled upon among the belongings of an English captain who had died in the Nawab's service.[149]

As *zamīndārs* the companies were obliged to steadily supply the imperial government with sailors and gunners. In times of crisis, the East India companies like other *zamīndārs* in the region were regularly solicited for manpower. As early as May 5, 1633, long before the EIC received its *zamīndāri*, Aga Muhammad Zamān, the Mughal governor of Orissa, rewarded the English a permit to carry out custom-free trade in the region, on condition that they "help, aid and assist the vessels of the Nawab, or any of his subject, in distress, either by foul weather or in danger of enemies to the best of their capacity."[150] Such requests continued. Again in 1677, the VOC had to send a boat and a sloop with twenty sailors to assist *faujdār* Malik Qasim's campaign against a rebellious chief in Orissa.[151] In 1711, Farrukh Siyar constantly pressed the VOC for manpower until they gave in and lent out a hundred sailors.[152] During the second Maratha attack, in 1743, the Nawab Ali Vardi Khan called in the company *wakīls*, or mediators, of the Dutch, English, and French companies and requested that each lend out two hundred men who would be put on the payroll of the Nawab's army.[153]

When recruitment failed to take the usual course of mutual agreement among the Mughal officials and the companies, Mughal armies depended on desertion. Other indigenous armies almost solely relied on desertion. Scottish ship captain Alexander Hamilton met two such Dutch deserters whom he called "renagadoes" while he was near Bengal in Cuttack, the capital city of Orissa. Although Hamilton stated very clearly that the place "is not frequented by Europeans," these two deserters had made their way into the army of the Nawab of Orissa as gunners.[154] Thus, the EIC at Kassimbazar, "cautious to prevent desertion," sent to Calcutta all extra European sailors and soldiers when, during the first Maratha invasion in 1740, the Nawab had asked for a hundred men.[155] Apart from aiding the imperial government, the companies as *zamīndārs* were not obligated to lend military support to any other political entities in the region. Nonetheless, European soldiers found their way into the Maratha army.[156] Both the VOC and EIC denied any knowledge of or responsibility for the seventeen European prisoners of war that the Nawab Alivardi Khan had captured from the retreating Maratha army in 1743. These were most likely sailors who aided Habibullah Khan, the military general for Alivardi Khan who had defected to the Maratha side.[157] In the 1757 battle of Plassey, as many as fifty-six Dutch soldiers defected to Siraj ud-Daulah's army.[158] Even in 1766, two soldiers of the EIC were lured by a "black man in the bazaar, who offered him fifty rupees a month for his service."[159] One might measure how entrenched European soldiers were in indigenous armies from one of the finest *maṅgalkābyas* of the eighteenth century, *Annadāmaṅgal*, composed under the patronage of Rājā Kṛṣṇachandra Rāẏ, the *faujdār* of Nadia. In the section on Bidya and Sundar's romance, the poet Bharatchandra Rāẏ describes a fort—Princess Bidya's residence—in which English, Dutch, Portuguese, French, Danish, and Germans filled the ranks of gunners.[160]

At Dhaka, when the shipwrecked sailors of the *Ter Schelling* met a Dutch man "from head to foot clad in Moorish (clothes)," they "thought inevitably that he was circumcised."[161] In fact, conversion to Islam was not unknown. It was quite common among the English.[162] In certain cases, conversion was used as a strategy by the deserters to garner protection from indigenous authorities against the companies. For example, the *faujdār* of Hugli, Malik Barkhordar, shielded a deserting VOC sailor who had converted to Islam in 1685. The company insisted that the *faujdār* issue a *parwānā* in order to hand over the deserter; Malik Barkhordar insisted that handing over a Muslim "[would] cost his head" if the Mughal emperor came to know about it, "or at least his service and well being."[163] The company then appealed to Nawab Shaista Khan for his intervention but to no avail. The next year VOC officials captured the same deserter in Balasore and hauled him back, only to lose him again, this time to the forces of Malik Barkhordar, who raided Chinsurah specifically to apprehend the converted deserter. A French soldier in the service of the EIC at Patna deserted to the imperial government and took a similar recourse, complaining that despite "being a Musselman, they [EIC] had obliged him to eat their victuals."[164] When Tambi van Makassar, a *mardijker* (freed slave-soldier), was caught trying to desert with two other slaves the trio faced severe whipping, branding, and twenty years of hard labor in chains. When Tambi managed to escape a second time, all efforts to convince the "villains of the Moorish government" to hand over the deserter proved fruitless as he had "taken the avowal of Mahomeddan faith."[165] Though there were instances when the local rulers did hand over deserters to the companies, it was rare and achieved only after paying a handsome bribe.[166]

The importance of Europeans in indigenous armies led to various settlements of Europeans in local Bengal communities outside the bounds of the East India company settlements. Europeans were known throughout the entire Mughal world as *firingī*. This term, which initially was used for the Portuguese and Portuguese-speaking elements in the Mughal Empire in the sixteenth century, was extended to all Europeans or European descendants residing in the realm. As Aniruddha Ray shows, the development of *zamīndārīs* in eastern deltaic lands involved the use of European military labor as well as Christian missionary activities.[167] Augustinian and Jesuit churches cemented together the communities of the rowdy groups of *firingī* who were mercenaries in the armies of various *zamīndārs*. Such settlements became part of the social geography of seventeenth- and eighteenth-century Bengal. In the seventeenth-century poet Rupram Chakraborty's *Dharmamaṅgal*, a *firingīpārā* (*firingī* colony) is mentioned alongside various place names and settlements during Ranjhābati's journey from the city of Mainā to Champa, the abode of Dharma.[168] The seventeenth-century poet Dbija Ramdev's *Abhayāmaṅgal* explicitly refers to these settlements as colonies of gunners. In the section on Kālketu's imaginary settlement, Gujarāt, he mentions that "*firingī* made their palaces, and their friends are all gunners."[169] It is quite likely that deserters flocked to these gunner colonies.

Even if they had not settled in these colonies, European deserters certainly joined the inner circle of indigenous armies and courts as *firingī*. Those deserters who were of European descent had a wide variety of origins, including indigenous roots. But as Sanjay Subrahmanyam argues, *firingis* were never fully accepted as natives, nor as fully Europeans either.[170] Indeed, gunner colonies of *firingī* in Eastern Bengal also had non-European runaways, such as Portuguese-speaking Africans. Thus, runaway European sailors and soldiers were absorbed into indigenous society within these heterogenous groups of *firingī*. The unique social space that Europeans occupied in Mughal Bengal enabled them to make an easier transition from being "European" workers to workers in Bengal, somewhat suspending their status as Europeans without completely "turning native." In Bengali vernacular imagination, European mercenaries as part of elite indigenous life survived well into the twenty-first century. Such consciousness is evident in the iconography of Jagadhātrī, one of the presiding deities of the Daws, a wealthy mercantile family in Calcutta. Conceived in the late nineteenth century, the idol of Jagadhātrī includes two armed European sentries flanking the goddess. As a semi-public annual event, the Jagadhātrī pujas of the Amritalal Daw family continue to this day, marking the social influence of a new elite born of a colonial economy in the culture of twenty-first century Kolkata. The Jagadhātrī idol along with its European sentries, poised in the middle of a *thakurdālān* (rectangular courtyard), built in the neoclassical style typical of wealthy merchant residences of nineteenth- and early twentieth-century Calcutta, collapses an early modern, precolonial experience into a colonial milieu.[171] The European sentries evoke the idiosyncratic splendor of the indigenous elite of a bygone colonial era within the public life of modern-day Kolkata (see figures 14 and 15).

The common seamen and soldiers of the East India companies were not alien to the socioeconomic hinterland of Bengal; it did not take long for newcomers to find their niche within indigenous society, an act of relocation that was always prejudicial to the interests of the companies. Not only were the interests of the indigenous state and those of the companies diametrically opposed to each other, their appreciation of the wage work of European sailors and soldiers was completely different as well. The indigenous armies as employers did not adhere to the European schema of waged work under the rule of capital, where burgeoning profits coincided with a sharp decline in workers' wages.[172] The social degradation that the rank and file of the Dutch and English armies experienced in Europe could be reversed in the indigenous armies. "Who merely carries a Christian name is here acknowledged as a full-fledged soldier," the sailors of the *Ter Schelling* observed. In certain places, as in the *zamīndāri* of Bhulua, they were "honored as lords and counts."[173] Set adrift because of enclosures of land, wars, and religious strife in Europe, sailors and soldiers were part of a large pool of mobile casual workers. This trend intensified in the second half of the seventeenth century in Europe.[174] As much-coveted gunners and cannoneers in the Mughal or other local armies, the displaced European proletariat in Eastern lands experienced an inversion of their social position—in fact, a "re-skilling" of their work.

FIGURE 14. Jagadhātrī idol at the Amritalal Daw estate. Photo by the author.

FIGURE 15. Close-up of one of the European sentries flanking the Jagadhātrī idol.

STRAGGLING IN BENGAL

Hardships at work or familiarity with Bengal did not necessarily lead European sailors to desert to inland indigenous armies. At nine in the evening of November 23, 1733 a police official of the VOC reported to the Hugli council's representative at Falta about a full-fledged strike at the waterfront. A "strong murmur" had spread among the sailors of all VOC ships harbored at Falta that they would not lift anchors because they had not received "according to old customs, baxies [*bakśiś*] for refreshments." In addition to rallying around their demands for customary pay or *bakśiś*, the striking sailors demanded payment of monthly wages even to those who were in debt to the company. These dual demands "interested the entire marine power" of the VOC stationed at Falta, rendering any violent measures against the aggrieved "inadvisable." The sheer number of the strikers also made it impossible to find replacements. Within three days the Hugli council gave in and resolved the grievances through sizeable payments. This incident of a unified strike action demonstrates moments when "customs" surpassed the conventions of indigeneity and becomes comprehensible to non-indigenous workers.[175]

Both European and indigenous sailors demanded *bakśiś*. The crews of two ships, *Slot Aldegonde* and *Pallas*, mounted the strike. Both ships had arrived in Bengal in early 1733 with a full European crew, but due to ravages from death and desertion, the VOC refitted both the ships with new crews of European and indigenous Bengali recruits. By November 1733, when the *Slot Aldegonde* was getting ready to embark on a journey to Punnekayal on the Pearl Fishery coast and the *Pallas* to Batavia, crews on both ships were two-thirds European, including fresh European recruits from among sailors residing on land, and one-third Bengali sailors. In Asia, sailors newly contracted and put into service from another ship or from land, whether they were Bengali or European, all expected at the beginning of their journey to receive payment of food money. VOC officials swapped the routinely used term for such payment, "kostgeld," for *bakśiś*. In Bengal *bakśiś* signaled an equivalence between the customary expectation for food money by sundry workers including Bengali seamen (and even boatmen) and that of European seamen who counted on food money as being a part of their pay. Moreover, demands for *bakśiś* as the basis of strike action allowed space for other demands which most likely concerned European sailors. While both European sailors and Bengali sailors expected their wages to be paid monthly, it was the European sailors who might not receive any wages in Asia because of long-standing debt to their many creditors. European workers thus considered *bakśiś* as a bridge, connecting notions of "customs" bred in different but intersecting contexts. Thus their demand for *bakśiś* became a platform to leverage their other, more specific demands.[176]

Bengal also offered respite from work. In and around Calcutta sailors engaged in the time-honored habit of straggling, thus reclaiming their "own" time away from work. Straggling represented how workers and their employers, especially the European companies, experienced time differently. While the companies perceived time as a measurement of how they used the labor of their workers, the sailors and soldiers always experienced time as an alternation between work tasks and "free" time. When Captain James Montgomery desperately searched for men for a voyage to Malabar, he urged the Calcutta council to recruit from among the "great many straggling seamen both of Dutch and English which belongs to no shipping lye sculking in the back parts of the town."[177] As an unused pool of labor, these stragglers were a nuisance for the VOC as well as the EIC. In June 1699, following the shipwreck of the EIC ship *Gracedieus*, Captain James Murvell dismissed all of his men. The EIC in turn offered to pay them 3 rupees per month unless they were recruited by another ship in order "to prevent their starving and any other inconveniences that may happen with their wandering idly about." However, when these men were offered employment by Captain Strutton, they refused to work unless they were given two months' wages, which was not the custom. The company then shipped them "two or three at a time" to Balasore and put them on a ship stationed there; apparently, there was no better way of dealing with such men who were "idleing about ready to starve and [would] not of their own accord accept of service." [178] These seamen, unlike the EIC officials, did not perceive time as money, and hence they preferred their penniless condition to laboring for a wage on disagreeable terms.

Some of these stragglers completely rejected the world of waged work. In 1677 two runaways were caught at Balasore who were seriously ill, and the surgeon doubted "they could outlive their treatment." One of them was Jacob Hendrikzoon from Harlinge, who had run away from service in the company four years prior with ten other mates from the sloop *De Roos*. They first arrived at Queda, where they converted to Islam. After avoiding service at sea for so long, to his misfortune, Hendrikzoon was hunted down in Balasore.

The other deserter, Cornelis Claeszoon, from Nieuwehoop, had escaped from the Dutch cargo ship *De Stadt Grave* in 1676 and ever since had "vagabonded."[179]

Resistance to waged work was manifest in the piratical activities carried out by fugitives. The EIC in 1715 anxiously noted that armed European bandits constantly attacked their boats passing through the forested deltaic lands off the coast of Chittagong. They were especially concerned about the luxury textile items coming out from Dhaka. The robbers, they reported, were "deserters from us because they have red coats." The EIC officials also identified some as "the Dutch soldiers discharged from our service."[180] The trajectory of the Dutch deserters thus finally took them to the limits of waged work in Bengal. Having served the EIC, they ultimately left it for high sea robbery. The spectacle of English soldiers committing piratical acts on EIC ships in red coats transgresses all conventions of waged work. Displaying the insignia of their erstwhile world of work, these soldiers defiantly mocked their service arrangements with the EIC while engaged in the act of stealing their former employer's property.

Authorities of every kind, including indigenous rulers, resented these masterless men. The companies often feared that the European renegades would harm the company vis-à-vis the local authorities, as the EIC feared that if the renegades "should plunder any boats belonging to the Mogull subjects," the Nawab's people will "take all opportunity of doing us ill offices." And in fact, such robberies were common. In January 1724, complaints of such activities in Chittagong prompted the EIC to send an ensign to the region. The band of robbers, comprising ten or twelve Europeans headed by two sergeants, were all deserters from company service, some of whom were hauled back by the ensign. Furthermore, the council of Chandernagore, headquarters of the French East India Company, complained about two deserters from the EIC at Patna, James Shaw and Abraham Blomer, who had been hiding in the French settlement, "from thence having got together twenty-five Europeans in a small vessel and were gone down the river." The deserters, the French feared, would "turn pirates." The EIC thus sent an army of three sergeants, four corporals, two drummers, and thirty private soldiers under the command of two ensigns to abort this act of recalcitrance.[181] Whether the EIC succeeded is not known. However, such rebels exemplify the many dimensions of desertion. These acts were sometimes informed by the need to negotiate for a better wage while at other times they were simply a bid to reject the world of labor for good. In all cases, flight prevented an orderly labor market from emerging in Bengal.

REINING IN THE SOLDIERS

As the EIC built its political fortune in Bengal in the 1750s and 1760s, the company substantially reformed its military. Within ten years, the EIC's momentous accomplishments included not just military victory in the battlegrounds of Plassey, eventually leading to the acquisition of revenue-collecting rights in the provinces of Bengal, Bihar, and Orissa, but also eradication of their chief European contenders in the region, the French and Dutch East India companies. These military victories depended on the recruitment of Dutch and French deserters and on the imposition of extreme military discipline under Robert Clive. From the beginning of the Carnatic wars (1743–64) the EIC realized that it needed to reform its military. Military reform entailed expansion of the army and the introduction of a hierarchical structure. But it also included imposing harsher discipline on European soldiers, which the EIC achieved by bringing the army under the purview of Mutiny Act in 1753. This law stipulated summary punishments against the slightest form of absconding among the European rank and file. By uprooting its competitors, increasing the ranks of officers in the army, and introducing the Mutiny Act, the company usurped the power of European sailors and soldiers to shape the military market in Bengal through the act of desertion.

Desertion of sailors and soldiers from rival companies to the EIC marked both the Battle of Plassey (1757) and the Anglo-Dutch War, or the Battle of Bedara (1759)—notably by strengthening the company's army—but most importantly, desertion to the EIC broke the backbone of its rivals' military power. By the end of 1757, after Plassey, the overwhelming majority of the EIC's surviving soldiers were French ex-prisoners of war and Dutch deserters.[182] Desertion of VOC soldiers to the EIC reached a fever pitch during and after the Battle of Bedara. By 1760, the VOC experienced massive leakages to the EIC, rendering them incapable of retrieving any of the deserters. The Chinsurah factory was ravaged by desertion; 139 European sailors and soldiers had fled. Better wages, which the VOC, by 1760, could not pay, was the prime factor behind the mass desertion. Defeat at the hands of the EIC also led to the forcible detention of many people, which could have spiked the number of deserters. In 1753 Batavia revised its laws regarding trials of deserters. *Fiscaals* in directorates were required to issue up to four public summonses, pleading for the deserter to return. If the deserter failed to appear after the fourth summon, the *fiscaal*'s court would pronounce judgment against them. In 1760, repeated summons for deserters failed. The Chinsurah council came up with a list of the names of deserters to be summoned and nailed it on the main gate of Fort Gustavus. When they failed to recapture the deserters, the company court passed rulings against them and made their sentences public. The sentences were harsh. The Hugli council of the VOC could seize half of the forfeited salary of the absentee deserters and half their belongings if they had left anything behind.[183] But even this did not persuade the deserters who remained at large. For the remainder of their presence in Bengal, the Dutch continued to suffer desertion of European workers to the EIC in massive numbers. After 1760, the imbalance of power regarding control over deserters became conspicuous. In the treaty of December 5, 1760, formally ending the Anglo-Dutch War of 1759, the Dutch promised their "deep solemn submission" to the English. The treaty stipulated that the VOC could not maintain more than 125 European soldiers in their factories in Bengal, Patna, and Balasore. Sure of their dominance, the EIC refused to even return the VOC's prisoners of war, not to mention the deserters.[184]

For EIC soldiers, the Carnatic wars and the other wars in Bengal precipitated reforms in the military structure, composition, and discipline which had important consequences for the practice of desertion by EIC soldiers. The loss of Madras to the French in 1746 resulted in the British Army's direct involvement in regulating and disciplining the EIC's European corps. The process ultimately prompted the EIC to adopt the British Army's code of martial law by bringing its army under the purview of the first Mutiny Act (1753).[185] These disciplinary measures were expedient because the size of the army had grown considerably by the 1760s. The total number of troops rose from 9,921 in 1763 to 27,762 in 1768.[186] Although the number of Indian soldiers grew exponentially, the number of European soldiers increased too. Under Robert Clive's untiring insistence, the expanding army in Bengal was streamlined into three infantry brigades, each consisting of one European battalion and seven *sepoy* battalions. A full colonel along with a lieutenant colonel commanded each brigade, with two majors as the third and fourth in command. Each battalion had five commissioned and five noncommissioned officers at its helm. An addition of thirty commissioned and eighty noncommissioned Indian officers backed the European officers of the *sipahi* battalions. Officer ranks surged to 830. Clive believed attenuated command at the top hindered discipline of those at the bottom of the army.[187] In 1772 the number of officers in the EIC army rose to 1,550.[188] Consequently, the increased number of officers, now with judicial powers, proved detrimental to the practice of desertion. Moreover, reforms in recruitment procedure two decades later, encouraging the company to recruit directly from England, further eroded the position of Bengal as a recruitment ground for European soldiers. From 1781, the EIC would maintain a regiment of a thousand men on British soil who supervised recruitment in England for the EIC army. The goal was to partake more substantially in the military labor market of the British Army and thereby avoid those recruits who were less motivated to serve the EIC army but desperate to make a living, anywhere. It was expected that such measures would curb disloyal acts, especially desertion, among the rank and file.

By 1753, when the EIC first embraced them, the Mutiny Acts had been providing the foundation of discipline for the British army both within England and in the colonies. The first Mutiny Act was born of the English Parliament's zealous efforts to contain military infractions when a section of the army had turned its allegiance to the deposed British monarch, James II, at the critical moment of the 1689 English Revolution. The act's primary goal was to curb desertion and the tendency for mutinies within army ranks and also to create a disciplined standing army to maintain order during peacetime. These acts were passed annually for over a century and half, with a few exceptions. From 1717 the Mutiny Acts recognized the legality of the monarch's Articles of War and authorized the use of death sentence by the General Courts Martial in times of peace, particularly for desertion. These laws put enormous arbitrary power in the hands of army officers of varying ranks particularly at regimental levels, where the use of extremely harsh corporal punishment was rife. From 1712 on, these laws were gradually introduced in different British colonies.[189] Even though both Indian and European soldiers were tried under the Mutiny Act, the European soldiers bore much of the brunt of this discipline in the early years after its introduction. Even in 1768, there were disputes with the army and the court of directors whether *sipahis* should be governed by the Articles of War and subject to capital punishment.[190]

But the EIC army officers utilized the Mutiny Act against their European rank-and-file runaways to its fullest severity. Even though regular records of General Courts Martial proceedings are hard to come by, the trial records of eight privates and one sentinel from 1765 and 1766 provide a valuable window into the use of the Mutiny Acts by the EIC army to impose unprecedented levels of discipline on the physical movement of common soldiers. All of the accused soldiers in these trials were convicted of the crime of desertion, even though their period of absence from their respective company was insignificant when compared to earlier acts of desertion. The mildest sentence was one thousand lashes on the bare back and the harshest sentence was death. Even though two officers of the company to which Private Abraham Russell belonged testified to his good character and sound behavior, Russell was given a sentence of two thousand lashes on a bare back for an absence of two days. John Christopher Lebot, who strayed for the longest period, was captured within two weeks of his absence from the morning roll call of January 15, 1766. Lebot pleaded that he had no knowledge of the Mutiny Act. Yet the General Courts Martial refused to believe him as "he saw a very recent instance of its [desertion's] consequence, as he was under arms on the 27th of November last when Frederick Greagor, private in Captain Barker's company was carried out to be shot by the sentence of a General Courts Martial for some crime." Like Frederick Greagor, John Christopher Lebot was shot to death in front of the regiment.[191]

These cases of desertion were not well-planned acts. Almost all these soldiers wandered off under the influence of alcohol. Sentinel Robert Wakefield, under alcoholic stupor, was unable to speak when he was found a few miles away from Allahabad where his company was stationed. John Akins "had no clothes on" when a *naik* and two *harcarrahs* captured him a few miles away from his regiment. None of these soldiers resisted arrest. In fact, one declared that he was very happy to see the *sipahis* as he could not find his way back to the regiment in his drunken haze. The company utilized native soldiers of various ranks to hunt down the missing European soldiers. Their familiarity with the region made the arrests swifter. None of these soldiers had been seeking alternative employment. Only John Riley, private in Captain Ahmutty's army, alleged that "a black fellow who offered fifty rupees for his service" lured him. However, after following him for sometime, Riley "lost him and never seen him since." Given how drunk Riley was when the *sipahis* found him, it is hard to trust his story. The EIC colonels, captains, and majors thus did not foil any daring acts of desertion. Their swift capture and sentencing made the rank and file aware of the army's ability to track their movements and also aware of the consequences of failure to adhere to the discipline the army superior demanded of their subalterns.

The use of the Mutiny Act to impose discipline was a class act. While common rank-and-file European soldiers bore the brunt of inhuman corporal punishment for the slightest unruly behavior, recalcitrant officers received much more lenient treatment. In 1766, a significant section of officers in Bengal threatened to stage a mutiny following Clive's reform, which had led to the reduction of their special pay (*batta*), an allowance drawn from the Bengal Nawabi's coffers which the European officers had been enjoying since their victory at Plassey. The officers revolted through mass resignation. Under the leadership of Clive, the EIC army primarily utilized *sipahi* manpower to monitor every movement of the officers of the recalcitrant "combination." The first brigade in which these officers belonged was sealed off from the second and third brigades. EIC military guards ensured these officers did not cause any disturbances while passing through upcountry roads. Clive advised the Calcutta council to follow each movement of these officers once they were in the presidency town so that at the slightest provocation of unrest they could be shipped back to Europe. Clive then alerted the Madras council to keep at the ready officers of various ranks who could replace the rebellious officers of Bengal. The mutiny subsided and Clive managed to calm all the aggrieved officers. Almost all the officers arrested in this conspiracy were convicted of the crime of desertion in the General Courts Martial and yet none received any harsh punishment. Sir Robert Fletcher, the lieutenant colonel who played an important role in fomenting the mutinous behavior among junior officers, was sentenced only to be cashiered. Even junior officers, such as Lieutenant William Vertue, was "cashiered with infamy, by having a sword and an espontoon broke over his head and his sash cut into pieces before him, at the head of all the troops cantoned at Bankipore."[192] The disparity in punishments between common soldiers and officers was necessary for a newly reformed army with a sharp hierarchy. The lenient treatment of officers shows that the EIC feared the disloyalty of these officers more than the desertion and unruly behavior of common soldiers. If a loyal officer class could be maintained, these officers in turn could take care of the supposed draeptomania of the common soldiers.

As both workers and subjects of the EIC state, European sailors and soldiers created several obstacles to the smooth functioning of the EIC in eighteenth-century Bengal. While their Dutch counterparts resorted to summary executions, the EIC struggled to implement the law that had already made desertion a penal offense in England. Faced with multiple competing political entities—such as the rival European companies which encroached upon the

EIC's sovereign control over its sailors and soldiers, the EIC depended upon a labor market of runaways in filling the ranks of its shipping crews and the army. Though such a strategy safeguarded the EIC from the damage that the VOC suffered, because the company was unsure of the commitment of its workers, the EIC's position as an employer and government remained precarious. Besides, deserting sailors and soldiers commanded a high rate of hire well into the mid-eighteenth century.

This situation started changing from the 1750s, as the EIC emerged as the supreme political force in the region. The EIC state eliminated its competitors and established effective discipline in its army. The European soldiers were the first group of workers over whom the EIC imposed undivided legal authority in punishing desertion. Since desertion as a form of criminal offense had origins in European armies, perhaps it is not surprising that the soldiers were the first to feel the brunt of the EIC's increasing political power. Even the smallest acts of absconding came with severe punishment. The EIC owed its ability to impose such discipline to the introduction of the Mutiny Acts, the military conquests that routed the major political/economic rivals of the EIC, and the reformation of the army through an increased hierarchical structure.

Nevertheless, by the 1760s the EIC had only partially tackled desertion of their European workers. The EIC state could not yet intercept deserting European sailors and hence the market for maritime labor in an effective legal way. Moreover, they still faced the problem of competing political powers recruiting European soldiers at the edges of their new political dominion. It was only in 1775 that the EIC was able to strike a deal with the Nawab of Awadh, Asaf-ud-Daulah, for the return of deserters.[193] Notwithstanding the difficulties, within the Bengal army at least, the EIC did succeed in instituting a labor discipline intolerant of desertion among its rank and file.

FOUR

"Less Than the Lowest Class of Laborers"

SILK REELERS AND THE COMPANY STATE, 1650–1779

SILK REELING WAS A UNIQUE FORM OF work in seventeenth- and eighteenth-century Bengal. It was the first artisanal work in the subcontinent organized into commercial manufactories. Unlike the local Mughal manufactories, or *karkhana*, which produced goods for elite households, the silk reeling units produced raw silk for foreign merchants, as well as local markets. Reelers were simultaneously artisans and workers, as VOC director Mattheus van den Brouk explained in 1662, "who had nothing to sell but the labor of their hands."[1] Even as the EIC and VOC tried to reorganize reeling work throughout the late seventeenth and early eighteenth centuries, the skills and demands of reelers constrained them. Just like with European sailors and soldiers, reelers played a key role in the intercompany rivalry between the VOC and EIC and in the rise of the EIC by the mid-eighteenth century. As it emerged as the supreme mercantile and political force in Bengal, the EIC revamped reeling work and expanded raw silk production by importing technology and experts from Europe. Consequently, they replaced one set of manufactory relations with another, and the artisan-waged worker-reelers lost their power to negotiate for their demands.

The silk reeling units in Bengal before the 1770s were unique innovations within the mercantile world. Mercantilism, in Marx's understanding, was an epoch where industrial capital and waged labor first arose in manufactories.[2] In the context of Europe and North America the links between manufacturing and industrial relations have been studied intensively.[3] Studies on manufactories in the Indian subcontinent are rare and in the case of silk reeling industry, scholars have only paid attention to the silk filatures (silk reeling factories) set up by the EIC beginning in the 1770s.[4] These studies assume that European social relations, or relations produced by European colonial domination, were the premise for the origins of manufactories. Frank Perlin rightly criticizes the literature on proto-industrialism for its teleology and Eurocentrism. However, due to the lack of an evidentiary base, even Perlin pays very little attention to manufactory work in Bengal and accepts silk filatures set up by the EIC, with European technology, as emblematic of "technical innovation and change in the organization of labour" in "proto-capitalist" Bengal.[5]

As this chapter demonstrates, the silk reeling units did not rely upon European technology and techniques. These were workplaces where a specialized group of reelers *re-reeled* already reeled silk bought from cocoon-producing peasant-reelers, to cater to the tastes of foreign merchants. European companies ran these establishments, but there was no parallel to re-reelers' work in Europe. Nonetheless, company officials strove to implement new technologies and work discipline in these units throughout the seventeenth century, often with little success. Existing literature neither sees nor explains the work of these re-reelers, not to mention the century-long struggle of the European East India companies to change this form of work. Moreover, in not understanding the work of the re-reelers, all existing scholarly literature on reelers conflates reeling work with that of re-reeling, misunderstanding the entire labor process. Understanding the indigenous organization of work is crucial to identifying what exactly was new with the coming of the filatures in the 1770s.

Within these reeling units the reelers' pre-industrial notions of work clashed with the industrial aspirations of the European companies. Though Eurocentric in his historical analysis, Marx called attention to the uneasy emergence of capitalist labor relations in manufactories like silk reeling units: "The original historic forms in which capital appears first *sporadically or locally* alongside the old mode of production while exploding them little by little everywhere, is on one side manufacture proper; this springs up where mass quantities are produced for export, for the external market—i.e. *on the basis of large scale overland and maritime commerce.*"[6] As a region highly attuned to the world economy ("the external market"), it is not surprising that Bengal witnessed the rise of silk reeling manufactories in the seventeenth century, long before colonial domination under the EIC. But just as the vision of order propounded in Ambrose Crowley's stringent seventeenth-century *Law Book*, the first manual of factory discipline in England, was still atypical in an English society soaked in precapitalist rhythms of artisanal work, so was the organized work in reeling units anomalous in seventeenth- and eighteenth-century Bengali society.⁷ Though reelers worked in these unique workplaces, they were part of a society that was a stranger to the discipline of industrial work. This uniqueness, or in Marx's words, "the local" or the "sporadic" nature of the reeling unit, intervened in the VOC's and EIC's early ambitions for expanding raw silk production. Because the companies depended on the skills, tools, and technology of the reelers, they were "compelled to wrestle with the insubordination of the workers."⁸ The major complaint of both the VOC and EIC was that the reelers refused to move to foreign parts of Bengal or Asia, which prevented the companies from expanding reeling operations. Only in the years 1758–62 did the EIC successfully establish monopolistic control over the reelers' labor by cutting out competitors and by encouraging reelers to desert from competing units. Yet in order to induce reelers to desert to their camp, the EIC still had to yield to reelers' demands on time, technology, and wages.

However, as the EIC overhauled manufactory work after the 1770s by importing foreign technology and experts from Europe to build silk filatures, they imputed the skills of the Kassimbazar reelers to the foreign technical know-how and European expertise. With the introduction of Piedmontese technologies of filature reeling in Bengal, the EIC was no longer dependent on the skills of the indigenous silk reelers—and their mobility practices as negotiating tools—for the expansion of silk yarn production. As Perlin says of "proto-capitalism" in eighteenth-century South Asia: "What is important about proto-capitalism is that under given conditions it maintains and intensifies a high rate of exploitation, driving prices given to producers lower than those available in a notionally open market, and thus fostering continued impoverishment at that level."⁹ The history of silk reeling work in Bengal reveals that even though such a tendency was present among various mercantile entities right from the seventeenth century on, it was frustratingly impossible to achieve. It was only between 1758 and 1770 that the EIC rallied political might to successfully realize their ends. In the process, the bargaining power of the reelers was destroyed, reducing them to one of the lowest-paid workers in the region.

RE-REELING UNITS IN SILK PRODUCTION

Silk reeling units before the 1770s were unique manufactories in South Asia and in the early modern world. Scholarship on Italian and French silk industries in the seventeenth and eighteenth centuries has demonstrated that silk reeling and throwing work were among the earliest forms of capitalist labor relations organized on factory floors.[10] The silk reeling units in Bengal, a much less known form of manufactory, emerged at a similar period as factory-like work places. These units formed a bridge between the local silk production and the overseas/overland silk markets. Not only European companies, but also local merchants serving a whole array of foreign traders within and outside Asia, maintained these units to prepare raw silk in a manner that suited the demands of the foreign markets.[11] Long-distance trade thus gave rise to this specialized labor. For the companies, the silk reeling units were their first major enterprise to organize indigenous labor on Indian soil.

Silkworm rearing developed primarily in the Western delta along the rivers Ganga, Padda, and Hugli. The surroundings of Kassimbazar became the most important region for procuring raw silk for the VOC and EIC. By the late 1670s, various official accounts of both companies indicate that the knowledge of silk rearing outside of Kassimbazar was present in Udaiganj and Khanakul, along the river Hugli; south of Kassimbazar, close to the VOC headquarters in Chinsurah; to the east of Kassimbazar in Kumarkhali, Boalia, and Sherpur; near Dhaka, along the river Padda; and to the north of Kassimbazar in Malda and Rajmahal.[12] Outside of these areas, silkworm rearing was virtually absent. Peasants did the work of silkworm rearing. They also possessed the knowledge of reeling silk.

With the help of family or hired labor, peasants who reared worms also reeled the first yarns out of the cocoons. There were three principal seasons or "bunds" for silk rearing—November, March, and July. The best cocoons came from the November bund and the worst from the July bund. After they hatched, the silkworms remained in baskets without food for a day. The next morning, they feasted on a treat of finely chopped tender mulberry leaves. While the healthy ones had an appetite, the weakest ones perished. The silkworm grower then moved these healthy worms into clean mats and fed them for around two weeks, at which time the worms stopped eating. This signaled that the worms were ready to spin their cocoons. Accordingly, the silkworm rearing peasant would move them to a special spinning mat with a spiral bamboo stick in the middle unto which the worms fastened their threads for making cocoons. George Williamson, an EIC servant who resided in Kassimbazar between 1756 and 1771, observed that members of the peasant household who fed the worm during this period of spinning did not cohabit or change clothes as the worms, which had a strong sense of smell, refused food from strangers.[13] Once the worms finished spinning, peasants exposed them to sunlight, thus killing the chrysalis. Next, the reeling process began. Ideally any member of the silkworm rearer's family could do this work. Alternatively, he could hire reelers either from the local village markets or "dispersed all over the country" to do the reeling work at their homes. The reelers cooked the cocoons with the dead worm inside in warm water, loosening the filaments. Each cocoon was made up of a single filament and the silkworm grower, his family members, or his hired reelers, using their nimble fingers, reeled out the filaments of ten to twenty-five cocoons at a time from a warm cooking pot, and compressed them to form yarn which they latched onto rudimentary bamboo reels. The best, most plump cocoons yielded *pattani* yarns while the inferior ones yielded *patti* yarns. After reeling the *pattani* yarns, the silkworm grower tied a knot with rope at the end.[14]

The European companies were unhappy with this process of reeling. They supplied a market where silk thread had reached a high degree of fineness, uniformity, and strength thanks to the technological advances and strict supervision of reelers in factories at Bologna, Piedmont, and Lyons. Pieter van Dam, the VOC historian, observed that in Bengal peasants never controlled the temperature of the water and hence produced uneven thread. He also complained that the peasants used unclean water which resulted in "dullness" of the thread. Williamson added that the method of killing the chrysalis left behind a lot of waste, for frequently the sky would be overcast or the worms would not finish spinning all at the same time, thus resulting in many worms piercing through their cocoons. The EIC preferred the Italian method of reeling, where cocoons were killed in warm water while reeling, to the less-controlled Bengali methods.[15]

As a consequence, the companies required that the irregularly-wound *pattani* and *patti* be re-reeled into yarns of raw silk fit for the European market, and in the case of the VOC, for both the European and the Japanese market. The companies never had direct contact with the growers and bought raw silk from local merchants (*paikars*), who had bought it from the peasants. The VOC created the highly paid post of "expert," an indigenous silk specialist who carefully noted the fineness of *pattani/patti* yarn, as well as color and weight, to ensure that the company was not cheated of its money.[16] In 1662, the company employed six other "experienced natives" who would test the silk alongside the silk expert.[17] The best *pattani* was rewound into *tanny* silk and also into *tanna banna* or *pangia* silk. *Patti* yarn could only be made into *tanna banna*. *Tanny* fetched a better price than *tanna banna*. The European companies sorted each variety into three qualities based on color and fineness—high (head), medium (belly), and low (foot).[18] Usually, either the *paikars* or the companies managed the work of re-reeling in their own reeling units. A specialized group of reelers, also known as *nacauds*, did this work.[19]

These re-reelers are the protagonists of this chapter. They came from the larger pool of reelers in the area and also engaged in reeling work as hired labor to silkworm rearers. The re-reelers in the Kassimbazar region worked in manufactories belonging to various merchants including the European companies. Some worked in the manufactories while simultaneously working from home for other merchants. Though almost all of these reelers owned land it is doubtful whether they earned a substantial living from agricultural work. Re-reelers in other regions supplemented re-reeling/reeling work with agricultural work. Both the companies simultaneously employed reelers to do the re-reeling work in their reeling manufacturing units while also buying finished re-reeled silk from local merchants.[20] Before the commencement of the seasons of silk buying and selling, the reelers in the VOC's unit produced carefully wound raw silk thread as "musters," or samples. The local merchants used these to instruct their reelers in their own re-reeling units as well as those reelers who worked on *pattani* from home. Even merchants not serving European markets seemed to have maintained reeling units. Notable here is the *nacaudkhana* (re-reeling unit) of the Armenian merchants in Sydabad, in the Kassimbazar region, mentioned by the Scottish private merchant, William Bolts.[21] In the re-reeling units *pattani* or *patti* was first washed in soap water. Pieter van Dam mentioned that native silk rearers smeared the *pattani* in ashes of banana trees to give the thread a white color. Hence, it was necessary to clean them first.[22] Additionally, the water softened the filaments in the thread, enabling the re-reeling process. The first step towards re-reeling was to separate the *pattani* onto small reels according to the fineness of the thread. Then they were wound onto large reels while reelers cleaned the silk of all impurities to achieve fineness and uniformity. On the large reels the color of the thread became conspicuous, depending on which the final sorting was done. The term *nacaud* comes from the use of a special tool the re-reelers used—an inch-long pin or *nakoān*—to pick out impurities from the thread while re-reeling. The VOC standardized the size of their reels—in 1758 their unit possessed 1,900 cylindrical reels: 400 three-foot-long, two-foot-wide reels and another 1,500 smaller reels.[23] The thread dried on the reels and then the reelers twisted them into skeins.[24]

These skeins, along with the skeins of re-reeled silk bought from the local merchant, were then graded. A Dutch sorter would do this work for the VOC. For the EIC, three people tested the silk: the Kassimbazar chief of factory, the second and third officer, and the warehouse keeper of the Kassimbazar factory. Initially, they all made their individual judgments silently on a piece of paper based on a skein of each variety of silk and then compared notes to finally decide the price of each sort.[25] They then put skeins of similar quality into the same bundle and sealed them in cloth bags. They gave the best-quality silk an "A" rating and an alphabetic order was followed for various lesser grades of silk. Reeling as manufactory work was thus a small but significant part of the complex process of producing raw silk yarn in Bengal for export.

THE VOC SILK RE-REELING UNIT, 1650–1760

The VOC silk re-reeling unit in Kalikapur, adjacent to Kassimbazar, was as Om Prakash notes, "the most ambitious of the company's manufacturing projects," leaving behind an impressive paper trail for reconstructing the nature of silk manufacturing in seventeenth- and early eighteenth-century Bengal.[26] Between 1653 and 1760, the silk re-reeling unit of the VOC was anything but stable. At times it produced all of its raw silk exported from Bengal, and at other times its operation came to complete standstill. At full capacity, 4,000 men reeled the full consignment of the VOC's raw silk export, and in slack times, the unit employed only sixty reelers, leaving the VOC to buy almost the entire consignment from local merchants (*paikars*). The VOC re-reeling unit is significant for two reasons. First, it provides a detailed picture of how European East India companies in Bengal organized reeling work, both in terms of transfer of foreign technology and employment of local workers before the coming of the filatures. Since, like the EIC, the VOC was attuned to the superiority of Italian silk yarns in European markets, what attempts did they make to introduce new technology in silk reeling and how successful were they in these efforts? To what extent were reelers "proletarianized," that is, as VOC officials observed, "had nothing to sell but the labor of their hands"?[27] Answers to these questions will enable us to appreciate the technological as well as the political-economic changes brought about by the EIC in Bengal's silk reeling industry beginning in the late 1750s. Second, as is elaborated later in the chapter, the VOC re-reeling unit with its reelers played a crucial role in the fierce mercantilist competition among the East India companies in the late 1750s, from which the EIC emerged triumphant. In other words, the EIC's transformation of reeling work in Bengal was premised upon the destruction of the VOC's silk re-reeling unit.

The VOC was aware of the fineness of the Italian silk thread in the European market and tried, unsuccessfully, to introduce technological changes in their re-reeling unit a century before the EIC introduced Italian-style filatures on Bengal's soil. These changes have gone completely unnoticed in both the scholarship on technological change in South Asia or in histories of European expansion and colonialism in India. In 1662, the VOC director of Bengal, Matheus van den Broecke, sent silk expert Daniel van Mollen to Kassimbazar "to prepare diverse sorts of silk in Italian method which will sell in our fatherland for 50 *schelling*." Van Mollen prepared 30 pounds of Italian varieties of silk, and also 300 pounds of *stik* and *naaij* silk, with the help of native workers. The Bengal council wrote to Batavia, "because this silk was never ever made in Bengal before, this consignment was extremely valuable." Van Mollen's technological input was likely in the realm of silk throwing. The Italian method of silk throwing was the key to the creation of the highest quality, most durable silk *organzine*, the most sought-after silk in Europe— the Piedmontese filature technology of reeling silk was still unknown at that time. As part of his contract, van Mollen created a small twining mill of 50 spools, presumably modeled after the small hand-driven circular Bolognese throwing machine.[28] In 1687 VOC commissioner Hendrik Adriaan van Rheede, on his inspection of the VOC's silk trade in Bengal, praised the *stik* and *naaij* silk prepared there.[29] However, the prohibitive cost—6 rupees and 12 anna per *pond* (Dutch measurement, a little more than an English pound)—over a rupee more expensive than *tanny* silk, did not allow *stik* and *naaij* silk to figure in the export items in the years to come. The same van Mollen had also reeled 30 ponds—12¾ ponds of superfine *organzine*, 6⅜ ponds of ordinary *organzine*, 4¾ ponds of *filado* and 6⅛ ponds of *tram*—of Italian silk.[30] But, as is discussed below, excessive labor costs forced the VOC to abandon their premature plans of preparing silk in the Italian method.[31]

Unlike the EIC, the VOC introduced and maintained the reeling of *florette*, also known as *mochta* or *matkā* yarns. This yarn, low in quality, was prepared from pierced cocoons. The VOC silk re-reeling unit had a separate section for preparing these yarns, known as the "mochta boiler house."[32] It seems that the yarns were prepared by boiling pierced cocoons, a method novel to the region as the local method of making *mochta* yarn precluded boiling. In

1687, van Rheede prodded the company to prepare all of its *matkā* silk in their re-reeling unit.[33] Though the VOC never reached that goal, *matkā*-making continued in the re-reeling unit well into the mid-eighteenth century.

Even while experimenting with silk yarns at their re-reeling unit, the VOC officials remained unsure of the profits of using the silk re-reeling unit during the first three decades of its existence.[34] In 1655, the unit produced 800 bales or 121,400 pounds of raw silk. In 1661, the amount nearly doubled to 1,457 bales, close to 98 percent of the total of exported silk. By 1662, the number of reelers in the unit rose to 1,500. Yet, "to our great bewilderment" the VOC in Bengal discovered that the silk prepared outside of the reeling unit was preferred in the Japanese and European markets to the painstakingly prepared silk at the company's re-reeling unit..[35] At the same time, the VOC had to face the thorny problem of cost reduction. The local merchants, or *paikars*, realizing that raw silk was a prized commodity among the European companies, hiked the price of *pattani* to almost 5 rupees per *ceer* (a little over a kilogram). Moreover, with the quick expansion in the number of reelers in the unit, the VOC lost supervisory power over their work. The result was a drop in the quality of reeled silk. Therefore, they decided to cut the size of the re-reeling unit in half. The actual reduction of the size of the workforce seems to have been more than half as only 158 bales or 11 percent of the total reeled silk, 1,388 bales, had been reeled in the unit. This figure went down to 7 percent in 1668–69. This trend continued into the 1670s. The master reeler as well as the reelers under him still produced substandard reeled silk. In 1674, the VOC decided to reduce the number of reelers to only 100. In the previous year, the unit had employed 500 reelers. In 1676, the VOC in Batavia complained that almost all the silk sent from Bengal was of poor quality, specifically mentioning the poor quality of the reeling. Moreover, since the VOC in Bengal at the time depended almost completely on reeled silk bought from the Bengal hinterland, they could not prepare the consignments for Batavia on time.[36] For a fleeting moment in 1676, officials of the Bengal directorate considered the idea of doubling the size of the workforce employed in the unit, but the idea was quickly abandoned. Instead, they decided that reliance on the silk re-reeling unit should be kept at a minimum.

The VOC resumed interest in preparing export-quality raw silk at their silk re-reeling unit beginning in 1700, when merchants raised the price of finished silk to 6 rupees per *ceer*. The VOC threatened that if the price remained high, they would reel their entire supply of silk in the unit. The threat worked. The price came down, and the unit continued to produce only

TABLE 1 Production in the VOC's silk re-reeling unit at Kalikapur

Year	Number of reelers	Reeler production as percentage of total raw silk exported from Bengal
1661	1,500	98
1669	—	7
1674	100	—
1718	—	83
1759	1,500	—

SOURCE: National Archive, The Hague, Netherlands, G.L. Vernet Collection, 1 (unfoliated), letter of July 28, 1756; Om Prakash, *Dutch East India Company and the Economy of Bengal* (Princeton: Princeton University Press, 1983), 113–117.

samples. When the price of reeled silk rose again in 1714, the VOC finally re-activated their re-reeling unit. Over the next four years, the VOC reeled in their own unit 83 percent of the silk they exported. The VOC prepared in their re-reeling unit all the silk sent in October and January 1718–19 to the European market. The interest in the re-reeling unit was such that in 1714, the Bengal directorate drew up plans for a major restructuring. The VOC increased the size of their re-reeling unit to accommodate 4,000 reelers at work. The transformed silk re-reeling unit was now a stone house immune to the risk of fire in the dry months from March to May.[37] The plan seems to have been carried out prior to 1722, when an all-engulfing fire destroyed the English silk re-reeling unit but spared the VOC unit.[38] This is also evident from renovation reports from 1756; the silk re-reeling unit was still a stone and wooden structure.[39] In 1734, the VOC tried bargaining with the *paikars* to bring down the price of prepared silk, for which they did not reach any satisfactory negotiation until November and so the entire order of *tanny* silk of superior (*cabessa*) and medium (*barriga*) quality "was prepared nowhere else but at the devices of our unit."[40] In 1759, 1,500 reelers continued to work regularly at the VOC silk re-reeling unit (see table 1). The unit at Kalikapur remained an important production center for VOC trade until 1760.

Working on a confined shop floor, under rigid discipline and supervision, the reelers of the VOC came close to resembling the proletarianized workers of nineteenth-century factories. Silk re-reeling units were extremely hierarchical workplaces, where the reeler labored under the supervision of a master reeler. Demands on a master reeler's vigilance were high, as one VOC director, Constantijn Ranst, made crystal clear: "The master reeler should check the reeled silk thrice a week at least and point out the problems so that they could be redressed. [He should] remind and see that reelers only put four skeins of raw silk in water at once and immediately reel it."[41] The most important quality of the master reeler was his ability to "keep the reelers in awe."[42] Any small mistake by the common reelers received the whip, "without any excuse."[43] Additionally, in 1673, the VOC records listed 49 head reelers working under the master reeler in the unit. These 49 head reelers supervised the work of 350 common reelers.[44] The master reeler recruited common reelers, most of whom were local. However, sometimes reelers were migrant workers. The VOC tried to recruit reelers for their Kalikapur unit from places further away such as Rajmahal. In 1712, when the VOC officials faced trouble in recruiting silk reelers from Kassimbazar and Hugli, to reel the best-quality silk, *pattani* and *adhapanji*, they looked towards Rajmahal. The director, Anthonij Huisman, requested the VOC *wakil*, a company intermediary for local courts, to recruit one hundred reelers from Rajmahal and send them to Chinsurah.[45] The reeler recruitment process shows that the VOC required special skills of these workers. Thus, specifications such as "demands for 200 reelers for preparing *adhapanjia*" crept up in the VOC's recruitment drives.[46] The VOC also endeavored to keep their units running year-round, thus laying exclusive claim over their reelers' labor. However, circumstances did not allow the VOC to impose such a work regime. Even though they obliged their master reelers to such a time commitment, they failed to procure enough silk to keep the unit going throughout the year. All reelers received money wages. The Kassimbazar council appointed a Dutch delegate who would "oversee the payment of the wages" by master reelers to common reelers. In 1670, the VOC decided that the common reelers would receive their entire pay in money wages. Except for the master reeler, who got extra pay in unsold silk waste (*porsia*), none of the other reelers received their wages in kind. In his contract, the master reeler Abhayram was forewarned not to use the silk waste as a way of reducing the money wage of the reelers.[47] Even the rewards of reeling thread satisfactorily went to the master reeler. The VOC seldom trusted such alienated workers. In their eyes, the reelers were "shrewd, poor and always in need," always suspect for their contumacy.[48]

The reelers are the earliest documented contract workers of the subcontinent. In 1670, the master reeler Abhay Ram signed a contract with the VOC in the presence of two indigenous reelers, Deep Chand and Jai Chand. The contract mentioned that he would receive a wage of 12 annas along with unsold silk waste for every *maund* of re-reeled silk. He also received an additional amount of 5 rupees to be distributed as wages among the common reelers who he would recruit to work under him. The contract, even while enshrining the indigenous practice of advance payment, introduced a system of debt bondage, similar to the system of procurement and extraction of labor introduced widely by the EIC after 1765.[49] In 1687, the VOC commissioner van Rheede suggested that the reelers should receive their wages only after delivering the re-reeled silk, but such a measure was never implemented.[50] The contract detailed that in case the re-reeled silk did not pass muster the master reeler, collectively representing the other reelers, would be held responsible for the loss in weight or the egregious mixture of different sorts of silk yarns, and fined accordingly. The master reeler and other reelers could pay the debts in money or in labor. In 1670 Abhay Ram mortgaged his son and all his moveable and immoveable property as security in lieu of fines that he might accrue.[51] The VOC had devised a very complex system of recovering their debts. In 1675, when the VOC reduced the size of their unit to just 100 reelers, the dismissed reelers stood indebted to the tune of 1,662 rupees and 14 annas. The VOC ensured that "the above-mentioned debts of reelers had been taken over by merchants who will supply the company." The reelers would "work for these merchants" and the merchants, Deep Chand and Jai Chand, in turn "had given their security" to the VOC.[52] VOC's use of contracts with a master reeler and local merchants as debt bondage for reelers was a prelude to a system that the EIC state used in all spheres of work beginning from the mid-eighteenth century.

Even though the VOC enjoyed remarkable power to enforce debt bondage, in a setting where no European company had such widespread political power, from time to time it had to write off debts. Since company standards for reeled thread were difficult to achieve and with every misstep, severely penalized, reelers often accumulated massive debts. The first master reeler, Balaram, whose name often comes up in the official accounts, contracted a sizeable debt of over a thousand rupees. The VOC utilized the security of local merchants in recovering that debt. In 1673, after the death of Balaram, the merchant Deep Chand took responsibility for recovering Balaram's unpaid debt of 1,000 rupees.[53] Abhayram, who succeeded Balaram as master reeler, amassed an insurmountable debt of 3,614 rupees within three years. The VOC maneuvered the local Dīwān, Rai Bal Chand, to give out a number of orders (*parwānā*), enabling it to recover its debts. With the local government on their side, the VOC imprisoned Abhay Ram, compelling him to pay off his debts in the following years. As a respite, the VOC pardoned some parts of Abhayram's debts because, as they admitted, "according to our contract with the master reeler we were bound to continuously provide the re-reeling unit with the silk, which we could not and so he (Abhayram) had suffered because of the work stoppage at the unit."[54] The VOC's inability to supply enough silk had prevented Abhayram from building a steady pace of work with common reelers over the year. Records from 1676 show that Abhayram paid at least part of his debt and the VOC expected to get 705 rupees more in recovery, which, nonetheless, they wrote off as a loss.[55] It is quite likely that Abhayram worked off his debt because the VOC had earlier mentioned that he was "too poor to pay the money in cash." Ghanashyam and Nimoe, sons of the late master reeler Balaram, succeeded Abhayram and like their predecessors, soon got enmeshed in the same debt trap. Not only were they unable to pay off their father's debt, but they further incurred a hefty debt of 771 rupees and 14 anna.[56] Transfer of debt across generations was a well-known practice in indigenous society. The VOC was the first European concern in Bengal to implement this practice in the realm of manufacture.

Even when the VOC utilized debt as an avenue for demanding more labor from their reelers, chronic indebtedness spurred the company to rethink the role of the master reeler. They toyed with the idea of removing the position completely but did not follow it through.[57] Instead, they redefined the payment system of the master reeler in the contract with Balaram's sons Ghanashyam and Nimoe, whereby the master reelers received a fixed wage of 200 rupees per annum instead of piece wages.[58] This was probably the only time in the history of Bengal's silk reeling industry that reelers received a time wage and not a piece wage. Wage information from 1759, however, shows that the VOC had discontinued this system of time wage and reverted to the payment of piece wages. Even when the VOC organized mechanisms to recover debts, extending their command over labor, the process created bottlenecks of unrequited capital harmful to the smooth running of business. They occasionally had to relieve master reelers of their debts. Moreover, reelers did not always wait for the VOC to relieve them of their debts. Fourteen of the forty-nine head reelers working under Abhayram ran away from Kalikapur without paying off their 642 rupees of debt.[59]

It is significant that the VOC restructured the role of the master reelers at a time when their re-reeling unit's contribution to overall raw silk exports was at its lowest. In all likelihood, the debts signify the reelers' uneasy transition to getting familiarized with a new kind of demand for raw silk thread and the skills and labor associated with it. Accounts of these uncertain years also reveal that the VOC received robust support from the local government, which enabled them to carry on and even at times experiment with new technologies.

Full-time hired work, contracts, and a money wage came to define the labor of the silk reeler. They worked in a highly hierarchical workplace where they owned neither tools nor the raw silk. The silk reelers' work conditions also presaged the quintessential colonial master-servant relationship, dictated through debt bondage. However, even as wage laborers, reelers were skilled workers, and the VOC continually reckoned with their skills. This reckoning often meant that the VOC had to pardon debts as there were only a limited number of reelers with limited capacity in their lifetimes to pay off the debts. Until 1760, the unit remained an important enterprise of the VOC trade in Bengal. The fluctuations in the size of the re-reeling unit somewhat stabilized in the eighteenth century. However, stability did not translate into a completely docile work force. Reelers made their demands unrelentingly well into the mid-eighteenth century.

CONTROL OVER REELERS

Though reelers were impoverished day laborers, the companies nevertheless depended upon their special skills. This mutual dependence gave the reelers leverage over the companies, which they frequently expressed through mobility. As is discussed in chapter 1, the artisan in eighteenth-century Bengal was a highly mobile subject. This is a noticeable pattern in different regions in India, and often such mobility was unconstrained by mercantile capital.[60] If artisans made a choice to move, they also made a choice not to move. Often scholars have focused on the propensity of artisans to move and have assumed that lack of mobility is an indicator of external (state or mercantile) use of force on artisans. It is true that precolonial states exerted their power in restraining or pressing artisanal labor, as is evident from the use of artisans in Mughal *karkhanas*. Yet artisans, and in this case, reelers, also weighed their odds and decided whether or not to move according to their employers' wishes. Through their choices over mobility, the otherwise destitute reelers made various demands regarding their working conditions—from wages in kind to control over time. Neither the VOC nor the EIC, even with their own state power and the support of the Mughal imperial government, could control the mobility of the reelers.

VOC officials faced the tribulation of moving reelers to different destinations within Bengal immediately after the creation of their silk re-reeling unit in Kassimbazar, in 1653–55. The VOC's quest to enlarge their raw silk exports from Bengal spurred them to set up units in different silk-growing areas of Bengal. In 1651 they set up a factory in Udaiganj close to their headquarters in Chinsurah, where they bought raw silk. This move coincided with the unprecedented expansion of the Kassimbazar silk re-reeling unit. At a time when their re-reeling unit was growing from strength to strength, the VOC faced fierce competition from the EIC. VOC director Johan Verpoorten reported that "the English, our competitors are chasing away as many [silk reelers] as they possibly can.... such a situation has given rise to the necessity of the company (VOC) to be very alert or else it will not reach its competence." In order to build its "competence," Verpoorten tried "many times" to send silk reelers from the surroundings of Kassimbazar to Udaiganj to build a new unit there. Alas, it was "all in vain," as "these people are not happy to live away from their wives and children."[61] The reelers would not agree to migrate as single able-bodied male workers. Additionally, they ran into debt presumably through their lack of interest in reeling work. Verpoorten abandoned the plan of relocating Kassimbazar reelers and instead employed the very few reelers the company could recruit from the *zamīndārī* of Udaiganj to work at the new unit to finish re-reeling silk for the Japanese market. Even this plan ran aground when, in 1658, after a dispute with the *zamīndār* of Udaiganj, the VOC shut down their factory in Udaiganj for good.[62] The VOC had run into an oft-encountered problem of recruiting labor in a foreign *zamīndārī* where they had little political power. The work force in Kassimbazar did not help either through their reluctance to move away from their families, under the VOC's employment terms.

If family ties underpinned choices over mobility for Kassimbazar reelers, for Khanakul reelers, control over time and modes of payment shaped their mobility choices. Soon after the failure of the Udaiganj factory, the VOC set up a factory in 1669 in Khanakul, an adjacent area.[63] Here it was not the VOC, but their supplying merchants, who had the intention of setting up two re-reeling units in two different villages. In 1670, VOC merchant Pieter Hoffmeester visited Khanakul and reported that the merchants were already behind in supplying the company with the amount of silk stipulated in their contracts. Apart from having a very bad crop of silkworms that season and stiff competition from Gujarati and Muslim merchants involved in upland trade as well as from local weavers who bought silk for their looms, they faced the increasing difficulty of getting hold of reelers. They recruited barely 400 reelers. Hoffmeester was not happy with the reelers' productivity; together they could reel only 15 maunds of silk in a month. Moreover, Hoffmeester noted, "some of them finding more advantage in agriculture during harvest time, do not bother with reeling." Thus, reeling was only seasonal work for some; they chose how much time they would spend in reeling for the merchants.[64]

Mobility came on the heels of demands for wages in kind. The year 1670 was special because the entire region faced a severe drought, the likes of which "people have no memory of." In such a situation the reelers stayed on the reels, unlike other years. But they demanded their wages "in rice instead of money." The contract merchants of the VOC had to spend 300–400 rupees to buy rice from other places and only then could they "stop the desertion of these reelers."[65] At times when grain prices were high, demanding payment in grains made more sense to reelers. Reelers again used their choice of mobility as a bargaining chip. Kassimbazar reelers too demanded wages in kind. Though contracts between master reelers and the VOC in Kassimbazar from the 1670s reveal that reelers got a full money wage, in 1713 the VOC reported that "the worst form of silk ketsjer, coutihael etc . . . [is] usually given to our reelers for reducing their wages."[66] Through retaining control over their mobility, reelers gained small but significant privileges that the VOC and their contract merchants had to indulge.

During a turbulent period of armed conflict in the summer of 1712, the VOC again failed to move their reelers to a safe haven where they could continue reeling silk for the overseas market. In July 1712, Farrukh Siyar's army marched towards Murshidabad against Dīwān Murshid Quli Khan, whom Farrukh Siyar suspected of opposing his claim to the Mughal throne. In the midst of this political rivalry, the VOC continually lost their European sailors and soldiers to the various indigenous armies (see discussion in chapter 3). In this situation, the VOC tried moving their reelers from nearby Kassimbazar to Kushtia, further down the river Padda. The VOC left their *wakil* Ramnanth Ray and their broker Ram Chandra Poddar with the "difficult" task of moving the reelers. On July 23, Ray and Poddar reported that the master reeler, Kalia, told them that there was "no fair way of moving them, but only by hook or crook," that is, by force. The *wakil* and the broker, reluctant to take up the task, waited for the VOC to give them further orders.[67] The plans were not carried out. However, the resolution of regional conflicts the following year made the undertaking redundant. Again, the reelers made strong choices over their mobility. They chose to stay in a politically volatile zone rather than relocate to safeguard the needs of the VOC.

The VOC tried to mobilize reelers within their larger imperial nodes in Asia. In the early 1660s, the VOC wanted to expand silk production not only within Bengal but also in other territories in Asia under its direct political control. In early 1662 the Bengal directorate sent silkworms with mulberry shrubs to Jafnapatam, in VOC-held Ceylon. Though the mulberry trees survived the journey and adjusted to the soil in Jafnapatam, the silkworms perished. On the request of Anthonij Pavilioen, the VOC commander of Ceylon, the VOC in Bengal in January 1663 sent another special consignment of silkworms under the care of four silkworm growers from Bengal. The "honorable worms" took passage on the ship *Hercules*, with no other commodities in its hold so as to give the worms "enough room." That same year, Daniel van Mollen prepared 30 pounds of silk in the Italian method using his twinning mill. Though producing satisfactory results, the costs remained high. The Bengal directorate blamed labor costs for such high expenses and thus sent some raw silk to Batavia, "to research whether or not (on account of a good number of slave children) [the raw silk] can be twinned cheaper than in Bengal." VOC officials wanted to bring down the price by driving down labor costs to a bare minimum.[68] The effort to procure cheap or unpaid labor failed, and silk was never again reeled in the Italian way either in the re-reeling unit in Bengal or elsewhere in the Dutch empire.

Yet, the VOC kept alive the hope of building a silk industry in its empire well into the eighteenth century.[69] On November 30, 1734, the silkworms in Jafnapatam miraculously increased in number under the care of five Europeans and some native Bengali silk growers—though remaining "still unremarkable" as a crop. With their eyes on the growing crop, the VOC decided to get a dozen silk reelers and the necessary instruments from Bengal to set up reeling work. Though the Bengal directorate promised help initially, two years down the line, the Hugli council reconsidered. The silk reelers had a very different temperament from the silkworm growers. In these two years, the VOC tirelessly tried to recruit a dozen silk reelers who would move to Batavia or Ceylon, but in vain. Even when they doubled the wages of the reelers, they refused.[70] The VOC officials blamed the workers' reluctance to move on the "Bengali" mentality. Unlike the Muslim Bengali seafarers and silkworm growers, who were "a special group of people," the Bengali silk reelers "being heathens had no interest in crossing the sea." The caste Hindu fear of crossing the sea (*kālāpāni*) was probably a good reason for their failure, but the VOC report also added that the reelers "having their coffee at home with their family they are least likely to survive in foreign lands."[71] The reelers were not coffee drinkers. The acerbic comment explains the reelers' parochialism not in religious terms but attachment to a family life that reelers did not want disturbed. Family ties of the Kassimbazar reelers once again ordained their decisions over mobility, frustrating the grand plans of the VOC.[72]

The EIC too faced similar problems of moving reelers well into the years after the company had received Dīwāni rights. In the 1760s, the EIC made conscious efforts to expand raw silk production in Bengal for the British market. Since they were still in the process of introducing the Piedmontese filature technology in Bengal, they had to depend on local reelers for this expansion drive. In such a situation, George Vansittart, collector of Midnapore, a western district known for its salt production, tried hard to build a silk industry in the area. On April 19, 1768, he reported that he had successfully convinced a few *zamīndārs* to extend silkworm cultivation by 400 bighas of land. The EIC increasingly entered into contracts with *zamīndārs* asking them to increase silkworm cultivation in their areas. Extension principally took place in the *parganas* of Kutubpur, Narranjole, and Cossijurah. Vansittart had reclaimed 500 more bighas of wasteland to lease it out to anyone interested in silkworm rearing. He requested the Fort William council to send him "any Calcutta people who are willing to take them ... from where silk has never before been cultivated." Such efforts yielded results. In 1768 he had gathered a good crop of silkworms. But instead of sending the worms to well-known reeling areas in Radhanagore in Burdwan, Vansittart harbored ambitions of developing the silk reeling industry in his district. So, he requested the Fort William council to send some silk reeler families from either Calcutta or Burdwan. The collector of Burdwan, Mr. Graham, flatly declined this request. He elaborated, "I do not think it would be practicable to effect a removal of the winders, admitting it could be done without prejudice to the company's investments." Since it was the norm to "afford all the winders we can possibly entertain full employment at home, they would hardly I imagine be prevailed upon to remove from their family habitations into another province." The request to remove families is impossible where family life was intertwined, beyond the walls of hearth and home, in the entire village life. Again, the reelers' preference for stability in their family life conflicted with the company's interest in and demands for mobility. When he received no help from Calcutta or Burdwan, Vansittart under his own initiative trained a few people who grew silk in Kutubpur, Narajole, and Cassijarah to reel silk as well. Spending over 4,000 rupees, George Vansittart was finally successful in getting the silk rearers of Midnapore to transition into reeling, though, he admitted, "they make rather awkward piece of business of it at present." Silk was never again reeled in Midnapore until the introduction of the filature system.[73]

By the end of seventeenth century William Petty observed, "Those who predominate in Shipping and Fishing have more occasions than others to frequent all parts of the World, and to observe what is wanting or redundant everywhere; and what each people can do, and what they desire; and consequently to be the Factors and carriers, for the whole world of trade."[74] Merchants, including the VOC and EIC companies, well aware of "the whole world of trade," found the reeling techniques in Bengal "wanting." The re-reeling manufactories in Bengal were responses to this transregional rationale of the mercantile interests. Petty had in mind especially the Dutch enterprises as the "factors and carriers for the whole world of trade." Indeed, the VOC pioneered experiments in silk production on a global scale by bringing Italian silk reeling methods to the Bengali reeling industry as well as by introducing Bengali silkworms and mulberry plants to Batavia and Ceylon. Soon, the EIC followed in their footsteps. However, between 1650s and 1760s such efforts failed repeatedly. At the heart of this failure were the mobility practices of the reelers. Reelers made choices about their working conditions, sometimes informed by particularistic and parochial values. Such choices proved a roadblock to the companies' ambitions. So long as the companies remained dependent on the skills of Bengali re-reelers, their capacity to expand the reeling industry remained limited, because the reelers refused to move.

REELERS AND THE ANGLO-DUTCH WAR, 1758–62

The EIC's efforts to restructure their silk industry, especially by introducing filature technology beginning in the 1770s has received much scholarly attention.[75] These and similar studies reveal the mercantilist basis for the EIC's interests in Bengal's silk industry, that is, expanding the production of raw silk in a dependent territory in order to strengthen the silk industry in England.[76] Though the EIC did not attain its goal of producing raw silk comparable to the finest quality of raw silk from Italy, it produced an enormous quantity of filature-made raw silk yarns. However, unknown to historians, this process of restructuring and expansion had begun earlier, in the late 1750s. The first step towards expansion required monopolization of the reelers' labor market between 1758 and 1762. This was a period when Kassimbazar became the theater of violent competition among the EIC, VOC, and other Asian merchants from which the EIC emerged victorious over the VOC by capturing the labor of the silk reelers. Historians of the eighteenth-century silk industry in Bengal have paid most attention to the silkworm *rearers* and their resistance to the monopsonistic efforts of the EIC and the introduction of filatures. However, silk *reelers*, especially the re-reelers, also played a crucial role in this transformative process. Their uncontrolled mobility—in the form of "desertion," as the VOC called it, played a key role in ramping up mercantile competition during the turbulent years of 1758–62.

The same reelers who refused to relocate in order to expand the silk reeling industry also ran away from work as a response to the companies' efforts to impose discipline. In 1662, when the VOC entered its first phase of decline, the master silk reeler protested to the VOC director, then residing in Kassimbazar, that "the flog has been used too much." The master reeler, under strict orders from the VOC officials, had to flog the reeler "without excuse" if he detected that the silk was spun roughly. The master reeler worried that the use of the flog for every "small fault" was such a "misuse" that he could "no longer hold them [reelers] together as a result of which a good number of them have escaped."[77] That VOC officials found no reliable solution to the problem is evident from the 1670 contract between the VOC and Abhay Ram, the master reeler. One provision stated that the company would provide exclusive foot soldiers to hunt down deserting reelers and bring them back to work.[78] The VOC always feared that reelers would run off at the smallest pretext. In 1714, when the VOC asked the governor general and his council at Batavia to provide funds for building a stone house for the silk re-reeling unit, they cited retention of the reelers as one of the main reasons for such renovations. If the older straw-roofed unit caught fire, the reelers would run away, and the VOC would lose its precious workforce.[79] This problem continued into the turbulent years after 1759, when the Dutch struggled with the EIC, whose political power in the region was on the rise.

Mercantilist competition to monopolize reelers' labor led up to the Battle of Bedara in November 1759, whereby the VOC lost their political and economic power in Bengal for good. In 1614, Jan Pieterzoon Coen, the founder of the Dutch empire in Asia, famously remarked, "One cannot do war without commerce, nor commerce without war."[80] Less than a century and half later, the EIC enhanced its hold over the raw silk industry in Bengal by following this very principle. The victory at Bedara against the VOC was a significant event in the history of the EIC's political ascendancy in Bengal, as it was a decisive victory against EIC's competitors, which already had been advanced by Clive's victory against the French (along with the Nawabi forces) at the Battle of Plassey in 1757. Scholars have discussed various aspects of that war, starting with the nineteenth-century accounts of Arthur Broome and Klerk de Reus.[81] However, while the military strategies, geopolitical implications, and conflicting personalities among the English, Dutch, and the Nawab of Bengal have been discussed in minute detail, there has been no discussion on the impact of the war on the VOC's trade and its workers themselves. The correspondence between Adriaan Bisdom, the VOC director at Chinsurah, and George Lodewijk Vernet, the VOC chief at Kassimbazar, reveals the conflict in the months leading up to the Battle of Bedara and right after it ended. Their letters indicate that the silk re-reeling unit featured prominently in the strategic plans of the VOC in Bengal and Batavia vis-à-vis the EIC within Bengal. No histories of the VOC in Bengal mention the fate of the unit after 1715. In the aftermath of the battle, the VOC suffered the complete ruin of their silk re-reeling unit. More significantly, the reelers of the VOC played an important role in the intercompany rivalry. While they endured impressment, they also made significant gains in their wages. In this atmosphere of fierce competition, they used the strategy of desertion to demand high wages and retain control over their time, ultimately destroying the re-reeling unit.

Political upheavals in the 1750s loosened the grip of the European companies over their reelers. The Maratha raids, which continued throughout the 1740s and into the 1750s, affected many reelers. The EIC reported disarray in the raw silk business in 1751, when the Maratha raiders burnt the houses of workers, compelling them to flee elsewhere. As hostilities between the Bengal Nawab Siraj-ud-Daulah and the EIC came to a head, Siraj's troops marched through Kassimbazar and Calcutta in 1756. The impact of these hostilities went far beyond the capture of the English factory in Kassimbazar. As Vernet reported, the "wantonness" of the soldiers of Siraj-ud-Daulah's army resulted in the flight of several silkworm-rearing peasants and silk reelers residing in and around Kassimbazar, affecting work at the VOC re-reeling unit in Kalikapur.[82] Most of the reelers ran to the other side of the river Padda. At least a third of the EIC's reelers had migrated to that region. On February 11, 1758, the EIC reported that they had enough reelers to complete work for only one sixth of their investment. A month later they counted only enough reelers to finish work on thirty bales of silk. Deserting reelers, far from giving up their trade, began working from home. The EIC resented this practice: "the method [of working from home] has been long complained of by all the considerable merchants of Cassimbazar as it is not only the case of silk being badly wound but occasions the great difficulty of getting workmen to wind it in their [merchant's] respective houses." This method enabled reelers to work for multiple merchants without subjecting themselves to the factory-like discipline of the re-reeling units. For the companies this meant complete loss of their supervisory control over raw silk production. They dreaded the resulting volatility in the labor market as well as in the work process itself.[83]

The VOC primarily blamed the EIC for both the loss of their reelers and the growing practice of working from home. In January 1758, Vernet wrote Bisdom and the Hugli council that work at the re-reeling unit was not going well at all because the English were "pressing reelers from all directions." There were only six hundred reelers available in the vicinity of the VOC factory, nine hundred less than the usual number of men employed. Moreover, only three hundred of these men could be put to work.[84] It is significant that Vernet used the term "pressing" to describe the EIC tactic of poaching their workers. Pressing or impressment were terms commonly used to describe the forceful recruitment of sailors, especially for naval ships at various ports in Europe.[85] The Dutch and English had evidently adopted such means of "recruitment" for silk reeling as well. The British Navy employed doubtful legal sanctions to carry out this practice during wartime, but the practice continued not just within the Navy but also among private British merchants, especially colonial British officials in the Anglo-American world in the seventeenth and eighteenth centuries.[86] Vernet's use of the term in 1758 signals the importance of the Kassimbazar silk reelers to Anglo-Dutch relations in Bengal. Like the seamen in the Anglo-American world in wartime, reelers too played a critical role in the conflicts which arose from the political ambitions of the two largest European companies fighting over the control of silk production in Asian lands.

By "impressment" Vernet also meant that EIC servants visited the houses of reelers every night, supplying them with *pattani*, the highest quality silk, which they then reeled, in addition to working for the VOC.[87] The EIC men surreptitiously went to the houses of the head reelers and supplied them with the *pattani*, which the head reelers then distributed among the other reelers. Moreover, the EIC's ruse opened the floodgates for other merchants in the region to bring their silk by stealth to the VOC reelers. As a result of the reelers' multiple engagements, the reeling work at the VOC's re-reeling unit suffered. Vernet complained that less *tanny* silk could be sent compared to the previous year's consignment. The quality of work became so bad that a good portion of the silk had to be re-reeled. Thus, the EIC too, contrary to its own proclaimed distaste for their own reelers working from home, actively induced VOC reelers to work from home in a bid to dominate the labor market.

The EIC's efforts to turn reelers away from the VOC re-reeling unit coincided with aggressive efforts to control *pattani* production. In order to improve the quality of raw silk, the EIC obtained from the Nawab in 1758 an order to oblige all silk growers who reeled *pattani* from cocoons "to work only with reels to the same dimensions as those in general use in the neighbourhood of Cossimbazar; to wind off a quantity of silk on each skain sufficient to prevent from separating or being tangled in the carriage from place to place and to tie the knot in the middle, instead of the end, which is the practice with the Laskypoor and other fine putney." They also obliged local *zamīndārs* to enter into bonds with the EIC to ensure that the reelers residing in their territories took proper measures. The *zamīndārs* around the Laskarpur *aurungs* were specially targeted. On February 18, 1758 the EIC reported that the *pattani* silk received from Laskarpur was so loosely wound as to damage filaments. As a remedy they asked *zamīndārs* from Laskarpur to give signed assurances (*mutchlekha*) stating that the reelers in their territories would use only hard *narnis* (wooden reels). Within a month Rani Bhawani, *zamīndār* of the *pargana* of Rajshahi, Narendra Narayan, *zamīndār* of the *pargana* of Tarpoor, and Madan Narayan and Narendra Narayan Chowdhury, *zamīndārs* of the *pargana* of Laskarpur declared in writing, "to cause all the putney made within their several districts to be made conformable to the musters deliver'd by us each skain to contain 24 fingers in circumference weight 1½ tolas the silk to be free from catcher and chattah." The EIC made these stipulations paying close attention to the complaints of the re-reelers who were unhappy with the excessive presence of the *chattahs* (impurities) in *pattani* skeins which resulted in the silk yarn getting entangled.[88] The EIC thus took special care to manage and organize various steps in the production of raw silk.

Even as the EIC tightened its hold over reeling work by quietly taking workers away from the VOC re-reeling unit or obliging *zamīndārs* to sign bonds, they still lacked supervisory power over those who re-reeled *pattani* from home. Work from home dismantled the factory organization that had structured re-reeling work for a century. It not only ended the supervisory role of the company officials but also disrupted the discipline of the workday. The EIC elaborated: "Arising from the knavery of the surdars or the undertakers who have thereby an opportunity of embezzling and changing the silk entrusted to their charge, which it is very old crime they have always been guilty of, and from the advantages they reap thereby encourage the winders to hurry over their work by which carelessness the latter are enabled to earn their livelihood with more ease than those who are better looked after and therefore will always decline taking employ anywhere else."[89] At home reelers could add to their meager earning the scraps of silk they "embezzled." Most importantly, they obtained control over their time—"hurry over their work"—in the absence of the factory supervision. The VOC similarly complained about the reelers: "Our reelers are now working in the night on their silk and so they come to our unit very late and then they work in such an unenthusiastic and roguish way that they break most of the finest threads into pieces and then hide them in the ground and also reel the rest so unequally that many threads which should get the stamp of first letters are getting a stamp of lower letters."[90] Even though catering to both rival companies meant that their workday literally never ceased, the exhausted reelers still designed their own work time and gleaned a few snippets of silk yarn contrary to the monopolistic aims of both the EIC and VOC.

Putting a stop to work from home ultimately became a concern for both companies. On March 30, 1758 the EIC felt the need to open a discussion with important merchants in the region, including the Dutch, to find solutions to this problem. Even while they induced reelers to run away from the VOC silk re-reeling unit, they acknowledged that "their concurrence is absolutely necessary" to find a solution of ending reelers' practice of working at home. They took the initiative to assemble "all the principal merchants, Guzaratters, Multannas, Armenians, Lahores &ca" to discuss "proper measures" to re-induce reelers to work at re-reeling units.[91] The VOC, on the other hand, always suspicious of the EIC's motives, took action on their own to tackle the problem. They made regular inspections of reelers' houses and cleared out any *pattani* they found. From April 1, 1758 they officially started registering silk traffic that passed through Kalikapur and made every transient silk merchant sign a bond stating they would not give any silk to reelers residing in Kalikapur.[92]

The EIC dominated the negotiations among all merchants of Kassimbazar to stop giving *pattani* to reelers at home. On April 6, 1758, the EIC convened a meeting with various silk merchants and drew up an accord with assent of all parties, prohibiting any merchant from delivering *pattani* to the houses of the head reelers or *sirdars*. If any *pattani* was found in the houses of the head reelers it would be immediately confiscated and distributed among all subscribers to the accord. Like all other merchants, the VOC agreed to the terms of the accord. Recall that the VOC previously had signed contracts with the French East India Company and EIC to return their deserting European servants. They did the same for an equitable share of saltpeter procured in the region.[93] But this time Vernet wanted to put the VOC's name as the first name on the contract. The EIC was unwilling to comply and stated outright, "it [Vernet's request] is derogatory to the honor of the company to allow of any precedency and as we knew of no power we had to give up a point which hereafter might be made use to the prejudice of the company." The EIC clearly viewed this contract as not just a negotiation among all merchants, but also a means to proclaim their mercantile and political supremacy. The VOC officials were fully aware of their weakness vis-à-vis the EIC. Vernet wrote to Bisdom in a conciliatory tone, "it is useful to embrace (the contract) and leave the rank to the English. Moreover, in 1736, when the Company was more powerful in this directorate ... we made a contract with other nations, regarding saltpeter we gave the first rank to the French or the English." Beneath the surface of the self-congratulatory note there was an acknowledgement that the days of the VOC power in Bengal were ending.[94] The VOC conceded first place to the EIC, and all merchants signed the contract.

In enforcing the contract, the EIC made clear its edge over the other mercantile interests in commanding the labor of the reelers. As the enforcer of the contract, the EIC gave five days for merchants to collect the *pattani* from the reelers' houses. Not all indigenous merchants signed the contract. The Gujarati merchants were especially concerned with this arrangement as "they had given out putney and advanc'd money to the surdars for the whole year's investment." They asked for at least a month to finish off their business with the head reelers, but the EIC only allowed fifteen days, on the condition that they sign the contract. The Gujarati merchants refused and within five days the EIC confiscated their silk.[95] In all probability these measures led to the decline of the Asian merchants' share of the raw silk trade in Bengal from 1758 onwards well into the 1760s.[96] Vernet best described the full force and consequence of the contract in his letter to Bisdom on June 16, 1758: "five days after signing the contract as the English started to clear houses of head reelers of their *pattani*, when suddenly the English had captured all head and common reelers by force and ... we are necessitated by these circumstances to hide in our factory the reelers who have come to work for us on their own free will."[97] Taking advantage of their position as enforcer, the EIC thus forcibly prevented reelers from working for other employers. The private merchant William Bolts vividly described the EIC's exertion of power: "This last kind of workman [reelers] were pursued with such vigour during Lord Clive's late government in Bengal, from a zeal for increasing the company's investment of raw silk, for it was a common thing for the company's seapoys to be sent by force of arms to break open the houses of Armenian merchants established at Sydabad... and forcibly take the nagaads [reelers] from their work, and carry them away to the English factory."[98] The use of the contract ultimately served only the purpose of the EIC in prohibiting merchants, both European and Asian, from accessing and hence extending their own reach over the labor of the reelers.

High wages too proved critical in this process of expansion. Beginning in February 1758, the EIC had been offering an extra 3 anna per *ceer* to attract runaway reelers from the VOC grounds.[99] When positive incentives failed, they kidnapped reelers from the vicinity of the VOC factory, as they did in June 1758. In July 1758, when the EIC had built a new re-reeling unit on the opposite side of the river Padda, reelers there demanded as high a wage as reelers working on the finest silk at Kassimbazar. Confident of their power to monopolize labor, the EIC only partially obliged. After a lull, wages rose again in early 1759.[100] This strategy of offering higher wages to lure workers continued well into the 1770s.

The EIC achieved its goal of extending control over reelers' labor not only by force or by offering high wages but also by erecting new re-reeling units in different places. In February 1758, in their report to the Fort William council, Kassimbazar officials wrote that the EIC ought to take action at Paddapar, the haven of runaway reelers since the days of Maratha raids. They observed that many intermediary merchants (*paikars*) had set up small re-reeling units there. The EIC was advised either to set up its own re-reeling unit or terminate reeling in that area. On March 26, 1758 the Fort William council ordered the Kassimbazar factory to build an additional re-reeling unit at Paddapar, under supervision of a company servant. A special official, Mr. Marriott, came from Calcutta and was sent on April 30, 1758 to the other side of Padda to seek out a proper place to build a re-reeling unit. By September 16 the EIC was employing six hundred reelers under the supervision of Mr. Marriott at Paddapar. It is significant that the first European experts on Piedmontese filature technology sent by the EIC in 1769 also visited Paddapar to inspect working conditions there. Apart from building their own re-reeling unit, the EIC also brought under their control several re-reeling units via their *gomastahs*, or salaried indigenous agents. These *gomastahs* controlled re-reeling units on behalf of the EIC. By 1759, in Rangpur, far away from the EIC factory at Kassimbazar, a company *gomastah* managed the re-reeling unit. With the change of the *gomastah* in service, supervisory posts too changed hands. In February 1759 when a new company *gomastah*, Nainsook, took up service in Rangpur, the former *gomastah*, Sanatan, had "deliver'd to him all his winders and given him an account of what money had been advanced (to) them."[101] Thus, the EIC by 1759 had extended their silk reeling operations by building multiple re-reeling units and seizing workers from rival merchants.

The VOC's fate is illustrative of the reeling operations of other merchants in the area. They first decried, resisted, and fought the EIC's encroachments upon their reelers, but finally accepted with resignation the EIC's ascendancy over silk production in Bengal. The impressment of reelers presaged armed conflict between the VOC and the EIC. The VOC found that just putting indigenous guards or peons around the houses of reelers was not enough to thwart the mighty armed force of the EIC. By November 1758, reelers willing to work for the VOC resided in their Kalikapur factory. Production suffered significantly. Given this situation, Vernet reported to Hugli: "We are asking the English with politeness, but it is fruitless, and so at last we are going to meet violence with violence."[102] Contracts and acts of self-defense ultimately gave way to the language of violence. It is significant that Vernet made such a comment in November 1758, a year before the battle at Bedara. Vernet's report from December 1758 signaled an unchangeable situation: the VOC could not create favorable conditions for silk production. He puts the war in a broader perspective. The two companies collided violently, not only on the battlefield at Bedara, but in their cutthroat competition to control the laboring bodies of their reelers.[103] In February 1759, seven months before the Battle of Bedara, Vernet reported that the tide had turned against the VOC. The quality of silk reeled had improved but the chronic shortage of reelers remained a major problem. That was the last mention of the silk re-reeling unit in Vernet's letters to Hugli until the end of the war. Six months after the formal end of the Battle of Bedara, in the months of June and July 1760, the VOC faced an acute scarcity of reelers. While able to gather enough reelers to prepare the full order of the *matka* variety of silk, for reeling *adapangia* silk, the VOC could get only fifty reelers, enough to supply only a very small fraction of the order. To prepare the best-quality silk, *pattani*, they found no reelers at all. Meanwhile, the EIC put a notice on the front door of their headquarters in Kassimbazar and made their *goldaars* (announcers with kettle drums) proclaim throughout the area that whoever would reel *pattani* silk for the EIC would get a special "acknowledgement fee."[104]

Desertion irreversibly ruined the VOC's Kassimbazar silk re-reeling unit. Reelers deserted the straw huts of Kalikapur and crossed to the other side of the Ganga in large numbers.[105] Throughout 1758, many reelers secretly worked for the English, precariously serving both companies. By 1760, they decided to migrate away from Kalikapur, abandoning the VOC altogether. Vernet's letter from June 1762 revealed that the entire silk industry around Kassimbazar had collapsed. Famine was one significant factor among many contributing to desertions from the VOC silk industry. From September to November 1762, many peasants, including silk reelers and rearers, died of starvation, and many others, faced with rising food prices, chose to run away, causing the death of most of the silkworms. This ensured the continued downfall of the VOC silk industry. In 1762, Vernet canceled the entire silk order, sent from Amsterdam via Batavia and Hugli.[106] A decade later, in a letter to Governor General Warren Hastings in 1775, the VOC noted the enormous power of the EIC in fixing the price of raw silk. With Warren Hasting's intervention, "an incredible alteration took place in the price of the pattenys from 5 to 9 tolas for the rupee." The VOC could not make any investment in silk in the region without the permission of the EIC's *gomostah*. As for employing reelers, the VOC had "no occasion to carry our attention further than to the late involuntary rise in the *haspelloon* [reeling wages] ... that the company's business might stand still from the desertion of the work people."[107]

In this tremendous whirlwind of events, reelers did not profess their allegiance to any one company, but instead tried to reap benefit from whomever they could while safeguarding their own practices. Even while the VOC provided protection to reelers willing to work for them, Vernet complained that the "rise in price is not only because of the rise in reeling wages as we have written to your honor in our successive letters but also because of the devilish behavior of our reelers to break the fine thread in small pieces and throw them away or hide in the ground."[108] Clearly the reelers siphoned off silk even as they chose to work for the VOC. As is discussed in the preceding section, demanding wages in kind was an old practice of the reelers. In a climate where they felt emboldened to ask for higher wages, they stealthily took away finer thread from the re-reeling unit. Moreover, even when they deserted to the EIC's re-reeling unit or were pressed into service, they resisted any attempt by the EIC to introduce changes in the workday. In 1757, the EIC sent a silk expert from England, James Wilder, to improve reeling methods in Bengal. One of the significant changes he implemented was a method of knotting silk yarn while re-reeling it. At the same time as the VOC reelers were taking away broken bits of fine silk from their re-reeling unit, the EIC tried to introduce Wilder's method. The reaction from the reelers was explosive. The EIC council at Kassimbazar reported: "The method of knotting silk propos'd by Mr. Wilder being introduced by the EWHK into the nacaud connah caus'd a great mutiny and desertion amongst the winders as they were not able to wind off so great a quantity as they formerly could by the great delay caus'd in endeavouring to make the knot proposed by Mr. Wilder."[109] The knot made work days longer and reelers resisted tooth and nail. Wilder suggested that a further raise in the wages would perhaps encourage reelers to warm up to the new technique. Kassimbazar council reluctantly assented. It is questionable to what extent such measures augmented the interests of the company. In faraway Rangpur, the *gomastah* Nainsook had only partial success in implementing the knot. The winders refused to knot A-quality silk, but agreed to knot the B, C, D, and E varieties of silk "upon condition that their present allowance be increas'd 8 annas per maund."[110] Even as the EIC extended its hold on reeling work in Bengal, changing the ways of the reelers proved hard and costly.

The EIC became the supreme force within the mercantile landscape of Bengal following the Plassey Revolution of 1757. Its impact on the silk reeling industry was felt by the years 1759–62 when the EIC accomplished its first step towards fully controlling silk reeling work by precluding competitors, most significantly the VOC, from hiring reelers. In this process, reelers played a key role through desertion. Not all, however, joined the EIC on their own volition—many were impressed. Most remarkably, even when their mobility in this period advanced the EIC's fortunes, the reelers preserved their methods of reeling silk, control over their time, and bargained hard for better wages.

FILATURE AND REELERS

Reelers lost their long-established customs of bargaining for better wages at the very moment factions within the imperial power structure in Bengal and London, after the gaining of Dīwāni rights (1765), debated how to preserve the "ancient constitution" of the newly conquered lands.[111] In his scathing report on the EIC's endeavors in India, Edmund Burke noted that the primary goal of the EIC's investments in the silk industry in Bengal was expansion of raw silk production so as to "render it a field for produce of crude materials subservient to the manufactures of Great Britain." Writing in 1783, he carefully outlined two steps in the company's expansion process. The first was a "perfect plan of policy, both of compulsion and encouragement" to secure a "bounty," or monopoly, over the labor and raw material in the production of raw silk, even at the cost of destruction of silk piece-good manufacture.[112] Indeed, reelers experienced both "compulsion and encouragement" to move to the EIC. However, Burke noted, the results of this first step were paradoxical to the intention of the Court of Directors. In the peculiar colonial setting of EIC rule in Bengal, "investments" were simply "a flow of cash" from revenues into the commercial spending of the EIC. The "encouragement" of raw silk production by means of "investment" from revenues into high wages and tax exemptions for reelers in fact had an adverse effect on revenue collection. Because EIC rule in India after 1765, as part of the "second British Empire," was underpinned by revenue collection, loss of revenue undermined the raison d'être of empire building.[113] The second step in the expansion of raw silk production, according to Burke's observation, was the introduction and spread of Piedmontese filature technology. Alongside the new filatures, the EIC maintained older units of re-reeling for the processing of *pattani* that it continued to buy. Thus the EIC significantly increased its capacity for raw silk production. All previous studies have treated workers (*nacauds*) of re-reeling units as the same as workers of filatures (*cuttanies*). *Nacauds* and *cuttanies* were distinct categories of workers, even though they came from the same neighborhoods.[114] The transition from Burke's step one to two had a profound impact on the reelers. As the number of filatures exploded, reelers in both filatures and re-reeling units lost the high wages they had negotiated in the 1750s and 1760s. Low wages for reelers was the bottom line for the transfer of filature technology in Bengal. In the absence of monetary incentives, the EIC could never bring reeling skills in filatures up to par with their Italian counterparts. Yet, low reeling wages ensured they got full return on their investments. Additionally, by spreading foreign technology, the EIC completely undermined re-reelers' use of mobility as a means to negotiate their conditions of work. The second step of expansion, unlike the first, was independent of the skills of the re-reelers, and hence their mobility practices became inconsequential to the EIC.

In 1769, the EIC's Court of Directors in London made a concerted effort with the EIC administrators in Bengal and silk reeling experts in Europe to introduce filature technology from the Novi region of Piedmont. A number of Italian silk reelers came to Bengal, under the leadership of Giacomo, better known as James Wiss. The first silk superintendents were sent to Boalia, Rangpur, and Paddapar. By the 1770s the first filatures were set up at Kassimbazar, Komarkhali, and Boalia.[115] For the next fifty years the EIC continued to send silk experts from Europe to examine and guide silk filature work in Bengal. Silk experts and EIC officials expected that production would increase in the filatures through removal of the various steps previously involved in the preparation of the silk yarn for European markets. As a Kassimbazar official noted, "filature silk is wound off at one operation from the pod and of any size and letter that may be prescribed," replacing the indigenous method of first reeling cocoons into *pattani* and then again re-reeling them into equal skeins.[116] "By the method of spinning silk with Italian machines," James Wiss pointed out, "two men make as much and better silk in a day than nine men could make of a bad quality by the old Bengal method."[117] In Bengal, filature work never fully replaced the re-reeling work of the *nacauds*. Nonetheless, along with the re-reeling units, filatures expanded massively the EIC's capacity for procuring raw silk in Bengal.

As in the 1750s, the EIC offered good reeling wages well into the late 1760s in order to increase the number of re-reelers/*nacauds* as well as to gather a new workforce of reelers for the filatures. All other strategies from the 1758–62 period, such as cutting out merchants from the market for reelers' labor or the procurement of raw silk, continued into the late 1760s. By then, the Court of Directors at London had decided that there was "no branch for trade which we more ardently wish to extend than that of raw silk." Such encouragement came on the heels of urging "manufacturers of wrought silk to quit that branch and take to winding of raw silk."[118] The 1760s thus saw large-scale involvement of the EIC state in promoting and expanding mulberry and raw silk cultivation. During this period, the collector of Midnapore, George Vansittart, brought ever more land under mulberry cultivation. Ancillary to the encouragement for mulberry and silkworm cultivation was also the plan to completely stop the EIC's investments in silk piece goods. From being a silk thread and textile-producing region, Bengal soon became merely a supplier of raw material to the British silk industry. In order to "induce the manufacturers of wrought silk to quit that branch and take to winding silk" and also to increase production of raw silk thread, the EIC increased the wages for silk reeling.[119]

Wage benefits also came in the form of revenue exemptions. This was a particularly enticing incentive for a peasant population either uninitiated in the art of reeling or used to reeling only as a part-time work to take up full time reeling. As the commercial resident of Rangpur, Edward Smith, the EIC official managing commercial activities, remarked in 1778, the exemption of *zamīndārī* levies on reelers' land was a "strong inducement for them (the reelers) to continue in the company's employ and remain in the pergunnahs." Such a privilege led to the swift proliferation of reelers, which was necessary, especially for the new filature technology. The number of reelers in one *pargana* of Rangpur alone rose to two thousand. In one village of this *pargana*, the number of reeler households rose from 17 out of 308 in 1768, to the entire village by 1777.[120] Up until the late 1760s, wages went up, leading to the expansion of raw silk production.

But with the implementation of filature technology, the wages of reelers/winders soon went back down, never exceeding the wages of unskilled day laborers. Diffusion of filature technology depended not only on the EIC but also on private merchants, both indigenous and European, linked to the EIC's trade. As Gautam Bhadra observes, "The pace of diffusion of filatures was linked with private trade, European and indigenous, in silk." The primary customer of privately owned filatures was the EIC and hence their mutual dependence played a crucial role in the diffusion of filatures. High-level European servants down to indigenous salaried agents, *gomastahs*, made investments in filatures of various sizes. The pace of filature expansion was occasionally thwarted by conflicts between the private merchants and the company, the reluctance of silk rearers to sell cocoons to filatures at a loss, and the company's efforts to stop overproduction of filature-made silk. Nonetheless, by 1831 in the Kassimbazar region alone there were over seventy privately owned filatures. The biggest paradox of the spread of filature technology was the inability of Bengali reelers to produce silk yarn comparable to the quality of Italian silk yarn. Karolina Hutkova explains this paradox in two ways—first, the reluctance of the EIC in improving the wages of the reelers and second, the mismanagement by the lower-level company officials in supervisory roles. Hutkova argues that the premise for the transfer of Piedmontese technique to Bengal was the assumption that Bengal was a low-wage region and hence, transfer of technology could be achieved on the backs of the reelers' cheap labor.[121] The EIC did not feel the need to give higher wages for reelers to adopt the new technology. Cheap labor guaranteed full return on their investments, regardless of silk quality. Low wages for filature reelers meant even lower wages for the reelers of the re-reeling units. With the introduction of the filatures the EIC thus reversed their older practice of monopolizing reelers' labor through high wages, once and for all.

The experience of wage reduction was seismic for both the reelers and the company, as a series of violent events from the Rangpur district between 1773 and 1778 reveals. These events were reminiscent of the "counterterror" organized by London silk weavers in defense of their wages and customary practices in the 1760s and 1770s.[122] In 1769, the commercial Resident of the silk factory at Rangpur, Mr. Wright, ordered the collector of revenues, Madan Gopal, to stop the *zamīndārs* in the region from exacting *abwabs* (levies) from the silk reelers. The government had never explicitly endorsed this exemption to the silk reelers, including both the *nacauds* (re-reelers) and the *cuttanies* (reelers at filatures). Nonetheless, over time, both the EIC authorities and the reelers came to consider the exemption as an "indulgence." The reelers further claimed that they enjoyed the exemption from "the first establishment of the factory." Whenever forced to pay their levies they "took protection of the factory." In other words, whenever the power of the collector was used to oblige them to pay the *zamīndārs*, they ran to the factory under "the express declaration that if they had not the protection they sought by coming into the nacaud connah, they would leave it." Indeed, reelers in their petition to the factory in April 1778 threatened that a re-imposition of the levies would lead them to "be drawn to the necessity of quitting their places of abode and employment at the factory." The Council of Revenue resented this privilege accorded to the reelers and clearly stated that "should any additional indulgence be absolutely necessary it will more properly become a charge of the factory than a diminution of revenue." In 1775, when the *zamīndārs* sent "people to demand the payment of our rents from the brothers and relations of *nacauds*, they collect 10 or 12 together and beat those we send." As a response, the collector published a public notice stating that all reelers had to pay their land revenue just like other peasants, who had no benefit of exemption. Three days after the publication a *zamīndār* in the *pargana* of Coondy sent two of his men to collect the fresh tax burdens from the reelers. These men put a few of the relations of the reelers, who were unable to pay the taxes, under confinement. In the middle of the night, they earned the wrath of the detained reelers, who broke out of their confinement, severely beat up the two *zamīndār*'s men, and then took shelter in the silk factory. The collector intervened and arrested only seven of the accused. Soon, the commercial resident protested "how extremely prejudicial to the company's investment this would prove, if the *zamīndārs* were permitted to lay hold of the factory people." Until 1776, the reelers would play off the interests of the silk industry against the interests of the revenue collection machinery of the EIC state, attempting to secure their "privilege." But following the incident at Coondy, the collector of Rangpur negotiated fruitfully between these two branches of the company. He released all the abused members of the reeler community on a written condition that the commercial resident of the silk factory would collect the extra taxes from the reelers in the factory for the year 1777. In the meantime, he also requested the governor general to resolve the matter. In consultation with the Board of Trade the governor general, Warren Hastings, came to the decision that "you [the collector] will proclaim the abolition of the exemption hitherto allowed to the *nacauds* from the beginning of the present year and authorize the *zamīndārs* to lay the same rents from them as they are permitted to receive from the other *ryots* [peasants], but as the faith of government has been either expressly or virtually pledged for their former exemption, we direct that no demands be made upon the *nacauds* for arrears of the exempted taxes." This declaration marked the end to an EIC–silk reeler relationship based on "privileges" or "encouragement." No longer did the EIC feel the need to protect its reelers with better wages or exemptions.[123]

The events resolved the contradictory demands of revenue collection and the promotion of trade and industry that Burke had pointed out, to the detriment of the reelers. Revenue exemptions were necessary "encouragement" at a time when the EIC needed to monopolize the labor of reelers for the expansion of silk production. "Indulgence" of Rangpur reelers was not an exception as reelers in Berhampore in Murshidabad and Dinajepur received similar privileges. Between 1765 and 1780, both these places witnessed disputes between the commercial and revenue branch, very similar to the incidents in Rangpur. Though the governor general formulated different solutions for each case, all decisions curbed the special privileges of the reelers.[124] The demands of revenue collection did not permit for such allowances. Reelers in all places struck work. Reelers' protests in these years were mostly a losing battle. They were especially in a vulnerable position as rent payers after the devastating famine of 1770. In an atmosphere of extreme penury, and frequent outbreaks of the Sanyasi rebellion in Rangpur, the reelers in the *pargana* of Coondy retaliated against the armies of the *zamīndār*. These were also trying times for many *zamīndārs*. who found themselves at default in collecting revenues. In Rangpur, many were personally indebted to an EIC officer, Captain Mckenzie. Since the 1770s many *zamīndārs* had faced loss of income when the EIC abolished their levies, especially the ones which ate away at the EIC's revenue share.[125] When it came to levies on reelers' lands, the EIC state deemed it more expedient to increase the income of their revenue-collecting intermediaries than to provide protection to its reelers. Thus, in this situation of acute distress the EIC now decided such disputes in favor of the *zamīndār*, not the reeler.[126]

The settlements were uneasy because manufacturers including reelers did not suffer revenue burdens silently. In 1783, Rangpur and Dinajepur became the focal point of a large-scale rebellion against the EIC's revenue collection machinery. While the primary target was the EIC's contracted revenue farmer, Devi Singh, many *zamīndārs* too bore the brunt of the peasants' ire. Since manufacturers were the hardest hit with the increasing revenue burden, it was quite likely that the reelers participated in the rebellion. A few years after the rebellion was crushed the EIC issued a fresh regulation on July 19, 1786 which stipulated that manufacturers in EIC service such as weavers and reelers were to pay only the rent "specified in their pottahs ... according to the stated established dues of government" and that "they shall be subjected to no arbitrary occasional tax of zemindars, farmers or collectors." Notwithstanding these safeguards subsequent records remain silent on any further demands of reelers for "indulgences" of revenue exemption or the EIC state's active role in protecting the reelers from excessive taxation. If judged from the condition of the reelers, the EIC state clearly decided to sacrifice their manufacturers to their revenue-collecting interests. By 1778 the collector of Rangpur himself had noted that "a good workman in the nacaud connah cannot earn half a rupee a month." In the 1790s the commercial resident of the same district saw no signs of reversal in this trend.[127]

Along with foreign technology, lowered wages, and the end of tax exemptions came the greater division of labor and more extreme supervision. The three-tiered hierarchical worker-supervisor relationship in the VOC re-reeling unit continued in the re-reeling units where the *nacauds* worked. In some cases, as in the Kumarkhali factory, the commercial resident asked for extra superintendents (*jogandars*) to monitor the master reeler (*sirdar*), the head reeler (*tageedar*), and the reelers. In the newly formed filatures, children too worked as apprentices to the reelers. The most important supervisory role in the filatures went to the EIC's paid agent or the *gomastahs*. One appreciative note specifies that the *gomastah* "would stay throughout entire days watching, guiding and instructing the winders."[128] From James Wiss onwards, the silk experts that the EIC sent out from London were not happy with the level of superintendence.[129] In 1824, John Wilkinson, another silk expert from London, also specified that supervision should be kept in the hands of Europeans, who had superior knowledge of the European market for silk thread.[130] Comparing the level of superintendence in Italian filatures to that of the EIC-controlled factories in Bengal, another silk expert despaired, "the superintendence, so close and so attentive ... I apprehend, never can be obtained under the agency of a large company." The experts thus desired far more supervision than had been achieved, for the further regimentation of work. In some cases, the EIC succeeded in employing European supervisors, as in the Bauleah filature in the 1790s. The commercial resident of the factory noted that the supervisor was particularly oppressive towards the reelers. Although he was "apt to be lazy," never reaching the filature on time, he "obliged the *cuttanies* to purchase cloths of him at an advanced rate." The reelers paid him through deductions in their wages.[131] Supervisors were thus necessary to intensify work at the filature and with the power that they exercised over the reelers, they instituted personalized, highly exploitative relationships.

Low-paid reelers engaged in re-reeling work continued their "devilish" practices of "making away" with silk waste. In 1791, the commercial resident at Rangpur advocated a slight rise in the wages of the *nacauds*, who earned less than a rupee per month (12 annas 3 pice). He added even after his recommended raise in their wages (to 1 rupee 6 pice), that the *nacauds* will still earn "less than the lowest class of daily labourers ... even boys and women." He believed the slight raise would "prevent their stealing the silk to make themselves amends for the low price paid for their labor." Stealing was not only a problem in the Rangpur factory. The commercial resident of Rampur Boalia in 1775 complained of the frequent loss of silk to the *nacauds*. The sloppy knot of the *pattani* towards the end of the skein enabled *nacauds* "to destroy and make away with the putney, which affects gross produce and enhances the price of the silk." Even though the Board of Trade assented to the suggestion of the Rangpur commercial resident, in 1799, the master reelers in the Rangpur factory petitioned the board to complain that they had not received any raise. The next year a master reeler with eight *nacauds* committed what the commercial resident called "a most daring robbery." In the middle of the night one of the reelers was caught red-handed in the re-reeling unit with three bags of silk. After interrogation the guards of the re-reeling unit hunted down his accomplices and handed them over to the magistrate. As wages dipped, reelers relied on "many petty thefts" as well as the occasional "robberies of a grand scale."[132]

Reelers at filatures received only slightly better wages. With the expansion of filature technology to places where there was no prior existence of the silk industry, the EIC had to convert sections of a peasant population into reelers. As the commercial resident at Rangomally factory reported: "For as many people they were collected from the Hoe but not without some compulsions on my part and more reluctance on theirs. When set to basons, there is little difference between the best and the worst spinners for some days, their fingers hardened by manual labour, are totally unsusceptible to the touch of a fine thread. It requires certain time to exercise them and once their hands and eyes get settled in the manner most filature set to work on grand harvest." Poor wages prevented the emergence of filature reeling as a specialized occupation. Even as late as 1818, the filature reeler made a living simultaneously "by working at the indigo factory, by engaging as a dandy in different boats, and working as colleys, their hands get so much out as to . . . quickness in catching the thread of the cocoons, that if the turner winds quick he does not join the end as he ought." Sometimes reelers used their "carelessness" and apparent lack of hand skill to their advantage. John Wilkinson, the silk expert from London, when asked by the Select Committee of the Parliament whether reelers break the thread because of their "carelessness," noted "no it is their plan; they will not be beaten out of it." The purpose of the reelers' habit of cleaning the silk while it was on the reel, which caused the silk yarn to break, Wilkinson explained was to "pull off what they (reelers) call a gout."[133] The "gout" was the reeler's small gain above his abysmal pay. Apart from immiserated reelers collecting silk waste, or "gout," little remained the same in silk reeling work for European companies a hundred and fifty years after the establishment of the VOC silk re-reeling unit.

Reeling work, independent from peasant production, was the earliest form of work that resembled capitalist wage relations. It was born entirely out of the needs of the overland and overseas trade and was propped up through a nexus of foreign and indigenous merchants. Even though workers were thoroughly immiserated, often having no more than their labor as a resource, their skills were important for the global market. The European East India companies, especially the VOC, tried to expand raw silk production in Asia, but failed because they were reliant upon the skills of these silk reelers and had no means to establish monopolistic control over them. The EIC achieved this end between 1758 and 1762. Through use of force, they removed various competitors from the labor market of reelers, thus cornering them for their grand plans of expanding raw silk production in Bengal. This process also saw the demise of the VOC re-reeling unit.

Reelers' mobility played an important role in the EIC's triumphal transforming of raw silk production in the region. For almost a century, both the VOC and EIC had failed to move reelers on the terms the companies desired. Reelers' reluctance to move prevented the VOC from extending their raw production in Asia. In the critical years of 1758 to 1762, reelers used their practice of desertion to join the EIC's camp, but only for a better wage and terms of employment and work that they primarily decided for themselves. In monopolizing their labor and consolidating Bengal as a raw silk-producing region, feeding the needs of the British silk industry, the EIC offered them lucrative wages until 1760s. However, with the introduction of the Piedmontese filature technology, mobility of reelers became inconsequential for the EIC's expansion. Even though re-reeling work in older style units continued, the EIC now completely depended upon an imported technology for the expansion of raw silk production. Since the basic assumption that undergirded the transfer of this technology was the low wages of the reelers, wages collapsed beyond recovery. This new technology proved the truth of what Andrew Ure, the Scottish propagandist of the factory system, later described: "when capital enlists science in her service, the refractory hand of labor will always be taught docility."[134] Even as the EIC taught the legs of the reelers a harsh lesson, their hands were not fully tamed. Well into the late 1700s the reelers, struggling under abysmal wages, took from the re-reeling units and filatures the fragments of silk they claimed as their own.

FIVE

"Prisoner" of the Magistrate

BOATMEN, EUROPEAN SAILORS, AND THE
COLONIAL POLICE, 1790–1817

BOATMEN AS WELL AS EUROPEAN SAILORS and soldiers experienced the EIC state from the 1790s as a surveillance machinery which clamped down on their mobility in order to create disciplined workers for state service. Their lot was slightly different from the lot of the silk reelers, who experienced the advent of the colonial state through a restructuring of the reeling industry which forcefully devalued their work. There has been a long-standing debate about when precisely the EIC founded a colonial state in India, divorced from its earlier conception of sovereignty, while also removed from the Mughal political system.[1] Structurally the EIC state underwent massive transformations after 1757. Apart from gaining the Mughal imperial office of Dīwāni, the EIC state successfully routed all its European competitors. Even as the EIC state fashioned itself as the preserver of the "Mughal constitution," in 1773 the EIC state in Bengal was brought for the first time under the metropolitan supervision of the English Parliament. Bengal thus became, albeit indirectly, the colonial possession of Britain. Between 1793 and 1820, boatmen and European sailors and soldiers experienced the EIC state as a new form of state power, which unlike the Mughal and Nawabi states, was much less unconstrained by the local power of the *zamīndārs*. Crucial to this new colonial state power was a centralized civilian surveillance system under the police magistrate, which intervened in the local labor market by forcefully recruiting workers, ascertaining their wages, monitoring their movements, and apprehending them when they absconded. In doing so, by the early 1800s the police emerged as the most efficient labor market manager of the EIC state. This success was in stark contrast to the failure of the EIC state in mitigating frequent depredations in the countryside or protecting their peasants from the excesses of the *zamīndārs*.[2]

Existing scholarship emphasizes the violence perpetrated by the EIC army and the failure of the police to maintain law and order; yet for boatmen, European sailors, and even for European soldiers, it was the police themselves who formed the most formidable and hence the most violent face of labor discipline. Such a major oversight by scholars is a result of their accepting state regulations as the beginnings of new labor relations. Thus, following the 1806 Regulation XI, Nitin Sinha concludes that the EIC state assigned the police the task of recruitment to mitigate the violence perpetrated by the army's interactions with boatmen.[3] Such an argument is neither aware of the many years of violent recruitment of boatmen by the police prior to 1806 nor of the years of official discussions around the topic of recruitment methods by the army prior to the drafting of the regulation wherein the police were granted the sole right to deploy violent means. Through police intervention in their everyday lives, boatmen became "public labor" of the colonial state. Police power, propped by a number of draconian regulations, eroded the negotiating power of these workers and restricted their mobility, including criminalization of desertion. In controlling desertion of European sailors, soldiers, and boatmen, the EIC state finally realized what the Mughal and Nawabi states had only hoped for—resolution to the tension between the controlled and uncontrolled mobility of their subjects. This achievement was predicated on what I call the EIC state's despotic control over workers' labor power.

The EIC state's despotic control over labor in the early 1800s was distinguishable from the Mughal, Nawabi, and *zamīndāri* control over labor. Though no stranger to the use of contracts in hiring workers, the Mughal and Nawabi states lacked the legal framework to coerce their hired workers. Despite its frequent laments on the use of coercion, the EIC state, on the other hand, created several legal provisions for coercive control over the labor power of its workers through contracts, centralized police force, and regulations. The autocratic power of the early EIC state is a much discussed subject.[4] Recent scholarship shows that even European Enlightenment intellectuals and philosophers criticized the EIC's unbridled extractive rule by monopoly capital.[5] In discussing the EIC state's criminal justice system, Radhika Singha argues that the company state was founded on a British notion of "indivisible sovereignty" and articulated this sovereign right of the state by legally establishing violence as the sole prerogative of the state. Singha borrows Thomas Babington Macaulay's term for identifying the early colonial state—"paternal despotism"—in characterizing the standardized colonial procedures of policing and prosecution which significantly narrowed the possibilities of local elites to utilize their power. In effect, the sovereignty of the colonial state expressed in terms of a centralized legal system removed the problem of fragmented or contested jurisdiction of the precolonial period.[6] In a similar vein, through the utilization of a centralized police force and harsh regulations, the EIC state subsumed the power of the *zamīndārs* and established exclusive control over the labor power of boatmen and European sailors and soldiers. In this sense, this chapter offers a mild rectification of Ranajit Guha's claim on the nature of transition in forced labor under colonial rule, that "what had been a matter of custom . . . acquired a sort of statutory dignity under the raj."[7] The colonial state not only removed older "customs" of state-worker relationship but also *innovated and introduced* for the first time in the region their power over workers as a complete control over their life, liberty, and labor power.

Contracts and the new police force were the touchstone of this despotic control over labor. As the 1670 contract between the master silk reeler and the VOC discussed in chapter 4 demonstrates, the European companies had struggled with only limited success to introduce and enforce formal contractual relationships as the basis of organization and discipline in work places. The EIC state's simultaneous use of centralized police power and laws modeled after the Master and Servant Act strengthened their implementation of contracts as never before. Douglas Hay and Paul Craven show that employment laws modeled after the several English Master and Servant laws proliferated globally after the 1780s and well into the nineteenth century.[8] The basic thrust of such laws in nineteenth-century colonial India was to create relationships of extreme hierarchy between workers and employers, with active intervention of the state under the guise of protecting the "sanctity of contractual relations."[9] But, in order for the colonial state to institute private employers' unbridled power over workers' labor, it had first to establish the state-as-employer's control over labor through vigorous criminalization of breach of contract propped up by a centralized police force. Legalistic contractual relationships made both boatmen and European sailors and soldiers "waged" workers—the Latin root of *wage* (*wadium*) means pledge or contract. In effect, workers pledged to suspend their power to decide conditions of work including time, hire, customary payment, and mobility to state control.

The EIC state disciplined European sailors and soldiers even as they emerged as "white" racialized subjects, privileged by the colonial justice system. The emergence of a racialized order which put the Europeans at the topmost rung of social hierarchy did not mean that the EIC state was lax in imposing work-place discipline upon on its white working class. Only in the aftermath of the rebellion of 1857 and the extension of manhood suffrage in 1867 in Britain did the British colonial state in India feel the urgency of hardening racial distinctions between the European rank and file and the natives. Until then the EIC state inflicted harsh disciplinary measures on its European workforce, sometimes harsher than the punishment meted out to their native workforce.[10] The experiences of low-ranking European sailors and soldiers described in this chapter are thus juxtaposed with the experiences of native boatmen. Just like the boatmen, these European workers could no longer use flight to negotiate their conditions of work, for the EIC state circumvented their movements through the use of draconian regulations backed by a strong, centralized law-enforcement machinery.

BOATMEN, "PUBLIC SERVICE," AND THE COLONIAL POLICE

As the boatmen's service for the state became increasingly vital, the EIC state machinery, particularly the police, intruded further and further into the lives of boatmen. By the late eighteenth century, the English Parliament, following decades of debates, bolstered the political power of the EIC state but slowly eroded its commercial monopoly. By 1813, except for the EIC branch involved in the China trade, trade in India was opened up to private traders from Britain.[11] In this changed scenario, the EIC required boats not just for trading purposes, but also for the transport of the military and the establishment of civil administration. Boatmen, henceforth, were engaged in maintaining the infrastructure—or in the words of the EIC state, "public works"—of the state. Recent research on transport and communication networks in early colonial Bengal shows that the colonial state's involvement in maintaining and improving communication lines predates the coming of railways by at least half a century.[12] Riverine communication work not only involved the movement of military personnel but also the maintenance of police stations and the functioning of public ferries.[13] As the colonial state spread its tentacles to the remotest parts of the region in the name of "public works," it had a profound impact on the lives of boatmen. With the growing number of police outposts and guard boats, boatmen entered public service on a full-time basis. They were at the constant beck and call of state officials to deliver a wide range of services from paying bribes to fulfilling job duties. Boatmen experienced the presence of colonial police in their immediate neighborhoods as a source of extreme terror. Both as fulltime workers whose livelihood solely depended on coerced public service, and as workers who were conscripted for public service against their will, the boatmen's position became extremely vulnerable. Although they remained mobile, they increasingly lost control over their mobility practices to the colonial state.

After 1765, the EIC state, as well as private individuals associated with the EIC state, phenomenally increased their access to various inland transport routes within Bengal and between Bengal and other provinces and states in the subcontinent. The EIC gained access to land routes, which meant a reduction in the frequency of fleet movements during the year. Consequently, the military employed fewer boats.[14] The labor of the military fleet, as is described in chapter 2, remained more or less the same.[15] Nonetheless, communication work as part of "public service," or the groundwork for the EIC state's military endeavors, metamorphosed into a much larger sector in the late eighteenth century. Public ferries, for instance, became an integral part of the transport sector, and were used primarily by the native populations. The military board maintained quite a few of these public ferries, out of concern for control over the manpower supply, especially boats and boatmen, and to protect the movement of their fleets.

The military received continuous assistance from a newly created police system in controlling and maintaining communication networks, including riverine communication. On December 7. 1792, Governor General Cornwallis created a new centralized police force for the EIC state with a magistrate at the helm of police forces in each district of the provinces of Bengal, Bihar, and Orissa.[16] Scholars argue that "public works" from the 1820s were no longer maintained by the military board, but by civil authorities—headed by magistrates alongside the collectors—thereby giving colonial economic extraction an ever so slightly benevolent face and assuaging a native constituency in favor of the state.[17] But, as records indicate, long before the 1820s the colonial state reckoned with the importance of civil administration in maintaining infrastructure, especially in sectors where civilian use was common. In the eighteenth century, either private individuals or the EIC's military maintained the ferries, embankments, and roads. From the beginning of the new century, in a bid to defray costs, the Military Board expected the police administration to take charge of many public ferries. For instance, in June 1806, the magistrate of Patna started a ferry service at Futwah with four boats.[18] In a discussion about how to cut costs in 1809, the military's quartermaster general mentioned that the boat establishment at Agra had been transferred to the local magistrate.[19] A year earlier, the assistant secretary of the Military Board suggested that the costs for repairing pier heads and roads leading to embankments at Agra should be transferred to the accounts of the Civil Department, either to the magistrate or the collector. The secretary of the Military Board accordingly asked the Judicial Department to issue orders to the magistrate of Agra to take over the repairing responsibilities and charges.[20]

Long before the civil administration formally took control over the public ferries, the magistrates held responsibility for several aspects of their operation, especially in regulating boats and boatmen. The primary motive behind such attention was surveillance. "Boats may with the spying glass be observed and ascertained," wrote one magistrate.[21] Magistrates took the lead in designing the legal contours of work discipline along the riverine transport system. For example, they strictly managed the size of boats. Regulation XXII of 1793 prohibited the manufacture of boats of a certain measurement without the prior permission from the magistrate. The goal was to limit the number of boats which could be used for robbery. Violation of the rule entailed confiscation of the boats and imprisonment of the carpenters and workmen of such boats.[22] Magistrates of different districts coordinated among themselves in the verification and confiscation of unpermitted boats, as well as arrest of the builders.[23] Accidents at ferries were common, and the magistrates used them as occasions to tighten their grips over the movement of boats. Following an accident, the magistrate of Hooghly in 1795 issued a regulative order for inspecting boats and monitoring the number of passengers and weight of goods on boats at Sulkia, Hooghly, and Ulubarya.[24] For similar ends the magistrate of the district of twenty-four *parganas* deployed guards under the supervision of Mr. Cooper, who monitored the conditions of boats, the number of oarsmen employed on each boat, the number of passengers, and, finally, made sure all the boats at the ferry cooperated with each other.[25] In fact, certain magistrates recommended that control over ferries should be completely handed over to the police force—the administrative arm of the EIC state most capable in "the guidance and observance of the manjees [*majhis*], and registry of their boats."[26] The EIC state added this suggestion to Regulation XIX of 1816.[27] According to this regulation, public ferries came under the jurisdictions of magistrates, who could determine the ferry's toll rates as well as the number and descriptions of boats being operating.. This power of the magistrate was reiterated in the Regulation VI of 1819.[28] Thus, the surveillance power of the police over the movement of boats had been intensifying since the 1790s.

The EIC police steadily increased their use of boats throughout Bengal. Magistrates divided districts into police jurisdictions of an area of 10 square kos (or 900 square kilometers). Each police jurisdiction would have one police station headed by a *darogah* (principal native supervisor), assisted by a *jamadar* and *bakshy*, and in some cases a *naik* presiding over an armed corps of *burkandazes*. In Bengal alone, by the 1820s, there were over 253 police stations (*thanas*). A number of these police stations, which were sited along the banks of rivers, possessed guard boats. Oftentimes, a *jamadar* along with a few *burkandazes* were posted on these guard boats. Government spies, or *girdwars*, who received a bounty on successfully leading police to a robber's hot trail, also used guard boats.[29] Guard boats were not always anchored adjacent to the *thanas*. They were also used in patrolling public ferries used daily by hundreds, and sometimes thousands, of civilians. Until 1801, three guard boats patrolled twelve public ferries in the city of Dhaka. Other than patrol work, police boats performed a range of law-keeping activities. Magistrates maintained government boats to escort witnesses from the interior of districts.[30] Police even used boats as floating jails. In July 1820, the Rangpur magistrate decided that a large boat was a sturdier option than a makeshift jail for thirty detainees. Inmates were primarily accused people who had been brought from various parts of the district for examination.[31] Police boats were special vessels built with copper bottoms, and usually Europeans received the contracts for building them. With their flashy, heavy metallic bottoms, the police boats became notorious fixtures on the rivers, from Calcutta to the interior districts of Bengal and Bihar.

The use of guard boats required the hire of a large number of boatmen, who were waged workers with precarious links to their work places and generally without the security of long-term sustenance. As government property, guard boats of the police station did not belong to the boatmen working on them. Police establishments hired these boatmen either seasonally or on a permanent basis but terms of employment varied widely. The *majhi* Unwar's petitions to the Nizamat Adalat (superior criminal court) provide a narrow window to this world of precarity. Unwar migrated from his homeland, Sylhet, to Rajmahal to work as a guard boatman at the Rajmahal police station. He was already working as a boatman in Calcutta when he came in contact with John Tombelle, the future magistrate of Bhagalpur. On a colleague's recommendation, Tombelle hired Unwar as the head *majhi* of the two boats that took Tombelle, his belongings, and his family to Bhagalpur. Pleased by his service, Tombelle appointed Unwar as the *majhi* of a guard boat at Rajmahal police station. He offered Unwar a monthly wage of 5 rupees and specifically assured him that he should "possess this employ for life." Unwar, happy with this settlement, brought his entire family from Sylhet to Rajmahal. As is shown in chapter 1, migration of peasants and artisans to new villages or *zamīndāris* was very common within the social context of the indigenous state. However, unlike in Unwar's case, such moves bore the additional security of a plot of land for settlement, known as *mirasi*. Even the menial castes, who rarely had rights over agricultural lands, sometimes got a small plot of land where they lived. In Rupram's *Dharmamaṅgal*, Kālu Dom had a hovel by a pond on the outskirts of the village, which was his hereditary allotment (*mirās*).[32] Unwar's only security was the good will of Tombelle but that had no effect on Tombelle's successor, William Armstrong. When Armstrong came to office a fire destroyed the Rajmahal police station. For three weeks, Unwar worked tirelessly alongside other boatmen and several hired workers to get the station back on its feet, under the supervision of the *darogah*, Abdullah Khan. A few days later, without giving any reason, Abdullah Khan dismissed Unwar and ten other boatmen.[33] In the same year that Unwar faced his ordeal, Thomas Hayes, the magistrate of Hugli, discharged two *majhis* who had been employed during his predecessor's time, on the ground that the boats they served on were too decayed. The *majhis* were not blamed for the condition of the boats, yet overnight they lost their means of livelihood.[34]

Unwar's precarious migration was a radical departure from the older mobility practices in general and particularly of boatmen in the region. Unlike the prevalent practice among various state entities, especially the *zamīndārs* in Bengal (including the EIC), whereby the state induced mobility of artisans and workers in exchange for providing them with the certainty of land settlement, the police force of the EIC state, in the early 1800s, did not provide any security to its migrant labor. In addition, Unwar's migration did not follow the long-standing circulatory practices of boatmen in the region, distinguishing upcountry boatmen from deltaic boatmen, which had shaped the labor market for both the VOC and EIC in the early eighteenth century. Such practices were resilient. Even in 1766, military officers complained to Fort William that "every black fellow has his peculiar province beyond which he cannot serve." Yet, Unwar had broken these old "provincial" habits when he and his family made a "journey from the native to a strange country" for a waged position, which he ultimately lost. His multiple petitions bear evidence to the desperation of joblessness that this migration outside the older circuits of boatmen's movement had brought.[35]

RECRUITING UNDER THE COLONIAL STATE

The colonial state, as understood from the vantagepoint of workers, was a set of symbiotic relationships among the *darogah*, the magistrate, and the military board. Historians have long focused on the fissures within the ruling class to expose the vulnerability of the early colonial state. In the history of crime and the colonial state, the *darogah* has been depicted as a local despot, often eschewing the control of the magistrate,[36] which was an embarrassment for the colonial state, ultimately resulting in the futility of enforcing English law.[37] Such scholarship sees the failure of colonial legal and police reforms along two axes—first, in spite of the erosion of the semi-sovereign power of the *zamīndārs* in Bengal, the colonial state seldom checked the oppressions of the *zamīndārī* retainers against their peasants, and second *darogahs* took over the mantle of mini-despots in the countryside and, in fact, often were in cahoots with the now-weakened *zamīndārs*, engaging together in various illegal activities. The upper-level colonial officials or judicial branches had to step in from time to time to shorten the leashes on the *darogahs*. Dismissal of *darogahs* remained common throughout the nineteenth century. Yet, it did not mitigate the terror they inflicted on the inhabitants under their jurisdictions.[38] More importantly, dismissal did not necessarily reveal a dysfunctional relationship between the magistrate and the *darogah*. Magistrate-*darogah* networks of cooperation becomes clear in the EIC state's intensified efforts to discipline work of various kinds in the early 1800s. This cooperative relationship was not always necessarily smooth, and only from the early nineteenth century do examples of the *thana*-magistrate coordination in recruitment appear.[39] Nevertheless, the expanded capacity of the colonial state to extract labor from the native population depended upon the police force to a very large extent. In this sense, to argue that the police system was "inefficient" would be wrong. The thin effort of the centralized state in preventing frequent damage of life and property for rural subjects demonstrates "inefficiency" or the reluctant and limited reach of the state, but the steady supply of a workforce for public service indicates quite the opposite. Moreover, by concentrating on boatmen, one can see the synergy between the military board and the magistrate-*darogah* nexus. While fissures existed and sometimes expanded within and between different bureaucracies, leading to major transformations in the nature of EIC rule, the early "garrison state" depended upon its civilian police for a steady and cheap supply of manpower.[40]

The recruitment procedures for the EIC's fleet underwent significant changes from the 1770s with experiments in recruitment by private agencies, *ghat majhis*, and the police in quick succession. In the early 1770s the EIC maintained a large number of boats as fixed establishments, besides hiring new crew from time to time. This resulted in the EIC state spending the exorbitant amount of 567,190 rupees in 1772. The following year, the EIC state reduced drastically its boat establishment to thirty-seven boats, reserved for official purposes. Henceforth, hiring boats each year especially for the transport of the military became an imperative, as had been the norm in the early eighteenth century. Evidence from the 1770s and 1780s suggest that European middlemen and agencies were new entrants into the business of recruiting boatmen. Between 1772 and 1774, the Military Board depended on "Messrs Share and Dellial" for recruitment of boatmen.[41] The Military Board discontinued this partnership and in 1774 signed a contract with Mr. Fraser, stating that he would provide the EIC fleet with 116 boats and their crews. Again in 1809 Archibald Murphy contracted boats, *majhis*, and *dandies* for the military from Allahabad to Agra.[42] European contractors thus creep up sporadically as boat recruiters for the military. The Military Board was also dependent on the *ghat majhi* for recruitment.

Assessment of *ghat majhis* as important recruitment agents begs for two important caveats so far completely unnoticed in existing literature—first, their role in the transportation sector far exceeded recruitment and second, the EIC state so designed their role as recruiters that they were heavily dependent on other EIC officials. As chapter 2 shows, by the 1740s, *ghat majhis* regularly recruited boats for the EIC in Calcutta. By the late 1700s the *ghat majhis* were also de facto superintendents of *ghats* (ferry points) not only in Calcutta but also in the districts. Wherever the ferries came under the purview of the Military Board or the magistrates of the concerned district, the *ghat majhi* was an entrepreneur working directly for the colonial state. Magistrates always complained of the "mercenary motives" of the *ghat majhis*—who made a huge profit from collections, while paying the government a pittance.[43] Some suggested a complete abolition of the post,[44] while others wanted them to become full-time government servants with fixed income.[45] However, all agreed on the important position held by the *ghat majhis*, especially in prominent places, because of their proximity to other *dandies* and *majhis*. In certain places, as in Hugli, the *ghat majhi* was the only "communication with the collector's department, in preparing the ferries for the troops and other contingencies."[46] At ferries under the control of the Military Board, the *ghat majhis* were obliged to provide the army with men and boats free of charge. The *ghat majhi* at Falta handed a bill of charges for the boats he recruited for Lieutenant Weston, who was passing through the region. His request was turned down on grounds that "it is the condition of the ghaut that sepoys and troops pass free from charges."[47] Regulation VI of 1819 transformed this practice into law, directing that magistrates would ensure the passing of military through public *ghats* free of charges, obliging *ghat majhis* to do recruiting work for the EIC military for free.

The enormous (coercive) power of the police behind the *ghat majhi* propped up his position as an efficient recruiter. *Ghat majhis* often secured the help of the military and the police in strong-arming the EIC's competitors for hiring boatmen. On November 25, 1795, Jetoo, the EIC's *ghat majhi* at Patna, went with six *sipahis* to the Danish factory to forcibly hire six boatmen. The commercial resident of the Danish factory wrote a letter to the magistrate, H. Douglas, protesting that "it had never been customery to send sepoys armed to the factory." While the Patna magistrate protected Jetoo, in January 1796, Douglas accused the *ghat majhi* of the Danish factory, Moinuddin, of forcefully hiring boats. Not only did Douglas oblige the Danish commercial resident, Schielke, to hand over the two allegedly pressed boats to the EIC *ghat majhi*, Jetoo, but also threatened to prosecute the commercial resident, a Danish man, if he sheltered Moinuddun. The governor general's office threw its weight behind the magistrate, stating that "should Mr. Schielke offer open and violent resistance to your authority you are authorized to have a recourse to the aid of a military force."[48] Jetoo's power to recruit thus depended upon the support of the magistrate. Elsewhere in Bengal, *ghat majhis* worked in close connection with magistrates. In September 1803, in the city of Murshidabad, a number of *dandies* (oarsmen) fled from the fleet of Lieutenant Brooks. Immediately, Lieutenant Brooks contacted the commanding officer of the station, who then turned to the magistrate. The magistrate sent orders to the *ghat majhi*. The *ghat majhi* diligently replenished the troops even though he reported "that he had no other mode of obtaining dandies than by pressing them from the boats on the river."[49] Without the muscle power of the police, such recruitment operations were not possible. Such interdependence disproves claims that *ghat majhis* were the most important recruitment agents for boats in early colonial Bengal.[50] It not only elides the complex gamut of functions that *ghat majhis* performed, but also the importance of police force in enabling the *ghat majhis* to function as recruiters.

Police establishments along the river became the most reliable recruitment agents for the military. Magistrates recruited "workmen of every description" for the movement of troops.[51] They hired not just boats, but also bullock carts, hackeries, and doolies.[52] As one military superintendent for road construction noted, "it has been an invariable practice with the superintendent to apply officially to the several magistrates and collectors of the districts ... for purwanahs to their public officers to assist him in collecting labourers and grains."[53] The magistrates were confident of their capacity to collect men for labor and to standardize the practices of a recruitment. The magistrate of Rangpur I. Wordsworth's recommendation to the governor general is telling in this regard: "[The magistrate] may be authorized at the commencement of every month ... to draw out ... the daily and monthly allowances of coolies, and every descriptions of labourers & ca as well as bearers, and to keep a register of their names, places of residence, and occupation, which if admitted of will, obviate such impositions in future and enable individuals more readily to procure artificers and others."[54] The magistrate had in mind the captains of the troops marching through Rangpur as the prospective employers of "every descriptions of labourers." He was confident of carrying out the assiduous task of registering each and every worker in his district on a monthly basis, knowing fully well that for workers the process could only be an "imposition." The "imposition" was imperative, for the goal was to create a controlled market in labor, bringing down wages significantly. The magistrate of Murshidabad, Mr. Turner, brought down porterage wages from 4 annas per diem to 3 annas per diem in 1811. At least until 1817, the porterage wage in Murshidabad was capped at 3 annas per diem.[55]

The *darogahs* were the magistrates' recruiters on the ground. As the agents of the EIC state and alien to the villages, their personalized power over ordinary villagers created a violent rule of terror.[56] Two successive cases against the *darogah* of Nokeela, filed by the *majhi* Premnarain and Ramlochan Sharma in 1793 and 1794 in Rajshahi district, brings to light the exploitative relationship between the police heads and the villagers (*raiyats*), especially boatmen. Eighteen complainants, coming from at least ten villages, testified in the district criminal court (Fouzdary Adalat) that the *darogah* had extorted money for "expences of boat hire, equipage, and court" as well as "marriage fees and taxes on horses, palanquin, and purchase of articles of dress, on bearers and labourers for personal use." Of these complainants, eight were boatmen. The amounts demanded were exorbitant, and the penalties for failure to pay them were severe. According to complainant Premnarain, Biswanath Sundial, *darogah* of Nokeela, with the *burkandaz* Harilal and *paik* Budhia, raided his house in July 1793 making "demands for rent."[57] Premnarain was carried off to the police station and detained for a day. The next morning, he was released after paying the *darogah* 5 rupees and 1 rupee to the *burkandaz*. He also added that he had to sell his fishing boat to withstand the financial pressure of the bribe. The *majhi* Dayaram of the same village complained of being forcibly picked up from his home and confined in the police station for two days with his hands and feet tied up. The *burkandazes* allowed him to go after paying 4 rupees and 4 annas in fine. The next year the *darogah* extorted 19 rupees collectively from six *majhis* in Nokeela. The *darogah* asked these *majhis* to produce before him the maker of their boats, Mohammad Azeem. But Mohammad Azeem was long dead and so the *majhis* had to pay a fine for their inability to produce a dead man![58] Almost all the complainants attested that people fled their homes to remove themselves from the *darogah*'s arbitrary power and greed. Unlike the boatmen running away from company establishments in the early years of the eighteenth century, the boatmen under the jurisdiction of the police station at Nokeela were not just voting with their feet. Because these boatmen had sold off their means of livelihood, that is, their boats, long since, relocation meant starting a new chapter in their lives under conditions of extreme vulnerability.

Even if the EIC resented the arbitrary power of the *darogahs*, fearing that their excesses might contradict the magistrates' authority and embarrass Lord Cornwallis's aspirations to impose an impartial rule of law, the EIC was also profoundly aware that such an arrangement worked best for recruitment of a workforce long accustomed to hiring themselves out on their own terms. Assadullah's treatment of the *majhis* Banoo and Rahmatullah is illustrative of the *darogah*'s routine practice of pressing boats for various services to the state. Assadullah, *darogah* of Jafferganj in the Rajshahi district, confiscated the boats belonging to the merchant Hussain Chulky and the *majhi* Rahmatullah, using them to apprehend dacoits. On June 26, 1793 a gang of robbers had entered a market area of Jafferganj, located near the confluence of three rivers, and plundered two boats belonging to a Dhaka merchant and one to a local potter. Following the incident, Assadullah asked for help from the people of Jafferganj. Apart from his *thanadar* (subordinate police official), "the rest offered me no assistance whatsoever, and no boats too had at that time arrived."[59] In such circumstances, the *darogah* seized two boats and two *majhis*, Rahmatullah and Banoo, a *majhi* who worked on Hussain Chulky's boat. Police service for most boatmen was a drain on their time. Rahmatullah's livelihood depended upon ferrying people to different places locally. Serving the police, even with pay, diverted him from his daily routine, and was not worth the risk. When the *burkandazes* first approached him, he had on board Shaikh Shaqir, a tobacco merchant, returning home from the neighboring market of Karjanna. Rahmatullah, for the time being, successfully pleaded that his boat was old and needed repair. However, within a few hours the *burkandazes* returned while Rahmatullah and his wife were at dinner. They dragged him along with his boat to the police station. At the police station Assadullah detained Rahmatullah and Hussain Chulky's boats and detained Banoo and Rahmatullah. That night, once the policemen stepped out of the station, Rahmatullah and Banoo made their way home. The next morning, they were again dragged back to the police station. Assadullah was irate upon learning that Rahmatullah had left without notice. He gave Rahmatullah between three and ten strokes of rattan.[60] After their punishment was over, both the *majhis* sailed the *darogah* and his *burkandazes* to the confluence of three rivers where the robbery had taken place. The search proved futile and the party returned to the Jafferganj police station empty handed. Though Assadullah released Hussain Chulky's boat, he refused to return Rahmatullah's boat and held onto it for almost a month. Assadullah and Rahmatullah's relationship confirms John McLane's argument that the newly formed colonial police remained an alien force of terror in Bengali society.[61]

Both Assadullah's and Biswanath Sundial's stories exemplify the EIC state's capacity to monitor every movement of working people at workplaces and at home. Access to the hinterland where workers resided was the fundamental gain of the EIC state. In the early eighteenth century, neither of the companies nor the centralized Nawabi and the Mughal states had the privilege of access to village police through bypassing the *zamīndārs*. *Darogahs* possessed enormous power to intrude into the boatmen's home and hearth and force them into public service whenever the need arose. Any jurisdictional protection from the EIC state became difficult.

With increasing police involvement, instrumental violence came to play an important role in recruitment and discipline. Historians have blamed the EIC army for representing "the most overt and possibly most feared face of company power."[62] Army violence on the peasant population has been long understood as a mindless and unnecessary show of raw power by officials which was sometimes detrimental to the interests of the state. Such understandings of violence are egregious. First, it was not just the army but also the police force which used violence routinely for recruiting labor. Second, official discussions on (il)legitimate uses of violence often surfaced when different bureaucratic branches of the state were parsing out their jurisdictional power and autonomy. Finally, in thinking that violence ultimately negatively impacted the state, one fails to take note of the structural use of violence to discipline an extremely chaotic world of work into a streamlined labor market.

Magistrates condoned acts of violence by military officers against boatmen so long as these intrusions did not interfere with their own jurisdictional control over boatmen.[63] When Lieutenant John Burnett was indicted in the murder of Kurmoo, a *goleah* (a *majhi*'s assistant),[64] Tombelle, the magistrate of Bhagalpur, lamented that "it has been with extreme reluctance that I have been compelled by my duty to take any measures in the unfortunate business," and he anxiously anticipated the moment when "you (Burnett) will be relieved from the unpleasant state of suspence you must now be in by the result of a formal process which in my opinion cannot but prove favorable to you."[65] In 1793, Burnett travelled from Dacca to Dinapore, a military station where he was posted, not too far from Kalganj; close to Dinapore, Kurmoo's boat inadvertently rammed into Burnett's boat. Following an altercation with Burnett's *majhi*, Kurmoo and seven other boatmen fled to other side of the river, fearing Burnett's reaction. Predictably, an irate Burnett sent three or four men after them, and Kurmoo was brought to Burnett. Burnett then ordered his *khalasie* (servant) to give the captive thirty strokes of rattan, "in order that others may be deterred from behaving in the like manner to an English gentleman."[66] After twenty-seven strokes, Burnett asked his *khalasie* to stop. Six days later Kurmoo died. Except for Kurmoo's seven colleagues, everyone else, including the local police officials, found no fault with Burnett's conduct.[67] In fact, Tombelle's correspondence with the Nizamat Adalat portrayed Burnett as a benevolent and solicitous employer, who sent 5 rupees for the maintenance of his three servants when they were held up in the Bhagalpur Fouzdary Adalat for interrogation.

Nine years later, Tombelle's successor, I. Wintle, had a very different reaction to Lieutenant Hume, who had beaten a peon to death. In his letter to the governor general Wintle accused Hume of being "deranged in his intellects," a far cry from an "English gentleman."[68] The magistrate used such harsh words not only because he was perturbed by the "irregularities and improprieties" of the military, but also because Hume had crossed the Rubicon separating the jurisdictions of civil and military administration. Hume had proceeded upriver from Fort William with thirty to forty magazine boats. Near Rajmahal some oarsmen had run away and Hume had sent *sipahis* from his fleet directly to the Rajmahal bazaar to recruit men without informing the local police authorities. As the *sipahis* tried to kidnap two men, they fought back. In the scuffle that followed, one of the men, Gour Buksh, a peon, bit the cheek of a *sipahi*. On hearing about the fight from the *sipahis*, Hume ordered the *darogah* of the local *thana* to send some *burkandazes* to assist the *sipahis* in hunting down and bringing the two men to his fleet. He forced Gaur Buksh's family to pay a "fine" of 5 rupees and then flogged both the men until they bled. Twenty-six days later, Gour Buksh succumbed to his injuries.[69] There are several similarities among the circumstances surrounding the deaths of Gour Buksh and Kurmoo. Yet, unlike Burnett, Hume did not elicit any sympathy from the magistrate. What irked Wintle most were Hume's direct efforts at recruiting oarsmen, bypassing the police establishment. Reflecting on the conduct of the *darogah* he said: "The Darogah has acted very foolishly on allowing such an interference in his duties. When the Lt. sent to call him and ordered him to investigate this case, he ought to have told the Lt., that this was the province of the Magistrate."[70]

It was not just Hume, a man with a long history of assault, but also other military men of "honor" who bore the brunt of magistrate's displeasure whenever they meddled outside their jurisdictions. In 1819, Lieutenant Irvine of Major Brooke's fleet forcefully freed two oarsmen, who had been locked up in the Munger police station for getting into a scuffle with two *burkandazes* of that police station. Irvine was compelled to free the oarsmen, as the *majhi* of the boat to which these oarsmen belonged was unable to move without their help. The acting magistrate, when informed of the incident, wrote a strong letter to Major Brooke, ordering him to send back the oarsmen. But Major Brooke took affront at the tone of the letter, complaining to Fort William: "but I cannot help saying, that after 23 years service in the army, I did not expect that my pride as a soldier and my feelings as a gentleman could have been (to say the least of it) so trifled with and by one so young in service."[71] The magistrates were scathing in denouncing the violence inflicted by the military *only* when they felt that the military had violated police jurisdiction.

Magistrates complained that the army's uncalculated violence, without any coordination with the magistrate, exposed the EIC state to the rage of a civilian population plagued by forced recruitment. Native inhabitants were vocal in expressing their discontent regarding such recruitment practices by the military. Most often such resentments were directed against the police as unlike the military the police force had contact with the native population on a daily basis. In 1805, the magistrate of Allahabad reported to Fort William that the army could hardly recruit peacefully the 400–500 coolies and oarsmen needed for pulling boats through the confluence of the Yamuna and Ganga rivers. The indiscriminate pressing conducted by the *sipahis* of the fleet affected native population from all social backgrounds. On October 12, 1805, all merchants closed shops in Allahabad and about a thousand people from all walks of life congregated at Begum Bagh in the city center to discuss ways of addressing the issue of military pressing. The magistrate asked a Maulavi (Muslim clergy) to remonstrate with the crowd about "the impropriety of assembling in such a tumultuous body." But the crowd refused to listen to him. The magistrate had to present himself in person and promise every redress for such matters.[72] Poor and irregular wages had made matters even worse. The magistrates of both Bhagalpur and Allahabad pointed out that wages were either paid at a rate lower than what private travelers paid or never paid at all. Owners of boats seldom ever received any securities.[73]

Police criticism of army violence was premised upon the "inefficiency" of the army serving as recruiters, instead of the police. Not only were the army's recruitment procedures violent, but also they were ineffectual, because "the villagers were accustomed to take to flight on the approach of a military force."[74] The men in uniform were conspicuous, easily alerting the locals. The police, of course, also resorted to violent recruitment methods whenever the need arose. They often had to meet high demands—200–300 oarsmen—for which there was no other option but to force people into service. Several magistrates admitted that workers for the troops "are not procurable without coercion."[75] Some, stricken by the pangs of their conscience, lamented that such use of force "renders the magisterial authority a source of oppression to the people instead of protection."[76] The magnitude and "efficiency" of this coercion can be fathomed from the magistrate of Bhagalpur I. Wintle's report in 1805, where he stated that as a result of police-induced recruitments, the Bhagalpur district bordering on the Ganga "has been stripped of inhabitants to forward this service."[77] Thus, the magistrates' criticism of the army's use of violence served primarily to goad the army to coordinate better with the magistrates in matters of labor recruitment, on the premise that the police were best suited to use force to slake the labor needs of the EIC state.

While the police and military coordinated their efforts in the arena of forced recruitment, the early colonial state increased its ability to harness labor beyond that of any indigenous regime. As is discussed in chapters 1 and 2, forced recruitment by the Mughal and Nawabi states was not very effective, because of the weak control of the centralized state over the *zamīndārs*, who had access to forced labor and who primarily maintained policing forces. Imperial recruiters participated in the local market of boats and boatmen, which often drove hiring rates up. Thus, even in a prominent place like Patna, boatmen could play off contending recruiters for better wages, as they had done following the press for boats for the family of Nawab Nazim Alivardi Khan in 1739.[78] However, in 1812 Metcalfe, the resident of Delhi, capital of the now weakened Mughal empire though not yet part of the formal colony of the EIC, reported that not just the army but also informal state actors such as "English gentlemen, travelers, sepoys, sowars, chuprassies, hurkarras, the whole host of our dependents whether military or civil," exacted forced labor. The commercial resident went on to say that "under the native government the system is under regulation and a provision is made for the support of this class of people. Under the British Government no such provision is made and the system is avowedly exploded."[79] If the EIC state and its beneficiaries aggressively recruited forced labor in a peripheral outpost of the EIC state, then in the heartland of EIC rule— Bengal and Bihar—one could expect the capacity to harness forced labor to be far more magnified. And efficacy increased too, if we take into account the EIC's legislation on preventing workers from running away from work.

The colonial state, by statute law, had identified the police force as recruiters for public works by the early 1800s. Regulation XI of 1806, titled "A Regulation for facilitating the progress of detachment of troops through the Company's territories, for affording any requisite assistance to persons travelling through these territories," formally forbade the army and the police "to compel any persons not accustomed to act as bearers, coolies, or boatmen." However, the regulation identified the police as the main recruiters for the army. They were responsible for the "just compensation" for all the workers and also were responsible for "adjust(ing) their rates of hire."[80] Seventy-two years earlier a couple of VOC officials, frustrated in their efforts to bring down the boatmen's asking rate of hire, had deplored that Bengal had no "law for demanding a stipulated hiring rate."[81] Regulation XI of 1806 addressed such a concern by appointing the police as the final arbiter of wages. In light of the 1806 regulation as well as Metcalfe's observations and numerous evidence of the efficacious recruitment by magistrates, one has to rethink historian Dirk Kolff's sympathetic estimate of Frederick Shore, the magistrate of Dehradun. Kolff reaffirms Shore's self-description as a "rebel" within the colonial bureaucracy, to which he attributes Shore's noteworthy ability to exert control over his district as a magistrate, a rare achievement, in Kolff's opinion, among magistrates of the time. At least as a recruiter of labor, Shore was not an exception but the rule, doing his duty according to the letter of law, like many other magistrates. The contours of his administrative role and not just Shore's personal acumen or paternalism against the tenor of the Cornwallis reforms of 1793 made Shore a success story.[82] Remedial qualities of the 1806 regulation were limited because the demands of the army far exceeded the number of workers available for voluntary government service. Hence, forcible recruitment went on unabated.

Forced recruitment through the collusion of the police and the military had a long life in colonial Bengal. The first judge of the circuit court of Bareilly reported in 1810 that the police force was "more solicitous to establish a reputation for zealous exertion in procuring supply for encampment than studious of the means of protecting the people from oppression."[83] Following this observation, the governor general issued a circular to several magistrates, which did not address the most important issue of coercive police recruitment procedures. It asked magistrates to report only on the "unwarrantable practices" of "troops marching through the country."[84] In cases where force by the army was not employed and instead the *zamīndārs* were solicited for recruitment of labor, the *thanadar* was designated as the supreme authority in determining the wage.[85] Special orders from the commander-in-chief through 1810, 1815, 1818, and 1819 emphasize the imperative of coordination between military and magistrate for recruitment needs of the army.[86] The official termination of forced labor was effected through Regulation III of 1820. But, the Regulation VI of 1825 reinstated the magistrate's coercive power even though the police force no longer directly recruited boatmen and other transport workers for the army. According to the new regulation, the collector of the district would approach "landholder, farmer, tahsildar and other person" to provide the army with the requisite number of men including boatmen, and their "willful neglect or disobedience" could be met with " a fine not exceeding 1000 rupees."[87] After 1829, when the offices of the collector and the magistrate were merged into one, coercive recruitment by the police came full circle because the immediate recruiters were now answerable to the police for any setbacks.

NEGOTIATING THE EIC STATE

The boatmen were rendered helpless in the face of the tremendous brute force of the colonial state. Court records sometimes provide brief yet moving descriptions of how these workers experienced this rising tide of brutality. As soon as the boatman Kurmoo saw that he had picked the wrong fight with the *majhi* of an English military man, he tried to run away. Unfortunately, he did not succeed in escaping and had to endure flogging. After his flogging ended, Kurmoo went to Burnett's cook and asked for some butter to rub on his wounds. He then went to his boat where he sat smoking his hookah in silence. His back flayed and bleeding, Kurmoo would not eat or drink for the remaining six days of his life. Gaur Buksh's only defense when he bore the brunt of Lieutenant Hume's masochistic punishments were his words, "there is no blood in my body to flow, it is dried up." Both Gaur Baksh and Kurmoo died of their beatings. The outcome of only Gaur Baksh's case is known: the Supreme Court of Judicature acquitted his murderer. Burnett's case was to be tried before the Supreme Court of Calcutta, provided that all witnesses traveled to the presidency town and awaited patiently the commencement of the Oyer and Terminer session over a year after the incident.[88] It is unlikely that Gaur Baksh's case was ever tried. The considerable legal immunity that the Lieutenants Hume and Burnett enjoyed after their murders of Gaur Baksh and Kurmoo, casts a clarifying light on what Achille Mmembe has called the "spirit of violence" of the colonial state, routinely realized in the "tactile perception of the native."[89]

Caught between the pincers of forced recruitment and increasingly ruthless surveillance, the boatmen's power to use desertion as a negotiating tool suffered a blow. As prolific recruiters, the police force succeeded in stalling the damaging effect of desertion. This is evident in how the Military Board and the governor general responded to Lieutenant Brook's crisis situation in 1803. The commanding officer of the Murshidabad station had written to both the magistrate of Murshidabad and the governor general to help out

Lieutenant Brooks, who had lost quite a few oarsmen to desertion. To make sure that the military counted not only on the efforts of the Murshidabad magistrate, the governor general alerted magistrates in thirteen other districts. Within *six days* of receiving orders from the governor general, the Murshidabad magistrate expeditiously provided Lieutenant Brooks with his required manpower. In the same letter to the governor general, the magistrate boasted that in the past year, apart from Lieutenant Brooks, he had helped out Lieutenant Norford, Captain Vemvernon, and Lieutenant Stewart, by shoring up 40–50 boats with either both *majhis* and *dandies* or 30–40 *dandies*.[90] The phenomenal increase in the EIC state's capacity to recruit boatmen becomes clear when one is reminded that in 1730s it took the VOC *forty-four* days to recruit boatmen for eighty vessels.[91] The magistrate also noted that he had "taken all the necessary securities to obviate any risk of desertion." The increased recruitment capacity of the magistrate was now a weapon used against the boatmen's practice of desertion.

The EIC state's "public works" installed a surveillance machinery throughout Bengal and Bihar which made desertion difficult. Take for instance the Sunderbans, which, as is discussed in chapter 2, was a chosen place for most boatmen to act on their plans of deserting the fleet. For much of the eighteenth century, the Sunderban deltas were the heart of darkness, a frontier zone, with very little direct presence of Mughal, Nawabi, or even, in some places, *zamīndāri* state power, and they were infested with tigers and robbers of all stripes. The EIC's primary focus in the region was the route between Dhaka and Calcutta. By 1800, there were two ways of waterborne travel to Calcutta from Dhaka, one through the district of Jessore, thereby bypassing the Sunderbans, and the other through the Sunderbans via the district of Bakerganj. The route via the Sunderbans was further broken down into the inner passage and the outer passage. While the inner passage involved narrow channels cutting through the heart of the Bakerganj district, the outer passage demanded navigation through the torrents of the Meghna, one of the largest rivers in the Bengal deltas. While the outer passage was navigable throughout the year, the inner passage could be used only during the monsoons. In 1800, the judges of the circuit court at the Dhaka division, after meticulous study of the region, decided that eighteen guard boats would be posted at various points of these routes in the two districts of Dhaka and Bakerganj. While four guard boats were placed under the jurisdiction of the Dhaka magistrate, the remainder were assigned to the Bakerganj magistrate. One guard boat was placed at Rynabad, on the border of Jessore and Dhaka. The EIC state was hopeful that these guard boats would increase the strength of the salt *chowkey* (guard stations for securing the EIC's monopoly over the salt manufacture and trade). The rest were strategically placed at the confluences of two or more rivers. The magistrates of the various districts were required to use their power of discretion in shuffling boats from the inner passage area to the outer passage area, depending on the season.[92] Chittagong at the farthest end of the Sunderbans, where the much-feared Arakanese pirates carried out their depredations, was placed under the guard of two gunboats. The marine department in Madras supplied these gunboats, manned by an all-European crew. One of the boats, *Harriet*, had a crew of sixty men with the capacity of ten four-pounder carriage guns. It had two lateen sails—necessary for sailing against the wind—as well as two tiers of oars, making it sailable in both river and the sea.[93] By 1810s the collector in Chittagong reported peaceful civilian rule without any of the local or external disturbances which had been rampant in the years between 1760 and 1800.[94] Boatmen in the Sunderbans, a territory which long had languished with liminal state presence, now confronted an elaborate architecture of colonial police patrol.

Unsurprisingly, a magistrate, specifically, the magistrate of Bhagalpur, I. Wintle, with his intimate knowledge of surveillance and his reputation for stripping the banks of Ganga of its population to further recruit for the labor needs of the military fleets, bears responsibility for drawing up the original proposal for Regulation XI of 1806. The regulation passed at a moment when magistrates in several districts lodged a slew of complaints against the army's behavior as being a hindrance to the streamlining of the labor market. Thus, Wintle drew up the first design of this regulation in a bid to control army violence in his territory. His foremost recommendation was to allow only police personnel and not the army to conduct recruitment. While supplying documents to the judicial department in Fort William relating to Lieutenant Hume's merciless murder of Gaur Baksh in 1805, Wintle reflected on the difficulty of retaining oarsmen on army store boats. He emphasized in his letter "the regular and quick dispatch of these boats is at all times of great importance to the state" and hence suggested that the governor general "may perhaps deem it advisable to form some rules for that purpose." The governor general in turn requested Mr. Wintle to provide a "draft of any rules which he may consider calculated to facilitate the hiring of dandies or coolies for public service."

In his proposal, Wintle also offered detailed suggestions on how to stop desertion. He devised a two-pronged strategy. First, Wintle pointed out that better wages might act "as an inducement to the *dandies* to remain on board" especially because they were paid at the rate of 3 rupees per month, which was between 8 annas to 1 rupee less than the rate paid by private individuals. Second, he suggested penalties be severe if boatmen broke terms of service. Like other magistrates and army officials, Wintle observed that the *majhis* often had full knowledge of their *dandies'* plans for running away.[95] Wintle proposed that the town major and the commissary of stores, at the time of hire, pay the *majhi* two-thirds of their hire. In return the *majhi* would provide a list of names and places of residence of the *dandies* on his boat and sign a contract which would state that the *majhi* will be held responsible for the absconding of the oarsmen. In order to compensate for the loss of time, labor, and expenses for rehiring *dandies*, the *majhi*'s boat would be liable to confiscation. To make his point clear, Wintle designed a template for the contract (see figures 16 and 17). He further specified that the commanding officer would have the power to seize the boat and sell it. If an oarsman remained at large, then the commanding officer should inform the magistrate of the district where the oarsman lived as well as the magistrate of the district from where he ran away. If apprehended the oarsman was to receive a sentence of hard labor on the public roads for a period of three months. If the oarsman deserted after receiving his advance before the army boats arrived in their villages, he was to return the money to the magistrate and receive a sentence of imprisonment in a *fouzdari* jail not exceeding ten days or corporal punishment not exceeding fifteen strokes of the cane. Even in case of sickness of the oarsmen, the *majhis* would be held responsible. The commanding officer would give the invalid oarsman a written discharge and the cost of recruiting a replacement would be deducted from the remaining one-third sum payable to the *majhi*.[96] The proposed contract was unabashedly pro-employer, even to the stipulation that in case employers failed to pay wages to the boatmen they would not face any punitive measure other than payment of the arrears.

The next year, the EIC state copied almost all of Wintle's suggestions into Regulation XI of 1806. The regulation empowered "local officers of police" to do the recruitment work not only for the EIC army but also for private travelers. It prohibited army officials and all "badged" officers except the police from meddling in recruitment affairs. It also endorsed Wintle's suggestion of introducing and enforcing contracts for boatmen. Excepting his recommended increase in the wages of the boatmen, the EIC state paid heed to all his suggestions. Even the template for contracts was borrowed from

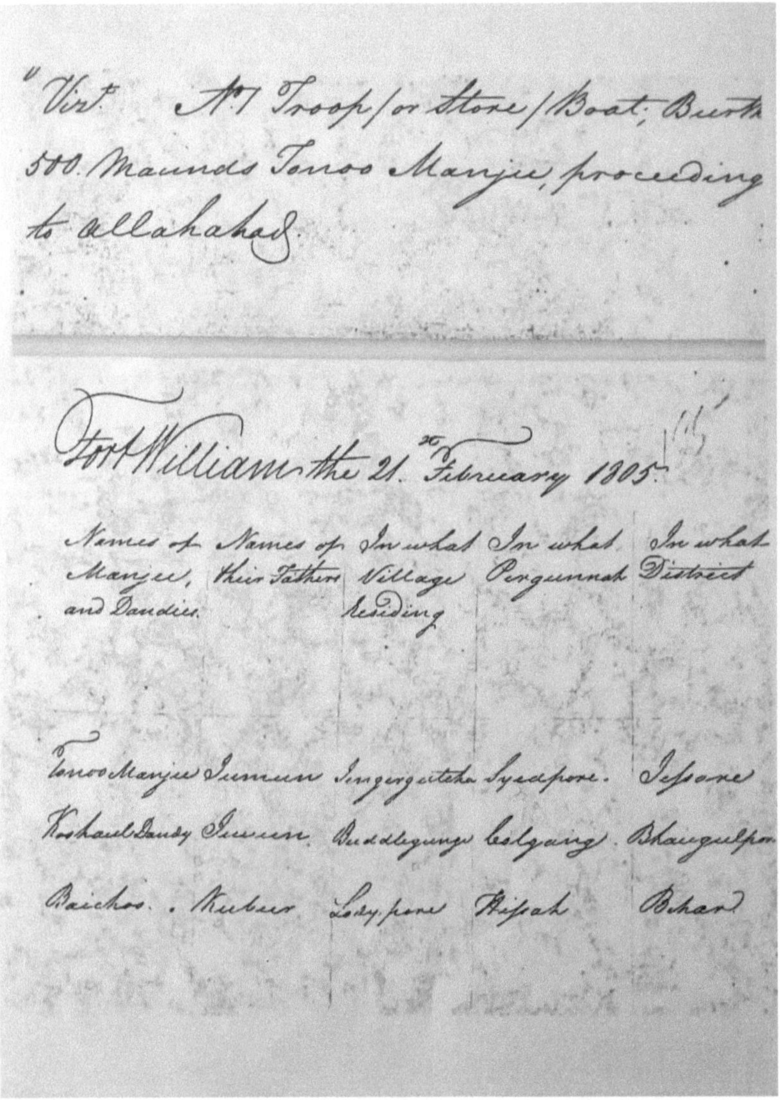

"Vizt. No. 1 Troop (or Store) Boat; Burthen 500 Maunds Tonoo Manjee, proceeding to Allahabad.

Fort William the 21st February 1805

Names of Manjee, and Dandies	Names of their Fathers	In what Village residing	In what Pergunnah	In what District
Tonoo Manjee	Sumun	Singergutcha	Syedpore	Jessore
Koshaul Dandy	Sewun	Buddlegunge	Colgong	Bhaugulpore
Baichoo	Kubeer	Lodypore	Hissah	Behar

FIGURE 16. Partial template of a contract for boatmen, drawn up by I. Wintle, the magistrate of Bhagalpur, February 21, 1805. Source: West Bengal State Archives, Kolkata.

Wintle's proposal. Thus a magistrate, not the Military Department, masterminded the regulation that tackled desertion in the severest manner.

Regulation XI of 1806 demonstrates that in spite of the mistrust between *darogah* and magistrate on one hand and magistrate and military men on the other, the state acted as a unified entity in stamping out boatmen's strategies

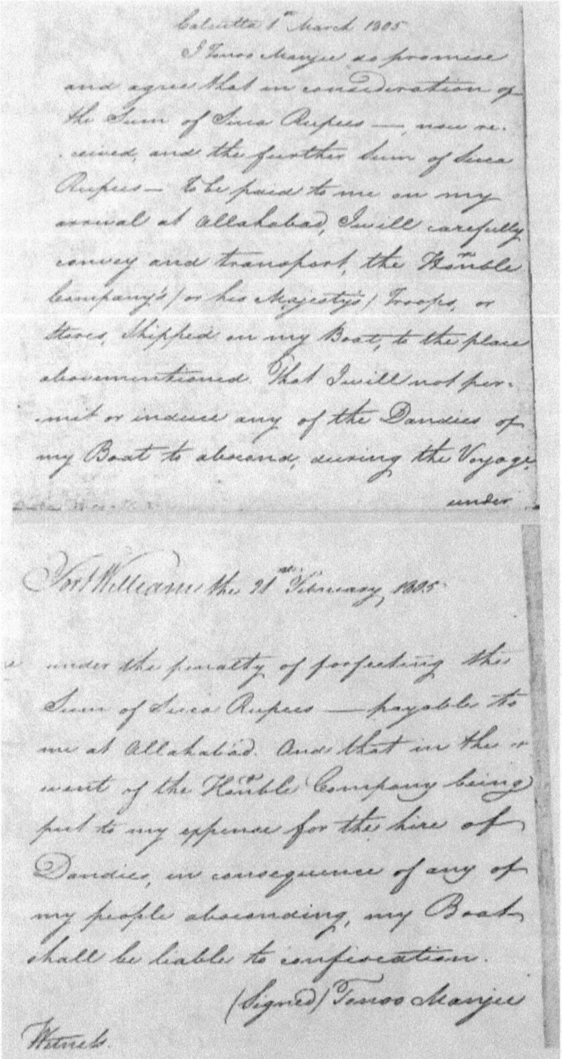
Calcutta 1st March 1805
I Tinoo Manjee do promise and agree that in consideration of the Sum of Sicca Rupees —, now re-ceived, and the further Sum of Sicca Rupees — to be paid to me on my arrival at Allahabad, I will carefully convey and transport, the Hon'ble Company's (or his Majesty's) Troops, or Stores, Shipped on my Boat, to the place abovementioned. That I will not per-mit or induce any of the Dandies of my Boat to abscond, during the Voyage, under

Fort William the 21st February 1805

under the penalty of forfeiting the Sum of Sicca Rupees — payable to me at Allahabad. And that in the event of the Hon'ble Company being put to any expense for the hire of Dandies, in consequence of any of my people absconding, my Boat shall be liable to confiscation.

(Signed) Tinoo Manjee

Witness

FIGURE 17. Continuation of template for boatmen's contract. Source: West Bengal State Archives, Kolkata.

of negotiation. Unlike in the eighteenth century, when better pay was the only means of stalling desertion, coercion became the most important tool for the colonial state to redress the problem. Both military and police agreed to apply force for recruitment and retention of the work force. However, the police force, as law enforcement agents who had intimate knowledge of the local population and no-holds-bar access to the boatmen, took responsibility for the "effective" use of force. Thus, they came up with blueprints of laws that would legitimize violence, create pressure on the workforce and increase their vulnerability, and finally, criminalize their practices of negotiations vis-à-vis the employers.

The 1806 regulation changed the relationships of hired work for Bengal's boatmen beyond recognition. The contract as defined in the regulation played an instrumental role in modifying the long-standing practice of advance payments by holding the head boatman legally responsible (liable to criminal charges) for the desertion of any oarsman. The English Master and Servant Acts inspired such regulations, as generations of historians have repeatedly pointed out.[97] In the Indian context, the irony of such regulations is evident in the fact that laws regarding breach of contract long preceded the Contract Act, passed in 1874.[98] The 1806 regulation also instituted a hierarchical relationship between the *majhi* as an intermediary gang-labor leader and the oarsman as the subordinate worker. From various examples of hiring practices in the early eighteenth-century, discussed in chapter 2, it is clear that boatmen, whether *majhi* or oarsmen, directly negotiated with EIC officials or private travelers. Only from the 1740s did the EIC engage *ghat majhis* in Calcutta and Kassimbazar as labor recruiters for boatmen, penalizing them for the desertion of boatmen. The 1806 regulation improved on such practices through the introduction of contracts, which could hold the head boatman responsible for the desertion of any oarsmen. It thereby formalized a hierarchy which worked towards the creation of a multi-tier security system, taking the risks of damages and losses off the shoulders of the EIC and heaping them upon the head boatmen.

In the case of boatmen, we can definitively say that the EIC efforts leading up to the 1806 regulation laid the basis for a hierarchical intermediary-worker relationship and a mechanism for mass recruitment. In fact, the military department subsequently applied the head boatman–oarsmen relationship instituted in the 1806 regulation to other segments of public labor. An order by the commander-in-chief in 1819 created the positions of *sirdar* (master) bearer and *sirdar* (master) coolie "for the express purpose of obtaining the several descriptions of carriage."[99] Moreover, although the contract recognized the legal personhood of the head boatman, on behalf of himself and all other rowers, the regulation also served to negate the individuality of the *majhi* and the oarsmen. Instead, the contract solidified an unequal relationship between the state and a disembodied, congealed mass of labor.

The 1806 regulation, as well as other regulations, had an adverse economic effect on the boatmen, especially if one examines wage payment. The newly standardized wage payment system precluded food money. A trend towards removing the food money was already evident during the famine years. Beginning in 1771 the EIC had discontinued payment of food money to boatmen in the Murshidabad area, the transshipment zone for the fleets of the European companies in the early eighteenth century, wherein boatmen vigorously had haggled for their food money. The pretext was the removal of "the various imposition to which the ryots [peasants] are made liable." Since all expenditure of the EIC state came out of its revenue collection the EIC could provide some relief on the tax burdens of a famine-stricken population only by scrapping away the food money from boatmen's and cartmen's hire. While *zamīndāri* levies for the same years were maintained, leading to the depression of the wages of the reelers, boatmen saw no such concession for their wages. Thus much like the silk reelers, the boatmen of Murshidabad witnessed a depression in their wages during this period.[100] The 1806 statute formalized this omission.

The advance payment system also underwent changes following the Regulation of 1806, after which boatmen were paid only two-thirds of their wages in advance, on the pain of criminal liability if they broke the contracts.[101] Instances of advance payment of full wages as had been practiced in the early eighteenth century disappeared. The variety of customary wages that *majhis* demanded in the early eighteenth century disappeared completely. Not only did the EIC not pay these wages, but also, as is evident from various travel accounts, private individuals, too, did not pay any previously customary wages. Even though European travelers in early nineteenth-century Bengal and Bihar constantly complained of the boatmen's propensity to steal, which they saw as a sign of their "moral depravity," never once did the travelers mention any payment of customary wages.[102] Even indigenous men of means, such as Raja Kṛiṣṇachandra Ghoṣāl, in his travels to and from Benares, did not pay any reward to his *majhis*. Ghoṣāl had tasked one of his fleet members, Bijayrām Sen, a doctor, with writing down the "merit" Ghoṣāl acquired not just through his pilgrimage but also through the various donations he had made to Hindu and Muslim religious figures, numerous beggars, and all the fellow passengers he sponsored on his journey. Despite the fact that their pilotage work was meticulously described, no mention is made of any honorarium to boatmen or for that matter any workers in Bijayrām's account of extravagant displays of "giving" and donation. Even though

Bijayrām celebrates Ghoṣāl's merits as an employer—"service people have no sorrows before him"—he precludes any description of the *zamīndār* "honoring" his artisans.[103]

The illegal salt trade, as a customary practice of boatmen to supplement their income, became much harder under the colonial state. The EIC state had not only monopolized the trade but also the manufacture of the product. Regulation X of 1819, a comprehensive legislation addressing the illicit manufacture and sale of salt, devoted an entire section to the transportation of salt. EIC salt agents registered all boats transporting salt to or from the company's stores. Any private individual carrying salt exceeding 5 seers required three different kinds of special passes from the Board of Customs, Salt and Opium. One of the passes, *rowannah*, mentioned "the quantity of salt intended to be transported under them, the date of the sale, and number of the lot in part or in full of which the salt is deliverable, the name of the purchaser, the place whence the salt is deliverable, the mode of conveyance, the place to which the salt is to be transported, and the route by which it shall be conveyed."[104] Inspection centers for salt, or salt *chowkies*, thoroughly examined all movement of salt within their respective jurisdictions. Failure to produce any of these passes led the proprietors of salt to pay a fine up to 10 rupees per maund of salt.[105] The regulation specifically mentioned that *majhis* and oarsmen transporting contraband salt were liable to a prison sentence not exceeding six weeks and a fine not exceeding 50 rupees. Carrying salt illegally in the holds no longer remained a "customary" privilege that employers, especially the military, willingly tolerated. Such major transformations in the customary payment system, alongside a specific legal innovation of contractual labor and criminal liability for breaking contracts, effectively eliminated the opportunities and incentives to run away from work.

The regulations sanctioned a discipline through articulation with various levels of state authority hitherto unknown in the region. By 1784, the EIC state and the British Parliament had jettisoned the need to rule India according to the "ancient Mughal constitution." The cornerstone of Cornwallis's reforms was a centralized, impersonal, and impartial rule of law. As the Supreme Court judge and renowned Orientalist William Jones has imagined it, Cornwallis, in creating a compendium of law and gleaning through the thicket of Indian customs, had become the "Justinian of India." Fundamentally, centralization of state power by removing all vestiges of the coparcenary system of precolonial rule, and in particular removing oversight by *zamīndārs*, was key to this rule of law. The regulations placed a hierarchical chain of command within the existing state functionaries, from the village level to the districts to Calcutta, committing them all to one rule. The EIC state thus put an end to the system of multiple overlapping jurisdictions they were once merely a part of. The new rule of law discomfited many. On the one hand, utilitarians were not satisfied by the level of centralization and the lack of uniformity, or "simplicity," of law, as regulations on the same subject varied from one presidency to another, even within the same presidency. On the other hand, at the very local level, as a judge and magistrate in Bengal had observed, awareness of the new method of rule showed "no tendency whatever to improve among the native, except their increasing knowledge of the Regulations, which, in speaking of the progress of political philosophy, is scarcely worth mentioning." To Indians, the "political philosophy" underpinning this rule was unexceptionally alien, as they were kept out of the middle- to high-ranking positions of the administration. For most, their undoubted "knowledge of the Regulations" came largely through the experience of coercion and punishment. Boatmen did not always experience this new state as an impersonal force. The *majhi* Unwar's aborted career as a guard boatman is testimony to the personalized power of magistrates over boatmen. Yet the personal power of magistrates and the *darogahs* was aligned with the larger system of discipline spelled out in regulations regarding recruitment, terms of hire, and conditions of labor of boatmen for the purposes of the EIC state. The alien nature of the new regulatory and contractual regime struck boatmen, long accustomed to moving between conflicting jurisdictions and thereby negotiating on their own for favorable terms of work, as an unprecedented form of labor discipline.[106]

Boatmen had few avenues to maneuver within the constraints they faced. Occasionally, they knocked on the doors of the law. Petitions from Unwar, Rahmatullah, Premnarain, and Dayaram show that, despite all odds against them, boatmen sought justice. Very little is written about subaltern petitioning practices in early colonial India. Boatmen's petitions are rare in the archives, but they significantly crop up in a period when desertion increasingly became a difficult or ineffective weapon of negotiation. In this sense, the boatmen's practice of petitioning resembled petitioning among weavers in colonial Andhra. As Potukuchi Swarnalatha argues, "petitions draw attention to the colonial juridical structure and the mechanisms that were put in place to discipline the so-called 'fugitive' or 'rebel' weavers."[107] Unlike the subaltern petitioners from other regions, boatmen petitioned individually. Since in Bengal boat rowing was never an occupation of any particular caste or community, and there are multiple examples of boatmen hiring themselves out individually and directly to both European or indigenous employers without any mediation of caste institutions or leadership, it is not surprising that boatmen petitioned individually. Boatmen, as petitioners, exposed the limits of the EIC state's "enlightened despotism" because justice remained elusive even after the boatmen followed all the difficult and expensive legal procedures.[108] Rahmatullah received compensation probably because his adversary was a *darogah* at a time when the magistrate's office busied itself purging lower-level police officers, following Cornwallis's reforms. Unwar, on the other hand, fought an exceptional legal battle against the most formidable force, the magistrate. Unwar's case only affirms a longstanding position among historians of crime and justice in early colonial Bengal that working or poor people seldom reported crime, due to the fear that legal matters would involve long periods of absence from their places or means of occupation. The overwhelming majority could not afford such loss of earnings.[109] After Unwar's petition to the Fouzdary Adalat in Bhagalpur failed to garner any response from the magistrate, he decided to petition the Nizamut Adalat in Calcutta, the highest criminal court of appeal for any native person in EIC-controlled India. He arrived at Calcutta in December 1806. He filed his first petition on December 27 and repeatedly petitioned the Nizamat Adalat on February 5, March 1, and March 16. In his third petition Unwar emphasized "his distress upon having expended the whole of the money he had brought with him to the Presidency."[110] The circuitous movement through the Fouzdary Adalat and then the Nizamat Adalat reduced him from being unemployed to complete destitution. Unwar's case conclusively shows that any amount of legal recourse was not enough to resolve the boatman's terms of employment in a conflict involving a magistrate.

Even outside of the meanderings of the legal system, boatmen made known their anger against unjust treatment. After the death of the boatman Kurmoo, the boatmen Biju, Dukhim, Jhugroo, Tufani, Bughalu, along with Kurmoo's eight-year-old son, Bharosee, under *majhi* Jayram's leadership carried their dead colleague from Chhapra to Dinapore. Jayram sought out Lieutenant Burnett and tried to hand the "slightly swollen body" of Kurmoo over to his boat. When he refused, Jayram reproached Burnett: "The man whom you ordered to be flogged has died in consequence." He further exhorted Burnett to take Kurmoo's corpse and go before the colonel stationed at Munger to confess his act. Jayram and the rest cremated Kurmoo's remains after the confrontation with Burnett. Even when they were reluctant to take police action, Jayram and his companions did not stop short of indicting Burnett of his crimes.[111] One sees similar glimpses of collective action in the congregation of sundry workers who protested military pressing at Begum Bagh in 1805. Finally, even though boatmen no longer demanded any form of customary wages, they continued to carry out clandestine trade in monopoly commodities such as salt, precariously, and at far greater risk than they had faced in the previous century.

Synchronization of work under the factory system required supervisors of workers on the shop floor to exert disciplinary control "like real army officers (managers) and N.C.Os (foremen, overseers) who command during the labour process in the name of capital."[112] As part of the "public service" sector, boatmen experienced synchronization of their work under the literal supervision of the army and the police. The despotism in this new discipline of hired work can be measured in the wider meaning of "public service," a term synonymous with convict labor within the realm of the EIC state in India and the Indian Ocean world. Even though they remained formally "free" hired workers, statute laws and police control of the boatmen's "public service" created harsh parameters reminiscent of convict labor. These parameters included below-market wage rates as decided by the police, increased hierarchy within the workplace, criminal breach of contract, and formal criminalization of the clandestine salt trade. These measures aborted the potentialities of boatmen to utilize unsupervised mobility to retain control over their work time and the substance and methods of their pay. In short, as hired labor, boatmen were successfully restrained from "quiet encroachment" upon state power.

THE COLONIAL STATE AND EUROPEAN SAILORS AND SOLDIERS

European soldiers had already felt the weight of aggrandized state power with the reforms in the military beginning in the 1750s—especially with the implementation of the Mutiny Acts (see chapter 3). Such reforms were further bolstered by the expanding surveillance apparatus of the EIC state's police force. In recapturing deserting sailors and punishing them, and even in recruiting them, the police emerged as the most important institution for regulating European sailors. Special regulations dating from the 1810s targeted sailors and reinforced the functions of the police. Army officials too depended on the police to punish their refractory European-born common soldiers as well as in recruiting them. While the wide chasm of racial privilege Europeans in India had experienced since the 1770s separated the social trajectories of indigenous boatmen and European sailors and soldiers, as workers both found their fates sealed in the hands of the EIC state's police. The police, armed with special statutes, steadily encroached on both the boatmen's and European sailors and soldiers' power to shape their labor market in Bengal through their mobility practices.

Despite reforms, the early colonial state faced difficulties recruiting European soldiers for its army in Bengal. As is discussed in chapter 3, army reforms under Robert Clive included use of the Mutiny Acts, an increase in (mainly European-controlled) officer ranks, recruitment in Britain, and a proportional increase in the ratio of indigenous to European soldiers. The 1796 reforms instituted by Cornwallis further reduced the number of European regiments to one in each presidency. However, from 1788, a royal troop comprised of primarily English soldiers were stationed on Indian soil. By 1850, the number of European soldiers in the EIC state or British royal army service stood prominently at 30,000. Nevertheless, throughout this period, recruiting difficulties persisted. Plans for sending recruits directly from Britain proved less than fruitful. In 1758, the Court of Directors reported that they were "under greatest difficulties in raising recruits" and exhorted the Bengal government to "form your designs and schemes" and "not depend upon numbers which will be impracticable to send" from Britain.[113] Consequently, the EIC recruited European soldiers well into the early nineteenth century not only from Europe but also from Bengal. Their backgrounds as "laborers" indicate that the freshly recruited privates came from the ranks of the laboring poor in England, defeating the purpose of recruitment in Britain, namely to avoid enlisting economically "desperate" people in the army (see figure 18). As the lowest-ranked European-born personnel, these infantry privates were an anomaly in an army in which Europeans usually served as officers, commanding a vast rank and file of indigenous soldiers or *sipahis*.

Even though Asian sailors entered the service of the EIC in ever-greater numbers by the late eighteenth century, European sailors remained a substantial segment of the wooden world of the EIC. The Navigation Acts defined only those ships as "British" whose crew numbered at least three-fourths European-born. The Navigation Acts especially discouraged Asian sailors on ships bound for Britain. This emphasis on a majority-European crew clashed

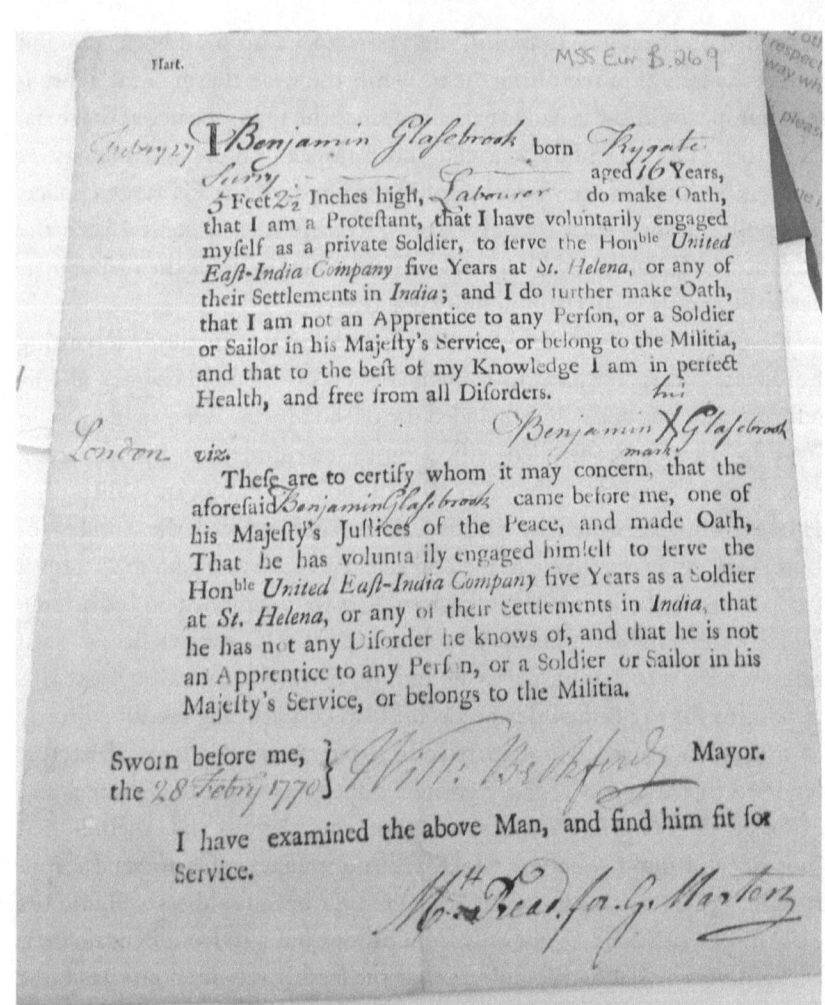

FIGURE 18. Contract of indenture for a private in the EIC army, 1770. Source: British Library, London, MSS Eur B 269.

with the reality on the ground. Many European sailors were lost to desertion. In 1814, the captain of the EIC ship *Forbes* wrote to the office of the governor general about the "distress" caused from "men by their repeated desertions." About to leave for Bombay, the ship lost at least four men in two bouts of desertion.[114] Men often fled in the dead of the night, sometimes using the ship's jolly boats.[115] During the Napoleonic wars, when more and more European sailors were pressed into the army, the British government relaxed the Navigation Acts so that only one British sailor onboard a ship weighing twenty tons was required to call that ship British.[116] Ship captains could replenish their depleted crews by hiring Lascars, or Asian sailors. British sailors still remained an important workforce for European shipping. Especially after 1813, when the EIC largely lost its commercial monopoly. many sailors came out to the East as crew on privately owned British vessels. Harald Fischer-Tine has noted that even as late as in 1866, 200,000 sailors were "transient members of white Calcutta" as opposed to 11,000 settled members.[117]

Sailors often "changed flags," inordinately benefitting the EIC especially after the 1759 Battle of Bedara, when the EIC extinguished intercompany rivalry. In 1804, when two sailors of the American ship *Minerva* were imprisoned on charges of "mutinous behavior," they declared themselves Englishmen and quickly entered the crew of EIC's armed ship *Les Freres Unis*.[118] Even though the EIC state allowed American ships into their ports, they imposed protective tariffs against American products and importantly for sailors, they refused to recognize US consuls in India until the middle of the nineteenth century.[119] Sailors on American ships, aware of this political divide, used it to their own benefit. The captain of the *Minerva* protested that the runaway sailors from his ship could not be British as they had declared themselves as American citizens before the American counsel in Lisbon. The same year two other sailors from an American vessel ran away to an EIC ship on the pretext that "they were Britons born."[120]

Deserters remained as resourceful as ever. Often sailors ran away with assets of the ship, presumably to sell them. When David Brown and Laborn Hodgson deserted from the EIC ship *Phoenix* they carried away Captain John Pyle's valuable belongings.[121] As Calcutta grew into a significant colonial settlement—a census report from 1837 reveals there were 3,138 "English" residents of Calcutta—European sailors could utilize their family networks for their escape plans.[122] A different David Brown, a deserter from the EIC ship *Ely*, had his wife come out to Calcutta in 1815. She resided in the house of a provisioner and country trader, Mr. Murray, in Entally.[123] The Calcutta police suspected this house of hosting another deserter, Richard Murray, from the ship *Ann* and a brother of Mr. Murray's.[124] It is quite possible that the proprietor of the house used both deserters in his business. Notwithstanding their interests, family links brought both the deserters surreptitiously to the same house. Of the various means and modes of running away in the Calcutta docklands, only a few were significantly new.

While the motives and modes of desertion had not changed much, life opportunities for deserters in early nineteenth-century Bengal had been transformed over the previous century. Deserters found fewer opportunities to play competing employers off one another in the early nineteenth century, following the elimination of rival companies and *zamīndāri* armies. Though British private traders came out in rising numbers to India after 1813, when the EIC lost its trading monopoly over the India trade, these private traders nevertheless relied on the EIC state to stem desertion of their sailors and introduce an orderly labor market. Loss of monopoly over trade was thus not a loss of control over the labor market for sailors. As the EIC state managed the waterfront—recruiting sailors for its own ships as well as for private ship captains and fixing wages generally—desertion as a means to spike wages was pointless. Instead, sailors and soldiers often deserted to escape legal penalties. The two sailors from the American ship *Minerva*, facing imprisonment for insubordination of shipboard authority, managed to escape. Similarly Joseph Thomas, a private soldier from the 1st European Regiment, ran away after he was drummed out of the cantonment at Dinapore and received a sentence of corporal punishment from the General Courts Martial.[125] For others, flight offered opportunities to find new occupations. The intrusion of the EIC into the Indian heartland opened up many alternative careers for runaways. The three sailors who fled the EIC ship *Monarch* in May 1811 took up different jobs in Calcutta and beyond. A carpenter, Robert Blaker, a joiner, Joseph Cadly, and a steward, John Bailey, immediately took up work at the shipbuilder Kydd's yard. A month later, after much enquiry and contradictory reports, the Calcutta police confirmed that the steward was still working at Kydd's shipyard, while the carpenter had made his way up north towards Patna. Thanks to the lapse by the Calcutta magistrate, the third deserter got off the hook even though the Calcutta police had managed to arrest him from Kydd's shipyard.[126]

Rare glimpses into the itinerancy of deserters reveal their extravagant, sometimes harebrained, entrepreneurial adventurism. Since the time of his desertion in 1785 and his capture in 1794, Martin, an EIC sailor, claimed that he had changed occupations nine times. He formed business partnerships with three different men, including a native merchant, and tried his hand at trades as wide-ranging as confectioner, liquor maker, and seller of cloth and salt. He had also worked as a clerk at the Revenue Department in Calcutta and in the judge and magistrate's office in Bhagalpur. Besides, the town adjutant reported, "it is well known among the lower class of people in the settlement that the said Martin and John Adams are the heads of a gang of thieves who have long been a pest to the settlement." John Adams had terrorized the suburb of Calcutta around Cox's Bungalow. He was apprehended and received a sentence of deportation to Europe. However, the town adjutant's four attempts to send him back failed as Adams either jumped ship or the crew, aware of his reputation, refused to take him on board. Adams finally escaped and made his way to Bhagalpur. The town adjutant reluctantly admired, "Adams is a young, good-looking man. Speaks English well but most languages are equal to him. He had been examined in French, Italian, Spanish and Portuguese."[127] Martin and John Adams lived the adventurous, multicultural, albeit low, life of the European underclass in Bengal. Unlike Martin and John Adams, Gardiner Thomas settled for a somewhat more respectable life as a librarian in the College of Calcutta after deserting from his ship. But he decided to try his luck one more time when he met Richard Roger Curbs on the streets of Calcutta. Richard Roger Curbs had come to Calcutta as a part of the crew of a ship which the Calcutta police had confiscated for carrying a cargo of African slaves from Mozambique. Thomas and Curbs decided to buy an old longboat from an East Indiaman and set off for Madras "in expectation of entering into a commercial concern to the Malay coast." However, they had no papers, not even a license for lawful residence in the Bengal presidency. The EIC army posted at Balasore soon caught them.[128] Such trajectories of deserters, ranging from dodging criminal persecution to adventurism, met with surveillance from the EIC state.

Deserting sailors were part of a larger group of European vagrants. Until the early 1790s the EIC military took responsibility for managing deserters and vagrants. After the escape of nine prisoners of war, the town adjutant of Calcutta on the night of October 29, 1794 issued "3 search warrants for apprehending all vagrants and others who would not give a good account of themselves." The ensuing catch was "one hundred and three persons . . . vizt thirty-five British subjects, forty eight foreigners, and twenty eight natives including Coffries (Africans)." Though the town adjutant did not capture the escaped prisoners, he did ensure that men "such as belonged to ships [were] sent to their respective captains and commanders."[129] Apart from deserters, a substantial number of white "loafers" were unemployed or "distressed" seamen with no affiliation to a ship. William Patton, third officer of the ship *Asia*, and two common soldiers, Thomas Stevens and Allys Buchtar, came to Calcutta from Penang to testify against five Manila seacunnies who allegedly had burnt and destroyed the *Asia*. After the trial was over all three remained unemployed. In his petition to the governor general, Patton wrote, "I am become a ruined man, and laboring under great embarrassments."

Patton had a knowledge of the Malay language and so could work on a temporary basis as an interpreter of Malay to the judge of the Supreme Court, but this employment was not enough for his subsistence. Others were destitute on the streets of Calcutta. Patton and the other sailors were lucky to receive three months' maintenance from the governor general's office. But even the governor general's office could not guarantee employment for a law-abiding (former) officer of one of its ships so as to keep him off the streets.[130]

The licensing system introduced on January 1, 1774 directly addressed the itinerancy of unwanted Europeans in the early colony.[131] The British Parliament by the 1770s had doused the imperial vision of the British Radical Whigs to turn EIC-controlled India into a settler colony.[132] The EIC thus carefully regulated the movement of those English men and women into Bengal who were not directly employed by the EIC state's military or civil administration. This people, the "unofficial Europeans," who constituted a considerable segment of the population within EIC territory, required licenses. The Board of Control in London, via the Court of Directors, granted indentures to free merchants or free mariners to reside in India, who on arrival received a "license" against the indenture. Anyone aspiring for the mariner's indenture had to show that he had served at sea for over three years or as an officer on an EIC ship. Many sailors often abused mariner's indentures to gain their residence permit, or "license," in India to do businesses of other kinds. For this reason, the Court of Directors in their letters to the governor general in Calcutta on April 2, 1807, mentioned that Edward Henry Tullah had been granted mariner's indenture provided "it is his intention to follow the seafaring line during his continuance in India."[133]

Elizabeth Kolsky argues that the licensing system was put in place to counter unchecked white violence in the interior of the colony, through the deportation of the unofficial population. Once in Calcutta, sailors would head to the areas of Lal Bazar or Bow Bazar where all the punch houses and brothels were located. Their alcoholism and rowdiness, often involving violence, was a source of inconvenience and shame for EIC officials and for the respectable non-official population of the city.[134] Additionally, the class divide within the European population underpinned the EIC's lack of trust in the intents and actions of poor Europeans. In order to protect the Europeans' interest in maintaining appearances as a monolithic entity in India, the EIC devised a complex system of registration and permission to weed out financially weak (and embarrassing) elements. In fact, the Marine

Board paid the passage fare for indigent Europeans to go back to England, as they did for Thomas William Thompson in 1815.[135]

Moreover, deserters, who were a substantial section of the vagrants, formed the most dangerous people among the European poor; they often were fortune seekers and had over the past two centuries regularly joined the armed forces of the EIC's enemies. Even as late as 1767, two soldiers, Nicole and Davie, ran off to the territory of the Nawab of Awadh, Shuja-ud-Daulah, with a small amount of arms "with which they not only supplied the country powers, but were actually training up a body of men for their service to our discipline."[136] Only in 1775 did the EIC strike a deal with Shuja-ud-Daulah's son, the Nawab Asaf-ud-Daulah, for the return of deserters.[137] The licensing system complemented such deals. A strict immigration system with a sufficient mechanism of frequent deportation ensured that poor Europeans who lacked sympathy for EIC interests could be kept at bay. The strictness of the license system resulted in only a small number of Europeans residing in Bengal—in 1814 the number was 1,455 and by 1830, three years before the cancellation of the license system, it had risen to 2,149.

Magistrates played a critical role in the successful enforcement of the licensing system. Both the Court of Directors in London and the governor general in Calcutta depended upon magistrates to scrutinize the official and non-official European presence in India. In their letters to the governor general the Court of Directors provided lists of names of persons receiving indentures and expressed concerns regarding anomalies in official presence.[138] In their letter of March 10, 1803, the Court of Directors requested the governor general in Bengal to deport five people who had entered the service of Bombay Marine as volunteers in 1794, but were missing from service as of December 1800. The governor general in turn sent out orders to the magistrates of Calcutta and other districts to hunt down these people and send them to the presidency town.[139] In order to ensure that the licensing system functioned, the governor general in Calcutta devised a local registration system heavily involving the police. On reaching Calcutta, all resident Europeans had to gather a local license from the magistrate for their stay in the provinces of Bengal, Bihar, and Orissa. In gathering these licenses, the aspiring residents paid a small fee to the magistrate of Calcutta. Between February 7 and March 7, 1815, George Inglis, William Green, Charles Moore, Arnold Matthews, and Stephen Rolt paid the Calcutta magistrate 16 rupees each to obtain "permission to proceed into the interior of the country."[140] On reaching the provinces, they had to report to the respective district magistrates of their stay. From time to time, magistrates of all districts were required to send in lists of European residents within their jurisdictions with details about the validity of their licenses, duration of stay, and occupation.[141] Anyone without a local license was sent back to Calcutta and then to England. Mr. Leland was sent back to England in 1805 when he failed to produce his license.[142] C.L. Maddox could not avoid deportation even though he pleaded that he was born of European parents in India.[143] The magistrates of Calcutta and the districts thus provided the necessary scaffolding for an intricate immigration system connecting London and Bengal via Calcutta.

With such elaborate surveillance measures, police personnel ensured the imprisonment and deportation of deserting sailors to destinations selected by their employers. As early as in 1784 the Calcutta *Gazette* reported that the superintendent of police kept under his "strict custody" seamen who had committed "irregularities and outrages."[144] These efforts continued into early 1800s. When apprehended, a magistrate of Calcutta sent I. Lewis, a former mate in the pilot service. back to England.[145] But deserting sailors did not always get sent back to England. The Calcutta magistrate had to send John Prentice, steward to the captain of the ship H.C.S. *Broxburnebury*, to Madras. He had run away from his ship in January and was apprehended five months later when the ship was harbored at Madras. Prentice was put back on his former ship.[146] Since apprehended sailors as punishment faced service on the ships from which they had ran away, the choice of destination remained in the hands of the ship owners or ship captains. This sometimes created confusion for the Calcutta magistrate. When William Phillips, who absconded from the *Larkins*, was captured in the suburbs of Calcutta, the ship had already left Calcutta. On asking the captain of the *Larkins*, Commodore Hayes, the magistrate of the suburbs, found out that the sailor Phillips was no longer needed on the *Larkins*, and so the magistrate put him on the ship H.C. *Cruizers*. Much to the magistrate's displeasure, Hayes then retracted his words and demanded that Phillips be put into service with one of the captains of the H.C. *Indiamen*. Finally the Council Chamber in Calcutta ordered that Phillips be put on board the ship *Lady Carrington* and taken to Bencoolen, where he would be handed over to Commodore Hayes.[147] The magistrate of the suburbs of Calcutta was particularly unsure of what to do with his prison population of deserted sailors, as he was short of funds to provide for the subsistence of these men in custody, who were most often destitute.[148] The magistrate of Calcutta proper was far more equipped to handle such prisoners because he could act as the recruiter of seamen for the ship captains.

The EIC subsequently passed legislation which formally defined the magistrate's law enforcement role as an enabler of the interests of ship owners and ship captains. In the early 1800s the EIC no longer suffered from a lack of legal mechanisms to enforce regulations criminalizing breach of contract. The Better Regulation and Government of Seamen in the Merchants Service Act of 1729, in fact, inspired the April 1814 regulation which punished, with two months' imprisonment, defaulting native artisans working for English manufacturers in Calcutta. To further strengthen the grip of state and employer over seaman, the EIC additionally passed the Regulation of April 13, 1816, which specified that any seaman who received an advance payment for a certain duration of work was bound to labor in any other ship as specified by the captain or owner of vessel with whom he had signed the contract. The regulation applied to cases where the ship met with accident or the seaman absconded before the duration of his labor contract expired. Further, if proven that the seaman failed to comply with such rule the justices of the peace in Calcutta could punish the offenders with up to two months of imprisonment.[149] Thus seamen could be put to work on vessels belonging to owners different from the ones with whom they had signed a contract. The 1816 ordinance came on the heels of a number of ship-burning incidents for which the EIC held their Lascar crews responsible.[150] However, the legislation was not only directed against Lascars but also "all and every such seaman, mariner, or person other than the captain and mates." As late as 1855, 486 inmates of the Calcutta House of Corrections were sailors convicted of breach of contract.[151] Similar to Regulation XI of 1806, the April 13, 1816 regulation denied legal individuality to seamen and reduced them to an undifferentiated mass of labor over which employers had despotic control. The 1816 ordinance unlike the 1806 regulation also conceptualized the employer as an undifferentiated interest group who could command or utilize the labor power of the seaman. The magistrates mediated between the undifferentiated interest group of private employers of sailors and the mass of congealed labor of seamen. In practice, though, magistrates often consulted the ship captains before putting captured deserters to work. As is evident from William Phillip's case from 1815, the practice of placing absconders in a workplace of the captain's choice was already in vogue before the law was put on paper in 1816.

Other regulations devised systems of police superintendence over vagrant sailors. A public notice on April 24, 1789 stated that "all Commanders of ships either from Europe or any port in India or from China shall on their arrival at this port deliver at the police office a list of sailors in their respective ships and the Countries of which they are subjects or they shall not be permitted to land their goods."¹⁵² In 1817, the EIC passed further legislation which propped up an even stronger surveillance system against the seamen. The Ordinance of July 14, 1817 introduced an intricate registration system which monitored seamen's every movement. It required seamen sailing from or belonging to the port of Calcutta to obtain a character certificate from the Marine Registry office. The governor general declared the Marine Registry office to be "the exclusive medium for supplying not only natives but European seamen for the government vessels and those of the merchants."¹⁵³ Only those seamen with detailed character certificates from the Marine office were deemed employable. The character certificates specifically mentioned the number of times seamen had absconded. If they misplaced their certificates, seamen had to pay a fine as high as 5 sicca rupees to get a duplicate. In order to prevent fraud, the ordinance stipulated that any action "with intent to defeat or obstruct the due execution of this ordinance" would be punished by a fine not exceeding 50 sicca rupees and prison time with hard labor not exceeding two months. The registrar at the Marine office also gained the power over any seaman who had embarked on a voyage or passed through the port of Calcutta, to extract on their return to port any balance the seaman might owe to the ship owner, either through labor or cash payment. The state thus stepped in to provide extra safeguards for employers using maritime contractual labor. Apart from the Marine Registry office, the EIC state made the Calcutta police responsible for movements of seamen. In fact, prior to the July 1817 regulation, the Calcutta magistrates carried out the registration work, providing character certificates to seamen stating "that they are not deserters from the army nor seamen under engagement to any ship, but at liberty to tender their services for employment."¹⁵⁴ The 1817 regulation stipulated that on reaching Calcutta, if any seaman ventured out into Calcutta or any other region for a period over forty-eight hours, he had to report his place of residence and his own details to the nearest police station within that division. If he failed to register his presence with the local police, the justices of the peace in Calcutta could punish him with a fine of 5 sicca rupees and commit him to hard labor in prison not exceeding fifteen days.¹⁵⁵

The July 1817 regulation not only restricted the mobility of seamen but also eroded their power of collective bargaining. The Marine Registry office intervened to fix wages for seamen sailing from or belonging to the port of Calcutta. If the seamen made a voyage to any port of Europe they would receive an advance of three months' wages and if they traveled to any port in Asia, Africa or America, they would receive an advance of two months' wages. The Marine Board stipulated the wages of the seamen, which were non-negotiable. The 1817 regulation deemed illegal any combination of actions that "any gunner, carpenter, boatsmen or other inferior officer or seafaring man or lascar shall enter into ... to exact a greater impress or advance of wages than is allowed in and by this rule, ordinance and regulation." Modeled after the 1798 anti-combination laws in England, this regulation negated any form of collective action by sailors, both Asiatic and European. Any two justices of the peace in Calcutta could punish seamen engaged in collective bargaining with a fine not exceeding 50 sicca rupees and a prison term of up to two months at hard labor.[156] All avenues for negotiation, whether flight or strike, had become fully criminalized.

Like European sailors, European common soldiers became racially privileged subjects at the same time that the EIC military penalized their unwanted mobility with sentences of penal labor. European soldiers committing acts of violence against their European counterparts were punished far more harshly than European soldiers inflicting violence on native members of the army or the indigenous population in general.[157] As Britons, European soldiers retained the privilege of trial by a jury in the Crown courts of the presidency towns. As a result, European soldiers committing crimes against native population could easily dodge trial because native victims often had no means of traveling to the presidency towns from remote provinces where these crimes had occurred. Yet this leniency did not extend to acts of insubordination in workplaces—desertion, most commonly—which were promptly tried by courts-martial set up by the military. Well into the 1810s the Mutiny Acts specified that General Courts-Martial could sentence captured deserters to capital punishment. In England, the imposition of brutal army discipline had aroused vocal public criticism since the 1740s.[158] Perhaps under the pressure of such criticism, the Mutiny Acts included provisions for commutation of capital punishment to transportation to penal colonies at the discretion of the Courts-Martial.[159] For European soldiers in EIC territories, transportation to penal colonies became more or less the standard punishment for desertion. Graver sentences of capital punishment were reserved for crimes such as murder of other European soldiers. For repeated desertions David Frew, a matross, received a sentence of transportation with hard labor to the penal colony of Botany Bay for life from a Courts-Martial assembled in Fort William in May 1816. Similarly Francis McHugh, a private in the 1st Battalion of His Majesty's 66th Regiment of Foot, was penalized with seven years of hard labor at Botany Bay for desertion by a Courts-Martial assembled in Dinajepur.[160] The same year, John Dougherty, a private in His Majesty's 86th Regiment of Foot, for mutinous behavior received from a General Court-Martial a sentence of fourteen years of hard labor as a convict in New South Wales.[161] Given the length and intensity of these prison terms, deserting European soldiers endured punishments harsher than European sailors or even native boatmen. The Calcutta sheriff, a special executive police, took responsibility for deporting the convicted soldiers.[162]

The police, especially in Calcutta, played a seminal role in monitoring every movement of the European sailors and soldiers—in limiting their vagrancy in and outside of the docklands, apprehending them if they absconded, putting them in jails, deporting them wherever necessary, and last but not the least in recruiting them.[163] The deep involvement of the police in recruitment of sailors (and even soldiers) is evident from Lodevick Printz's experience as a crimp for the British Army in Calcutta during the early years of the Napoleonic Wars. Printz, a German law-abiding "respectable gentleman" and a resident of Calcutta for thirteen years, according to his own words, "supplied government with more than 1500 men during the last war, both by seas and land."[164] In 1803 he responded to a lucrative offer made by the EIC government to enlist recruits for the company's service for three years at a bounty of 100 rupees per man. The Napoleonic Wars had created a shortage of European army personnel and so the EIC state was ready to pay a fat price for new recruits. Major Grace and Colonel Green granted Printz's application on the condition that in case he failed to recruit men, he would serve in the artillery for three years. Printz failed miserably and was reduced to serving as a matross in the artillery when he wrote a letter to the Military Department explaining the cause of his failure: the noncooperation of the magistrate of Calcutta. Soon after receiving the commission for recruiting soldiers, Printz realized that he had irked the magistrate by not consulting him before receiving the commission. All private shipowners and ship captains or military recruiters had to belong to the magistrate's favorable network to get any access to the European workforce in Calcutta.

The magistrate and his subordinates within the police maintained an iron grip over the labor market in European sailors and soldiers. The town sergeants along with the guards went on rounds through the streets of Calcutta, kidnapping any loitering European who they thought fit to be a sailor. These kidnapped men were prisoners of the magistrate, held in custody sometimes for two to three months on bread and water. The ship captains who ultimately used this labor bore the costs of maintaining this reserve labor pool at the rate of one rupee per day for the prisoners' bread, water, and shelter. One of the town sergeants even owned a punch house and recruited seamen for a commission from ship captains as high as one gold mohur per man. The biggest grievance of the Calcutta magistrate and sergeants against Printz was that "if I [Printz] was to remain in the recruiting service, they would not be able to get any sailors for the ships."[165] Printz was competing with the magistrate. The police were extremely concerned about keeping their exclusive control over the labor market of European sailors and soldiers. A town sergeant kidnapped one of Printz's recruits and threatened to put him on board a frigate. Printz had to pay a hefty sum to free the man. In such an adverse climate, Printz could only recruit fifteen men. Before writing to the Military Department Printz complained about the Calcutta magistrate to Major Grace and Colonel Green but to no effect. Because army officials, like ship captains, depended heavily on magistrates for securing and disciplining their men, taking any action against the Calcutta magistrate was out of the question.

The "frontiers" of the colonial world, in Frantz Fanon's description, "are shown by barracks and police stations."[166] In Bengal a coalition of police and military violence created the cordon sanitaire fastening boatmen and European sailors and soldiers to their positions as workers in a colonized world. Unlike in Fanon's appraisal, this brutal regime was not only directed against the indigenous population but also against working class Europeans. Racial privilege for European sailors and soldiers went hand in hand with redoubled discipline in the workplace, put into effect by a police state they had never before encountered in this part of the world. By the early nineteenth century, contested legal or police jurisdiction by various state entities was not a problem for the EIC state. It had removed or superseded all other competitors for state power—the Nawabi state, the rival European companies, and the *zamīndārs*. In the process the EIC administration had brought localized police forces under centralized control. As the reach of the police extended from the streets of Calcutta to the creeks of the Bengal countryside, the police emerged as the chief recruiter of boatmen as well as European sailors and soldiers for the colonial state and private employers. The "language of pure force" considerably counteracted the use of desertion as a means for boatmen and European sailors and soldiers to influence the value of their labor. The impact is most evident in the disappearance of customary wages and the introduction of a standardized wage payment system. In addition to losing their power of mobility to influence hiring practices, boatmen lost control over their rhythms of work. A number of regulations—Regulation XI of 1806, the April 13, 1816, regulation, and the July 24, 1817, regulation—legally validated the role of the police in monitoring the labor market for boatmen and European sailors and soldiers.

While institutionalizing the police as the hatchet men of the labor market these regulations reproduced boatmen as well as European sailors and soldiers as a new kind of worker-subject. As workers they found their occupations beset with new hierarchical relationships never experienced before. Apart from subjecting them to these new hierarchies, the regulations converted the boatmen and European workers' subjecthood into an incorporeal mass of labor, both real and spectral, to be utilized by the state and private employers. In discussing the nature of subjectivities of the ruled that colonial legislation prohibiting specific indigenous practices had created, Dirks notes that "subjectivity presented itself as an absence; it was only there when it was totally suppressed"; men and women, he explained, were passive victims of the devious customs of an alien country and their passivity defined their subjectivity.[167] The colonial state's labor laws articulated a similar form of negation—boatmen and sailors were colonial subjects, reduced to disembodied units of "labor."

Conclusion

A COLONIAL RULE OVER LABOR

IN THE SUMMER OF 1798, the English legislature created the Thames River Police. a special police force for the City of London. This was the brainchild of Patrick Colquhoun, magistrate and manufacturers' advocate, and John Harriott, seaman, soldier, manufacturer, and army recruiter. Coming from an aristocratic Scottish family, Colquhoun spent five years in the Virginia colony at an early age, acquainting himself with the legal and commercial world of the British empire. On his return to Scotland he entered public office and rose to the position of magistrate of Glasgow in 1782. Over the next ten years Colquhoun became the voice of manufacturing interests in Scotland and England. In these years of agitation, he came to ponder East India's place in Britain's commerce and empire. Soon after, he joined London's magistracy and occupied himself with the prospect of rectifying the police administration in the city, where he met John Harriott. Harriott came from an upwardly mobile family of tanners. At a young age he joined the merchant marine and went to the Americas. Thereafter he found employ in the EIC army, which took him to India. Steadily Harriott rose the social ladder to become a farmer, manufacturer, army recruiter, and finally the first magistrate of Thames River Police. He wrote his memoirs in two volumes detailing his experience in Britain and the world. Colquhoun, on the other hand, was a prolific man of letters with at least twenty-seven books and pamphlets to his credit. In their various works on police, commerce, and empire Colquhoun and Harriott envisioned a hierarchical, orderly world with Britain at its center. For both, the moral and practical purpose of the Thames River Police was to guard the "floating property" of merchant capital that plied the river Thames every day, and to instill a morality of respect towards this property in the heart and minds of the "rough, ignorant multitude" laboring on the river. This new police force put into effect regulations to rid the river of "masterless men" by putting all laboring poor under hierarchical supervisory control, monitoring their wages while criminalizing all extra earnings through "privileges" and "perquisites," and registering and licensing all public houses, crimps, and sailors. While disciplining labor on London's waterfront, Colquhoun and Harriott, with their experience of service in the far-flung corners of the British empire, were also conscious of the conditions of labor in the colonies. In Colquhoun's schema of the global division of labor, the colonies were solely producers of agricultural commodities. More specifically, colonial workers should labor to produce agricultural bounties in the form of raw material to augment British manufactories.[1] Such visions of labor at home and out in the world also underpinned the EIC state's attitude towards work in Bengal. The EIC state combined the wisdom of labor control in the metropole accumulated over four centuries with their specific experience in Bengal for a century and half to craft a colonial governance over labor which was patently alien to Bengal.

In Bengal, the EIC found a plenitude of hired workers, but no social or political mechanism to make them bound to contracts. As this book elucidates, hired work of various kinds was integral to rural and urban life in Bengal, including company settlements. Companies had played an integral role beginning in the seventeenth century in organizing large-scale hired work in the region. This organization was possible because of a readily available workforce both accustomed to and willing to work for a hire in crucial zones of company activities. In fact, both the VOC and EIC could regularly hire workers on contract, as was the case with silk reelers. For some workers, such as long-distance shipping crews, the companies could negotiate contracts for as long as five years with considerable ease.[2] Yet, binding workers to contracts created an unprecedented challenge for the companies in India. Historians have explored in detail the frequent breakdowns in contractual negotiations between indigenous brokers working for the companies or intermediary merchants and European companies.[3] These disputes required the exertion of the companies' own state powers but more importantly the assistance of the imperial government. Sometimes the companies found the imperial state on their side, as was the case with Emperor 'Alamgir's *farmān* of 1662 permitting the VOC to recover its debts or Dīwān Balchand's *parwāna* allowing the company to force their reelers to pay off their debts.[4] The strength of these orders was such that VOC could imprison their defaulting intermediary merchants and workers. Yet, such orders were few and far between and hence bore little disciplinary weight. Moreover, both the imperial government as well as the companies as state entities faced jurisdictional limitations on enforcing these contracts. Thus, lack of fastidious enforcement of contractual obligations coexisted uncomfortably with the widespread use of contracts in matters of commerce and its concomitant labor.

The English state's fear of "masterlessness," a condition wherein the poor "lay idle" with their mobility uncontrolled, had no parallel in the Indian subcontinent. The ordinance of 1349, which for the first time legislated that all "idle men and women" be "bound to serve anyone who requires his/her services," was used against people without property who were identified by the courts as "vagrants." In the Indian subcontinent, caste servility perhaps comes closest to such stringent state-sanctioned servility. By the late eighteenth century, processes of centralization in several indigenous states stiffened caste boundaries and imposed unpaid forced labor (*begār*) on untouchable caste groups.[5] Yet, the indigenous states did not always intervene to determine the rigidity of caste relations. In Marwar, the artisanal caste councils zealously guarded the exclusivity of their caste profession, preventing outsiders from entry independent of the state.[6] Moreover in those cases where states did police caste boundaries they did not regulate mobility practices. Thus, in the Malabar region where the rulers of Cochin, Calicut, and Travancore granted special certificates to untouchable menial servile dependents of high-caste masters, these certificates did not specify or restrict the mobility practices of the servants. Mobility was left to the unequal negotiations between the lords and their lower-caste servants.[7] In Bengal, one does not come across such state-regulated, individuated servitude as is evident from the caste certificates of Malabar. Even though land grants often attached the labor of residents of land to a donee, these grants did not specify mobility nor did they criminalize recalcitrant mobility. The itinerant poor were a permanent fixture of rural and urban life, as chapter 1 shows. Although indigenous states often feared the mobility of the roving poor, unlike the English state they did not criminalize vagrancy. After all, begging was not a crime, and paying beggars often brought merit to benevolent patrons, cutting across religious affiliations. On the contrary, in England fear of vagrancy resulted in statutes between the 1570s and 1590s which banned individual begging, tethered the poor to "abiding places," and made work compulsory for state-sanctioned "able-bodied poor" in order to receive state support.[8] Similarly labor laws such as the Statute of Artificers of 1565 ensured that men and women who were forced into service could not leave employment without their employers' consent under penalty of imprisonment. Such master-servant relations imposed by the state were not built on social negotiations. Thus, influential political and literary figures of the eighteenth century such as Daniel Defoe and Jonathan Swift feared that, without such forceful regulations, "order is inverted, subordination ceases" as "servants be governours of their masters." Swift's satire specifically mocked servants' uncontrolled mobility and their propensity to "stay out" of their masters' home, a proclivity that servants' "flesh and blood cannot always resist."[9]

Direct intervention of a centralized state by its police force was one solution to masterlessness and uncontrolled mobility, a phenomenon remarkably absent in Bengal. The 1349 English Ordinance of Laborers succeeded in compelling masterless men and women into service, regulated wages, and enforced contracts, prioritizing the power of the centralized state in deciding labor relations in the country. The statute not only introduced the centralized state's ability to enforce compulsory labor but also subsumed the ability to fix wages and contracts, once the domain of village-level governance. In Bengal company officials pined for such legislation. Individually both the VOC and EIC were armed with legislation to tackle the rowdy mobility of their workers. Yet, as *zamīndārs* in Bengal their ability to enforce these laws was much eroded not only by their limited jurisdiction but also the contrary role of the central imperial Mughal/Nawabi state. Mughal jurisprudence did not criminalize desertion. Legally the imperial government could impose restricted mobility on tax-evading peasants but not any possessive claim over the workers' labor power. Moreover, the imperial state shared military and police governance with localized *zamīndāri* power centers, making it difficult for the imperial government to intervene in matters of labor control. Thus Bengal remained a sore spot in company governance even though elsewhere in Asia where the companies could muster aggrandized state power, such laws were liberally enforced. As early as the 1740s even Bengali sailors of the VOC recruited in Bengal but who deserted in and around Batavia and suffered the misfortune of recapture were put to tens of whip lashes behind the council house in the city center and then banished to the island of Edam (present-day island of Damar Besar, off the coast of Jakarta) for years of unpaid penal labor.[10] Neither Mughal nor *zamīndāri* governance of Bengal could come to their rescue in such far-off lands. On the river Thames, from the mayor down to the headmen of workmen and wherrymen, the centralized state regulated years of apprenticeship, boat wages, and passenger numbers. In Bengal, after 1792, the EIC created a similar interventionist state apparatus with a combination of the army, centralized police under the magistrate and the *darogah*, as well as regulations which oversaw every aspect of work by boatmen and European sailors, from their wages to their mobility. The centralized state assigned separate juridical status to boatmen and European sailors and designed the mechanism of policing accordingly.

"Systematic colonization" in Bengal entailed putting the worker "on the right road by means of police."[11] Police involvement went beyond direct control over recruitment, wage control, and enforcement of penalties according to the statutes. Police surveillance, by itself, re-oriented the mobility of hired workers. Surveillance ensured that boatmen could not use flight to negotiate better wages and considerably reduced the EIC state's time and efforts in recruiting them. The licensing system created a nexus of information from Calcutta to the districts via the magistrates. This same network of surveillance was used against deserters. In Calcutta, wartime recruiters like Lodevick Printz learned the hard way the power of the Calcutta magistrate over recruitment of European sailors. Sometimes, surveillance measures in Bengal exceeded England's surveillance of its working population. Although a statute to register sundry seamen in England was repealed in 1711, the ordinance of July 24, 1817 introduced the same registry system in Bengal. When the governor general decided to offer all sailors in Bengal a character certificate, Colquhoun contemplated a magistrate-led licensing of all crimps to mediate the recruitment of seamen both on behalf of merchants and sailors. Police intervention, Colquhoun suggested, would goad men "to conduct business honestly and in moderate terms."[12]

The centralized state further imposed hierarchical relationships in workplaces as a cure for masterlessness. During the reign of Philip II and Mary I, in the mid-sixteenth century, statutes were passed that transformed watermen and wherrymen, making a living as "masterless men, and single men of all kinds of occupation and faculties," into a specialized, disciplined workforce. Eight of the best watermen, who were also "householders," were selected to serve as "overseers and rulers of all the wherrymen and workmen on the river Thames." Subsequent monarchs, irrespective of political differences, passed statutes which introduced an increasingly straightjacketed apprenticeship system among the watermen and wherrymen.[13] In Bengal, the EIC state similarly instituted a hierarchical relationship among boatmen, first through the creation of the recruiter *ghat majhi*, in the 1740s, and then through defining the relationship between head boatman (*majhi*) and oarsmen in Regulation XI of 1806. The hierarchy enabled the EIC to delegate power and distribute risk onto the head boatman in the disciplining of oarsmen. The head boatmen as supervisors shared responsibility with the EIC state in preventing all forms of infractions of oarsmen, including desertion. Mobile workers, on both the rivers Thames and Ganga, could not be left masterless.

As boatmen became part of "public service," they experienced hired work as a form of waged work unique to the English tradition. In rural England, "service" had created a class of farm laborers attached to landowning masters through waged service. Servants, distinct from domestics, were a common part of the English labor force. The terms and conditions of their work were harsher than those for "laborers," who enjoyed shorter contracts and more freedom. Besides, regulations such as the Ordinance of Labourers of 1349, distinguished between "work" and "service," the latter always entailing force or compulsion. In the British empire in Asia, service as a form of unfree labor was most explicit in "public service," a domain of work reserved almost exclusively for convicts. Though the British colonial officials shied from calling convicts "workers" even as they used their labor in infrastructure projects, convicts considered themselves as "company *ke naukar*" (servants of the company).[14] Boatmen too entered this domain. But, unlike convicts, boatmen as "free" hired labor for "public service" experienced the specific English implications of "service." All contemporary English political imaginations of the "free-born Englishman" excluded servants. Their freedom was deferred to their masters, for servants were "virtually comprehended in their master's covenant with God."[15] Service ensured a condition of subservience and unfreedom. Boatmen's loss of control over their work hours, wage rates, customary privileges, and mobility were in line with this condition.

With "slaves" in Xenophon's *Oeconomicus* becoming "servants" in Gentian Hervet's sixteenth-century English translation of *Oeconomicus*, a cognitive identification of slavery with service had already been established in English thought and practice. This resemblance, apart from the realm of household work, was not noticeable in other forms of hired work in Bengal until the end of the eighteenth century.[16] For much of the eighteenth century enslaved people and formerly enslaved people or manumitted slaves, of whom an overwhelming majority were women, did the care work and sexual labor in the EIC or VOC settlements. The pathway from slavery to hired help for household work continued even in the late eighteenth century when many more women with no prior history of slavery entered care work. Because these women, whether enslaved or freed and working for hire, continued to do the same work, as household workers they confronted a unique situation where the distinction between slavery and hired work remained dim. Court records thus present multiple instances of affinity among formerly enslaved and now enslaved workers. Sometimes, in rare instances of interaction with workers from other domains of work, household slaves learned that the condition of slavery was anomalous in the world of work in Bengal. This was the case for Simon van Orissa, an enslaved worker in the household of a junior merchant of the VOC, who planned his escape in June 1739 at the instigation of a mason. The mason had suggested that it was only natural for slaves in Bengal like Simon to flee from their master's home. Yet by the early nineteenth century hired work in other domains experienced the increasing collapse of the boundaries between slavery and hired work, and between freedom and unfreedom. In this respect the boatmen's experience as hired labor was much akin to that of the women who since the early eighteenth century had worked in European households under analogous conditions of slavery and hired work.[17]

Police on the rivers Thames and Ganges also redefined the "customs" of work. "Customs," as Sumit Guha and Nandita Sahai show, are highly dynamic and highly sensitive to historical contexts.[18] The historicity of "customs" not only explains caste as a political and economic institution but also how it was possible for caste to sometimes become the resource for collective bargaining among even untouchable caste groups.[19] Guha and Sahai's works belong to the larger literature which addresses the egregious assignment of seemingly immutable "customs" or interchangeably, "caste customs," to historically specific practices, stemming in large measure from the collections and catalogues of "customs" by colonial bureaucracy. In eighteenth century Bengal, caste alone is an inadequate label for explaining the customs of hired work. Not all occupations were strongholds of one or a few castes, such as inland shipping or silk reeling.[20] While boatmen in company fleets maintained their caste rules, they did not utilize caste collectives as the medium for collective bargaining. As pay became the site for claiming customs even European sailors' demands for food money or pay despite debt could easily be couched in the indigenous terminology for customary pay, or *bakśiś*. The antiquity of these "customs" is irrelevant; rather, they illuminate the historical nature of state-worker and employer-worker relationships in the seventeenth and early eighteenth centuries. Thus, the practices of boatmen or silk reelers and even European sailors and soldiers, which the European companies catalogued as "customs," belied any nineteenth-century colonial definitions of customs. As this book intends to show, when it came to the customs of hired workers such as boatmen, the "Herculean task" for the colonial state was not a meticulous cataloguing, but abolition.[21] Along the river Thames too abolition of customs was legion. John Harriott recalled, in the following words of bravado, his success in putting an end to the "half savage" Irish coal heavers' perquisite of reserving for themselves two or three bushels of coal while unloading ships: "It was a labour not unworthy of Hercules and we succeeded by our joint efforts in bringing into reasonable order some thousands of men who had long considered plunder as privilege."[22] At a similar time in Bengal, the EIC state issued regulations which not only criminalized walking away from work but also made the boatmen's practice of carrying salt on board for their private sale a criminal offense. Like the Thames River Police, separate branches of surveillance—salt *chowkies* and the centralized police force under the magistrates—ensured the implementation of these regulations. The "Herculean" police force in London and Bengal saw in the customs of the hired worker a "hydra" to be vanquished.

Straightjacketing conditions of work was a global process of capitalism. More and more domains of work which heretofore remained outside the reach of the surveillance state whether in Bengal or in England entered its grasp. In Bengal the EIC state minted regulations beginning from the 1750s to standardize wages, create workplace hierarchy, and penalize breach of contract. Workers affected by such regulations ranged from domestic servants to European sailors.[23] The hierarchical relationship between head boatmen and rowers became a regulatory model for disciplining porters and bearers. In England where similar regulations for workers had been in effect for at least several centuries the development of the surveillance state was still far from complete, as the creation of the Thames River Police in 1798 suggests. If both the City of London and Bengal saw extension of police control over workers at a similar time, and if in Bengal both European and indigenous workers were being subjected to ruthless standardization of conditions of work simultaneously, one needs to rethink Gopalan Balachandran's definition of the colonial waged worker: "S/he had therefore to be mobilized, deployed, immobilized, and afterwards de-mobilized in a manner as to be available for re-mobilization, using apparatuses of control that were densely authoritarian even when they were not overtly penal. No matter how firmly locked into place, the coolie's immanent condition was always one of apparently random mobility."[24] Coercion through control over mobility was at the heart of the creation of the waged worker everywhere in the metropole and in the colony at the end of the eighteenth century. The chasm between the metropolitan and colonial waged worker had to wait for at least half a century when laws criminalizing breach of contract were fading away in the metropole while they continued to thrive in the colony, or when distinct difference in wage levels between colonial and metropolitan workforce had emerged.[25] During the eighteenth century the "wages of whiteness" for European sailors and soldiers remained confined to judicial immunity for inflicting violence on the natives. Thus proliferation of regulations and statute laws and the burgeoning use of the police and military forces for labor control on the London waterfront and Bengal simultaneously perhaps allows us to appreciate colonial rule as co-constitutive of Eurocentric capitalism.

Yet, colonial governance was not merely an implementation of a metropolitan culture of work. For one, the regulations for workers in the colony took note of the colony's specificity of work. In certain cases, as is evident from registration of sailors, the surveillance state was far more aggressive in the colony than in the metropole. But most significantly the EIC state created a workforce peculiar to the colony. This special workforce serviced the economic interests of Britain but would find no counterpart in Britain. Both Colquhoun and Harriott wrote about the fate of the subcontinent under EIC rule. Harriott during his years as a soldier in Golconda noted "the difference between the prosperity of the country that did not belong to the Company . . . and the fertile plains of Golconda to the eastward belonging to the company."[26] The former was decidedly better off than the latter. He diagnosed the company's revenue regime as the cause of this contrast. Colquhoun's careful study of Bengal aptly noted the EIC state's conundrum of the "investments" in trade in Bengal: "At present, the sovereign is the exporting merchant. The capital he employs is not like the capital of a merchant. It is furnished only from the taxes which the people pay. Under such a system the people must always remain poor, where the sovereign himself exports the produce of labour of the people without any return."[27] Such discerning observations on the plight of people in Bengal were juxtaposed with other ideas, such as "The surplus exportable labour produced in the British Isles will always consist chiefly of manufactures; that of the colonies will arise entirely from agricultural pursuits."[28]

Despite the awareness of the situation of manufacturers such as silk reelers in Bengal, it is unsurprising that Colquhoun as a champion of the manufacturers' cause in Britain would assign such difference between manufacturing in the colony and the metropole. Ultimately, Colquhoun's schema denied silk reelers of Bengal the subject position of manufacturers. The origins of silk reelers lay in "skilled" manufacturing work attached to the overseas commerce of Bengal, and subsequently the peculiarity of the EIC's rule, sealed its destiny. The EIC state removed the majority of competing employers, introduced foreign reeling technology, and created an ever-increasing burden of revenue extraction on its subject population, ensuring the silk reelers' descent into the lowest class of impoverished hired workers. This descent involved a unique experience of heavily constrained access to a market, inability to use their skills in the expansion of reeling operations and hence, as leverage vis-à-vis the EIC, reductions in revenue rates as a wage benefit, and the subsequent loss thereof. A "rule of difference" had paved a special path for the silk reelers' decline into the condition of a "daily laborer" wherein the distinction between "skilled" and "unskilled" work became superfluous, befitting only a hired laborer of the colony.

A combination of the English tradition of disciplining masterless men with the creation of a unique group of workers, maladjusted to the EIC state's ravenous needs for revenue as capital and a constrained market, defined the colonial repertoire of the EIC state's rule over labor in Bengal. Both mobilization and immobilization of labor were central to this governance; specifically, state power in the form of regulations, police, and military; and revenue requisition by *zamīndārs*, collectors, and silk residents followed closely the footsteps of the EIC state's hired workers and redirected them. State-labor relations as prevalent in England informed such governance with the goal of stabilizing recruitment, wages, and the master's control over labor. Any previous customs of work that came in the way of this goal were directly or indirectly removed. Police and the military actively intervened to fence off the market from their workers' labor. In the early nineteenth century, unfreedom of service for European sailors and soldiers and indigenous boatmen in Bengal existed alongside a labor market ruled by the Master and Servant Laws and the police in England. It was only with the repeal of these laws in England in 1875 that the gulf between colonial and metropolitan governance of labor was cast in sharp relief. Aside from state-imposed discipline, the squeeze of revenue extraction signified the domain of experience of the indigenous worker as colonial subject. For silk reelers the "privilege" of nonpayment of revenue had once determined their wages. With the introduction of filatures, the EIC state deemed their skills "outdated" and quickly removed their privileges and reduced their wages. Direct state intervention in determining the wages of reelers deliberately intertwined the subject of the reeler-worker with the revenue-paying subject. In England, no worker in manufacturing suffered this fate. Colonialism created unique laboring subjects while extending the metropolitan logic of labor control over them.

GLOSSARY

BAKSHY Assistant to a *darogah* in a police station after 1793

BAKŚIŚ Customary payment

BEGĀR Corvee, or forced labor

BERUNIYĀ Hired worker

BIGHA Unit of land measurement (in the colonial period, one *bigha* equaled one-third of an acre)

BURKUNDĀZES Native police corps equipped with firearms

CĀṬHĀH Unit of land measurement, smaller than a *bigha* (approximately one-twentieth of a *bigha*)

COMMERCIAL RESIDENT Agent of the English East India Company supervising the company's investments

CUTTANIES Reelers in a silk filature

DANDIES Oarsmen

DAROGAH Superintendent; after 1793, head of a police station

DIRECTORATE Bureaucratic designation of a VOC settlement headed by a director

DĪWĀN Head of Mughal provincial revenue administration

EIC English East India Company

FARMĀN Order issued by the Mughal emperor

FAUJDĀR Mughal imperial official primarily tasked with maintaining law and order

FIRINGĪ Term for all Europeans in the Mughal world

FISCAAL Chief judicial official in a VOC directorate

FLORETTE, MOCHTA, MATKĀ Silk yarns reeled from pierced cocoons

FOUZDARY ADALAT Criminal court in EIC-controlled Bengal; cf. Nizamat Adalat

GANDĀ Monetary measurement (1 anna = 4 gandās)

GHAT MAJHI Ferryman; sometimes a recruiter of *majhis*

GOLEAH Assistant to a *majhi*

GOMASTAH Salaried agent of the English East India company

GOUVERNAMENT Bureaucratic designation of a VOC settlement bigger than a directorate but smaller than a *commandement*

HARCARRAH Intelligence agent

JĀGĪR Temporary assignment of revenue proceeds from a certain area as salary and expenses for holding a state office in centralized Mughal imperial administration

JĀGĪRDAR Holder of *jāgīr* with judicial and police responsibilities, usually a rank-holding Mughal imperial official

JAMADAR Assistant to a *darogah* in a police station after 1793

JOGANDARS Superintendents in silk filatures

KĀMĀRA Ironsmith

KĀRIKAR Artisan

KARKHANA Mughal imperial workshop

KARMAKĀR Artisanal caste

KOTWĀL Police chief of a town

MAJHI Head boatman and/or pilot

MAUND Unit of weight (100 maunds = 4.5 tons)

MUCHLEKHA Bond

NACAUD Silk re-reeler

NACAUDKHANA Silk re-reeling workshops

NIZAMAT ADALAT Superior criminal court in EIC-controlled Bengal; cf. Fouzdary Adalat

NAIK Leader of *burkandazes*

ORGANZINE Best-quality Italian silk

PAIK Armed attendant employed by EIC police

PARGANA Subdivision of a *sarkār* and also a cluster of villages

PARWĀNĀ Order issued by higher-level imperial officials other than the emperor

PATTANI Best-quality silk yarn reeled directly from the cocoon by silkworm-rearing peasants or reelers hired by silkworm-rearing peasants

PATTI Second-best-quality silk yarn reeled directly from the cocoon by silkworm-rearing peasants or reelers hired by silkworm-rearing peasants

PĪR Title for a local saint venerated in the Bengal delta

PORSIA Silk waste used as customary payment over and above contracted wage to re-reelers

QĀẒĪ Judge working closely with *faujdārs* and *kotwāls*

RESIDENT Political representative of the English East India Company in Indian courts

SĀRI Boatmen's song

SARKĀR Subdivision of a province

SEER Unit of measurement for weight (1 seer = approximately 1 kilogram)

SIRDAR REELER Master silk re-reeler

SUBAHDAR Mughal provincial governor; also referred to by the English and Dutch India companies as a nawab

TA'ALLUQDĀR Smaller *zamīndār*, often with revenue farming rights

TAGEEDAR Head reeler working under master reelers in a filature

TANNA BANNA Second-best-quality silk yarn re-reeled from *pattani* and silk yarn re-reeled from *patti*

TANNY Best-quality silk yarn for the warp re-reeled from *pattani*

TRANSPORT BRIEVEN Certificates of salary consignment issued by the VOC to multiple creditors of their recruited sailors in the Dutch Republic

VOC Vereenigde Oostindische Compagnie (Dutch East India Company)

WAKĪL Representative of any East India company to Mughal courts

ZAMĪNDĀR A person under Mughal revenue administration, often with hereditary claims over a piece of land, entitled to collect revenue, with judicial and police responsibilities

ZAMĪNDĀRI Area administered by a *zamīndār*

NOTES

INTRODUCTION

1. "Resolution re: Repeal of Workmen's Breach of Contract Act and Certain Sections of the Indian Penal Code," British Library, London, Economic and Overseas Department Annual Files L/E/7/1339/1142. Emphasis mine.

2. D. Kooiman, "Jobbers and the Emergence of Trade Unions in Bombay City," *International Review of Social History*, XXII, 3 (1977): 313–28; Sumit Sarkar, *Modern India 1885–1947* (New York: Palgrave Macmillan, 1989), 244–47; R. Chandavarkar, "Workers' Politics and the Mill Districts in Bombay between the Wars," *Modern Asian Studies*, XV, 3 (1981), Special Issue, *Power, Profit and Politics: Essays on Imperialism, Nationalism and Change in the Twentieth Century*, ed. C.J. Baker, G. Johnson, and A. Seal: 603–47.

3. "Resolution."

4. The earliest work on early colonial labor legislation comes from R.K. Das. However, for Das the early colonial legislation instituting relations of servility were "premodern" laws enacted under "old" government of the East India Company (EIC) different from the "modern" factory laws under the "new" British government of the late nineteenth century. See R.K. Das, *Principles and Problems of Indian Labour Legislations* (Calcutta: Calcutta University Press, 1938), 104–14. Later scholars have identified such legislation as part of a unified colonial labor policy. See Tanika Sarkar, "Bondage in the Colonial Text," in *Chains of Servitude: Bondage and Slavery in India*, ed. Utsa Patnaik and Manjari Dingwaney (Madras: Sangam Books, 1985), 97–126; Amiya Kumar Bagchi, "Workers and the Historians' Burden," in Irfan Habib, K.N. Panikkar, T.J. Brynes and Utsa Patnaik, *The Making of History: Essays Presented to Irfan Habib* (London: Anthem, 2002), 298; Ravi Ahuja, "The Origins of Colonial Labour Policy in Late Eighteenth-Century Madras," *International Review of Social History* 44 (1999): 159–95; Michael Anderson, "India, 1858–1930: The Illusion of Free Labor," in *Masters, Servants, and Magistrates in Britain and the Empire, 1562–1955*, ed. Douglas Hay and Paul Craven (Chapel Hill: University of North Carolina Press, 2004), 422–54; Prabhu Mohapatra, "Regulated

Informality: Legal Constructions of Labour Relations in Colonial India 1814–1926," in *Workers in the Informal Sector: Studies in Labour History 1800–2000*, ed. Sabyasachi Bhattacharya and Jan Lucassen (Delhi: Macmillan India Ltd., 2005); for a more recent work on factory laws see Aditya Sarkar, *Trouble at the Mill: Factory Law and the Emergence of the Labour Question in Late Nineteenth-Century Bombay* (New Delhi: Oxford University Press, 2018).

5. The only exceptions are a few studies based on Southern India: David Washbrook, "Land and Labour in Eighteenth-Century South India: Golden Age of the Pariah?"; Peter Robb, ed., *Dalit Movements and Meanings of Labour in India* (New Delhi: Oxford University Press, 1993), 68–86; Ravi Ahuja, "Labour Relations in an Early Colonial Context: Madras, 1750–1800," *Modern Asian Studies* 36, no. 4 (2002); and Prasannan Parthasarathi, *The Transition to a Colonial Economy: Weavers, Merchants and Kings in South India, 1720–1800* (Cambridge: Cambridge University Press, 2004).

6. Dipesh Chakrabarty, "Translating Life-Worlds into Labor and History," in Dipesh Chakrabarty, *Provincializing Europe: Postcolonial Thought and Historical Difference* (Princeton: Princeton University Press, 2000), 72–96.

7. Partha Chatterjee, "Whose Imagined Community?" in *Nation and its Fragments: Colonial and Postcolonial Histories* (Princeton: Princeton University Press, 1993), 10.

8. Edmund Burke, "Ninth Report from the Select Committee appointed to take into consideration the state of administration of justice in the provinces of Bengal, Bahar and Orissa. Printed in the Year 1783," British Library, London, Parliamentary Papers, (hereafter, L/Parl), 15, 27.

9. Douglas Hay and Paul Craven, eds., *Masters, Servants, and Magistrates in Britain and the Empire* (Chapel Hill: University of North Carolina Press, 2004), 58, 59–116, 422–53; Prabhu Mohapatra, "From Contract to Status: Or How Law Shaped India's Labour Relations in Colonial India, 1780–1880," in *India's Unfree Workforce: of Bondage Old and New*, ed. Jan Breman, Isabelle Guerin and Aseem Prakash (New Delhi: Oxford University Press, 2009).

10. P.J. Marshall, "The British in Asia: Trade to Dominion," in *The Eighteenth Century*, ed. P.J. Marshall and Alaine Low (New York: Oxford University Press, 1998), 488; K.N. Chaudhuri, *The Trading World of Asia and the English East India Company, 1660–1760* (London: Cambridge University Press, 1978), 508, 510, 533; Om Prakash, *Dutch East India Company and the Economy of Bengal* (Princeton: Princeton University Press, 1983), 70.

11. Discussion of Marx's Asiatic model is extensive. For different evaluations see Irfan Habib, in *Essays in Indian History: Towards a Marxist Perception* (New Delhi: Anthem Press, 2002); Jairus Banaji, *Theory as History: Essays on Mode of Production and Exploitation* (Leiden: Brill, 2010), 15–40; Kevin Anderson, "Colonial Encounters in the 1850s," in *Marx at the Margins* (Chicago: University of Chicago Press, 2016), 9–41.

12. In fact, Marx did start revising his understanding of the village community in Indian society.

13. Scholarship on caste is vast. Recent research has historicized the emergence and transformations in caste relations contingent upon construction of kingship, ruling circles, patriarchal control, fiscal needs of state, organization of labor services, and individual and group negotiations vis-à-vis the state. Some representative works include Susan Bayly, *Saints, Goddesses and Kings: Muslims and Christians in South Indian Society, 1700–1900* (Cambridge: Cambridge University Press, 1989); Suvira Jaiswal, *Caste: Origin Functions and Dimensions of Change* (New Delhi: Manohar, 1998); Nicholas Dirks, *The Hollow Crown: Ethnohistory of an Indian Kingdom* (Ann Arbor: University of Michigan Press, 1993); Irfan Habib, *The Agrarian System of Mughal India, 1556–1707*, 3rd ed. (Oxford University Press, 2012); Sumit Guha, *Beyond Caste: Identity and Power in South Asia, Past and Present* (Leiden: Brill, 2013); Divya Cherian, *Merchants of Virtue* (Oakland: University of California Press, 2022).

14. Indrani Chatterjee, *Gender, Law and Slavery in Colonial India* (New Delhi: Oxford University Press, 1999), 1–33.

15. For the importance of commercialization in India in the eighteenth century see Christopher Bayly, *Rulers, Townsmen and Bazaars: North India in the Age of British Expansion* (Cambridge: Cambridge University Press, 1983); Sushil Chaudhury, *From Prosperity to Decline: Bengal in the Eighteenth Century* (New Delhi: Manohar, 1995); Muzaffar Alam, *The Crisis of Empire in Mughal North India: Awadh and the Punjab, 1707–1748*, 2nd ed. (New Delhi: Oxford University Press, 2013); Prasannan Parthasarathi, *Why Europe Grew Rich and Asia Did Not* (Cambridge: Cambridge University Press, 2011).

16. R.S. Sharma, *Sudras in Ancient India* (New Delhi: Motilal Banarassidas, 1990), 11, 168, 206; Habib, *Agrarian System of Mughal India*, 135–44.

17. Parthasarathi, *Transition to a Colonial Economy*; Nandita Prasad Sahai, *Politics of Patronage and Protest: The State Society and Artisans in Early Modern Rajasthan* (New York: Oxford University Press, 2006); Washbrook, "Land and Labour in Eighteenth-Century South India."

18. Sanjay Subrahmanyam, *The Portuguese Empire in Asia, 1500–1700: A Political and Economic History* (Malden: Wiley Blackwell, 2012).

19. Notable exceptions are two: Alessandro Stanziani, *Sailors, Slaves and Immigrants: Bondage in the Indian Ocean World, 1750–1914* (New York: Palgrave Macmillan, 2014) and Anthony Cox, *Empire, Industry and Class: The Imperial Nexus of Jute, 1840–1940* (Milton Park, UK: Routledge, 2013).

20. N.A.M. Rodger, *The Wooden World: An Anatomy of Georgian Navy* (New York: W.W. Norton, 1996); Marcus Rediker, *Between the Devil and the Deep Blue Sea: Merchant Seamen, Pirates and the Anglo American Maritime World, 1700–1750* (New York: Cambridge University Press, 1987); Gopalan Balachandran, *Globalizing Labour? Indian Seafarers and World Shipping, c. 1870–1945* (New Delhi: Oxford University Press, 2012); Matthias van Rossum, *Werkers van de Wereld: Globalisering, arbeid en interculturele ontmoetingen tussen Aziatische en Europese zeelieden in dienst van de VOC, 1600–1800* (Verloren: Hilversum, 2014); Aaron Jaffer, *Lascars and Indian Ocean Seafaring, 1780–1860: Shipboard Life, Unrest and Mutiny* (Woodbridge, UK: Boydell Press, 2015).

21. Christopher Hawes, *Poor Relations: The Making of a Eurasian Community, 1773–1833* (London: Routledge, 1996); Kenneth Ballhatchet, *Race, Sex, and Class Under the Raj: Imperial Attitudes and Policies and Their Critics, 1793–1905* (London: St. Martin's Press, 1980); Elizabeth Buettner, "Problematic Space, Problematic Races: Defining 'Europeans' in Late Colonial India," *Women's History Review* 9, no. 2 (2000): 277–98; Clare Anderson, "Discourses of Exclusion and the 'Convict Stain' in the Indian Ocean (c. 1800–1850)"; Harald Fischer-Tine, "Flotsam and Jetsam of Empire?: European Seamen and Spaces of Disease and Disorder in Mid-Nineteenth Century Calcutta," in *The Limits of British Colonial Control in South Asia*, ed. Ashwini Tambe and Harald Fischer-Tine (New York: Routledge, 2009); Elizabeth Kolsky, *Colonial Justice in British India: White Violence and the Rule of Law* (Cambridge: Cambridge University Press, 2010); Sharmistha De, *Marginal Europeans in Colonial India, 1860–1920* (Kolkata: Thema, 2008).

22. Antoinette Burton, *Empire in Question: Reading, Writing and Teaching British Imperialism* (Durham: Duke University Press, 2011), 277.

23. Stanziani, *Sailors, Slaves and Immigrants*.

24. Jairus Banaji, *Theory as History: Essays on Mode of Production and Exploitation* (Leiden: Brill, 2010), 131–54.

25. Stanziani, *Sailors, Slaves and Immigrants*.

26. Debendra Bijoy Mitra, *Cotton Weavers of Bengal* (Calcutta: Firma KLM, 1978); Hameeda Hossain, *The Company Weavers of Bengal: The East India Company and the Organization of Textile Production in Bengal 1750–1813* (New York: Oxford University Press, 1988). The literature on this debate is large. Some representative works include: Romesh Dutt, *The Economic History of India, vol. I, Under Early British Rule*, 2 vols. (London: Kegan Paul, Trench, Trubner, 1902); Morris D. Morris, "Towards a Reinterpretation of Nineteenth-Century Indian Economic History," *Journal of Economic History* 23 (1963): 606–18; Amiya Bagchi, "Deindustrialization in India in the Nineteenth Century: Some Theoretical Implications," *Journal of Development Studies* 12 (1976): 135–64; Tirthankar Roy, *Traditional Industry in the Economy of Colonial India* (Cambridge: Cambridge University Press, 1999).

27. Titas Chakraborty, "Slave Trading and Slave Resistance in the Indian Ocean World: The Case of Early Eighteenth-Century Bengal," *Slavery and Abolition* 40, no. 4 (2019): 706–36; Titas Chakraborty, "The Household Workers of the East India Company Ports of Pre-Colonial Bengal," *International Review of Social History*, 64 (2019): 71–93. For hired household workers in the late eighteenth century, see Nitin Sinha, "Domestic Servant and Master-Servant Regulations in Colonial Calcutta, 1750s–1810s," *Past and Present*, 25 (2022): 141–88.

28. Jan Lucassen, "Working at the Ichapur Gunpowder Factory in the 1790s, Part I," *Indian Historical Review* 39, no. 2 (2012): 19–56, 251–71; Chitra Joshi, "Dak Roads, Dak Runners and the Reordering of Communication Networks," *International Review of Social History* 57 (2012): 169–89; Nitin Sinha, "Contract, Work and Resistance: Boatmen in Early Colonial Bengal," *International Review of Social History* 59 (2014): 11–43.

29. Sudipta Sen, *Empire of Free Trade: East India Company and the Making of the Colonial Market Place* (Philadelphia: University of Pennsylvania Press, 1998), 32.

30. Philip Stern, *The Company State: Corporate Sovereignty and the Early Modern Foundations of the British Empire in India* (New York: Oxford University Press, 2011).

31. C.E. Luard assisted by H. Hosten, trans., *Fray Sebastien Manrique, Travels, 1629–1643, Vol. I* (London: Hakluyt Society, 1927), 44–45, 140; Basil Coppleton Allen, *Dacca: Eastern Bengal District Gazetteer* (New Delhi: Logos Press, 2009), 44; Prakash, *Dutch East India Company and the Economy of Bengal*, 39.

32. Christopher Bayly, *The Birth of the Modern, 1780–1814* (Malden, MA: Blackwell, 2004), 86–100; David Armitage and Sanjay Subrahmanyam, eds., *The Age of Revolutions in Global Context, 1760–1840* (New York: Palgrave Macmillan, 2010), xxii.

33. Historians, depending on their focus on regions and sections of society, do not agree on any single timeline for the colonial transition in India. For a good review regarding differing positions, see Robert Travers, "The Eighteenth Century in Indian History," *Eighteenth Century Studies* 40, no. 3 (2007): 492–508.

34. Robert Travers, *Ideology and Empire in Eighteenth-Century India: The British in Bengal* (Cambridge: Cambridge University Press, 2007), 20.

35. P.J. Marshall, *Bengal: The British Bridgehead: Eastern India, 1740–1828*, Vol. 2 of *The New Cambridge History of India* (Cambridge: Cambridge University Press, 1987), 2.

36. Barun De, "Early Manifestation of the Colonialist Premise in the British Occupation of Bengal," *Proceedings of the Indian History Congress*, 38 (1977): 474–88; Sen, *Empire of Free Trade*; James Vaughn, *The Politics of Empire at the Accession of George III: East India Company and Crisis and Transformation of Britain's Imperial State* (New Haven: Yale University Press, 2019).

37. Seema Alavi, *The Sepoys and the Company: Tradition and Transition in Northern India, 1770–1830* (New Delhi: Oxford University Press, 1995).

38. Bayly, *Rulers, Townsmen and Bazaars*; Chaudhury, *From Prosperity to Decline*; Kumkum Chatterjee, *Merchants, Politics and Society in Early Modern India; Bihar, 1733–1820* (Leiden: Brill, 1996); Sen, *Empire of Free Trade*; Rajat Datta, *Society, Economy and the Market, Commercialization in Rural Bengal, 1760–1800* (New Delhi: Manohar, 2000).

39. Sudipta Sen and Kumkum Chatterjee emphasize use of violence but Rajat Datta differs. Sen argues that the EIC introduced a new idea of a market governed through centralized control usurping *zamīndāri* governance; Datta argues that the EIC extended commercialization by removal of *zamīndāri* controls. Chatterjee emphasizes the displacement of certain groups of merchants by others and removal of certain sectors of trade as a result of company governance. See note above.

40. Hameeda Hossain, "The Alienation of Weavers: Impact of the Conflict between the Revenue and Commercial Interests of the East India Company, 1750–1800," *Indian Economic and Social History Review* 1, no. 3 (1979): 323–45.

41. Eric Stokes, *English Utilitarians and India* (Oxford: Oxford University Press, 1959), 4.

42. Jon E. Wilson, *The Domination of Strangers: Modern Governance in Eastern India 1780–1835* (Basingstoke: Palgrave Macmillan, 2008), 182; Dirk Kolff, *Grass in Their Mouth: The Upper Doab in India under the Company's Magna Charta, 1793–1830* (Leiden: Brill, 2010), 22.

43. Karl Marx, *Capital Volume 1* (New York: Penguin, 1976), 899.

44. Joshi, "Dak Roads"; Sinha, "Contract, Work and Resistance."

45. Clare Anderson, "British Indian Empire, 1789–1939," in Clare Anderson, ed., *A Global History of Convicts* (London: Bloomsbury, 2018); Hugh Tinker, *A New System of Slavery: The Export of Indian Labour Overseas, 1830–1920* (London: Oxford University Press, 1974); Clare Anderson, "Convicts and Coolies: Rethinking Indentured Labour in the Nineteenth Century," *Slavery and Abolition* 30, no. 1 (2009), 93–109; Chitra Joshi, "Public Works and Questions of Unfree Labour," in *Labour, Coercion and Economic Growth in Eurasia, 17th-20th Centuries*, ed. Alessandro Stanziani (Leiden: Brill, 2013), 273–88; Anand Yang, *Empire of Convicts* (Oakland: University of California Press, 2021), 11–50.

46. Irfan Habib, "Forms of Class Struggle in Mughal India," in *Essays in Indian History: Towards a Marxist Perception* (New Delhi: Anthem Press, 2002), 233–58, Dilbagh Singh, "Contesting Hegemony: State and Peasant in Late Medieval Rajasthan," in *Rethinking A Millennium: Perspectives on Indian History from the Eighth to the Eighteenth Century*, ed. Rajat Datta (New Delhi: Aakar Books, 2008), 300–315; Michael Adas, "From Avoidance to Confrontation: Peasant Protest in Precolonial and Colonial Southeast Asia," *Comparative Studies in Society and History* 23, no. 2 (1981): 217–47; James Scott, *Weapons of the Weak: Everyday Forms of Peasant Resistance* (New Haven: Yale University Press, 1985), 30–33, 304–50.

47. Richard Eaton, *The Rise of Islam in the Bengal Frontier, 1204–1760* (Berkeley: University of California Press, 1997), 194–225.

48. Jon E. Wilson, "'A Thousand Countries to Go to': Peasants and Rulers in late Eighteenth-Century Bengal," *Past and Present* 89 (2005): 84.

49. Raffaele Laudani, *Disobedience in Western Political Thought : A Genealogy* (Cambridge: Cambridge University Press, 2013). For discussion on institutionalized dissidence in Indian polities see Andre Wink, *Land and Sovereignty in India: Agrarian Society and Politics under the Maratha Swarajya* (Cambridge: Cambridge University Press, 1986); Norbert Peabody, *Hindu Kingship and Polity in Pre-Colonial India* (Cambridge: Cambridge University Press, 2003).

50. Kolsky, *Colonial Justice in British India*, 75-76.

51. M.H. Starling and F.C. Constable, *Indian Criminal Law and Procedure* (London: W.H. Allen, 1887), 416.

52. Clive Dewey, "The Influence of Sir Henry Maine on Agrarian Policy in India," in *The Victorian Achievement of Sir Henry Maine: A Centennial Reappraisal*, ed. Alan Diamond (Cambridge: Cambridge University Press, 1991), 364–75.

53. Amiya Bagchi, *Private Investment in India, 1900–1939* (Cambridge: Cambridge University Press, 1972), 133–38.

54. In particular, Henry Maine's theory of legal evolution is influential in this context; Mohapatra, "From Contract to Status." Some economic historians have

accepted Maine's premise. Tirthankar Roy, *Traditional Industry in the Economy of Colonial India* (Cambridge: Cambridge University Press, 2004), 30–41. On imperialist implications of Maine's theory of legal evolution see Karuna Mantena, *Alibis of Empire: Henry Maine and Ends of Liberal Imperialism* (Princeton: Princeton University Press, 2010) and Mahmood Mamdani, *Define and Rule: Native as Political Identity* (Cambridge, MA: Harvard University Press, 2012).

55. Nicholas Dirks, *The Scandal of Empire: India and Creation of Imperial Britain* (Cambridge, MA: Harvard University Press, 2006), 296.

56. Stokes, *English Utilitarians and India*, 1–46; T.H. Baglehole, *Thomas Munro and the Development of Administrative Policy in Madras, 1792–1818* (Cambridge: Cambridge University Press, 1966), 136–37.

57. Utsa Patnaik, "On Capitalism and Agrestic Unfreedom, a Reply to Tom Brass, 'Some Observations on Unfree Labour, Capitalist Restructuring, and Deproletarianization,'" *International Review of Social History* 39 (1994), 255–75; Jan Breman, *A Footloose Proletariat: Informal Sector Labour in the Rural and Urban Landscape of West India* (Cambridge: Cambridge University Press, 1994); V.K. Ramachandran, *Wage Labour and Unfreedom in Agriculture: An Indian Case Study* (Oxford: Oxford University Press, 1990). Especially Patnaik and Ramachandran have argued that full fledged capitalist relations of wage labor did not evolve in India as a result of persistence of semi-feudal relations such as caste bondage. This thesis has been challenged differently by Tom Brass and Jairus Banaji. For Brass, the persistence of such precolonial relations was a method by capital to wage class struggle on workers, a process he has called "deproletarianization." See Brass, "Some Observations." For Banaji all forms of wage relations are unfree; see Jairus Banaji, "Fictions of Free Labour: Contract, Coercion and So-called Unfree Labour," in Jairus Banaji, *Theory: Essays on Modes of Production and Exploitation* (New Delhi: Aakar, 2013), 131–54.

58. See note above. Also see Andrew Liu, *Tea War: A History of Capitalism in China and India* (New Haven: Yale University Press, 2000).

59. Nicholas Dirks, *Castes of Mind: Colonialism and the Making of Modern India* (Princeton: Princeton University Press, 2001), 172.

60. This approach is different from Gyan Prakash's method of critically analyzing the impact of Enlightenment thought in the construction of colonial discourse on free and unfree labor. Gyan Prakash, *Bonded Histories: Genealogies of Labor Servitude in Colonial India* (Cambridge: Cambridge University Press, 1990). My method is Thompsonian and follows the works of Edward Thompson and Peter Linebaugh; see detailed discussion in chapter 2.

CHAPTER ONE

1. The story has been collected by Pika Ghosh. Pika Ghosh, *Temple to Love: Architecture and Devotion in Seventeenth Century* (Bloomington: Indiana University Press, 2005), 44.

2. Sukumar Sen, ed., *Brindāaban Dās birachita Chaitanyabhāgabat* (New Delhi: Sahitya Akademi, 1982), 193; in Krisnadasa Kaviraj's biography, Chaitanya convinces the Qazi to join the procession. Sushil kr De, *Early History of Vaishanava Faith and Movement in Bengal* (Calcutta: General Printers, 1942), 60.

3. Nandita Prasad Sahai, *Politics of Patronage and Protest: The State Society and Artisans in Early Modern Rajasthan* (New York: Oxford University Press, 2006).

4. Prasannan Parthasarathi, "Rethinking Wages and Competitiveness in Eighteenth-Century Britain and South India," *Past and Present* 158, 1 (1998): 79–109.

5. Dipesh Chakrabarty, *Provincializing Europe: Postcolonial Thought and Historical Difference* (Princeton: Princeton University Press, 2000), 47–96; Robert Gregg and Madhavi Kale, "The Empire and Mr Thompson: Making of Indian Princes and English Working Class," *Economic and Political Weekly* 32, no. 36 (September 1997): 2273–88.

6. Antonio Gramsci, *Subaltern Social Groups: A Critical Edition of Prison Notebook 25*, ed. Joseph A. Buttigieg and Marcus E. Green (New York: Columbia University Press, 2021), 10.

7. Stratification of peasant holdings in precolonial Bengal leading to hired labor has been studied to a certain extent by Gautam Bhadra, *Mughal yuger Kriṣi Orthonīti O Kriṣak Bidraha* (Calcutta: Subarnarekha, 1983); Philip Stern's study of Calcutta *zamīndāri* emphasizes the EIC government's effort to create civic governance. However, neither of these works examine the political power of the Calcutta *zamīndāri* in creating civic governance within the larger context of *zamīndāri* and Mughal/Nawabi political control over Bengal. Philip J. Stern, *The Company-State: Corporate Sovereignty and the Early Modern Foundations of the British Empire in India* (New York: Oxford University Press, 2011), 164–84.

8. On pastoral power see Michel Foucault, "The Subject and Power," *Critical Enquiry* 8, no. 4 (1982): 777–95.

9. Jack Cohen, trans., *Karl Marx: Pre-Capitalist Economic Formations, Part I, 1857–58* (1964), 68.

10. Jacques Le Goff, "Labor, Techniques, and Craftsmen in the Value Systems of the Early Middle Ages (Fifth to Tenth Centuries)," in *Time, Work and Culture in the Middle Ages*, trans. Arthur Goldhammer (Chicago: University of Chicago Press, 1980), 71.

11. Sukumar Sen, *Bangla Sahityer Itihās* (Calcutta: Modern Book Agency, 1948), 98; Kumkum Chatterjee, *The Cultures of History in Early Modern India: Persianization and Mughal Culture in Bengal* (New Delhi: Oxford University Press, 2009), 92.

12. Kumkum Chatterjee, "Goddess Encounters: Mughals, Monsters and the Goddess in Bengal," *Modern Asian Studies*, 47, no. 5 (2013): 1435–87.

13. This process was already under way in the creation of Puranic literature in Bengal; Kunal Chakrabarty, *Religious Process: The Puranas and the Making of a Regional Tradition* (New Delhi: Oxford University Press, 2001).

14. For this discussion I have followed Sukumar Sen, *Bangla Sahityer Itihās* and Sukhamay Mukhopadhyaya, *Madhyayuger Bāṃlā Sahityer Tathya o Kalakram* (Calcutta: Ji Bharadwaj, 1960).

15. For a detailed discussion on the antiquity of *maṅgalkābyas*, see Sukumar Sen, *Bangala Sahityer Itihās*; Asutosh Bhattacharya, *Bangla maṅgalkābyeritihas*, 12th ed. (Kolkata: A. Mukherjee, 2009); T.W. Clark, "Evolution of Hinduism in Medieval Bengali Literature: Siva, Candi, Manasa," *Bulletin of the School of Oriental and African Studies*, 17, no. 15 (1955): 14; Hitesranjan Sanyal, "Literary Sources of Medieval Bengali History: A Study of a Few Mangalkavya Texts," *Occasional Paper 52* (Calcutta: Center for Studies in Social Sciences, 1982).

16. Regional Sanskrit poetry showed different strands of vernacularization in the compositions of late twelfth-century Sena court poets. See Jesse Ross Knutson, *Into the Twilight of Sanskrit Court Poetry* (Berkeley: University of California Press, 2014).

17. Bharatchandra is seen as an exception working in the *maṅgalkābya* genre. Even though his poem was ostensibly meant to praise Annada, his main purpose was to eulogize his patron. See France Bhattacharya, "The Poet and His Patron: Bharat Chandra Ray (1712–60) and Raja Kriṣna Chandra Ray of Nadia (1728–82)," in *The Varied Facets of History: Essays in Honor of Aniruddha Ray*, ed. Ishrat Alam and Syed Ejaz Hussain (New Delhi: Primus Books, 2011), 215–28.

18. Satyanarayan Bhattacharya, ed., *Kabi Kriṣnarām Dāser Granthabalī* (Kolkata: Calcutta University Press, 1958), 167.

19. For a discussion on mortal and divine aspects of the *maṅgalkābyas* and their ability to legitimize divine and political power, see Clinton Seely with Fredrika Miller, "Secular and Sacred Legitimation in Bharatchandra Ray's Annada-Mangal (1752 C.E.)," *Archiv Orientalni* 68 (2000): 327–58. For discussions on the relationship between lower castes and *maṅgalkābyas* see Sanyal, "Literary Sources of Medieval Bengali History" and France Bhattacharya, "Rupram's Dharmamangal: An Epic of the Low Castes?" *Archiv Orientalni* 68 (2000): 359–86.

20. David Curley, *Poetry and History: Bengali Mangalkabya and Social Change in Precolonial Bengal* (New Delhi: Chronicle Books, 2008), 1–70.

21. Tapan Raychaudhuri, *Bengal Under Akbar and Jahangir: An Introductory Study in Social History* (Kolkata: A. Mukherjee, 1953); Aniruddha Ray, "Urbanization in Medieval Bengal (AD 1200–1600)," Address of the President, Medieval Indian Section, Indian History Congress, 1992–93; Gautam Bhadra, *Mughal yuger Kriṣi Orthonīti O Kriṣak Bidraha* (Calcutta: Subarnarekha, 1983).

22. Chatterjee, *The Cultures of History in Early Modern India*, 101–15; Curley, *Poetry and History*, 1–70.

23. Edward Dimock and Ronald Inden," The City in Pre-British Bengal," in Edward Dimock, *The Sound of Silent Guns* (New Delhi: Oxford University Press, 1989), 118.

24. Dusan Zbavitel, "Bengali Folk-Ballads from Mymensingh and the Problem of their Authenticity" (PhD diss., University of Calcutta, 1963).

25. For example, the ballad of Isa Khan Masnad Ali, which Richard Eaton uses to understand the "folk" perception of Isa Khan as a rebel against Mughal rule. Richard Eaton, *The Rise of Islam and the Bengal Frontier, 1204–1760* (Berkeley: University of California Press, 1993), 149.

26. Some experiences depicted in the ballads clearly chronicle late eighteenth-century or nineteenth-century developments. For example, indebtedness in several ballads has been associated with eviction from land, which was a novelty brought about by colonial land settlement and land revenue policies especially since 1793. Sugata Bose, *Peasant Labour and Colonial Capital: Rural Bengal Since 1770* (Cambridge: Cambridge University Press, 1993), 114–18.

27. The concept of coevality is influenced by Ajay Skaria, *Hybrid Histories: Forest, Frontiers and Wildness in Western India* (New York: Oxford University Press, 1999), 14–17.

28. For a discussion on plot function of the *maṅgalkābyas* see, Seely with Miller, "Secular and Sacred Legitimation."

29. Muzaffar Alam, "Eastern India in the Early Eighteenth Century 'Crisis': Some evidence from Bihar," *Indian Economic and Social History Review* 28, no. 1 (1991): 66.

30. Sukumar Sen, ed., *Kabikankan Mukunda birachita Chaṇḍīmaṅgal* (New Delhi: Sahitya Akademi, 2007), 68.

31. Ibid., 76–77.

32. Irfan Habib, *The Agrarian System of Mughal India, 1556–1707*, 3rd ed. (Oxford: Oxford University Press, Oxford India Perennials Series, 2012), 136–37.

33. Land measurement. In the colonial period, 1 bigha = 1/3rd acre.

34. Dinesh Chandra Sen, *Purbabaṅga Gītikā*, 2 volumes (hereafter, *PG*) (Kolkata: Dey's Publishing, 2009), 179–80.

35. Alam, "Eastern India in the Early Eighteenth Century 'Crisis,'" 66.

36. Purnachandra Chakraborty, ed., *Srī Srī Padmapurān bā Biṣaharir Pnāchali* (Kolkata, undated), 59–60. I am extremely indebted to Professor Satyabati Giri of Jadavpur University for sharing this reference with me.

37. Achintya Biswas, ed., *Bipradās Pipilaier Manasāmaṅgal* (Kolkata: Ratnabali, 2002), 62.

38. Habib, *Agrarian System of Mughal India*, 131–32.

39. Panchanan Chakraborty, ed., *Rameśwar Rachanābali* (Calcutta: Bangiya Sahitya Parishat, B.S. 1371, 1964), 449.

40. Ibid., 447.

41. Biswas, *Bipradās Pipilaier Manasāmaṅgal*, 152; Bijanbihari Bhattacharya, ed., *Ketakadās Kṣhemānandar Manasāmaṅgal* (New Delhi: Sahitya Akademi, 2011), 14; Sukumar Sen, *Visnupala's Manasamangal* (Kolkata: Asiatic Society, 2002), 76

42. Jayantakumar Dasgupta, ed., *Kabi Bijayguptar Padmapurān* (Kolkata: Calcutta University Press, 2009), 294.

43. Shirin Akhtar, *The Role of Zamindars in Bengal 1707–1772* (Dhaka: Asiatic Society of Bangladesh, 1982), 129; John R. McLane, *Land and Local Kingship in Eighteenth Century Bengal* (Cambridge: Cambridge University Press, 1993), 52–53.

44. Chakraborty, *Rameśwar Rachanābali*, 453.

45. Panchanan Mandal, ed., *Mukuṅdarām Chakrabortyr Chandīmagal* (Kolkata: Bharabi, 1991), 8.

46. Dasgupta, ed., *Kabi Bijaygupter Padmapurān*, 294.
47. R.S. Sharma, *Sudras in Ancient India* (New Delhi: Motilas Banarasidass, 1990), 112.
48. Chakraborty, *Rameśwar Rachanābali*, 453.
49. Akṣaya Kumar Kāyal and Chitra Deb, eds., *Ketakadās Kṣemānandar Manasāmaṅgal* (Kolkata: Lekhapara, B.S. 1384, 1977), 145.
50. Biswas, *Bipradās Pipilaier Manasāmaṅgal*, 149–52.
51. Barbers are higher in caste status than fishermen. Brahmins can accept water from barbers' hands but not from the hands of fisherfolk (*PG*, 604).
52. David Washbrook, "India in the Early Modern Economy: Modes of Production, Reproduction and Exchange," *Journal of Global History* 2 (2007): 96.
53. See Kāyal and Deb, *Ketakadās Kṣemānandar Manasāmaṅgal*, 138–43; Sukumar Sen, *Visnupala's Manasamangal* (Kolkata: Asiatic Society, 2002), 51.
54. Sen, *Kabikankan Mukunda birachita Chaṅdīmaṅgal*, 76.
55. Ibid., 76, 330; Sri Sri Kumar Bandopadhyay, *Kabikankan Chaṅdī, Part I* (Calcutta: Calcutta University Press, 1952), 342.
56. Ratnalekha Ray, *Change in Bengal Agrarian Society, 1760–1850* (New Delhi: Manohar, 1979), 23.
57. Dasgupta, *Kabi Bijaygupter Padmapurān*, manuscript *kha* and *ga*, 348.
58. Dasgupta, *Kabi Bijaygupter Padmapurān*, 348.
59. Max Weber, *Theory of Social and Economic Organization* (New York: Free Press, 1947), 230.
60. Irfan Habib, *Essays in Indian History: Towards a Marxist Perception* (New Delhi: Anthem Press, 2002), 375–77.
61. Mohammad Yusuf Siddiq, *Historical and Cultural Aspects of Islamic Inscriptions of Bengal: A Reflection on Some New Epigraphic Discoveries* (Dhaka: The International Center for Study of Bengal Art, 2010), 193–94.
62. Piyushkanti Mahapatra, ed., *Ghanaram Chakraborty rachita Dharmamangal* (Calcutta: Calcutta University Press, 1961), 346–48.
63. Overgekomen Brieven en Papieren in the Archives of the Dutch East India Company, National Archive, the Hague, Netherlands (hereafter, VOC), 8787, 569–573. There were several other carpenters and sawers who worked for a smaller span of time, between eight and twenty days.
64. For example, in 1730 there were 657 carpenters assisted by 74 sawers, VOC 8870, 280.
65. Dasgupta, *Kabi Bijaygupter Padmapurān*, 351.
66. Dasgupta, *Kabi Bijaygupter Padmapurān*, 349.
67. Coolies who worked as carpenters' assistants got a wage of 1.5 annas while the normal wage for any other coolie was 1 anna, VOC 8758, 69–76.
68. Dasgupta, *Kabi Bijaygupter Padmapurān*, manuscript *kha*, 348.
69. VOC 8787, 191.
70. Om Prakash, "Trade and Politics in Eighteenth-Century Bengal," in *The Eighteenth Century in India*, ed. Seema Alavi (New Delhi: Oxford University Press, 2002), 142.

71. Jonathan Israel, *The Dutch Republic: Its Rise, Greatness, and Fall, 1477–1806* (Oxford: Oxford University Press, 1995), 322; Pepijn Brandon, *War, Capital and the Dutch State (1588–1795)* (Leiden: Brill, 2015), 104; Femme S. Gaastra, *De geschiedenis van de VOC* (Zutphen: Walburg Pers, 2001); George Winius and Markus Vink, *The Merchant-Warrior Pacified: The VOC and Its Changing Political Economy in India* (New York: Oxford University Press, 1995), 47–84; Adam Clulow, *The Company and the Shogun* (New York: Columbia University Press, 2014).

72. Philip J. Stern, "'A Politie of Civill & Military Power': Political Thought and the Late Seventeenth-Century Foundations of the East India Company-State," *Journal of British Studies* 47, no. 2 (2008): 263–64.

73. Stern, "A Politie of Civill & Military Power," 282; Stern, *Company-State*, 24.

74. I have more or less paraphrased Ratnalekha Ray's definition of a *zamīndār*. Ray, *Change in Bengal Agrarian Society*, 21–22.

75. Akhtar, *Role of Zamindars*, 15, 32.

76. McLane, *Land and Local Kingship*, 134.

77. For previous presence of the VOC in the region, see Om Prakash, *Dutch East India Company and the Economy of Bengal* (Princeton: Princeton University Press, 1983), 24–40.

78. VOC 2849, 156.

79. West Bengal State Archives, Kolkata, Dutch Pattas, Bundle 1, Patta no. 340, 344..

80. For an analysis of Schulyenburgh's knowledge of native culture in Bengal and his painting, see Byapti Sur, "The Dutch East India Company Through Local Lens: Exploring the Dynamics of Indo-Dutch Relations in Seventeenth-Century Bengal," *Indian Historical Review* 44, no. 1 (2017): 73.

81. Farhat Hasan, "Indigenous Cooperation and the Birth of a Colonial City: Calcutta, c. 1698–1750," *Modern Asian Studies* 26, no. 1 (1992): 67–70.

82. Aniruddha Ray, *Towns and Cities in Medieval India* (London: Routledge, 2016), 460.

83. Hasan, "Indigenous Cooperation," 79–81.

84. Pieter Souman, the muster roll keeper of the VOC, bought the house of a dead mardijker, Jan Dirksz. He had as his neighbor a *firingi*, Nicolas Alve, and a free burger, Jan Brengman. National Archive, The Hague, Tamil Nadu State Archives (hereafter, TNSA 1.11.06.11)/1677A, 157. Simonia, widow of the pilot Leendert Dirksz Staalman, sold her house to the pilot Jan de Bruijn on May 18, 1743. She had as her neighbors a Muslim man, Piroe, a Hindu man, Souram, and a free burgher, Alexander. TNSA 1.11.06.11/1693, 229. See Bibliography for full identification of these and other archival citations.

85. Property sold by Jan Drabbe to an Armenian, Khwaja Keeuwen, on July 27, 1734, TNSA 1.11.06.11/1677B, 285; sale of house by Harmanus Blom, junior merchant to the head cooper, Jan Reijkewaart, on June 10, 1941. TNSA 1.11.06.11/1677B, 708.

86. House sold by Christian Edel to Jacobus Brakel on October 6, 1741. TNSA 1.11.06.11/1694, 775.

87. Nisith Ranjan Ray, *Calcutta: The Profile of a City* (Calcutta: K.P. Bagchi, 1986), 36.
88. British Library, London, Calcutta Factory Records (hereafter, G/7)/4 (unfoliated), Consultation of September 6, 1703.
89. British Library, London, Bengal Public Proceedings (hereafter, P/1)/1, 379v-380r.
90. P/1/9, 5v-6r; P/1/3, 195r,
91. P/1/1, 301r-v.
92. Harisadhan Mukhopadhyay, *Kalikātā: Sekāler o Ekāler* (Calcutta: P.M. Bagchi, 1985), 293.
93. P/1/1, 77r-78v, 173r-v; Mukhopadhyay, *Kalikata*, 304.
94. Mukhopadhyay, *Kalikata*, 302.
95. Pradip Sinha, *Calcutta in Urban History* (Kolkata: Firma KLM, 1978),18.
96. P/1/1, 352r.
97. P/1/6, 260v.
98. Ibid.
99. Farhat Hasan, "Indigenous Cooperation,"72.
100. P/1/1, 398v.
101. P/1/1, Part II, 50v.
102. National Archive, The Hague, Kopie-generale landmonsterrollen van de VOC-dienaren in de VOC-vestigingen in Indië (hereafter, Generale Monsterrollen VOC) 11539, 419; the VOC did not fortify their settlements until 1743, though they continued to maintain their standing armies. Prakash, *Dutch East India Company*, 50.
103. Prakash, *Dutch East India Company*, 48–49. For Mir Jumla's Assam expedition, see Frans Janszoon van der Heiden and Willem Kunst, *Vervarelycke Schipbreuk van"t Oost-Indisch Jacht ter Schelling onder het landt van Bengale* (Amsterdam: Jacob Meus en Johannes van Someren, 1675) (hereafter, *Ter Schelling*).
104. After the death of Sobha Singh, the mantle of rebellion fell onto his uncle Maha Singh and the Afghan chieftain and *zamindar* Rahim Khan. According to Jadunath Sarkar, the rebellion was conclusively crushed by Prince Azim, the new *subahdar* (governor) of Bengal in 1698. Jadunath Sarkar, ed., *History of Bengal, Vol II: Muslim Period 1200–1757* (Dacca: University of Dacca, 1943). Aniruddha Ray is skeptical of this conclusion; he suspects the rebellion was not fully crushed because Murshid Quli Khan reported disturbances in Chandrakona as late as 1704. Aniruddha Ray, *Adventurers, Landowners and Rebels: Bengal c. 1575–c. 1715* (New Delhi: Munshiram Manoharlal, 1998), 153–57.
105. Generale Monsterrollen VOC 11542, 449; 11547, 406.
106. Four soldiers and ten peons accompanied a boat with 445 bales and chests from Kassimbazar to Calcutta in October 1701. British Library, London, Kassimbazar Factory Records (hereafter, G/23)/4 (unfoliated), October 15, 1701. Subsequent references, from 1702 onwards, to soldiers on boats are found in the British Library, London, Bengal Public Proceedings, P/1 series (1702/3).
107. Generale Monsterrollen VOC 11542, 449.
108. Generale Monsterrollen VOC 11627, 117; 11636, 97–104.

109. P/1/16, 410v-411r.

110. National Archive, The Hague, Radermacher Collection (hereafter, CR) 486 (unfoliated). Troop numbers extracted from the report of the commandeering Colonel Roussel on the expedition in Bengal sent to the High Government (at Batavia) and also parts of a letter sent by the same person.

111. Alam, "Eastern India in the Early Eighteenth Century 'Crisis,'" 66.

112. Shireen Moosvi, "Reforming Revenue Administration: Aurangzeb's Farman to Rasikdas, 1665," in *People, Taxation and Trade in Mughal India* (New Delhi: Oxford University Press, 2008), 180.

113. Ray, *Change in Bengal Agrarian Society*, 22.

114. See clauses 6 and 9 of Moosvi's circular, "Reforming Revenue administration"; the clash between the *zamīndārs* and the Mughal state stemmed from the issue of share in revenue. While the Mughal state wanted to increase their share of the revenue, they also wanted to abolish *zamīndāri* demands on peasants to relieve them of the burden. The *zamīndārs* on the other hand from time to time cheated on their payment of revenue to the Mughal state. See Dilbagh Singh, "Contesting Hegemony: State and Peasant in Late Medieval Rajasthan." in *Rethinking a Millennium: Perspectives on Indian History from the Eight to the Eighteenth Century*, ed. Rajat Datta (New Delhi: Aakar Books, 2008).

115. Judith Bennett, "Compulsory Service in Late Medieval England," *Past and Present*, 109 (2010): 9.

116. Ann Kussmaul, *Servants in Husbandry in Early Modern England* (New York: Cambridge University Press, 1981), 60–61.

117. William Chambliss, "A Sociological Analysis of the Law of Vagrancy," *Social Problems* 12, no. 1 (1964): 67–77; Peter King, *Crime and Law in England, 1750–1840: Remaking Justice from the Margins* (New York: Cambridge University Press, 2006), 18–20.

118. Marjorie Kensinton Mcintosh, *Poor Relief in England 1350–1600* (Cambridge: Cambridge University Press, 2012), 228.

119. Steve Hindle, *On the Parish? The Micro-Politics of Poor Relief in Rural England c. 1550–1750* (Oxford: Oxford University Press, 2004), 171.

120. Menno Witteven, *Antonio van Diemen: De Opkomst van de VOC in Azie* (PhD diss., Leiden University, 2011), 147–62; van Rossum, "Werkers van de Wereld," 94–97.

121. J.A. van der Chijs, ed., *Nederlandsch-Indisch Plakaatboek, 1602–1811, Negende Deel* (Bataviaasch Genootschap van Kunsten en Wetenschappen met medewerking van de Nederlandsch-Indische Regering, 1891), 203.

122. Ibid., 193.

123. Ibid., 412.

124. Ibid., 201–2.

125. Jadunath Sarkar, "The Regulations of Aurangzib," *Journal of Asiatic Society of Bengla*, 2, no. 6 (1906): 224.

126. B.R. Grover, "The Position of Desai in the Pargana Administration of Subah Gujarat under the Mughals," *Proceedings of the Indian History Congress*

24 (1961): 152; Nandini Chatterjee, *Negotiating Mughal Law: A Family of Landlords Across Three Indian Empires* (Cambridge: Cambridge University Press, 2020), 242.

127. Zafarul Islam, "Aurangzeb's Farman on Land Tax—An Analysis in the Light of Fatawa-i-Alamgiri," *Islamic Culture* 52 (1978): 117–26.

128. For examples of runaway peasants returned to their land, see Habib, *Agrarian System of Mughal India*, 130–31; for jurisdictional control over labor, refer to Robert Steinfeld, *Coercion, Contract and Free Labor in the Nineteenth Century* (Cambridge: Cambridge University Press, 2001).

129. Naveen Kanalu Ramamurthy, "Mirror and Masks of Sovereignty: Imperial Governance in the Mughal World of Legal Normativism, c. 1650s-1720s" (PhD diss., University of California Los Angeles, 2021), 319-22.

130. Hiroshi Fukawaza, "A Note on the Corvee System (Vethbegar)," in *The Medieval Deccan: Peasants, Social Systems and States Sixteenth to Eighteenth Centuries* (New Delhi: Oxford University Press, 1991), 131–47.

131. Julius Jolly, ed. and trans., *Nāradiya Dharmaśāstra or The Institutes of Narada* (London: Trubner, 1876), 66. It should be noted that Brahmaninical conduct texts were seldom the basis for law and order in precolonial India.

132. Ray, *Change in Bengal Agrarian Society*, 20; Kumkum Chatterjee, *Merchants, Politics and Society in Early Modern India Bihar 1733–1820* (Leiden: Brill, 1996), 34.

133. Akhtar, *Role of Zamindars*, 90–116; Ray, *Change in Bengal Agrarian Society*, 19.

134. Akhtar, *Role of Zamindars*, 117–46.

135. Shah Nawaz Khan and Abdul Hayy, *Maathir ul Umara*, vol. 1, trans. H. Beveridge and B. Prasad (Kolkata: Asiatic Society, 1941), 392.

136. Ray, *Adventurers, Landowners and Rebels*.

137. The Portuguese in Bengal also enjoyed such judicial powers. H. Hosten, "A Week at the Bandel Convent," *Bengal Past and Present* 10 (January-March 1915): 106–18, and also in J.J.A. Campos, *History of the Portuguese in Bengal* (Calcutta: Butterworth and Co., 1919), 143–44. Arthur Mitchell Fraas, "'They Have Travailed into a Wrong Latitude': The Laws of England, Indian Settlements, and the British Imperial Constitution, 1726–1773" (PhD diss., Duke University, 2011), 66.

138. Sources of the Mayor's Court and especially the Court of the Oyer and Terminer and Gaol Delivery in Calcutta has been extensively used by Fraas, "They Have Travailed into a Wrong Latitude"; Titas Chakraborty, "The Household Workers of the East India Company Ports of Pre-Colonial Bengal," *International Review of Social History*, 64 (2019): 71–93; Titas Chakraborty, "Slave Trading and Slave Resistance in the Indian Ocean World: The Case of Early-Eighteenth Century Bengal," *Slavery and Abolition* 40, no. 4 (2019): 706–36.

139. I have seen some such cases. For example, the case between Choppa and Sattee plaintiff and Santose defendant, hearing of July 7, 1747 at Mayor's Court, Calcutta, British Library, London, Mayor's Court Records (hereafter, P/154)/46 (unfoliated). Also see Hannah Weiss Muller, *Subjects and Sovereign: Bonds of*

Belonging in the Eighteenth-Century British Empire (New York: Oxford University Press), 182–83.

140. Akhtar, *Role of Zamindars*, 166.
141. VOC 8787, 539–541.
142. VOC 2849, 155.
143. Ray, *Change In Bengal Agrarian Society*, 176.
144. Akhtar, *Role of Zamindars*, 143.
145. VOC 8752 (Part II), 193–237.
146. VOC 8762, 61–65.
147. The conflict lasted until the end of August 1719, when the Fort William council received news that "the engagement" between Hunt's army and the Chakwars was "very hott for sometime." The casualties on the side of the Chakwar army were much greater than the company's. A sergeant, a soldier, and a drummer of the EIC were killed, whereas the Chakwars had their boats burnt and several men were taken as prisoners of war. P/1/4, 105r, 124v.
148. P/1/4, 473v.
149. VOC 8774, 742–744.
150. Akhtar, *Role of Zamindars*, 161.
151. Muzaffar Alam and Sanjay Subrahmanyam, *The Mughal State, 1526–1750* (Oxford: Oxford University Press, 2011), 46–55.
152. This number is from Maulavi Abdus Salam, trans. and ed., *Riyazu-s-Salatin* (Calcutta: Baptist Mission Press, 1902), quoted in Ray, *Change in Bengal Agrarian Society*, 27.
153. Akhtar, *Role of Zamindars*, 32, 91, 94, 95.
154. Akhtar, *Role of Zamindars*, 97.
155. Hasan, "Indigenous Cooperation," 76.
156. P/1/9, 99r.
157. Kalikinkar Datta, *Alivardi and His Times* (Calcutta: University of Calcutta, 1939), 144–63.
158. P/1/14, 65v.
159. P/1/4, 31r-v, 83v.
160. VOC 8752 (Part II), 197–215; the name is not mentioned. Salimullah does not make any reference to any such *jagirs*. However, he mentions that Seif Khan extended agriculture.
161. Francis Gladwin, *A Narrative of the Transactions in Bengal (a translation of Salimullah Munshi's 'Tarikh-i-Bangala')* (Calcutta: Stuart and Cooper, 1788), 68–69; VOC 8752 (Part II), 197–215.
162. Quoted in Akhtar, *Role of Zamindars*, 30.
163. Akṣaya Kumār Kayāl, ed., *Ruprām Chakraborty birachita Dharmamaṅgal*, 294.
164. Monetary measurement: 1 anna = 4 gandās.
165. Unit measurement for weight: 1 seer equals approximately 1 kilogram.
166. *Ter Schelling*, 104.
167. Ramamurthy, "Mirror and Masks of Sovereignty," 132.

168. Ibid., 278-79.

169. Patrick Olivelle, ed. and trans., *Dharmasutras: The Law Codes of Ancient India* (New York: Oxford University Press, 1999); P.V. Kane, *History of Dharmashastra (Ancient and Medieval Religious and Civil Law)*, vol. III (Poona: Bhandarkar Oriental Research Institute, 1973), 187.

170. Richard Eaton, *The Rise of Islam and the Bengal Frontier, 1204–1760* (Berkeley: University of California Press, 1993), 194–265.

171. The majority of evidence for forced labor by precolonial regimes come from Eastern Rajasthan and Maharashtra. Of these, the state of the Peshwas in Maharashtra in the late eighteenth century demonstrates best the capacity of the centralized states. In Eastern Rajasthan the central and local government officials competed with each other in exacting forced labor from villagers. In both places forced labor seems to have been organized according to caste relations, with the menial castes carrying out almost of all of the forced labor tasks. Even though porterage is mentioned as one of the forms of forced labor, there is no mention of boatmen rendering forced services. Furthermore, there were stipulations or "customs" regarding who could exact forced labor and the time spent on it, to which both the worker and the oppressor agreed. V.S. Kadam, "Forced Labour in Maharashtra in the Seventeenth and Eighteenth Centuries: A Study of its Nature and Change," *Journal of the Economic and Social History of the Orient*, 1991 (34): 55–87; Hiroshi Fukawaza, "A Note on the Corvee System (Vethbegar)," in *The Medieval Deccan: Peasants, Social Systems and States Sixteenth to Eighteenth Centuries* (New Delhi: Oxford University Press, 1991), 131–47; Harbans Mukhia, "Illegal Extortions from Peasants, Artisans and Menials in Eighteenth Century Eastern Rajasthan," in *Perspectives on Medieval History* (New Delhi: Vikas Publishing House, 1993), 192–213.

172. Sen, *Kabikankan Mukunda biracbita Chaṇḍīmaṅgal*, 65–66.

173. Kane, *History of Dharmashastras*, 416.

174. *PG*, 458.

175. The Maratha penal system was riddled with the same problems. See Sumit Guha, "An Indian Penal Regime: Maharashtra in the Eighteenth Century," *Past and Present* 147, no. 1 (1995): 101–26.

176. Prakash, *Dutch East India Company*, 240–49. For discussion on deep monetization in early modern India see Jan Lucassen, ed., *Money of the Masses: Copper Coin Production and Circulation in India 1500–1900* (New Delhi: Manohar, forthcoming).

177. Achintya Biswas, ed., *Jagajjiban Ghoṣaler Manasāmaṅgal* (Kolkata: Ratnabali, 2002), 68.

178. In Kumar Bandopadhyay's edition, "Mahābir tomar beruneẏ nāhi sadh" (Mahabir we have no interest in doing your hired work." In Sen's edition, "Mahābir tomar beruneẏ nāki sādh." Tailors in one of Kumar Bandopadhyay's ms versions say "Darji kapaṛ siye, berān kariẏā jiẏe" (Tailors sew clothes, and live by doing hired work); another version mentions "Darji kapaṛ siye, betan paiẏa jiẏe" (Tailors sew clothes, and live on wages). Sen's edition also mentions this second version. Kumar

Bandopadhyay, *Kabikankan Chaṅḍī, Part I*, 301, 359; Sen, *Kabikankan Mukunda birachita Chaṅḍīmaṅgal*, 67, 81.

179. Sen, *Empire of Free Trade*; Chatterjee, *Merchants, Politics and Society*, 13–37, 65–100, 205–230.

180. Patrick Olivelle, "Social and Literary History of Dharmaśāstra: Commentaries and Legal Digests" in *The Oxford History of Hinduism: Hindu Law*, ed. Donald Davis Jr. and Patrick Olivelle (Oxford: Oxford University Press, 2018), 19.

181. David Washbrook, "India in the Early Modern Economy," 100.

182. Biswas, *Bipradās Pipilaier Manasāmaṅgal*, 152.

183. Biswas, *Jagajjiban Ghoṣaler Manasāmaṅgal*, 79.

184. Bhattacharya, *Ketakadās Kṣhemānandar Manasamangal*, 13–14.

185. *Xenophon's Treatise on the Householde, translated by Gentian Hervet* (London: Thomas Berthelet, 1532), 58.

186. Raffaela Sarti, "'The Purgatory of Servants': (In)Subordination, Wages, Gender and Marital Status of Servants in England and Italy in the Seventeenth and Eighteenth Centuries," *Journal of Early Modern Studies* 4 (2015): 347–72.

187. For the connection between economy and polity in seventeenth- and eighteenth-century England see Karen Harvey, *The Little Republic: Masculinity and Domestic Authority in Eighteenth-Century Britain* (Oxford: Oxford University Press, 2012), 24–63.

188. Maulavi Abdus Salam, trans. and ed., *Riyazu-s-Salatin* (Calcutta: Baptist Mission Press, 1902), 21.

189. Chetan Singh, "Forest, Pastoralists and Agrarian Society in Mughal India," in *Nature Culture Imperialism: Essays on the Environmental History of South Asia*, ed. David Arnold and Ramachandra Guha (New Delhi: Oxford University Press, 1995), 21–48.

190. Binay Bhushan Chaudhury, "Tribal Society in Transition: Eastern India 1757–1920," in *India's Colonial Encounter: Essays in Memory of Eric Stokes*, ed. Mushirul Hasan and Narayani Gupta (New Delhi: Manohar, 1993), 65–120.

191. Willem van Schendel, ed., *Francis Buchanan in South East Bengal, 1798: His Journey to Chittagong, Chittagong Hill Tracts, Noakhali, and Comilla* (Dhaka: University Press, 1992), 35, quoted in Eaton, *Rise of Islam and the Bengal Frontier*, 250.

192. A similar association of forest and subsistence/trade existed amongst the Dangis. Skaria, *Hybrid Histories*, 45–46.

193. Chetan Singh, "Forest, Pastoralists and Agrarian Society in Mughal India."

194. Biswas, *Bipradās Pipilaier Manasāmaṅgal*, 149–50.

195. Bhattacharya, *Ketakadās Kṣhemānandar Manasamangal*, 11–12.

196. In a folk tale from Bengal, the great Sanskrit scholar Kalidasa is seen cutting wood. For English translation see Edward Dimock, ed. and trans., *The Thief of Love: Bengali Tales from Court and Village* (Chicago: University of Chicago Press, 1963), 179–83.

197. VOC 8748 (Part II), 145-148.

198. VOC 8777, 291–293.

199. Shireen Moosvi, "The World of Labour in Mughal India (1500–1750)," *International Review of Social History*, 56 (2011): 245–61.

200. "The artisan brought the fourteen ships to the trader's house ... [Chand] gave the artisan priceless treasure" (coudda diṅgā kare āge baniar thnai ... Karmakare dilā tabe amulya ratan), quoted in Biswas, *Jagajjiban Ghoṣaler Manasāmaṅgal*, 63; "If you make all the ships, I will give you lots of money" (gathile sakal diṅgādibā ratna kaṛi), quoted in Sri Shubhendu Singha Ray and Sri Subalchandra Bandopadhyay, "Mukunda Kabichandra krita *Biśallocanīr Gīt*," *Sāhitya Pariṣat Patrika* 61, no. 2 (B.S. 1361, 1954): 185.

201. "Ek lakhya tākā diba ihār dakṣiṇā," quoted in Akṣaẏa Kumār Kayāl, ed., *Rupram Chakraborty birachita Dharmamaṅgal* (Kolkata: Bharabi, B.S. 1393, 1986), 103.

202. Sri Tamonash Chandra Dasgupta, ed., *Nārāyan Deber Padmapurān* (Calcutta: Calcutta University Press, 1947), 260.

203. Dirk Kolff, *Naukar, Rajput and Sepoy: The Ethnohistory of the Military Labour Market in Hindustan, 1450–1850* (Cambridge: Cambridge University Press, 2008), 19–20; Stewart Gordon, "Robes, Kings and Semiotic Ambiguity," in *Robes of Honor: Khil'at in Pre-colonial and Colonial India*, ed. Stewart Gordon (New Delhi: Oxford University Press, 2003), 380–83; Eaton, *Rise of Islam and the Bengal Frontier*, 162–65.

204. The robe-giving ceremony (*khil'at*) was a well-known custom throughout Eurasia and North Africa by the eight century A.D. However, the custom became an integral part of courtly culture in South Asia with the coming of Ghanznavid (tenth century) and Ghurid (twelfth century) invaders. Gavin Hambly, "The Emperor's Clothes: Robing and 'Robes of Honour' in Mughal India," in Gordon, *Robes of Honour*, 31–35.

205. Akhtar, *Role of Zamindars*, 15.

206. Dasgupta, *Nārāyan Deber Padmapurān*, 257; in another seventeenth-century text, Jagajjiban Ghosal's *Manasāmaṅgal*, the artisan who is commissioned to make the ships received *pān* from Chand. Biswas, *Jagajjiban Ghoṣaler Manasāmaṅgal*, 63.

207. David Curley, "'Voluntary' Relationships and Royal Gifts of Pan in Mughal Bengal," in Gordon, *Robes of Honor*, 65.

208. Ibid., 61–63.

209. Biswas, *Bipradās Pipilaier Manasāmaṅgal*, 165.

210. Ray and Bandopadhyay, "Mukunda Kabichandra krita *Biśallocanīr Gīt*," 185.

211. Hambly, "The Emperor's Clothes," 42–43.

212. Biswas, *Jagajjiban Ghoṣaler Manasāmaṅgal*, 98. The same was done with artisans who manufactured the seven ships, ibid., 63. In Narayan Deb's *Padmapuran* the ironsmiths get jewelry (*sobarno abharan*). Dasgupta, *Narayan Deber Padmapuran*, 261.

213. The patron-client relationship of Murshidabad has been dealt with in detail in Ratnabali Chatterjee's *From Karkhana to the Studio: A Study of the Changing Social Roles of Patron and Artist in Bengal* (New Delhi: Books and Books, 1990), chap 1.

CHAPTER TWO

1. VOC 8782, 401, 511–561.
2. Nitin Sinha, *Communication and Colonialism in Eastern India* (London: Anthem, 2012); Tilottama Mukherjee, *Political Culture and Economy in Eighteenth Century Bengal: Networks of Exchange, Consumption and Communication* (Hyderabad: Orient Blackswan, 2013); Ravi Ahuja, *Pathways of Empire: Circulation, "Public Works" and Social Space in Colonial Orissa (c. 1780–1914)* (Hyderabad: Orient Blackswan, 2009).
3. Michael Fisher, "Working across the Seas: Indian Maritime Labourers in India, Britain, and in Between, 1600–1857," *International Review of Social History* 51, special issue (2006): 21–45; Matthias van Rossum, *Werkers van de Wereld: Globalisering, arbeid en interculturele ontmoetingen tussen Aziatische en Europese zeelieden in dienst van de VOC, 1600–1800* (Verloren: Hilversum, 2014); Aaron Jaffer, *Lascars and Indian Ocean Seafaring, 1780–1860: Shipboard Life, Unrest and Mutiny* (Woodbridge: Boydell Press, 2015).
4. James Rennell, *An account of the Ganges and Burrampooter Rivers* (London, 1781), 105–106.
5. Tilottama Mukherjee, "Of Rivers and Roads: Transport Networks and Economy in Eighteenth-Century Bengal," in *Coastal Histories: Society and Ecology in Pre-modern India*, ed. Yogesh Sharma (New Delhi: Primus, 2010), 22.
6. William Petty, *Several Essays in Political Arithmetick* (London, 1755), 107–12.
7. Karl Marx, *Capital Volume 1* (New York: Penguin), 443.
8. Generale Monsterrollen VOC 11539, 439.
9. Rennell, *An account of the Ganges and Burrampooter Rivers*, 107.
10. VOC 8752 (Part II), 198.
11. VOC 8752 (Part II), 197–199.
12. This is the route followed by VOC vessels from Patna for both saltpeter and opium in 1660, 1662 and 1674, VOC 1304, 187, VOC 1236, 101. Similar patterns can be discerned from the movement of EIC boats from Patna for the years 1679, 1680 and 1681, British Library, London, Kassimbazar Factory Records (hereafter, G/23)/1 (unfoliated), December 17, 1679, and Hugli Factory Records (hereafter, G/20)/5 (Part II), 124–125; G/20/3, 51.
13. Rennell, *An account of the Ganges and Burrampooter Rivers*, 110, quoted in Jean Deloche, *Transport and Communications in India Prior to Steam Locomotion: Water Transport* (New Delhi: Oxford University Press, 1993), 25.
14. Sebastian Prange, *Monsoon Islam* (Cambridge: Cambridge University Press, 2018), 27–28.
15. VOC 8762, 196–197.
16. In September 1733, on his journey back from Patna, Jan Geldzak was ordered to go back to Patna to escort another fleet. While his ensign went on to Hugli, Captain Geldzak returned to Patna. His crew worked very long hours to cover the

upriver journey to Patna in just two weeks instead of a month, the time usually taken by the fleets. VOC 8776, 806–808.

17. Jayantakumar Dasgupta, ed., *Kabi Bijayguptar Padmapurān* (Kolkata: Calcutta University Press, 2009), 244.

18. Dasgupta, *Kabi Bijayguptar Padmapurān*, 277.

19. Bāridbaraṇ Ghoṣ, ed., *Nagendranāth Basu pracyabidyāmahārṇab sampādita Bijayrām Sen biśarad pranita Tirthamaṅgal* (Kolkata: Paraśpathar, 2009).

20. De Gennes de la Chanceliere's accounts in Indrani Ray, "Journey to Casimbazar and Murshidabad: Observations of a French Visitor to Bengal in 1743," in *The French East India Company and the Trade of the Indian Ocean: A Collection of Essays by Indrani Ray*, ed. Lakshmi Subramanian (New Delhi: Munshiram Manoharlal, 1999), 153. See entire segment on boats in Henry Yule and A.C. Burnell, *Hobson-Jobson: A Glossary of Colloquial Anglo-Indian Words and Phrases, and of the Kindred Terms, Etymological, Historical, Geographical and Discursive* (London: John Murray, 1903); VOC 8752 (Part IV), 8739, 8740, 8742, 8769, 8770, 8776, 8777, 8785, 8792, 8796.

21. VOC 8757, 222–223.

22. VOC 8782, 529.

23. Ray, "Journey to Casimbazar and Murshidabad," 154.

24. Yule and Burnell, *Hobson-Jobson Glossary*, 558.

25. When Captain Geldzak's fleet reached Nadia in late September 1736. he sent out pilot vessels to inspect which stream of the Jalangi joining the Ganges was the most navigable. VOC 8782, 511–561.

26. VOC 8760, 38.

27. VOC 8762 (Part II), 29.

28. Ibid., 57–58.

29. In 1723 at Patna *bangelas* were hired for saltpeter at the rate of 3 rupees and 8 anna for 100 maunds (VOC 8751 (Part II), 54). In 1732, sixty vessels were hired for carrying 7,200 maunds of saltpeter at the rate of 8 rupees per 100 maund (VOC 8770, 123). In 1734, five vessels were hired for carrying 1,350 maunds of saltpeter at the rate of 16 rupees per 100 maund (VOC 8776, 655). In the same year vessels were hired for 15 rupees and 8 annas per 100 maunds of saltpeter (VOC 8777, 818).

30. G/20/5, Part II, 8; G/23/1 (unfoliated), December 11–17, 1679. The VOC too used the place for transfer. VOC 1324, 451r-v.

31. K.M. Mohsin, *A Bengal District in Transition: Murshidabad, 1765–1793* (Dacca: Asiatic Society of Bangladesh, 1973), 14–15.

32. VOC 8770, 122–123.

33. "Niet te uiterste verlegen te staan." VOC 8786, 518–519.

34. VOC 8752 (4), 32–33.

35. I will limit my discussion to boats of the Patna fleet. Several other kinds of boats used by the companies in and around the settlements are mentioned by the English traveler Thomas Bowrey and the EIC official Streynsham Master, who visited Bengal in the seventeenth century, including the *purgoo*, which is derived from

the Portuguese *barca, boora*, or *bhar*. These lighter-oared vessels were used for carrying saltpeter and other goods from Hugli and salt to Dacca and also as tow boats to smaller vessels bound up or down the river Hugli. Richard Carnac Temple, ed., *The Diaries of Streynsham Master, 1675–1680, Volume I* (London: John Murray, 1911), 317, and Temple, *Diaries of Streynsham Master, Volume II*, 44; Sir Richard Carnac Temple, ed., *Thomas Bowrey's A Geographical Account of Countries Round the Bay of Bengal, 1669 to 1679* (London: Hakluyt Society, 1905), 228–29; Robert Hardgrave, Jr., *Boats of Bengal, Eighteenth Century Portraits by Balthazar Solvyns* (New Delhi: Manohar, 2001).

36. Identifying vessels in South Asia is always a difficult task. As both anthropologists and historians agree, the nomenclature for boats was a purely local phenomenon. The same boat traveling down from Patna to the deltas could be called by different names at various stages of its journey. Having said that, a more or less standard array of vessels emerges from the company records. Sean McGrail, Lucy Blue, Eric Kentley, and Colin Palmer, *Boats of South Asia* (London: Routledge, 2003), 32.

37. Temple, *Thomas Bowrey's A Geographical Account*, 228.

38. VOC 8752 (Part IV), 33; VOC 8786, 590.

39. VOC 8752 (Part IV), 33 for 1725. The majority of boats hired by the VOC were employed on a monthly basis. We have information of different hiring practices of *ulaks* at Patna. They were hired for 14 or 15 rupees in the years 1729 and 1730. It is not clear whether the boats were hired on a monthly basis, but it is highly unlikely because in 1730 boats were hired for a journey to Fettua, which was at worst a two days sail from Patna. VOC 8661, 42; VOC 8764, 49–54.

40. Native to Bihar, *patellas* were used for ferrying bulk goods such as grains, salt, saltpeter, and beeswax and sometimes the luggage of soldiers and officials. Thomas Bowrey, an English traveler to Bengal in the late seventeenth century, mentions that Shaista Khan, the Subahdar of Bengal, employed sixty such boats for his journey to Agra. The companies used them for bringing saltpeter from Bihar. Some of them were 350 tons. Temple, *Thomas Bowrey's A Geographical Account*, 225.

41. Though exact descriptions of *bangelaars* are hard to come by, the *Hobson-Jobson Glossary* (the dictionary of Anglo-Indian words compiled in the late nineteenth century) described these boats as the same style of vessel as *patellas*. But VOC sources indicate they were two separate vessels. VOC 8752 (Part II), 54.

42. P/1/6, 702r; P/1/10, 9v-10r; P/1/13, 265v; P/1/16, 35r. For the year 1735, there is an instance of payment on a monthly basis: 61 *ulaks* were hired by the EIC at a slightly lower rate (23 rupees per month) than the VOC's. P/1/11, 50r. In 1737 *ulaks* were hired according to weight—27 rupees per hundred bags. P/1/13, 165v.

43. VOC 8777, 292; VOC 8776, 653–656.

44. VOC 8770, 122–123, showing 20 *polwars* hired for 6 anna per day.

45. Also, at the construction sites of boats or bridges, canoes were hired for moving the artisans and coolies back and forth between the banks and the vessels anchored in the river.

46. P/1/15, 329r, 377v.

47. VOC 8762, 267 and VOC 8777, 830. The VOC had two yachts, two *bajras*, and one sloop which they used for inland transport in 1729 and 1734. The sloop often made its way from Patna to Chinsurah on the long and windy route through the Sunderban deltas.

48. The *majhi* Sadaram declared that he had worked for Lakhhan Das, a merchant located in Calcutta, for over twenty years. P/154/46 (unfoliated), the case between Choppa and Sattee plaintiff and Santose defendant, hearing of July 7, 1747 at Mayor's Court, Calcutta.

49. In 1734, twenty-three *majhis* were hired at the rate of 6 rupees per month, and over two hundred rowers were hired for 4 rupees per month (VOC 8776, 653–656). In 1743, over 250 rowers were hired for a daily wage of 0.5 anna (VOC 8794, 269). In 1744, twelve *majhis* were employed for 2.8 rupees per month, and rowers were employed for 18 annas per month (VOC 8796, 551).

50. None of the rates that I have found corresponds to the rates cited by Nitin Sinha, according to a Home Public report of June 21 1773. Nitin Sinha, "Contract, Work and Resistance: Boatmen in Early Colonial Eastern India, 1760s-1850s," *International Review of Social History* 59 (2014): 13.

51. This fluctuation continued into the nineteenth century. Sinha, "Contract, Work and Resistance, 21–24.

52. For the *lascar-ghat serang* relationship, see Gopal Balachandran, *Globalizing Labour*. Michael Fisher has shown that until the mid nineteenth century the *ghat serang* as the intermediary recruiter had not replaced all other forms of direct recruitment. Michael Fisher, *Counterflows to Colonialism: Indian Travellers and Settlers in Britain, 1600–1857* (Delhi: Orient Blackswan, 2004), 69–71. For the *ghat majhi-majhi* relationship see Mukherjee, "Of Rivers and Roads" and Sudipta Sen, *Empire of Free Trade: East India Company and the Making of the Colonial Market Place* (Philadelphia: University of Pennsylvania Press, 1998) 41; for *sardar*-coolie relationship see Tirthankar Roy, "Sardars, Jobbers, Kanganies: The Labour Contractor and the Indian Economic History," *Modern Asian Studies* 42, no. 5 (2008): 971–98.

53. Matthias van Rossum, "Lost in Translation? Maritime Identity and Identification in Asia under the VOC," *Journal of Maritime Research*, 16, no. 2 (2014): 139–52.

54. G/23/2 (unfoliated), September 1679.
55. P/1/16, 321r.
56. P/1/9, 384v.
57. P/1/15, 416r.
58. P/1/15, 630v, 715r-v, 761v.
59. VOC 8770, 124.
60. VOC 8776, 654, 751.
61. VOC 8776, 655.
62. VOC 8793, 466.
63. VOC 8793, 467.
64. VOC 8805, 65. The accounts for this year were kept in stuivers. The equivalence between florins and sicca rupees was 1.5:1, hence 3.5 stuivers equals

approximately 2 annas. See Om Prakash, *Dutch East India Company and the Economy of Bengal* (Princeton: Princeton University Press, 1983), 130.

65. VOC 8760, 9–10; VOC 8776, 212 and 761; VOC 8782, 469; VOC 8786, 523.
66. P/1/13, 233v.
67. P/1/11, 111r-112v.
68. P/1/11, 191v.
69. Akṣaẏa Kumar Kāẏal and Chitra Deb, eds., *Ketakadās Kṣhemananda Manasamangal* (Kolkata: Lekhapara, 1977), 137.
70. P/1/14, 126r, 166v-167r.
71. Patrick Olivelle, ed. and trans., *Dharmasutras: The Law Codes of Ancient India* (New York: Oxford University Press, 1999), 95.
72. Jadunath Sarkar, *Life of Mir Jumla* (Calcutta: Thacker, Spink, 1933), 160; also quoted in Atul Chandra Roy, *History of Bengal: Mughal Period (1526–1765)* (Calcutta: Nababharat Publishers, 1968), 245.
73. Yusuf 'Ali, "āhwāl-i-Mahābat Jang," in *Bengal Nawabs*, ed. and trans. Jadunath Sarkar (Calcutta: Asiatic Society, 1952), 106.
74. Hitesranjan Sanyal, *Social Mobility in Bengal* (Calcutta: Papyrus, 1959), 39-42; and Gautam Bhadra, *Mughal yuger Kriṣi Orthonīti O Kriṣak Bidraha* (Calcutta: Subarnarekha, 1983), 125.
75. "Bengal: Its Castes and Curses," Independent Section, *The Calcutta Review*, vol. 101 (1895); Jogedranath Bhattacharya, *Hindu Castes and Sects* (Calcutta: Thacker, Spink, 1896).
76. Bhattacharya, *Hindu Castes and Sects*, 316.
77. William Wilson Hunter, Herman Michael Kisch, Andrew Wallace Mackie, Charles James O'Donnell, and Herbert Hope Risley, *A Statistical Account of Bengal, Vol. 14, Bhagalpur and Santhal Parganas* (London: Trubner and Co., 1877), 73.
78. Robert Montgomery Martin, *The History, Antiquities, Topography, and Statistics of Eastern India; comprising the districts of Behar, Shahabad, Bhagulpoor, Goruckpoor, Dinajepoor, Puraniya, Rungpor, and Assam. Vol. 1, Behar (Patna city) and Shahabad* (London: William H. Allen, 1838).
79. L.S.S. O'Malley, *Bengal District Gazetteers: Hooghly* (Calcutta: The Bengal Secretariat Book Depot, 1912), 101–102.
80. Bhattacharya, *Hindu Castes and Sects*, 316; L.S.S. O'Malley, *Indian Caste Customs* (London: Curzon Press, 1932).
81. Asim Roy, *Islamic Syncretistic Tradition in Bengal* (Princeton: Princeton University Press, 1983), 37–38.
82. Bhattacharya, *Hindu Castes and Sects*, 16; *Census of India*, 1931, vol. 5, part 1, 423.
83. L.S.S. O'Malley, *Bengal, Bihar, Orissa and Sikkim* (Cambridge: Cambridge University Press, 1917), 212.
84. O'Malley, *Bengal District Gazetteers: Hooghly*, 102.
85. Bhattacharya, *Hindu Castes and Sects*, 279; O'Malley, *Bengal District Gazetteers: Hooghly*, 102–103.

86. "Extract from Bengal Public Consultations, 24th April 1789" in the case of Michael Mcnamara, 1789, British Library, London, Europeans in India (hereafter, O/5)/2.

87. West Bengal State Archives, Kolkata, Bengal Judicial Criminal (hereafter, BJC), April 25, 1794 (no. 46).

88. Ibid. Cunjaram *majhi* stood security for two other *majhis*, Premnarain and Dayaram, from whom the *darogah* of the police station at Nokeela in Rajshahi district extorted money. Cunjaram's cousins were married to Premnarain and Dayaram. The same darogah extorted money from a raiyat, Bungoo, in the village Kumarpara. Nidhu, a *majhi* of the same village stood security for Bungoo. Nidhu along with other villagers who were all agriculturists had to pay special levies to the darogah. BJC February 28, 1794 (no. 11); BJC May 30, 1794 (no. 2).

89. For Islamization see Richard Eaton, *The Rise of Islam and the Bengal Frontier 1207–1760* (Berkeley: University of California Press, 1993).

90. Roy, *Islamic Syncretistic Tradition in Bengal*, 207–49.

91. Ibid., 229, 241.

92. Ibid., 207–49.

93. Ascribed to Zainuddin's Rasul Vijay, quoted in Roy, *Islamic Syncretistic Tradition in Bengal*, 35.

94. VOC 8776, 839.

95. Eaton, *Rise of Islam and the Bengal Frontier*, 194–226.

96. James Wise, *Notes on the Races, Castes and Trades of Eastern Bengal* (London: Her Majesty's printer Harrison and Sons, 1883), 17.

97. Ibid.

98. Wakil Ahmad, *Bāṃlā Lokasaṅgīt: Sārigān* (Dhaka: Bamla Akademi, 1998), 74.

99. Eaton, *Rise of Islam and the Bengal Frontier*, 71–94, 102–112, 268–302. The intersectarian commonality and borrowing can also be seen in northeastern India. Indrani Chatterjee, *Forgotten Friends: Monks, Marriages, and Memories of Northeast India* (New Delhi: Oxford University Press, 2013), 1–73.

100. This method has been adopted by Sumantra Banerjee in his study on the folk origins of the iconography of Rādhā. Sumantra Banerjee, *Appropriation of a Folk Heroine: Radha in Medieval Bengali Vaishnavite Culture* (Shimla: Indian Institute of Advanced Study, 1993)

101. Ratnabali Chatterjee, "Representation of Gender in Folk Paintings of Bengal," in *Social Scientist* 28, no. 3/4 (March-April 2000): 7-21

102. Ahmad, *Bāṃlā Lokasaṅgīt: Sārigān*; Asutosh Bhattacharya, *Baṃlar Lokasāhitya, Vol. 3* (Kolkata: Calcutta Book House, 1965), 585–634.

103. This song has been mentioned in Jaynarayan Ghosal's *Karunānidhan Bilās* (1813–1814). Based on the refined language of the verse, Wakil Ahmad is skeptical if the song was composed by any folk artist. Ahmad, *Bāṃlā Lokasaṅgīt*, 6–9.

104. Ahmad, *Bāṃlā Lokasaṅgīt*, 39–40. There are several other songs on the boat theme. See ibid., 39–42.

105. Ramakanta Chakravarti, *Vaisnavism in Bengal, 1486–1900* (Kolkata: Sanskrit Pustak Bhandar, 1985), 25; Banerjee, *Appropriation of a Folk Heroine*, 17–18.

106. Sati Ghosh, *Bāṃlā sāhitye Vaishnav Padābalīr Kramabikāś* (Kalikata: Saraswat Library, B.S. 1376), 88–89.

107. For a detailed discussion on the rhythm and tune of *sāri* songs, see Ahmad, *Bāṃlā Lokasaṅgīt*, 25–29.

108. Ibid., 78–86.

109. Banerjee, *Appropriation of a Folk Heroine*, 26.

110. For the theology of Gauṛiya Vaishnavism, see Shashibhushan Dasgupta, *Śrīrādhār Kramabikāś sahitya o darśane* (Kolkata: A Mukherjee), 261–75.

111. Bhattacharya, *Baṃlar Lokasāhitya*, 627.

112. Muslim authors of Vaishnava lyrics have given rise to a debate about the intersection of Islam and Vaishnavism. Svami Bhumananda has identified these authors as Vaishnavas. Enamul Haque has argued that Sufism was the bedrock of Chaitanya bhakti. J.M. Bhattacharya and Edward Dimock have come up with six categories of Vaishnav lyrics, based on their theological belief structure. Finally, based on the colophons of the lyrics, Roy has argued that wherever the poet is distant from the love-play of Radha and Kriṣna, the author is Vaishnav and wherever the authors participated in the love-play, they were speaking as a Sufi. Roy, *Islamic Syncretistic Tradition in Bengal*, 186–206.

113. Ralph Nicholas, *Fruits of Worship: Practical Religion in Bengal* (Delhi: Orient Blackswan, 2003), 28–46.

114. Chakravarti, *Vaisnavism in Bengal*, 349.

115. Ibid., 354.

116. Shashibhushan Dasgupta, *Obscure Religious Cults as Background to Bengali Literature* (Calcutta: Calcutta University Press, 1946), 1–128.

117. Ibid., 346–84.

118. Edward Dimock, *The Place of the Hidden Moon: Erotic Mysticism in the Vaisnavasahajiya Cult of Bengal* (Chicago: University of Chicago Press, 1966), 249–70; Deben Bhattacharya, *The Mirror of the Sky* (London: George Allen and Unwin, 1969), 23–38.

119. Dimock, *Place of the Hidden Moon*, 260.

120. Ahmad, *Bāṃlā Lokasaṅgīt*, 73.

121. Quoted in Bhattacharya, *Baṃlar Lokasāhitya*, 590.

122. Bhattacharya, *Mirror of the Sky*, 8.

123. On conscious aesthetic choice in music, see Steven Feld, "Aesthetics as Iconicity of Style, or 'Lift-up-over-sounding': Getting into the Kaluli Groove," *Yearbook for Traditional Music*, 20 (1988): 74–113.

124. Ahmad, *Bāṃlā Lokasaṅgīt*, 53.

125. Chatterjee, *Forgotten Friends*, 8.

126. H.R. Sanyal has calculated that 28 percent of the Vaishnav temples in Bengal have been commissioned by members of Antyaja castes. Hiteshranjan Sanyal, *Social Mobility in Bengal* (Calcutta: Papyrus, 1959), 65–81.

127. Hemanga Biswas, "Pallīsamājer saṃgīt o saṃhāt," in *Hemaṅga Biśwās Racanāsamagraha*, ed. Pranab Biswas and Rangili Biswas (Kolkata: Dey's, 2012), 267–68.

128. Bernard Cohn, "From Indian Status to British Contract," *An Anthropologist amongst Historians and Other Essays* (New Delhi: Oxford University Press, 1987), 463–82; Cohn borrows this idea from Henry Maine. In Maine's formulation, status (communal despotism) represented the polar opposite of contract (individual freedom). In his evolutionary schema contract represented a higher stage of development located in modern Europe over status-based traditional India. Evidence from Patna and Mircha shows that from the 1720s on there were frequent such instances of negotiations. Henry Maine, *Ancient Law: Its Connection with Early History of Society and Its Relation to Modern Ideas* (New York: Scribner, 1864); VOC 8751 (3), 21; VOC 8769, 68–69; for Patna, VOC 8764, 49–54; VOC 8776, 209–212; VOC 8777, 817–819; VOC 8786, 333–334, 516–517.

129. The term is taken from Raymond Williams, *Culture* (Glasgow: Fontana, 1981), 39. Ratnabali Chatterjee uses Williams's formulation in understanding the patronage of Murshidabad artists. Ratnabali Chatterjee, *From Karkhana to the Studio A Study of the Changing Social Roles of Patron and Artist in Bengal* (New Delhi: Book and Books, 1990), 17.

130. 100 maunds = 4.5 tons, roughly.
131. VOC 8751 (Part II), 54.
132. VOC 8777, 818–819.
133. VOC 8777, 789.
134. VOC 8787, 448–449.
135. P/1/15, 745r-v, 761v.
136. VOC 8739, 265–266.
137. P/1/11, 111v.
138. P/1/15, 745r-v, 761v.
139. VOC 8739, 265–266.
140. VOC 8776, 654.
141. VOC 8782, 469–471.
142. VOC 8786, 519–524.
143. VOC 8776, 761.
144. VOC 8776, 212.
145. P/1/15, 2r.
146. Prasannan Parthasarathi, *Transition to a Colonial Economy: Weavers, Merchants and Kings in South India, 1720–1800* (Cambridge: Cambridge University Press, 2004), 113; Nandita Prasad Sahai, "Artisans, the State, and the Politics of Wajabi in Eighteenth-Century Jodhpur," *The Indian Economic and Social History Review* 42 (2005), 41–69. The other discussions on collective rights and privileges are confined to the use rights over the commons in land. Gadgil and Guha have brought to our attention the use of commons. Their arguments are largely based on an anthropological study conducted by Gadgil and Malhotra. Serious questions about the historical claims in both these pieces have been raised by Sumit Guha. Madhav Gadgil and Ramachandra Guha, *This Fissured Land: An Ecological History of India* (New Delhi: Oxford University Press,1992), 90–95, M.M. Gadgil and K.C. Malhotra, "Ecology of a Pastoral Caste: The Gavli Dhangar of Peninsular India,"

Human Ecology, 10 (1982): 107–43; Sumit Guha, "Claims on the Commons: Political Power and Natural Resources in Pre-colonial India," *The Indian Economic and Social History Review* 39 (2002): 181–96.

147. E.P. Thompson, "Custom, Law and Common Right," in *Customs in Common* (New York: The New Press, 1993), 100.

148. Linebaugh has discussed customary practices and their relationship to wages in the urban setting of London. Peter Linebaugh, *The London Hanged: Crime and Civil Society in the Eighteenth Century* (London: Verso, 2006), 225–87, 371–442.

149. VOC 8770, 306.

150. On antiquity of customs see Sumit Guha, "Wrongs and Rights in the Maratha Country: Antiquity, Custom and Power in Eighteenth Century India," in M.R. Anderson and Sumit Guha, eds., *Changing Concepts of Rights and Justice in South Asia* (New Delhi: Oxford University Press, 1998).

151. VOC 8774, 152–153.

152. P/1/6, 510v-511r.

153. P/1/9, 129v.

154. P/1/9, 124r.

155. P/1/9, 384v.

156. P/1/10, 108r.

157. In 1756, similar work withdrawals were also evident among Madras boatmen. Ravi Ahuja, "Labour Unsettled Mobility and Protest in the Madras Region," *The Indian Economic and Social History Review* 35, no. 4 (1998): 396.

158. Since *Kaivartagīta* provides the only indigenous precolonial profile of a boatman in Eastern India and since a sizeable section of the boatmen working for the companies came from Kaivarta castes, I will use the text even though it does not precisely come from Bengal. Prabhat Mukherjee, *The History of Medieval Vaishnavism in Orissa* (New Delhi: Educational Services, 1981), 82–83; Kunjabehari Das, *A Study of Orissan Folklore* (Shantiniketan: Viswabharati Press, 1953), 56–57.

159. VOC 8782, 401; evidences of such payments come from 1725, 1728, and 1734. For both times, the VOC noted that these payments are "according to custom." VOC 8752 (4), 36; VOC 8760, 39; VOC 8776, 680.

160. VOC 8740, 49.

161. VOC 8782, 533–534.

162. P/1/10, 135v-136r.

163. VOC 8785, 571.

164. VOC 8776, 680.

165. "Bahre gābar bhāi daṛe bhār diyā. Kanchan balai dimu ratane jariya. Thekilum nidān dine ki kahimu bhāi. Magra tarile dimu gayer kāpāi." Asutosh Das, ed., *Dwija Rāmdev biracita Abhayāmaṅgal* (Kolkata: Kalikata Biswabidyalay, 2012), 279.

166. Asef Bayat, *Life as Politics: How Ordinary People Change the Middle East* (Palo Alto: Stanford University Press, 2010), 43–65, 60.

167. VOC 8769, 68–69.

168. VOC 8776, 755.

169. VOC 8776, 753–760: "Veel hassebassens met de coelijs." In 1739 coolies could be persuaded to carry opium chests from Badderpourgola to Jalangi at the previous year's rate of 9 annas per chest. VOC 8786, 516–517.

170. VOC 8762, 197 (emphasis is author's);

171. VOC, 8752 (Part II), 203; VOC 8770, 304–306; VOC 8774, 645–709; VOC 8776, 679–773; VOC 8787, 959–967; VOC 8792, 983–1000.

172. VOC 8752 (Part II), 203.

173. This incident is first described in the 1733 instruction. VOC 8774, 649–650.

174. VOC 8758, 25.

175. Thompson, "Time, Work Discipline and Industrial Capitalism," in *Customs in Common*, 61.

176. VOC 8776, 656; VOC 8777, 291.

177. VOC 8748, 162.

178. P/1/17, 630v, 658v-659r.

CHAPTER THREE

Chapter title quoted from Joost van den Vondel, "Lucifer: Het Tweede Bedryf," in *De werken van Vondel. Vijfde deel 1645–1656*, ed. J.F.M. Sterck et al. (Amsterdam: De Maatschappij voor goede en goedkoope lectuur, 1931), 635.

1. William Petty, *Several Essays in Political Arithmetick* (London, 1755), III, 122.

2. Kaushik Ray, "The Hybrid Military Establishment of the East India Company in South Asia: 1750–1849," *Journal of Global History* 6, no. 2 (2011): 206; Stuart Reid, *Armies of the East India Company* (Oxford: Osprey, 2009), 5.

3. Philip Stern, *The Company State* (New York: Oxford University Press, 2011), 121–41.

4. Philip Stern, "Soldier and Citizen in the Seventeenth-Century English East India Company," *Journal of Early Modern History* 15 (2011): 83.

5. Dirk Kolff, *Naukar, Rajputs and Sepoys: The Ethnohistory of the Military Labour Market in Hindustan, 1450–1850* (Cambridge: Cambridge University Press, 2008).

6. Frank Tallet, "Soldiers in Western Europe, c. 1500–1790" and Michael Sikora, "Change and Continuity in Mercenary Armies: Central Europe, 1650–1750," both in *Fighting for a Living: A Comparative History of Military Labour 1500–2000*, ed. Erik-Jan Zürcher (Amsterdam: Amsterdam University Press, 2013).

7. Peter Way, "'The scum of every county, the refuse of mankind': Recruiting the British Army in the Eighteenth Century," in *Fighting for a Living: A Comparative History of Military Labour 1500-2000*, ed. Erik-Jan Zürcher (Amsterdam: Amsterdam University Press, 2014).

8. Maria Augusta Lima Cruz, "Exile and Renegades in Early Sixteenth Century Portuguese India," in *Indian Economic and Social History Review* 23, no. 3 (1986).

9. G.V. Scammell, "European Exiles, Renegades and Outlaws and the Maritime Economy of Asia, c1500–1700," *Modern Asian Studies* 26, no. 4 (1992): 641–61.

10. Elizabeth Kolsky, *Colonial Justice in British India: White Violence and the Rule of Law* (New Delhi: Cambridge University Press, 2010), 8–9, 37–38.

11. Petty, *Several Essays*, 122.

12. Femme Gaastra, "Soldiers and Merchants: Aspects of Migration from Europe to Asia in Dutch East India Company in the Eighteenth Century," in *Migration, Trade and Slavery in an Expanding World: Essays in Honor of Pieter Emmer*, ed. Wim Klooster (Leiden: Brill, 2009), 101–2.

13. Matthias van Rossum, *Werkers van de Wereld: Globaliseering, arbeid en interculturele ontmoetingen tussen Aziatische en Europese zeelieden in dienst van de VOC, 1600–1800* (Hilversum: Verloren, 2014), 105.

14. Ibid., 136.

15. Jan Lucassen, "A Multinational and Its Labor Force: The Dutch East India Company, 1595-1795," *International Labor and Working-Class History* 66 (2004): 12–39; Jelle van Lottum, *Across the North Sea: The Impact of the Dutch Republic on International Labour Migration, c. 1550–1850* (Amsterdam: Aksant, 2014).

16. Matthias van Rossum, Lex Heerma van Voss, Jelle van Lottum, and Jan Lucassen, "National and International Labour Markets for Sailors in European, Atlantic and Asian Water, 1600–1850," in *Maritime History Global History*, ed. Maria Fusaro and Amelia Polona (Liverpool: Liverpool University Press, 2010), 58.

17. Generale Monsterrollen VOC 11636, 103–104.

18. Generale Monsterrollen VOC 11542, 455–459.

19. VOC 8792, 106.

20. Captain A. Broome, *History of the Rise and Progress of the Bengal Army* (Calcutta, 1851), 27–28.

21. VOC 8796, 545–546; for "toepas" see Teotonio de Souza, *Indo-Portuguese History: Old Issues, New Questions* (New Delhi: Concept, 1985), 152.

22. For Portuguese workers see Stefan Halikowski Smith, "Languages of Subalternity and Collaboration: Portuguese in English Settlements across the Bay of Bengal, 1620–1800," *International Journal of Maritime History* 28, no. 2 (2016): 237–67; Titas Chakraborty, "The Household Workers of the East India Company Ports of Pre-Colonial Bengal," *International Review of Social History* 64 (2019): 71–93.

23. Robert Orme, *History of the Military Transactions of the British Nation in Indostan from 1745* (1778), 81.

24. British Library, London, Robert Clive Collection (hereafter, Mss Eur G/37)/20/1, 11-v.

25. In January 1757 the Bengal Native regiment of 300–400 carefully chosen *sipahis* was created by Robert Clive. Seema Alavi, *The Sepoys and the Company: Tradition and Transition in Northern India 1770–1830* (New Delhi: Oxford University Press, 1998), 35.

26. P/1/3, 11; P/1/19, 188.

27. Van Rossum, *Werkers van de Wereld*, 231–32.

28. In the column for the name of the ship on which the European soldiers came to Asia, "in dienst" or "in service" or "in India aengenomen" or "taken in (to service)/contracted in India" is entered for the European recruits from Asia.

29. Generale Monsterrollen VOC 11621, 161, 166.

30. British Library, London, Military Department Records, Bengal Army, L/Mil/10/130 (Part II), 72-73.

31. Van Rossum, *Werkers van de Wereld*, 222–23.

32. Marcus Rediker, *Between the Devil and the Deep Blue Sea: Merchant Seamen, Pirates and the Anglo American Maritime World, 1700–1750* (New York: Cambridge University Press, 1987) 118–21.

33. Ibid., 77–115, 205–53.

34. Isaac Sunderman, *Isaac Sundermans: Zyn Geschriften* (Gedrukt voor den autheur: Den Haag, 1712), 40.

35. Ibid.

36. J.D. Hullu, *Op de Schepen der Oost-Indische Compagnie*, ed. J.R. Bruijn and J. Lucassen (Groningen: Wolters-Noordhoff, 1980), 57.

37. Sunderman, *Isaac Sundermans*, 66.

38. Ibid.

39. Ibid., 68.

40. Edward Barlow, *Barlow's Journal of His Life at Sea in King's Ships, East & West Indiamen, & Other Merchant Men from 1659 to 1703, Volumes I & II*, ed. Basil Lubbock (London: Hurst and Blackett, 1934; hereafter, *Barlow's Journal*), 339.

41. *Barlow's Journal*, 544.

42. In June 1737 the Fort William council received several complaints from his officers about misbehavior by their ship captain. Members of his crew designed a plan for desertion which finally did not take place. P/1/13, fol. 68v.

43. TNSA 1.11.06.11/1677B, 332–333. The Tamil Nadu State Archives are digitized by the National Archive, The Hague, Netherlands, and accessed through http://www.gahetna.nl/collectie/archief/ead/index/zoekterm/tamil%20nadu%20state%20archive/aantal/20/eadid/1.11.06.11#c01:2.

44. VOC 8744 (Part II), fol. 17.

45. *Barlow's Journal*, 338.

46. *Barlow's Journal*, 339.

47. Van Rossum, *Werkers van de Wereld*, 111.

48. "There being severall dead and deserted," P/1/1, 407r; "Mortality and deserters having lessened my ships company seventeen men," P/1/11, 177v; "Having had the misfortune since I came from England of burying seven of my men … have had seven more runaway," P/1/11, 338r.

49. VOC 8760, 33.

50. VOC 8762 (Part II), 25.

51. P/1/4, 124v.

52. *Barlow's Journal*, 439, 440.

53. VOC 1422, 1510–1515.

54. 8777, 268–269.

55. VOC 8753 (Part II), 189–191.

56. Chakraborty, "The Household Workers of the East India Company Ports of Pre- Colonial Bengal."

57. VOC 1422, 1450r-1451v.

58. P/1/10, 126r.

59. J.A. van der Chijs, ed., *Nederlandsch-Indisch Plakaatboek, 1602–1811, Negende Deel* (Bataviaasch Genootschap van Kunsten en Wetenschappen met medewerkingvan de Nederlandsch-Indische Regering, 1891), 568.

60. VOC 8774, 752–763.

61. VOC 8757, 396.

62. VOC 8764, 312.

63. VOC 8757, 394–399.

64. VOC 1320, 612v.

65. VOC1378, 1281v-1282r.

66. VOC 8742 (Part II), 105–106.

67. VOC 1328, 506v.

68. VOC 1320, 612v.

69. VOC 8742 (Part II), 105.

70. VOC 8743 (Part II), 40.

71. Ibid.

72. VOC 8774, 764–767.

73. VOC 8774, 765.

74. VOC 1328, 485r-v.

75. VOC 8737, 121.

76. VOC 8744, 73–74.

77. VOC 8752 (Part IV), 18–19.

78. W.P. Coolhaas, *Generale Missiven der V.O.C. van Governeurs-Generaal en Raden aan Heren XVII (deel 7, 1713–1725)* ('s Gravenhage: Martinus Nijhoff, 1979): 146; Frank Lequin, *Het Personeel van de Verenigde OOst-Indische Compagne in de Achttiende Eeuw, Meer in Het Bijzonder in de Vestiging Bengalen*, Deel I (PhD thesis, Leiden University, 1982), 136; VOC 8745 (Part I), 32–33; VOC 8745 (Part II), 74–75; VOC 8752 (Part II), 276–277; VOC 8754, 273–274; VOC 8756, 107–108; VOC 8764, 314; VOC 8777, 267–269.

79. VOC 8757, 140–143; VOC 8764, 313.

80. VOC 8774, 764.

81. Henry Davison Love, ed., *Vestiges of Old Madras, 1640–1800, Vol. I* (London: John Murray, 1913), 491–93.

82. G.T. Boag, *Records of Fort St. George: Diary and Consultation Book of 1738, Vol. 68* (Madras: Superintendent Government Press, 1930), 22.

83. VOC 8745 (Part II), 74–75.

84. VOC 8744 (Part II), 15–17.

85. W.P. Coolhaas, *Generale Missiven der V.O.C. van Governeurs-Generaal en Raden aan Heren XVII (deel 6, 1698–1713)* ('s Gravenhage: Martinus Nijhoff, 1968–1976), 773.

86. VOC 1320, 615r-v.
87. VOC 1328, 523r.
88. VOC 8754, 273–274.
89. VOC 1422, 1442v-1443v, 1450r-1451r.
90. VOC 1422, 1415v-1416r.
91. VOC 1320, fol. 548r.
92. J.A. van der Chijs, ed., *Nederlandsch-Indisch Plakaatboek, 1602–1811, Vierde Deel* (Bataviaasch Genootschap van Kunsten en Wetenschappen met medewerkingvan de Nederlandsch-Indische Regering, 1891), 191.
93. VOC 8737, 350–351.
94. VOC 8742 (Part I), 65.
95. VOC 8754, 73–75.
96. P/1/16, 239v.
97. VOC 8761, 108–109; VOC 8764, 312–313; VOC 8757, 395.
98. P/1/16, 101r.
99. Karam 'Ali, "Muzaffarnāmah," in *Bengal Nawabs*, trans. Jadunath Sarkar (Calcutta: Asiatic Society, 1952), 31–32.
100. Jan Parmentier, *"De Holle Compagnie": Smokkel en Legale Handel onder Zuidnederlandse Vlag in Bengalen, ca 1720–1744* (Hilversum: Uitgeverij Verloren, 1992), 86.
101. P/1/17, 239v.
102. P/1/17, 340v.
103. P/1/17, 588r-589v.
104. VOC 8755, 459.
105. P/1/6, 29v.
106. VOC 8755, 343–344.
107. P/1/17, 239v.
108. Michael Sonenscher, "Work and Wages in Paris in the Eighteenth Century," in *Manufacture in Town and Country before the Factory*, ed. Maxine Berg et al. (Cambridge: Cambridge University Press, 1983), 147–72.
109. VOC 8755, 344; van Rossum, *Werkers van de Wereld*, 237.
110. Barnaby Slush, *The Navy Royal: Or a Sea-Cook Turn'd Projector* (London, 1709), 92, quoted in Rediker, *Between the Devil and the Deep Blue Sea*, 116.
111. VOC 8742 (Part II), 107.
112. Van Rossum, *Werkers van de Wereld*, 190–96, 232–33.
113. Nicholas Rogers, *The Press Gang: Naval Impressment and its Opponents in Georgian Britain* (New York: Continuum, 2007); Ghulam Nadri, "Sailors, Zielverkopers, and the Dutch East India Company: The Maritime Labour Market in Surat," *Modern Asian Studies* 49, no. 2 (2014): 1–29.
114. VOC 1320, 549r.
115. Rediker, *Between the Devil and the Deep Blue Sea*, 82.
116. VOC 1307, 631v.
117. VOC 8742 (Part I), 157.
118. VOC 8755, 516.

119. VOC 8753 (Part II), 221.
120. VOC 8754, 74.
121. VOC 8757, 141.
122. Stern, *Company State*, 3–18.
123. Stern, *Company State*, 61–82.
124. P/1/5, 516v.
125. VOC 8737, 352.
126. VOC 8753 (Part II), 221.
127. P/1/5, 512r–513v.
128. VOC 8771, 1610–1615; VOC 8777, 274–275.
129. P/1/6, 617v–618r; P/1/10, 7r.
130. VOC 8770, 255.
131. VOC 8777, 266–267.
132. Sir Josiah Child, *A supplement, 1689 to a former treatise concerning the East-India trade, printed 1681* (London, 1689), 9–10.
133. Within the indigenous political cultures desertion was never considered a crime or a blow to their sovereignty. Kaushik Ray, "The Hybrid Military Establishment of the East India Company in South Asia," 216.
134. VOC 1361, 1378, 1422, 1470, 8737–8800 (all files).
135. Jadunath Sarkar, "Bengal under Murshid Quli Khan," in *History of Bengal*, vol. 2, *Muslim Period 1200–1757*, ed. Jadunath Sarkar (Dacca: BRPC Books, 1943), 397–421.
136. VOC 8743 (Part I), 512–513.
137. VOC 8743 (Part II), 40.
138. VOC 8743 (Part I), 513.
139. VOC 8743 (Part II), 40.
140. VOC 8743 (Part I), 513.
141. Frans Janszoon van der Heiden and Willem Kunst, *Vervarelycke Schipbreuk van 't Oost-Indisch Jacht ter Schelling onder het landt van Bengale* (Amsterdam: Jacob Meus en Johannes van Someren, 1675), 30 (hereafter, *Ter Schelling*).
142. VOC 8743 (Part I), 512–513; VOC 8743 (Part II), 39–40.
143. E.P. Thompson, "Time, Work Discipline and Industrial Capitalism," in *Customs in Common* (New York: The New Press, 1993), 372–78. For discipline in the Mughal army, see Subah Dayal, "Making the 'Mughal' Soldier: Ethnicity, Identification, and Documentary Culture in Southern India c, 1600–1700," *Journal of the Economic and Social History of the Orient* 62, nos. 5–6 (2019), 856–924.
144. Sanjay Subrahmanyam, *The Portuguese Empire in Asia, 1500–1700: A Political and Economic History* (Malden: Wiley Blackwell, 2012), 261–83; Tapan Ray Chaudhuri, *Bengal under Akbar and Jahangir: An Introductory Study in Social History* (New Delhi: Munshiram, 1969), 235–53.
145. Scammell, "European Exiles, Renegades and Outlaws," 642–46.
146. Iqtidar Alam Khan, "Nature of Gunpowder Artillery in India during the Sixteenth Century: A Reappraisal of the Impact of European Gunnery," *Journal of the Royal Asiatic Society*, Third Series, 9, no. 1 (1999): 27–34, 31.

147. Jorge Flores, *Unwanted Neighbors: the Mughals, the Portuguese and their Frontier Zones* (New Delhi: Oxford University Press, 2018), 217–19.
148. *Ter Schelling*, 111.
149. VOC 1240, 1405v.
150. Zaheeruddin Malik, "Mughal Official Documents Concerning the English Trade in Bengal, 1633–1712," *Proceedings of the Indian History Congress* 31 (1969): 248.
151. VOC 1328, 506r-v.
152. VOC 8743 (Part II), 39.
153. P/1/15, 212r.
154. Alexander Hamilton, *A new account of the East Indies, being the observations and remarks of Capt. Alexander Hamilton, who spent his time there from the year 1688, to 1723. trading and travelling, by sea and land, to most of the countries and islands of commerce and navigation, between the Cape of Good-hope, and the Island of Japon* (Edinburgh, printed by J. Mosman, 1727), 389–91.
155. P/1/14, 129r.
156. P/1/15, 317r-v.
157. 'Ali, "Muzaffarnāmah," 29.
158. Lequin, *Het Personeel van de Verenigde OOst-Indische Compagne*, 135.
159. Mss Eur G/37/1/2, 13–15.
160. Bhārātchandra Rayguṇākār, "Annadāmaṅgal," in *Bhārātchandra Granthābalī Vol. 2*, ed. Brajendranath Bandopadhyay and Sajanikanta Das (Kolkata: Bangiya Sahitya Parishat, 1944), 9.
161. *Ter Schelling*, 102.
162. *Ter Schelling*, 102; Scammell, "European Exiles, Renegades and Outlaws," 658.
163. VOC 7530, 799.
164. P/1/15, 332r.
165. VOC 8762, 95–97.
166. Five soldiers were returned by the "moors" to the VOC after paying an expensive gift to them. VOC 8756, 107.
167. Aniruddha Ray, *Adventurers, Landowners and Rebels, c. 1575-c. 1715* (New Delhi: Munshiram Manoharlal, 1998), 3–23.
168. Akṣaẏa Kumar Kāẏal, ed., *Rupram Chakraborty birachita Dharmamaṅgal* (Kolkata: Bharabi, B.S. 1393), 54–55.
169. "Firiṅgi bāṅdhila taṅgi, gulantāj tār saṅgi," Asutosh Das, ed. *Dwija Rāmdev birachita Abhaẏāmaṅgal* (Kolkata: Kalikata Biswabidyalay, 2012), 79.
170. Subrahmanyam, *Portuguese Empire in Asia, 1500–1700*, 261–83.
171. For the social history of pujas of influential families in late nineteenth-century Kolkata see Tithi Bhattacharya, "'Tracking the Goddess: Religion, Community and Identity in the Durga Puja Ceremonies of Nineteenth Century Calcutta," *Journal of Asian Studies* 66, no. 4 (2007).
172. Karl Marx, *Wage Labor and Capital* (New York: Labor News Company, 1902), 45–53.

173. *Ter Schelling*, 101.

174. Jan Lucassen and Jelle van Lottum, "Six Cross-sections of the Dutch Maritime Labour Market: A Preliminary Reconstruction and its Implications (1610–1850)" in *Maritime Labour: Contributions to the History of Work at Sea, 1500–2000*, ed. Richard Gorski, Hetty Berg, J. de Jong, and W. Koetsenruijter (Amsterdam: Amsterdam University Press, 2007), 13–42; Jelle van Lottum, "Labour Migration and Economic Performance: London and the Randstad, c 1600–1800," in *Economic History Review* 64, no. 2 (2011): 531–70; Page Moch, *Moving Europeans: Migration in Western Europe since 1650* (Bloomington: Indiana University Press, 1992), 31–60.

175. VOC 8775, 119–127.

176. Generale Monsterrollen VOC 1691–1791, accessed through www.dutchshipsandsailors.nl; Matthias van Rossum, *Werkers van de Wereld: Globalisering, arbeid en interculturele ontmoetingen tussen Aziatische en Europese zeelieden in dienst van de VOC, 1600–1800* (Verloren: Hilversum, 2014), 231–32.

177. P/1/11, 338r.

178. G/7/3, 171–172.

179. VOC 1330, 838r.

180. P/1/3, 53v-54r.

181. P/1/6, 4v, 18r, 170v.

182. G.J. Bryant, *The Emergence of British Power in India, 1600–1784: A Grand Strategic Interpretation* (Rochester: Boydell Press, 2013), 157.

183. VOC 3006, 1862–1909.

184. Mss Eur G/37/8, 32.

185. John McArthur, *Principles and Practice of Naval and Military Courts Martial with an Appendix Illustrative of the Subject, vol. 1* (London: Butterworth, 1805), 26.

186. Huw Boven, "The East India Company and Military Recruitment in Britain," *Historical Research: The Bulletin of the Institute of Historical Research* 59, 139 (1986): 79.

187. Bryant, *Emergence of British Power in India*, 183.

188. P.J. Marshall, "British Society in India under the East India Company," *Modern Asian Studies* 31, no. 1 (1997), 96.

189. David A. Schleuter, "The Court Martial: A Historical Survey," *Military Law Review* 87 (1980): 129–66; Arthur Gilbert, "The Regimental Courts Martial in the Eighteenth Century British Army," *Albion* 8, no. 1 (1976): 50–66; G.A. Steppler, "British Military Law, Discipline, and the Conduct of Regimental Courts Martial in the Later Eighteenth Century," *The English Historical Review* 102, 405 (1987): 859–86.

190. British Library, London, Parliamentary Papers (hereafter, L/Parl)/2/22, Minutes and Letters of the Governor and Select Committee of Bengal and of Colonel Richard Smith, Commander in Chief of the Army, in the year 1768, relative to the Trial of Sepoys by Courts Martial. Recent research on corporal punishment in the EIC army shows that before 1857, European common soldiers were more prone to corporal punishment than were the *sipahis*. See Radhika Singha, "The 'Rare

Infliction': The Abolition of Flogging in the Indian Army, circa 1835–1920," *Law and History Review* 34, no. 3 (2016): 783–97.

191. Mss Eur G/37/1/2, 31–54.

192. *Further Report from the Committee of Secrecy Appointed by the House of Commons Assembled at Westminster in the Sixth Session of the Thirteenth Parliament of Great Britain to Enquire into the State of the East India Company* (London, 1773).

193. Mentioned in Kolsky, *Colonial Justice in British India*, 38.

CHAPTER FOUR

1. VOC 1240, 1388v.
2. Karl Marx, *Grundrisse* (London: Penguin, 1973), 327.
3. Some sample works are Paul Mantoux, *The Industrial Revolution of the Eighteenth Century: An Outline of the Beginnings of Modern Factory System in England*, trans. Marjorie Vernon (London: Metheun, 1961); Maxine Berg, *The Age of Manufacture, 1700–1820: Industry, Innovation and Work in Britain* (London: Routledge, 1994); Sheilagh Ogilvie and Markus Cerman, *European Proto-Industrialization* (Cambridge: Cambridge University Press, 1996); Lawrence Peskin, *Manufacturing Revolution: Intellectual Origins of Early American Industry* (Baltimore: Johns Hopkins University Press, 2003).
4. Sabyasachi Bhattacharya, "Cultural and Social Constraints on Technological Innovation and Economic Development: Some Case Studies," *Indian Economic and Social History Review* 3, no. 3 (1966): 240–67; Gautam Bhadra, "Silk Filature and Silk Production: Technological Development in Early Colonial Context, 1768–1833," in *Science and Empire: Essays in Indian Context (1700–1947)*, ed. Deepak Kumar (Allahabad: Anamika Prakashan, 1991), 59–86.
5. Frank Perlin, "Proto-Industrialization and Pre-colonial South Asia," *Past and Present* 98, no. 1 (1983): 89.
6. Marx, *Grundrisse*, 510–11.
7. E.P. Thompson, "Time, Work Discipline and Industrial Capitalism," *Customs in Common* (New York: New Press, 1993), 382–85.
8. Karl Marx, *Capital Volume 1* (London: Penguin, 1976), 490.
9. Perlin, "Proto-Industrialization and Pre-colonial South Asia."
10. Carlo Poni, "The Circular Silk Mill: A Factory Before the Industrial Revolution in Early Modern Europe," *History of Technology* (1999): 65–85; Claudio Zanier, "Pre-Modern European Silk Technology and East Asia: Who Imported What?" in *Textiles in the Pacific, 1500–1900*, ed. Debin Ma (London and New York: Routledge, 2005), 134–41.
11. A wide variety of long-distance Asian traders bought raw silk in Bengal, see Sushil Chaudhury, "International Trade in Bengal Silk and Comparative Role of Asians and Europeans, circa 1700–1757," *Modern Asian Studies* 29, no. 2 (May 1995): 373–86.
12. VOC 1212, 218v-219v; VOC 1278, 2172–2173.

13. George Williamson, *Proposals Humbly submitted to the Considerations of the Court of Directors for affairs of the United Company of Merchants of England, trading to the East-Indies for improving and increasing the Manufactures of Silk in Bengal, so as to preclude the necessity of importing raw silk into England from Italy, Turky, etc, The whole being the result of Close Application, accurate observations and repeated experiments made on the spot during a residence in Bengal of fifteen years, from 1756 to 1771* (London, 1775).

14. This process has been reconstructed using Williamson, "Proposals" and F.W. Stapel and C.W. Th. Baron van Boetzelaer van Asperen en Dubbeldam, eds., *Pieter van Dam, Beschryvinge van de Oostindische Compagnie 1639–1701*, vol. 4 (1927–1954), 67–71; digital access through resources.huygens.knaw.nl/vocbescrijvingvandam (hereafter Van Dam, *Beschryvinge*). West Bengal State Archives, Board of Trade Proceedings (hereafter BoT), "Observations of Raw Silk and Remarks on the Observations," June 23, 1778; Om Prakash, Bhaskar Mukhopadhyay, and, more recently, Roberto Davini and Karolina Huktova have described the process of silk rearing and reeling in their works. However, all descriptions are incomplete and overlook or erroneously describe major steps in the rearing and reeling process. See Om Prakash, *Dutch East India Company and the Economy of Bengal* (Princeton: Princeton University Press, 1983), 55–57; Bhaskar Mukhopadhaya, "The Structure of Silk Production in Early Colonial Bengal, 1770–1833" (PhD diss., University of Calcutta, 1991); Roberto Davini, "A Global Commodity within a Rising Empire," *Commodities of Empire Working Paper* 6 (2008): 8; Karolina Hutkova, "The British Silk Connection: The English East India Company's Silk Enterprise in Bengal, 1757–1812" (PhD diss., University of Warwick, 2016).

15. Van Dam, *Beschryvinge*, 67–68; Williamson, "Proposal," 15.

16. VOC 1302, 351r.

17. VOC 1240, 1387r.

18. Van Dam, *Beschryvinge*, 69–70.

19. The VOC never used the term *nacaud*, unlike the EIC.

20. VOC 1313, 156r.

21. William Bolts, *Considerations on Indian Affairs, Particularly respecting the Present State of Bengal and its Dependencies* (Piccadilly, London, 1772), 195.

22. Van Dam, *Beschryvinge*, 69; this process of bleaching was noticed in indigenous methods of silk reeling in the late nineteenth century, K.M. Mohsin, *A Bengal District in Transition: Murshidabad, 1765–1793* (Dacca: Asiatic Society of Bangladesh, 1973), 45.

23. National Archive, The Hague, Netherlands, G.L. Vernet Collection (hereafter, Vernet), 1 (unfoliated), November 9, 1756.

24. Williamson, "Proposals," 16.

25. British Library, London, Home Miscellaneous (hereafter, H), vol. 47, 125–127.

26. Prakash, *Dutch East India Company*, 113.

27. VOC 1240, 1388v.

28. See Poni, "Circular Silk Mill," 69.

29. Van Dam, *Beschryvinge*, 65.

30. VOC 1240, 1484v-1485r.
31. VOC 1242, 648v.
32. VOC 8745 (Part II), 47.
33. Van Dam, *Beschryvinge*, 64.
34. For information in this paragraph and the next I have used Prakash, *Dutch East India Company*, 113–17, unless the notes indicate otherwise.
35. VOC 1240, 1388r.
36. VOC 1307, 502r-v.
37. VOC 8745 (Part II), 46–47.
38. VOC 8750, 24.
39. Vernet, 1 (unfoliated), letter of July 28, 1756.
40. VOC 8776, 324–325.
41. VOC 1313, 155r.
42. VOC 1307, 502v.
43. VOC 1240, 1387v.
44. VOC 1299, 555r; VOC 1291, 444r.
45. VOC 8744, 105, 121–122.
46. VOC 8744, 105.
47. VOC 1277, 1457v.
48. VOC 1313, 155r.
49. Irfan Habib and Tapan Ray Chaudhuri, *Cambridge Economic History of India, Vol. II* (New Delhi: Cambridge, 1983), 288; Bhaskar Mukhopadhyay, "Orientalism, Genealogy and the Writing of History: The Idea of Resistance to Silk Filature in Eighteenth Century Bengal," *Studies in History* 11, no. 2 (1995): 196–219.
50. Van Dam, *Beschryvinge*, 63.
51. VOC 1277, 1457r-1458v.
52. VOC 1313, 158r-v.
53. VOC 1291, 444r.
54. VOC 1313, 158v.
55. VOC 1320, 605v.
56. VOC 1313, 157v.
57. VOC 1291, 449r.
58. Prakash, *Dutch East India Company*, 116.
59. VOC 1299, 555r.
60. Jan Lucassen, "Working at the Ichapur Gunpowder Factory in the 1790s, Part I," *Indian Historical Review* 39, no. 2 (2012): 19–56; Nandita Sahai, *Politics of Patronage and Protest: The State Society and Artisans in Early Modern Rajasthan* (New York: Oxford University Press, 2006), 189–90; Joseph J. Brenning, "Textile Products and Production in Late Seventeenth Century Coromandel, in *Merchants, Markets and the State in Early Modern India*, ed. Sanjay Subrahmanyam (New Delhi: Oxford University Press, 1990), 86; Sinnapah Arasaratnam, *Maritime India in the Seventeenth Century* (New Delhi: Oxford University Press, 1993), 191–92.
61. VOC 1212, 219r.
62. Prakash, *Dutch East India Company*, 41.

63. Ibid.
64. VOC 1278, 2171-2172.
65. VOC 1274, 437r-438r.
66. VOC 8744, 45.
67. VOC 8743, 633-635.
68. VOC 1239, 1238v, 1629r-v; VOC 1242, 648v.

69. In 1727 the Bengal council sent silkworms to Batavia under the care of two growers. They sent a detailed report on how to look after the worms in order to avoid sickness, lest the growers fell sick or died during the voyage. VOC 8758, 12-15.

70. VOC 8785, 73-74.

71. There is no evidence to suggest that the silk reelers were all Hindus. Though all the head reelers of the VOC had Hindu-sounding names, there is no way of knowing the names or backgrounds of the common reelers who formed the majority of workers. Moreover, in the absence of caste information, it is impossible to ascertain the socio-religious disposition of these workers towards overseas travel. Information on the religious and caste backgrounds of silk reelers comes from responses to late-nineteenth- and twentieth-century surveys, in which silk reelers of Bengal were a heterogeneous group, hailing from "clean" castes such as Sadgopes and Gandhabanias and also from untouchable castes such as Chandala, as well as a good number of Muslims. Nitya Gopal Mukerji, *A Monograph on the Silk Fabrics of Bengal* (Calcutta: Bengal Secretariat Press, 1903), 3.

72. VOC 8785, 73-74; VOC 8777, 120.

73. British Library, London, George Vansittart Collection (hereafter, Mss Eur F331)/1, 65, 84, 109; Mss Eur F331/35, 7, 8,19; Mss Eur F331/28, 31; Walter Firminger, ed., *Bengal District Records, Midnapore, vol. II, 1768-1770* (Calcutta: The Bengal Secretariat Record Room, 1914), 81, 88.

74. William Petty, *Several Essays in Political Arithmetick* (London, 1755).

75. Bhattacharya, "Cultural and Social Constraints on Technological Innovation and Economic Development"; Harbans Mukhia, "Social Resistance to Superior Technology: The Filature in Eighteenth Century Bengal," *Indian Historical Review* 9, no. 2 (1985): 56-68; Bhadra, "Silk Filature and Silk Production"; Mukhopadhaya, "Structure of Silk Production in Early Colonial Bengal"; Mukhopadhyay, "Orientalism, Genealogy and Writing of History"; Pradip Kumar Majumdar, "The Silk Industry of Bengal: A Study of Relationship between the English East India Company and Silk Producers, 1773-1813," PhD diss., Kalyani University, 2007; Hutkova, "British Silk Connection."

76. Edmund Burke, "Ninth Report," L/Parl/15, 27-28; Hutkova, "British Silk Connection," 95-100.

77. VOC 1240, 1387r-1391v.
78. Prakash, *Dutch East India Company*, 115.
79. VOC 8745 (Part II), 46-47.

80. Quoted in Sophus Reinert, "Rivalry: Greatness in Early Modern Economy," in *Mercantilism Reimagined: Political Economy in Early Modern Britain and Its Empire*, ed. Philip Stern and Carl Wennerlind (New York: Oxford University Press, 2014), 351.

81. Captain Arthur Broome, *History of Rise and Progress of the Bengal Army* (Calcutta, 1851); G.C. Klerk de Reus, "De Expeditie naar Bengale in 1759," *Indische Gids*, 11, no. 2 (1889): 2093–118; (1890), 27–90, 247–78. Other accounts of the Battle of Bedara includes Kalikinkar Datta, *The Dutch in Bengal and Bihar, 1740–1825* (New Delhi: Motilal Banarassidas, 1968); C.R. Boxer, *Jan Compagnie in oolog en vrede. Beknopte geschiedenis van de VOC* (Bussum, 1977); Holden Furber, *Rival Empires of Trade in the Orient 1600–1800* (Minneapolis: University of Minnesota Press, 1976); F.S. Gaastra, *De Geschiedenis van de VOC* (Zutphen, 2002); George Winius and Markus Wink, *The Merchant-Warrior Pacified: The VOC and Its Changing Political Economy in India* (New Delhi: Oxford University Press, 1995); Om Prakash, *European Commercial Enterprise in Pre-Colonial India* (Cambridge: Cambridge University Press, 1998); Hugo s' Jacob, "Bedara Revisited: A Reappraisal of the Dutch Expedition of 1759 to Bengal," in *Circumambulations in South Asian History: Essays in Honour of Dirk H.A. Kolff*, ed. Jos Gommas and Om Prakash (Leiden: Brill, 2003), 117–32.

82. Vernet, 1 (unfoliated), letter of March 9. 1956.

83. G/23/13, Consultations, February 11, 1758, February 26, 1758, March 30, 1758.

84. Vernet, 2 (Part I), 5–6.

85. Denver Brunsman, *Evil Necessity: British Naval Impressment in the Eighteenth Century Atlantic World* (Charlottesville: University of Virginia Press, 2013).

86. Niklas Frykman, "Impressment, Kidnapping and Panyarring," in *The Princeton Companion to Atlantic History*, ed. Joseph C. Miller (Princeton: Princeton University Press, 2015), 240–42.

87. Vernet, 2, 4, 10.

88. British Library, London, English East India Company General Correspondence with India (hereafter, E/4/619, Letter from Court, March 17, 1769; G/23/13, Consultations, February 18, 1758, March 26, 1758.

89. G/23/13, Consultation of March 30, 1758.

90. Vernet, 2, 6.

91. G/23/13, Consultation of March 30, 1758.

92. Vernet, 2, 54.

93. Datta, *The Dutch in Bengal and Bihar*, 6.

94. G/23/13, Consultations, April 6, 26, and 30, 1758; Vernet, 2 (Part I), 62–63.

95. G/23/13, Consultations, April 30 and May 9, 1758.

96. Chaudhury, "International Trade in Bengal Silk," 381.

97. Vernet, 2 (Part I), 72.

98. Bolts, *Considerations on Indian Affairs*, 195; also quoted in N.K. Sinha, *The Economic History of Bengal: From Plassey to Permanent Settlement, Volume I* (Calcutta: Firma KLM, 1965), 19.

99. Vernet, 1, 72.

100. G/23/13, Consultations of February 25, March 26, July 8, 1758.

101. G/23/13, Consultations of February 25, 26 March, April 30, September 16, 1758 and February 6, 1759.

102. Vernet, 2, 73.
103. Vernet, 2, 142–143.
104. Vernet, 2 (Part I), 172–173; (Part II), 29–30, 34.
105. Vernet, 2 (Part II), 29.
106. Vernet, 2 (Part III), 20–21, 64.
107. Datta, *The Dutch in Bengal and Bihar*, 198–99, Appendix G.
108. Vernet, 2 (Part I), 142–143.
109. G/23/13, Consultation of October 7, 1758.
110. G/23/13, Consultations of February 28, 1759.
111. Robert Travers, *Ideology and Empire in Eighteenth-Century India: The British in Bengal* (Cambridge: Cambridge University Press, 2007); Partha Chatterjee, *Black Hole of Empire: History of a Global Practice of Power* (Princeton: Princeton University Press, 2012), 33–66.
112. Edmund Burke, "Ninth Report," L/Parl/15, 2, 28; for a detailed discussion on "investments" of the EIC post-Plassey, see N.K. Sinha, *The Economic History of Bengal: From Plassey to Permanent Settlement, Volume I* (Calcutta: Firma KLM, 1965), 6–34.
113. James Vaughn, *The Politics of Empire at the Accession of George III: East India Company and Crisis and Transformation of Britain's Imperial State* (New Haven: Yale University Press, 2019), 131–231. This paradox was present in the recruiting and employing of many other groups of workers. In the case of coolies in construction sites, see P. J. Marshall, "Company and the Coolie," in *The Urban Experience: Calcutta: Essays in Honour of Nisith R. Ray*, ed. Pradip Sinha (Calcutta: Riddhi-India, 1987), 23–38; for salt manufacturers (malangies), see K.N. Patra, "British Salt Monopoly in India," *Proceedings of Indian History Congress* 29, no. 2 (1967): 90–98.
114. For all previous works see note 75 above.
115. Hutkova, "British Silk Connection," 103–37.
116. Quoted in Bhadra, "Silk Filature and Silk Production," 61–62.
117. Quoted in Hutkova, "British Silk Connection," 196.
118. Mohsin, *A Bengal District in Transition*, 50.
119. L/Parl/15/2, Appendix no. 37.
120. Walter Firminger, ed., *Bengal District Records: Rangpur, Vol. I, 1770–1779* (Calcutta: The Bengal Secretariat Record Room, 1914), 42–54; BoT, Proceedings of May 13, 1778, Letter from Edward Smith to Robert Palk, April 23, 1778.
121. Hutkova, "British Silk Connection," 126–36, 165–98, 201–9.
122. Peter Linebaugh, *The London Hanged: Crime and Civil Society in the Eighteenth Century* (London: Verso, 2006), 256–88.
123. Firminger, *Bengal District Records: Rangpur, Vol. I*, 42–54; BoT, Proceedings of May 13, 1778 and April 23, 1778; "Petitions of the nacauds, cattanies etc employed on the service of the Honble Company," April 23, 1778.
124. In Dinajepur, the governor general specified that if any reeler occupied lands before 1765, he was liable to pay the levies. Also, if any reeler cultivated his land, he was obliged to pay the same. BoT, Proceedings of May 13, 1778, "Minute by Mr. Cottrell."

125. Sudipta Sen, "Internal Trade and Market in Bengal and Rise of the English East India Company," in *A Comprehensive History of Modern Bengal 1700–1950, vol. 1*, ed. Sabyasachi Bhattacharya (Delhi: Primus, 2020), 407–20.

126. BoT, Proceedings of December 14, 1780 (no. 62); BoT, Proceedings of May 13. 1778, "Minute by Mr. Cottrell"; Majumdar, "Silk Industry of Bengal," 78, 79; Ranjit Sen, "English Moneylenders and the Growth of Private Fortune in Bengal in the Second Half of the Eighteenth Century," *Proceedings of the Indian History Congress* 37 (1976): 30–36; Sugata Bose, *Peasant Labour and Colonial Capital: Rural Bengal Since 1770* (Cambridge: Cambridge University Press, 1993), 19; Majumdar, "Silk Industry of Bengal," 78, 79.

127. Hameeda Hossain, *The Company Weavers of Bengal: The East India Company and the Organization of Textile Production in Bengal 1750–1813* (Oxford: Oxford University Press, 1988), 130–39; Firminger, *Bengal District Records: Rangpur, Vol. I*, 42–54; J.E. Colebrooke, *A digest of Regulations and Laws Enacted by the Governor General in Council for the Civil Government of the territories of the Presidency of Bengal, Arranged in Alphabetical Order, Supplement to the Digest* (Calcutta, 1807), 458.

128. Bhadra, "Silk Filature and Silk Production," 78–79.

129. British Library, London, Home Correspondence (hereafter E/1)/66, 422v-423r.

130. L/Parl/2/74, 186.

131. BoT, Proceedings of February 1, 1780, "letter from I.I. Keeghly to Robert Palk, 17th December, 1779"; BoT, Proceedings of October 28, 1796, "Letter from S. Hasleby to Robert Palk, 23rd October, 1796"; L/Parl/2/62, 310.

132. BoT, Proceedings of March 29, 1791, "letter from B. Mason to Board of Trade, Fort William, 10th March, 1791"; "Extracts of a Letter from the Resident at Bauleah dated the 16th November, 1775," British Library, London, Murshidabad Factory Records (hereafter G/27)/10, December 4, 1775; BoT, Proceedings of July 16, 1799, "Letter from William Egerton to Board of Trade, Fort William, 13th July 1799"; BoT, Proceedings of August 1, 1800, "Letter from B. Mason to Board of Trade, Fort William, 8th April, 1800."

133. Bhadra, "Silk Filature and Silk Production," 77; Mukhopadhaya, "Structure of Silk Production in Early Colonial Bengal," 176; L/Parl/2/74, 192.

134. Andrew Ure, *Philosophy of Manufactures, or an Exposition of the Scientific, Moral and Commercial Economy of the Factory System of Great Britain* (London: Charles Knight, Ludgate Street, 1835), 368; also quoted in Peter Linebaugh, *Red Round Globe Hot Burning, A Tale at the Crossroads of Commons and Closure, of Love and Terror, of Race and Class, and of Kate and Ned Despard* (Oakland: University of California Press, 2019), 302.

CHAPTER FIVE

1. Recent contributors to the debate include James Vaughn, *The Politics of Empire at the Accession of George III* (New Haven: Yale University Press, 2019);

Robert Travers, *Ideology and Empire in Eighteenth-Century India: The British in Bengal* (Cambridge: Cambridge University Press, 2007); Jon E. Wilson, *Domination of Strangers: Modern Governance in Eastern India 1780–1835* (Basingstoke: Palgrave Macmillan, 2008); Philip Stern, *The Company State: Corporate Sovereignty and the Early Modern Foundations of the British Empire in India* (New York: Oxford University Press, 2011).

2. Anand Yang, *The Limited Raj: Agrarian Relations in Colonial India, Saran District, 1793–1920* (Berkeley: University of California Press, 1988); Basudeb Chattopadhyay, *Crime and Control in Early Colonial Bengal 1770–1860* (Calcutta: K.P. Bagchi, 2000).

3. Nitin Sinha, "Contract, Work and Resistance: Boatmen in Early Colonial Bengal," *International Review of Social History* 59 (2014): 19.

4. Ranajit Guha, *Dominance without Hegemony* (Cambridge, MA: Harvard University Press, 1997).

5. Siraj Ahmed, *The Stillbirth of Capital: Enlightenment Writing and Colonial India* (Palo Alto: Stanford University Press, 2012).

6. Discussed in details in Radhika Singha, *A Despotism of Law: Crime and Justice in Early Colonial India* (New Delhi: Oxford University Press, 2000).

7. Guha, *Dominance without Hegemony*, 27.

8. Douglas Hay and Paul Craven, eds., *Masters, Servants, and Magistrates in Britain and the Empire, 1562–1955* (Chapel Hill: University of North Carolina Press, 2004), 10, 27.

9. Michael Anderson, "India, 1858–1930: The Illusion of Free Labor," in *Masters, Servants, and Magistrates*, ed. Douglas Hay and Paul Craven, pp. 444–46.

10. Radhika Singha, "The 'Rare Infliction': The Abolition of Flogging in the Indian Army, circa 1835–1900," *Law and History Review* 34, no. 3 (2016): 785.

11. H.V. Bowen, "British India, 1765–1813," in *The Eighteenth Century*, ed. P.J. Marshall and Alaine Low (New York: Oxford University Press, 1998), 530–51, 548–49.

12. Ravi Ahuja, *Pathways of Empire: Circulation, "Public Works" and Social Space in Colonial Orissa (c. 1780–1914)* (Hyderabad: Orient Blackswan, 2009); Michael Fisher, "The East India Company's Suppression of the Native Dak," *International Review of Social History* 31, no. 3 (1994): 311–48; Joshi, "Dak Roads, Dak Runners and the Reordering of Communication Networks," *International Review of Social History* 57 (2012).

13. Nitin Sinha has argued that public works with the use of police in the ferries starts from the 1820s. As this chapter shows, it had a far earlier start, beginning in the 1790s. See Sinha, *Communication and Colonialism in Eastern India* (London: Anthem, 2012), 155–80.

14. Sinha, "Contract, Work, and Resistance," 14.

15. Nitin Sinha has utilized a number of private European accounts of riverine travel. See Sinha, "Contract, Work, and Resistance." For indigenous accounts of travel, see Bāridbaraṇ Ghoṣ, ed., *Nagendranāth Basu pracyabidyāmahārṇab sampādita Bijayrām Sen biśarad pranita Tirthamaṅgal* (Kolkata: Paraśpathar, 2009).

16. Before Cornwallis's reforms, *zamīndārs* maintained their own police forces as chapter 1 demonstrates. Alongside the *zamīndāri* police, from 1772 onwards, the EIC state vested police power in the executive head of the districts or in the collectors. In 1781 the EIC state created the position of the magistrate. Under Cornwallis the power of the magistrate was extended and in 1792, the police stations came directly under the control of the magistrates. After 1792, the dispute regarding the jurisdiction of the magistrate and the collector continued into the first decade of 1800. After 1829, the positions of the collector and the magistrate were merged into one person. B.B. Misra, *The Central Administration of the East India Company, 1773–1834* (Oxford: Oxford University Press, 1959), 320–34; Eric Stokes, *English Utilitarians and India* (Oxford: Oxford University Press, 1959), 143–44; Dirk Kolff, *Grass in Their Mouth: The Upper Doab in India under the Company's Magna Charta, 1793–1830* (Leiden: Brill, 2010), 68–85.

17. Ahuja, *Pathways of Empire*, 79–118; Sinha, *Communication and Colonialism in Eastern India*, 155–80.

18. West Bengal State Archives, Kolkata, Bengal Judicial Criminal (hereafter, BJC), July 3, 1806 (no. 45).

19. BJC, June 2, 1809 (no. 33).

20. BJC, January 13, 1809 (no. 20).

21. BJC, March 12, 1814 (no. 8).

22. Tilottama Mukherjee, *Political Culture and Economy in Eighteenth-Century Bengal: Networks of Exchange, Consumption and Communication* (Hyderabad: Orient Blackswan, 2013), 297.

23. The Bhagalpur magistrate withheld some boats coming from Dhaka. After a flurry of letters exchanged between the magistrates of Bhagalpur and Dhaka, the governor general intervened to release the boats. BJC, June 21, 1799 (no. 6).

24. BJC, August 28, 1795 (no. 12).

25. BJC, March 12, 1814 (no. 8).

26. BJC, January 25, 1815 (55).

27. D. Sutherland, *Appendix to the Regulations of the Bengal Code, Vol II* (Calcutta, 1864), 1347–53.

28. Richard Clarke, ed., *Regulations and Acts of the Bengal Government, 1793–1854* (London, 1855), 96–97.

29. Two *girdwars*, Khwaja Ahmed Ally and Bahadur Khan, were sent by the governor general to the magistrate of Hugli, who then sent the boats to patrol the area between Niasarai and Nuddea. BJC, August 28, 1795 (no. 13).

30. West Bengal State Archives, Kolkata, Bengal Judicial Civil (hereafter, BJCivil), August 20, 1835 (no. 16).

31. BJC, August 11, 1820 (no. 12).

32. Akṣaẏa Kumar Kāyal, ed., *Ruprām Chakraborty birachita Dharmamaṅgal* (Kolkata: Bharabi, B.S. 1393), 205.

33. BJC, March 27, 1806 (no. 5).

34. BJC, February 6, 1806 (no. 18).

35. James Long, *Selections from Unpublished Records of the Government for the years 1748 to 1767 inclusive, Vol. 1* (Calcutta: Office of Superintendent of Government Printing, 1869), 438.

36. Ranjan Chakrabarti, *Authority and Violence in Colonial Bengal, 1800–1868* (Calcutta: Bookland, 1997).

37. Chattopadhyay, *Crime and Control in Early Colonial Bengal.*

38. Examples of terror are many. See *The Confessions of Miajahn, Darogah of Police, dictated by Him and Translated by a Mofussilite* (Calcutta: Wyman and Co., 1869); Giriś Candra Basu, *Sekāler Dārogār Kāhini* (Kalikata: Pustak Bipani, 1958; first published 1888).

39. Kolff, *Grass in Their Mouth*, 84–86.

40. The term "garrison state" comes from the political scientist Harold Laswell and has been used by Douglas M. Peers to characterize the polity under the early East India Company's colonial state. According to Peers the early colonial state was marked by a total lack of independent civil administration. Douglas M. Peers, *Between Mars and Mammon, Colonial Armies and the Garrison State in India, 1819-1835* (London: I.B. Tauris, 1995); this concept has also been used by Thomas Metcalf in understanding the early company state. Thomas Metcalf, *Ideologies of the Raj* (Cambridge: Cambridge University Press, 1995), 37.

41. Private European agencies based in Calcutta were important recruiters of boatmen for private travel. Sinha, "Contract, Work and Resistance," 19.

42. British Library, London, Miliary Proceedings, P/23/16, consultation nos. 5-8.

43. BJC, February 21, 1815 (no. 53).

44. Magistrates of Murshidabad and Mirzapore were of this opinion. BJC, November 14, 1815 (no. 38); BJC, March 8, 1814 (no. 36).

45. The magistrate of Benaras of this opinion. BJC, February 21, 1815 (no. 52).

46. BJC, March 12, 1814 (nos. 8 and 9).

47. BJC, January 20, 1809 (no. 10).

48. K.K. Datta, ed., *Selections from Unpublished Correspondence of the Judge-Magistrate and Judge of Patna* (Patna: Superintendent Government Printing, 1954), 50–54.

49. BJC, September 22, 1803 (no. 16).

50. Mukherjee, *Political Culture and Economy in Eighteenth-Century Bengal*, 153–55.

51. Charles Elliot, Acting Magistrate of Agra to Fort William, BJC, July 3, 1806 (no. 3).

52. For doolies, BJC, November 6, 1806 (no. 36).

53. BJC, March 3, 1812 (no. 11).

54. BJC, October 14, 1802 (No.6).

55. BJC, June 6, 1817 (no. 46).

56. Basudev Chatterji, "The Darogah and the Countryside: The Imposition of Police Control in Bengal and Its Impact," *Indian Economic and Social History Review* 1, no. 18 (1981): 19–42; John McLane, "Bengali Bandits, Police and Landlords

after the Permanent Settlement, " in *Crime and Criminality in British India*, ed. Anand Yang (Tucson: University of Arizona Press, 1985), 28–29.

57. BJC, February 28, 1793 (no. 11).
58. BJC, May 30, 1794 (no. 2).
59. BJC, September 13, 1793 (no. 30).
60. Witnesses on both sides, including the plaintiff and the defendant, do not agree on the number of strokes.
61. McLane, "Bengali Bandits, Police, Landlords after Permanent Settlement."
62. Mukherjee, *Political Culture and Economy in Eighteenth Century Bengal*, 317.
63. It is important to remember here, that in spite of the tussles between the military and civil branches in EIC-ruled India, they were, as Douglas Peers has argued, "partners in empire." Douglas Peers, "Between Mars and Mammon: The East India Company and Efforts to Reform its Army, 1796–1832," *The Historical Journal* 33, no. 2 (June 1990): 386.
64. The figure of the *goleah* is absent in the EIC and VOC records in the early eighteenth century. The wage rate of the *goleah* in the late eighteenth century was slightly lower than the *majhi*'s, between 4 and 5 rupees. Sinha, "Contract, Work and Resistance," 13.
65. BJC, April 25, 1794 (no. 46).
66. BJC, February 28, 1794 (no. 2).
67. None of the boatmen were owners of the boat. The owner was an unnamed merchant. BJC, April 25, 1794 (nos. 45, 46).
68. BJC, January 3, 1805 (no. 28).
69. BJC, January 3, 1805 (no. 28); BJC, July 4, 1805 (no. 13); BJC, May 16, 1805 (no. 3); BJC, August 24, 1805 (nos. 10, 11, 12).
70. BJC, January 3, 1805 (no. 28).
71. BJC, August 27, 1819 (no. 31).
72. BJC, October 24, 1805 (no. 23).
73. BJC, January 3, 1805 (no. 28) and October 24, 1805 (no. 23).
74. BJC, January 3, 1805 (no. 28).
75. BJC, July 3, 1806 (nos. 3, 4).
76. BJC, July 3, 1806 (no. 3).
77. BJC, July 3, 1806 (nos. 2, 3).
78. See discussion in chapter 2.
79. BJC, December 19, 1812 (no. 68).
80. *The Bengal Code, Volume 1* (Calcutta: Superintendent of Government Printing, 1889), 96–102; Sinha, "Contract, Work, and Resistance," 39.
81. VOC 8777, 789.
82. Kolff, *Grass in Their Mouth*, 343–400.
83. BJC, July 27, 1810 (no. 20).
84. BJC, October 24, 1810 (no. 66).
85. BJC, February 14, 1814 (no. 17).
86. National Archives, New Delhi, General Orders by Commander-in-Chief (hereafter, GO), years 1818, 1819 (unfoliated).

87. "Regulation VI of 1825," in *The Bengal Code, Volume 1*, 217–19.

88. BJC, April 25, 1794 (no. 47).

89. Achille Mmembe, *On the Postcolony* (Berkeley: University of California Press, 2001), 175.

90. BJC, October 7, 1803 (no. 2).

91. See discussion in chapter 2, in the section "Recruiting Boats," and specifically note 59 (VOC 8770, 124).

92. BJC, July 24, 1800 (nos. 8–11).

93. BJC, March 1, 1799 (nos. 1–4).

94. James Lees, *Bureaucratic Culture in Early Colonial India: District Officials, Armed Forces, and Personal Interest under the East India Company, 1760–1830* (Oxford: Routledge, 2020), 111–48, 167–68.

95. Lt. Brooks too pointed this out. BJC, September 22, 1803 (no. 16).

96. BJC, February 21, 1805 (nos. 5, 6).

97. For historical scholarship on labor legislation, see note 4 in the Introduction.

98. Amiya Kumar Bagchi, "Workers and the Historians' Burden," in *The Making of History: Essays Presented to Irfan Habib*, ed. Irfan Habib, K.N. Panikkar, T.J. Brynes and Utsa Patnaik (London: Anthem, 2002), 298.

99. GO, year 1819.

100. West Bengal State Archives, Kolkata, Comptrolling Committee of Revenue, Murshidabad (hereafter, CCRM), April 1, 1771.

101. National Archives, New Delhi, Military Board Proceedings (hereafter, MB), February 21, 1806 (nos. 36, 37); and Military Department Proceedings (hereafter, MD), December 6, 1816 (no. 100).

102. Sinha, "Contract, Work and Resistance," 36–42.

103. Ghoṣ, *Nagendranāth*, 125.

104. Richard Clarke, *Digest or Consolidated Arrangement, Regulations and Acts of the Bengal Government, 1793–1854* (London, 1855), 65.

105. Clarke, *Digest*, 69.

106. Travers, *Ideology and Empire*, 25; Bernard Cohn, *Colonialism and Its Forms of Knowledge: The British in India* (Princeton: Princeton University Press, 1996), 70; Stokes, *English Utilitarians and India*; Rajat Kanta Ray, "Indian Society and the Establishment of British Supremacy, 1765–1818," in *The Oxford History of the British Empire, Volume II: The Eighteenth Century*, ed. P.J. Marshall, Alaine Low, and Wm. Roger Louis (New York: Oxford University Press, 1998), 508–29; Chittaranjan Sinha, "Personnel of Indian Judges in Bengal Presidency under the East India Company's Administration, 1793–1833," *Proceedings of Indian History Congress* 30 (1968): 340–51.

107. Potukuchi Swarnalatha, "Revolt, Testimony, Petition: Artisanal Protests in Colonial Andhra," *International Review of Social History* 46 (2001): Aparna Balachandran comes to similar conclusions, in "Petitions, the City and the Early Colonial State in South India," *Modern Asian Studies* 53, no. 1 (2019): 150–76. Other studies on subaltern petitioning come from eighteenth-century South India and Marwar.

108. Robert Travers, "Indian Petitioning and Colonial State Formation in Eighteenth Century Bengal," *Modern Asian Studies* 53, no. 1 (2019): 89–122.

109. Chattopadhyay, *Crime and Control in Early Colonial Bengal*.

110. BJC, March 27, 1806 (no. 5).

111. BJC, April 25, 1794 (no. 46).

112. Karl Marx, *Capital, Volume 1* (New York: Penguin, 1976), 450.

113. Long, *Selections from Unpublished Records*, 133–34.

114. BJC, January 29, 1814 (no. 11).

115. BJC, March 14, 1815 (no. 1).

116. Iona Man-Cheong, "'Asiatic' Sailors and East India Company: Racialisation and Labour Practices, 1803–1815," *Journal of Maritime Research* 16 (2014): 167–81.

117. Harald Fischer-Tine, "Flotsam and Jetsam of Empire?: European Seamen and Spaces of Disease and Disorder in Mid-Nineteenth Century Calcutta," in *The Limits of British Colonial Control in South Asia*, ed. Ashwini Tambe and Harald Fischer-Tine (New York: Routledge, 2009), 123.

118. BJC, July 26, 1804 (nos. 1, 2).

119. Panchanand Misra, "A Century of Indo-American Trade Relations, 1783-1881," *Proceedings of Indian History Congress* 27 (1965): 351–58.

120. BJC, December 13, 1804 (no. 2).

121. BJC, February 14, 1815 (no. 6).

122. P.J. Marshall, "White Town of Calcutta under the Rule of the East India Company," *Modern Asian Studies* 34, no. 2 (2000): 307–31.

123. Ibid.

124. BJC, February 21, 1815 (nos. 1, 2).

125. BJC, April 14, 1803 (no. 21).

126. BJC, June 18, 1811 (nos. 39, 40).

127. MD, November 28, 1794 (no. 8).

128. BJC, January 8, 1807 (no. 1).

129. MD, November 28, 1794 (no. 7).

130. BJC, January 22, 1814 (no. 15).

131. British Library, London, English East India Company General Correspondence with India (hereafter, E/4)/622, letter of March 30, 1774.

132. Vaughn, *Politics of Empire*, 198.

133. BJC, April 9, 1807 (no. 23).

134. Clare Anderson, "Discourses of Exclusion and the 'Convict Stain' in the Indian Ocean (c. 1800–1850)" in *The Limits of British Colonial Control in South Asia*, ed. Ashwini Tambe and Harald Fischer-Tine (New York: Routledge, 2009), 108; Fischer-Tine, "Flotsam and Jetsam of Empire?" 123–24.

135. BJC, March 7, 1815 (no. 29).

136. Long, *Selections*, 477–478.

137. Kolsky, *Colonial Justice in British India*, 38.

138. In their letter to the Public Department dated August 17, 1803, the Court of Directors mentioned two people proceeding to India under free mariner's inden-

ture, BJC, March 8, 1804 (no. 29). Similarly the letter of April 2, 1807, mentioned four people proceeding to India under similar conditions, BJC, April 9, 1807 (no. 23).

139. BJC, March 10, 1803 (no. 11).
140. BJC, March 7, 1815 (no. 23).
141. BJC, March 8, 1804 (no. 36).
142. BJC, July 11, 1805 (no. 1).
143. BJC, November 22, 1804 (no. 2).
144. Thankappan Nair, *Origin of the Kolkata Police* (Kolkata: Punthi Pustak, 2007), 63.
145. BJC, September 4, 1806 (no. 27).
146. BJC, January 16, 1813 (no. 20); BJC, June 26, 1813 (no. 12).
147. BJC, March 7, 1815 (nos. 2, 3).
148. BJC, March 21, 1815 (no. 2).
149. BJC, April 6, 1816 (no. 26).
150. For detailed discussion of the regulation of Lascars following the burning of ships see Michael H. Fisher, "Finding Lascar 'Wilful Incendiarism': British Ship-Burning Panic and Indian Maritime Labour in the Indian Ocean," *South Asia: Journal of South Asian Studies* 35 (2012): 596–623.
151. Harald Fischer-Tine, "Flotsam and Jetsam of Empire?" 141.
152. *Advertisement, notifying that the Town Major has been authorised to apprehend and confine in Fort all vagrant seamen and low Europeans who have no proper means of subsistence*, National Archives, New Delhi, Home Public (HP), April 24, 1789 (no. 8A). Also quoted in Abhishek Ray, "Archaeology of Vagabondage" (PhD diss., Trent University, 2014), 63–64.
153. BJC, May 24, 1816 (no. 30).
154. Ibid.
155. BJC, August 12, 1817 (nos. 5, 6).
156. Ibid.
157. This has been discussed in detail by Elizabeth Kolsky, *Colonial Justice in British India*, 54–56.
158. E.E. Steiner, "Separating the Soldier from the Citizen: Ideology and Criticism of Corporal Punishment in the British Armies, 1790–1815," *Social History* 8, no. 1 (1983): 21.
159. John McArthur, *Principles and Practice of Naval and Military Courts Martial with an Appendix Illustrative of the Subject, vol. 1* (London: Butterworth, 1805), 125–28.
160. BJC, March 28, 1817 (nos. 6, 7).
161. BJC, August 5, 1817 (nos. 2, 3).
162. BJC, March 28, 1817 (nos. 6, 7).
163. BJC, March 28, 1817 (nos. 6, 7).
164. BJC, March 14, 1805 (no. 3).
165. Ibid.
166. Frantz Fanon, *The Wretched of the Earth* (New York: Grove, 1963), 37.

167. Nicholas Dirks, *Castes of Mind: Colonialism and the Making of Modern India* (Princeton: Princeton University Press, 2001, 153.

CONCLUSION

1. Patrick Colquhoun, *A Treatise on the Commerce and Police on the River Thames: Containing a Historical View of the Port of London* (London: Joseph Mawman, in the Poultry, successor to Mr. Dilly, 1800), 1–80, 420–580; Patrick Colquhoun, *A Biographical Sketch of the Life and Writings of Patrick Colquhoun, Esq. LLD.* (London: Smeeton, 1818); John Harriott, *Struggles Through Life Exemplified in the various Travels and Adventures in Europe, Asia, Africa, and America, Vol II* (Philadelphia: James Humphreys, 1809), 256–67. For a detailed discussion on the role of police in labor discipline in the city of London refer to Peter Linebaugh, *The London Hanged: Crime and Civil Society in the Eighteenth Century* (London: Verso, 2006), 371–442; and Peter Linebaugh, *Red Round Globe Hot Burning, A Tale at the Crossroads of Commons and Closure, of Love and Terror, of Race and Class, and of Kate and Ned Despard* (Oakland: University of California Press, 2019), 301–16.

2. Van Rossum, *Werkers van de Wereld: Globalisering, arbeid en interculturele ontmoetingen tussen Aziatische en Europese zeelieden in dienst van de VOC, 1600–1800* (Verloren: Hilversum, 2014), 138–39.

3. Sushil Chaudhury, "Bengal Merchants and Commercial Organisations in the Second Half of the Seventeenth Century," in *Companies, Commerce and Merchant: Bengal in the Pre-colonial Era*, ed. Sushil Chaudhury (New York: Routledge, 2017); Om Prakash, "From Negotiation to Coercion: Textile Manufacturing in India in the Eighteenth Century," *Modern Asian Studies* 41, no. 6 (2007): 1331–68

4. Om Prakash, *Dutch East India Company and the Economy of Bengal* (Princeton: Princeton University Press, 1983), 110.

5. V.S. Kadam, "Forced Labour in Maharashtra in the Seventeenth and Eighteenth Centuries: A Study of Its Nature and Change," *Journal of the Economic and Social History of the Orient* 34 (1991), 55–87; Nandita Prasad Sahai, *Politics of Patronage and Protest: The State Society and Artisans in Early Modern Rajasthan* (New York: Oxford University Press, 2006), 124–65; Divya Cherian, *Merchants of Virtue* (Oakland: University of California Press, 2022).

6. Sahai, *Politics of Patronage and Protest*, 136–38.

7. Matthias van Rossum, Merve Tosun, and Alexander Geelen, "Enslaveability, Slavery and Global Micro Histories: Reflections through the Case of Cali," *Slavery and Abolition*, 43, no. 3 (2022): 482–98; nineteenth-century colonial accounts mention that in certain parts of Malabar masters faced restrictions on selling their servile workers to areas not contiguous to the village of origin of the servant or outside the district of his origin. Such restrictions did not apply to masters from Cochin, Travancore, or Calicut, as sale documents (*acten van transport*) kept by the VOC in the eighteenth century confirm. Moreover, it is not clear from nineteenth-century accounts what the legal enforceability of such restrictions were. See Dharma Kumar,

Land and Caste in South India: Agricultural Labour in the Madras Presidency during the Nineteenth Century (New Delhi: Cambridge University Press, 1965), 34–48.

8. Marjorie Keniston McIntosh, *Poor Relief in England 1350–1600* (Cambridge: Cambridge University Press, 2011), 275–76; Paul Slack, *The English Poor Law, 1531–1782* (Cambridge: Cambridge University Press, 1990).

9. Judith Bennett, "Compulsory Service in Late Medieval England," *Past and Present*, 109 (2010): 9; Christopher Hill, "Pottage for Freeborn Englishman: Attitude to Wage Labour," in *Change and Continuity in Seventeenth Century England* (Cambridge, MA: Harvard University Press, 1975), 188; Jonathan Swift, *Directions to Servants* (London: R. Dodsley, 1745), 3; Daniel Defoe, *The Great Law of Subordination Consider'd* (1724), 17.

10. Van Rossum, *Werkers van de Wereld*, 343.

11. Karl Marx, *Capital, Volume I* (New York: Penguin, 1976), 543–50.

12. Colquhoun, *A Treatise on the Commerce and Police on the River Thames*, 524.

13. Ibid., 419–36.

14. Anand Yang, "Indian Convict Workers in Southeast Asia in the Late Eighteenth and Early Nineteenth Centuries" *Journal of World History* 14, no. 2 (2003): 183; Anand Yang, *Empire of Convicts* (Oakland: University of California Press, 2021).

15. Ann Kussmaul, *Servants in Husbandry in Early Modern England* (New York: Cambridge University Press, 1981), 5; Bennett, "Compulsory Service in Late Medieval England," 9; Hill, "Pottage for Freeborn Englishman," 223.

16. See discussion in chapter 1.

17. Titas Chakraborty, "Slave Trading and Slave Resistance in the Indian Ocean World: The Case of Early Eighteenth Century Bengal," *Slavery and Abolition* 40, no. 4 (2019): 718; Titas Chakraborty, "The Household Workers of the East India Company Ports of Pre-Colonial Bengal," *International Review of Social History* (2019): 71–93.

18. Sumit Guha, "Wrongs and Rights in the Maratha Country: Antiquity, Custom and Power in Eighteenth century India," in *Changing Concepts of Rights and Justice in South Asia*, ed. M.R. Anderson and Sumit Guha (New Delhi: Oxford University Press, 1998); Sahai, *Politics of Patronage and Protest*.

19. Sahai, *Politics of Patronage and Protest*; Prasannan Parthasarathi, *The Transition to a Colonial Economy: Weavers, Merchants and Kings in South India, 1720–1800* (Cambridge: Cambridge University Press, 2004)

20. This trend was also noticeable in places where caste-based artisanal organization was very strong. David Washbrook, "Land and Labour in Eighteenth-Century South India: Golden Age of the Pariah?" in *Dalit Movements and Meanings of Labour in India*, ed. Peter Robb (New Delhi: Oxford University Press, 1993), 77; Sanjay Subrahmanyam, "Notas sobre a mão-de-obra na India pre-colonial (seculos XVI a XVIII)," in *O trabalho mestiço: Maneiras de pensar e formas de viver, séculos XVI a XIX*, ed. Eduardo França Paiva and Carla Maria Junho Anastasia (São Paulo: Annablume, 2002), 471–72.

21. For discussion of the "Herculean task" of the cataloguing of practices, see Sudipta Sen, *Empire of Free Trade: East India Company and the Making of the Colonial Market Place* (Philadelphia: University of Pennsylvania Press, 1998), 150.

22. Harriott, *Struggles Through Life Exemplified in the various Travels and Adventures*, 259.

23. Nitin Sinha, "Domestic Servant and Master-Servant Regulations in Colonial Calcutta, 1750s–1810s," *Past and Present*, 25 (2022): 141–88; Prabhu Mohapatra, "From Contract to Status: Or How Law Shaped India's Labour Relations in Colonial India, 1780–1880," in *India's Unfree Workforce: Of Bondage Old and New*, ed. Jan Breman, Isabelle Guerin, and Aseem Prakash (New Delhi: Oxford University Press, 2009); Radhika Singha, "Making the Domestic More Domestic: Criminal Law and the 'Head of the Household', 1772–1843," *Indian Economic and Social History Review* 33, no. 3 (1996).

24. Gopalan Balachandran, "Making Coolies, (Un)Making Workers: 'Globalizing' Labour in the Late-19th and Early-20th Centuries," *Journal of Historical Sociology* 24, no. 3 (2011): 268.

25. Gopalan Balachandran, *Globalizing Labour: Indian Seafarers and World Shipping 1870–1945* (New Delhi: Oxford University Press: 2012).

26. Harriott, *Struggles Through Life Exemplified in the various Travels and Adventures*, 152.

27. Patrick Colquhoun, "Appendix—British India Possessions," in *Treatise on the Wealth, Power and Resources of the British Empire in Every Quarter of the World including the East Indies* (London, Joseph Mawman, 1815), 58.

28. Colquhoun, *Treatise on the Wealth, Power and Resources*, 73.

BIBLIOGRAPHY OF PRIMARY SOURCES

ARCHIVES

National Archive, The Hague, Netherlands
  Archives of the VOC
    Overgekomen Brieven en Papieren (VOC)
    Kopie-generale landmonsterrollen van de VOC-dienaren in de VOC-vestigingen in Indië (Generale Monsterrollen VOC 11539–Generale Monsterrollen VOC 11636)
    Radermacher Collection (CR)
    Tamil Nadu State Archives (TNSA 1.11.06.11)
    G.L. Vernet Collection (Vernet)
British Library, London
  Bengal Public Proceedings (P/1)
  Calcutta Factory Records (G/7)
  Robert Clive Collection (Mss Eur G/37)
  Economic and Overseas Department Annual Files (L/E/7)
  English East India Company, General Correspondence with India (E/4)
  Europeans in India (O/5)
  Home Correspondence (E/1)
  Home Miscellaneous (H)
  Hugli Factory Records (G/20)
  Kassimbazar Factory Records (G/23)
  Mayor's Court Records (P/154)
  Military Department Records, Bengal Army (L/Mil/10)
  Military Proceedings (P/23)
  Murshidabad Factory Records (G/27)
  Parliamentary Papers (L/Parl)
  Proceedings of the Sessions of Oyer Terminer and Gaol Delivery (P/155)
  George Vansittart collection (Mss Eur F331)
National Archives, New Delhi

General Orders by Commander-in-Chief (GO)
Home Public (HP)
Military Board Proceedings (MB)
Military Department Proceedings (MD)
West Bengal State Archives, Kolkata
 Bengal Judicial Civil (BJCivil)
 Bengal Judicial Criminal (BJC)
 Board of Trade Proceedings (BoT)
 Comptrolling Committee of Revenue, Murshidabad (CCRM)
 Dutch Pattas

PUBLISHED BENGALI SOURCES

Ahmad, Wakil. *Bāṃlā Lokasaṅgīt: Sārigān*. Dhaka: Bamla Akademi, 1998.
Bandopadhyay, Sri Kumar. *Kabikankan Chaṅḍī, Part I*. Calcutta University Press, 1952.
The Bengal Code, Volume 1. Calcutta: Superintendent of Government Printing, 1889.
Bhattacharya, Bijanbihari. *Ketakadās Kṣhemānandar Manasāmaṅgal*. New Delhi: Sahitya Akademi.
Bhattacharya, Satyanarayan, ed. *Kabi Kriṣnarām Dāser Granthabalī*. Kolkata: Calcutta University Press, 1958.
Biswas, Achintya, ed. *Bipradās Pipilaier Manasāmaṅgal*. Kolkata: Ratnabali, 2002.
——— ed. *Jagajjiban Ghoṣaler Manasāmaṅgal*. Kolkata: Ratnabali, 2002.
Chakraborty, Panchanan, ed. *Rameśwar Rachanābali*. Kalikata: Bangiya Sahitya Parishat, 1964.
Chakraborty, Purnachandra, ed. *Srī Srī Padmapurān bā Biṣaharir Pnāchali*. Kolkata, undated.
Das, Asutosh, ed. *Dwija Rāmdev birachita Abhaẏāmaṅgal*. Kolkata: Kalikata Biswabidyalay, 2012.
Dasgupta, Jayantakumar, ed. *Kabi Bijayguptar Padmapurān*. Kolkata: Calcutta University Press, 2009.
Dasgupta, Sri Tamonash Chandra, ed. *Nārāẏan Deber Padmapurān*. Kolkata: Calcutta University, 1947.
Ghoṣ, Bāridbaraṇ, ed. *Nagendranāth Basu pracyabidyāmahārṇab sampādita Bijayrām Sen biśarad pranita Tirthamaṅgal*. Kalikata: Paraśpathar, 2009.
Kāyal, Akṣaẏa Kumar, ed. *Rupram Chakrabarty birachita Dharmamaṅgal*. Kolkata: Bharabi, B.S. 1393.
Kāyal, Akṣaẏa Kumar, and Chitra Deb, eds., *Ketakadās Kṣemānandar Manasāmaṅgal*. Kolkata: Lekhapara, 1977.
Mandal, Panchanan, ed. *Mukuṅdarām Chakrabortyr Chandīmaṅgal*. Kolkata: Bharabi, 1991.

Ray, Sri Shubhendu Singha, and Sri Subalchandra Bandopadhyay. "Mukunda Kabichandra krita *Biśallocanīr Gīt*," *Sāhitya Pariṣat Patrika*, 61, no. 2 (B.S. 1361): 161–90.
Rayguṇākār, Bhārātchaṅdra. "Annadāmaṅgal," in *Bhārātchaṅdra Granthābalī Vol. 2*, ed. Brajendranath Bandopadhyay and Sajanikanta Das. Kolkata: Bangiya Sahitya Parishat, 1944.
Sen, Dinesh Chandra. *Purbabaṅga Gītikā*, 2 volumes. Kolkata: Dey's Publishing, 2009.
Sen, Sukumar, ed. *Brindāban Dās birachita Chaitanyabhāgabat*. New Delhi: Sahitya Akademi, 1982.
———, ed. *Kabikankan Mukunda birachita Chaṅdīmaṅgal*. New Delhi: Sahitya Akademi, 2007.
———, ed. *Visnupala's Manasamangal*. Kolkata: Asiatic Society, 2002.

PUBLISHED DUTCH SOURCES

Coolhaas, W.P. *Generale Missiven der V.O.C. van Goverveurs-Generaal en Raden aan Heren XVII (deel 6, 1698–1713)*. 's Gravenhage: Martinus Nijhoff, 1968–1976.
———. *Generale Missiven der V.O.C. van Goverveurs-Generaal en Raden aan Heren XVII (deel 7, 1713–1725)*. 's Gravenhage: Martinus Nijhoff, 1979.
Stapel, F.W., and C.W. Th. Baron van Boetzelaer van Asperen en Dubbeldam, eds. *Pieter van Dam, Beschryvinge van de Oostindische Compagnie 1639–1701*. 's Gravenhage: Martinus Nijhoff, 1927–1954.
Sunderman, Isaac. *Isaac Sundermans: Zyn Geschriften*. Gedrukt voor den autheur: Den Haag, 1712.
van der Chijs, J.A., ed. *Nederlandsch-Indisch Plakaatboek, 1602–1811, Negende Deel*. Bataviaasch Genootschap van Kunsten en Wetenschappen met medewerkingvan de Nederlandsch-Indische Regering, 1891.
———. *Nederlandsch-Indisch Plakaatboek, 1602–1811, Vierde Deel*. Bataviaasch Genootschap van Kunsten en Wetenschappen met medewerkingvan de Nederlandsch-Indische Regering, 1891.
van der Heiden, Frans Janszoon, and Willem Kunst. *Vervarelycke Schip-breuk van 't Oost-Indisch Jacht ter Schelling onder het landt van Bengale*. Amsterdam: Jacob Meus en Johannes van Someren, 1675.

PUBLISHED ENGLISH SOURCES

Barlow, Edward. *Barlow's Journal of His Life at Sea in King's Ships, East & West Indiamen, & Other Merchant Men from 1659 to 1703, Volumes I & II*, ed. Basil Lubbock. London: Hurst and Blackett, 1934.

"Bengal: Its Castes and Curses," Independent Section, *The Calcutta Review*, Vol. 101 (1895).

Bhattacharya, Jogendranath. *Hindu Castes and Sects*. Calcutta: Thacker, Spink and Co., 1896.

Boag, G.T. *Records of Fort St. George: Diary and Consultation Book of 1738, Vol. 68*. Madras: Superintendent Government Press, 1930.

Bolts, William. *Considerations on Indian Affairs, Particularly respecting the Present State of Bengal and its Dependencies*. Piccadilly, London, 1772.

Bowrey, Thomas. *Thomas Bowrey's A Geographical Account of Countries Round the Bay of Bengal, 1669 to 1679*. Ed. Sir Richard Carnac Temple. London: Hakluyt Society, 1905.

Buchanan, Francis. *Francis Buchanan in South east Bengal, 1798: His Journey to Chittagong, Chittagong Hill Tracts, Noakhali, and Comilla*. Ed. Willem van Schendel. Dhaka: University Press, 1992.

Child, Sir Josiah. *A supplement, 1689 to a former treatise concerning the East-India trade, printed 1681*. London: 1689.

Clarke, Richard. *Digest or Consolidated Arrangement, Regulations and Acts of the Bengal Government, 1793–1854*. London, 1855.

Clarke, Richard, ed. *Regulations and Acts of the Bengal Government, 1793–1854*. London, 1855.

Colquhoun, Patrick. *A Biographical Sketch of the Life and Writings of Patrick Colquhoun, Esq. LLD*. London: Smeeton, 1818.

———. *A Treatise on the Commerce and Police on the River Thames: Containing a Historical View of the Port of London*. London: Joseph Mawman, in the Poultry, successor to Mr. Dilly. London, 1800.

———. *Treatise on the Wealth, Power and Resources of the British Empire in Every Quarter of the World including the East Indies*. London, Joseph Mawman, 1815.

The Confessions of Miajahn, Darogah of Police, dictated by Him and Translated by a Mofussilite. Calcutta, 1869.

Datta, K.K., ed. *Selections from Unpublished Correspondence of the Judge-Magistrate and Judge of Patna*. Patna: Superintendent Government Printing, 1954.

Firminger, Walter, ed. *Bengal District Records, Midnapore, vol. II, 1768–1770*. Calcutta: The Bengal Secretariat Record Room, 1914.

Further Report from the Committee of Secrecy Appointed by the House of Commons Assembled at Westminster in the Sixth Session of the Thirteenth Parliament of Great Britain to Enquire into the State of the East India Company. London, 1773.

Hamilton, Alexander. *A new account of the East Indies, being the observations and remarks of Capt. Alexander Hamilton, who spent his time there from the year 1688, to 1723, trading and travelling, by sea and land, to most of the countries and islands of commerce and navigation, between the Cape of Good-hope, and the Island of Japon*. Edinburgh: J. Mosman, 1727.

Harriott, John. *Struggles Through Life Exemplified in the various Travels and Adventures in Europe, Asia, Africa, and America, Vol II*. Philadelphia: James Humphreys, 1809.

Hunter, William Wilson, Herman Michael Kisch, Andrew Wallace Mackie, Charles James O'Donnell, and Herbert Hope Risley. *A Statistical Account of Bengal, Vol. 14, Bhagalpur and Santhal Parganas.* London: Trubner and Co., 1877.

Long, James. *Selections from Unpublished Records of the Government for the years 1748 to 1767 inclusive, Vol. 1.* Calcutta: Office of Superintendent of Government Printing, 1869.

Love, Henry Davison, ed. *Vestiges of Old Madras, 1640–1800, vol I.* London: John Murray, 1913.

Martin, Robert Montgomery. *The History, Antiquities, Topography, and Statistics of Eastern India; comprising the districts of Behar, Shahabad, Bhagulpoor, Goruckpoor, Dinajepoor, Puraniya, Rungpor, and Assam. Vol. 1, Behar (Patna city) and Shahabad.* London: William H. Allen, 1838.

McArthur, John. *Principles and Practice of Naval and Military Courts Martial with an Appendix Illustrative of the Subject, vol. 1.* London: Butterworth, 1805.

O'Malley, L.S.S. *Bengal, Bihar, Orissa and Sikkim.* Cambridge: Cambridge University Press, 1917.

———. *Bengal District Gazetteers: Hooghly.* Calcutta: The Bengal Secretariat Book Depot, 1912.

———. *Indian Caste Customs.* London: Curzon Press, 1932.

Rennell, James. *An account of the Ganges and Burrampooter Rivers.* London, 1781.

Starling, M.H., and F.C. Constable. *Indian Criminal Law and Procedure.* London: W.H. Allen, 1887.

Sutherland, D. *Appendix to the Regulations of the Bengal Code, Vol. II.* Calcutta, 1864.

Temple, Richard Carnac, ed. *The Diaries of Streynsham Master, 1675–1680, Volume I.* London: John Murray, 1911.

Williamson, George. *Proposals Humbly submitted to the Considerations of the Court of Directors for affairs of the United Company of Merchants of England, trading to the East-Indies for improving and increasing the Manufactures of Silk in Bengal, so as to preclude the necessity of importing raw silk into England from Italy, Turky, etc, The whole being the result of Close Application, accurate observations and repeated experiments made on the spot during a residence in Bengal of fifteen years, from 1756 to 1771.* London, 1775.

Wise, James. *Notes on the Races, Castes and Trades of Eastern Bengal.* London: Her Majesty's printer Harrison and Sons, 1883.

Xenophon. *Xenophon's Treatise on the Householde, translated by Gentian Hervet.* London: Thomas Berthelet, 1532.

TRANSLATED SOURCES

Ali, Karam. "*Muzaffarnāmah*," in *Bengal Nawabs*. Trans. Jadunath Sarkar. Calcutta: Asiatic Society, 1952.

Ali, Yusuf. "Āhwāl-i-Mahābat Jang," in *Bengal Nawabs*. Trans. Jadunath Sarkar. Calcutta: Asiatic Society, 1952.

Gladwin, Francis. *A Narrative of the Transactions in Bengal (a translation of Salimullah Munshi's 'Tarikh-i-Bangala')*. Calcutta: Stuart and Cooper, 1788.

Jolly, Julius, ed. and trans. *Nāradiya Dharmaśāstra or The Institutes of Narada*. London: Trubner and Co., 1876.

Kane, P.V. *History of Dharmashastra (Ancient and Medieval Religious and Civil Law), vol. III*. Poona: Bhandarkar Oriental Research Institute, 1973.

Khan, Shah Nawaz, and Abdul Hayy. *Maathir ul Umara, Vol. 1*. Trans. H. Beveridge and B. Prasad. Kolkata: Asiatic Society, 1941.

Luard, C.E., and H. Hosten, trans. *Fray Sebastien Manrique, Travels, 1629–1643, Vol. I*. London: Hakluyt Society, 1927.

Maulavi Abdus Salam, trans. *Riyazu-s-Salatin*. Calcutta: Baptist Mission Press, 1902.

Olivelle, Patrick. *Dharmasutras: The Law Codes of Ancient India: A New Translation*. New York: Oxford University Press, 1999.

INDEX

Abdallah Khan Bukhari, 32
Abdullah Khan, 193
Abhayram, 158–60, 167
abolitionism, 16
abwabs, 180
Achyutānanda Dās: *Gopālanka Ogāla*, 100; *Kaivartāgīta*, 100
Act for the Better Regulation and the Government of the Merchants Service (1729), 112, 121, 225
Adams, Martin and John, 220–21
Africans, 221; Portuguese-speaking, 136
Aga Muhammad Zamān, 134
Age of Sail, 66, 112, 126
agriculture: family labor in, 30; mobility of labor in, 30. *See also* crop failure; rice
'Ain-i-Akbari, 60
Akhtar, Shirin, 49
'Alamgir, 10
alcohol, 127–28, 130, 133, 145, 222
Ali Vardi Khan, 52, 125, 134–35
Allahabad, 202. *See also* India
allegory, 91
All India Trade Union Congress (AITUC), 1
'āmils, 43, 46
Amritalal Daw family, 137; Jagadhātrī idol at the Amritalal Daw estate, 138*fig.*
Amsterdam, 4, 175
Anglo-Dutch war (1759), 42, 142–43; silk reelers and the, 166–76
Anglo-Mughal war (1684–90), 37, 117, 123, 130

Ann (ship), 219
Apastambā Dharmasūtra, 30
Arakan, 42
Armenians, 52, 100, 105, 110; as merchants in Sydabad, 153
Armstrong, William, 193
art, 115. *See also* terracotta panels on temples
artisans, 32–34; as impecunious and powerless subjects, 62; as mobile hired workers, 33
Asaf ud-Daulah, 147, 222
Asia: British access to labor markets in, 14–15; creditors of sailors in, 127; desertion to foreign rivals in the lands of, 121; mobilization of silk reelers within the larger imperial nodes of the VOC in, 164; recruitment of European soldiers by the VOC in, 111–12. *See also* South Asia
Asia (ship), 221
Asiatic Mode of Production (AMP), 5–6
Aulchānd, Fakir, 90
Aurangzeb (emperor), 43, 46–47, 81, 131
Austrian war of succession, 12
'Azīm-ush-shān (Prince 'Azīm), 37, 51, 131

Badderpourgola, 65, 72, 86, 95
Baḍakhān Gājī, 86
Bahādur Shāh, 131
baithaks, 90
bajras, 74, 75*fig. See also* boats
Bakarganj, 60, 86, 206

bakshy, 192
bakśiś, 139–40, 237. See also wages
Balachandran, Gopalan, 238
Balaram, 159–60
Balasore, 140, 221. See also India
ballads: and company archives, 26; Eastern Bengali, 10, 23, 25–26; and historical events, 26, 254n26. See also *Dewāna Bhābnā*; *Mahiśal bandhu*; *Manik Tārā*; poetry; *Pūrbabaṅga Gītikā*
bandhu, 89
bangelas, 76, 94, 266n41. See also boats
banian, 79–80
Bankibazar settlement, 125
Bara Auliyā, 86
Barlow, Edward, 10, 113, 115; sketch of Hugli of, 113, 114*fig.*
Batavia, 9, 42–52, 110–12, 120–29, 139, 142, 155–56, 164–68, 175, 234. See also Dutch East India Company (VOC)
Battle of Bedara, 109, 142, 167–68, 174, 219
Battle of Plassey, 142, 146, 168
Bauls, 90–92
Bayat, Asef, 102
Bay of Bengal, 110
begār, 54–55, 233. See also labor
Bengal, 2–4, 6, 49, 101, 142; beruniÿas of, 20–63; as colonial possession of Britain, 186; Council of Revenue of, 180; eastern, 85, 90; European underclass in, 221; extension of the Mughal state's authority over major parts of, 85; as the gateway for bullion imports into Mughal India, 56; in the heartland of EIC rule, 203; history of the political ascendancy of the EIC in, 168; lower-level government of, 49; militarized inland fleets (VOC and EIC) in, 4–5, 65; Muslim dynasties ruling over, 23; Muslim population in, 83; peculiar law-and-order situation in, 98; political geography of, 11–12, 85; popular culture of medieval, 20–21; as separate VOC directorate, 35; seventeenth-century rebellion in, 48; socioeconomic and political life of late medieval, 21, 25; stratification of peasant holdings in precolonial, 252n7; as supplier of raw material to the British silk industry, 178; "systematic colonization" in, 235; western, 85. See also Bhagwangola; Bīrpur; Bishnupur; British empire; Chittagong; Dhaka; Hugli (Bazar Mirzapore); Kassimbazar; Kharagpur; Mahiṣadal; Mainā; Marwar; Nadia; Orissa; Patna; politics; Rangpur; Sitakund; states; Sunderbans
Berhampore, 181. See also India
berun, 56, 61. See also migrant workers
Bhadra, Gautam, 82, 179
Bhagalpur, 71–72, 101, 193, 203, 215, 220–21; boatmen of, 82; magistrates of, 200, 202, 207. See also India
Bhagirathi river, 67, 72–73
Bhagwangola, 72–73. See also Bengal
bhakti traditions, 92
Bhāratcandra, 91; *Annadāmaṅgal*, 24, 135
Bhattacharya, Ashutosh, 90
Bihar, 12, 26, 43, 46–49, 53, 64, 101, 142; boatmen of, 82, 84; in the heartland of EIC rule, 203; western Bengal and, 85. See also India
Bijay Gupta: *Padmapurān*, 30, 32–33, 57, 69–70
Bijayrām Sen, 70
Bipradās Pipilai: *Manasāmaṅgal*, 28–30, 57, 59, 62
Bir Hambir, 20
Bīrpur, 50. See also Bengal
Bir Shah, 53
Bisdom, Adriaan, 36, 168–69, 172
Bishnupur, 20. See also Bengal
Biswās, Hemaṅga, 93
blacksmiths. See smiths
boatmen, 36, 38, 63, 82, 186–230; acts of violence by military officers condoned by magistrates against, 200; from Calcutta, 100; caste belonging of, 83–84, 92–93, 106; collective bargaining power of, 99; customary labor practices of, 17–19, 41, 76, 92–94, 99–106, 188, 230, 237–38; daily allowance of food money for the, 96–97; daily schedule for fleet, 69–70; deltaic, 106, 193; in the early eighteenth-century company state, 64–106; European, 207; forcible hiring of, 196, 236–37; gifts given to, 102;

histories of boats and, 65, 70; individual petitions of, 214–15; larger system of discipline spelled out in regulations regarding recruitment, terms of hire, and conditions of labor of, 214; pilotage work of, 100–101; profitable stipulated hiring rate denied by, 95–96; public service on a full-time basis of, 189–94, 216; religious affiliations of, 84; rising tide of brutality against the, 200, 205; role in deciding their own terms of employment of, 96–100, 236; selling off their means of livelihood by, 198; in the social world of eighteenth-century Bengal, 80–93, 102; strikes of, 100; supervision of, 66, 100; as territorial, 95; upcountry, 65, 95–96, 106, 193; as worshippers of deltaic *pīrs*, 86. *See also* boats; caste/castes; *dandies*; desertion; indigenous peoples; labor; *majhis*; recruitment; salt; wages; workers

boats: cargo, 76, 77*fig.*; guard boats of police stations, 192–93; hiring by the EIC of, 195; involvement in the EIC colonial state in, 189, 207; large saltpeter, 95; pilot, 77*fig.*; pleasure, 74, 75*fig.*; plundering of, 198–99; recruitment of, 74–80, 195–98; rowing, 74, 75*fig.*; strict EIC management of the size of, 191; surveillance of the police over, 191–92. *See also bajras*; *bangelas*; boatmen; *majhis*; *patellas*; *polwars*; ships; *ulak* boats

Bodu Chandidāsa: *Sri Kṛṣṇa Kīrtan*, 89

Bolts, William, 153, 173

Brahminical pantheon, 24. *See also* Brahmins

Brahmins, 20, 29–31, 100, 255n51; conduct of, 30, 47, 57–58, 81, 83; inseparable nature of political and economic realms in the jurisprudence of, 56; as paternalistic landholder employers, 57; religion of, 85; as removed from agricultural labor, 31; widows of, 31. *See also* Brahminical pantheon; Hinduism

bratageet, 24

Britain: end of the rule of India according to the "ancient Mughal constitution" established by the EIC and the Parliament of, 213; extension of manhood suffrage of 1867 in, 189; Parliament of, 222; rebellion of 1857 in, 189. *See also* British empire; England; English East India Company (EIC)

British empire, 2, 7; Admiralty courts of the, 121; Bengal's subordinate position in the political economy of the, 3; General Courts Martial of the, 144–45, 220, 227–28; hired work in the, 15, 236; penal code as "the greatest gift" to India of the, 16; subjecthood of European sailors and soldiers in the, 7, 144. *See also* Bengal; Britain; British India; British Navy; colonialism

British India: "conservation of Indian customs" in, 17; Indian Penal Code of, 1; labor laws of, 1–2, 19; Legislative Assembly of, 1, 17. *See also* British empire; colonialism; India

British Navy, 169. *See also* British Empire

Brooks, Lieutenant, 205–6

Brooke, Major, 201

Broome, Arthur, 168

Buddhism, 85; Vajrayānā, 87, 90; sahajiyā beliefs traced back to the cults of Vajrayānā, 90

bullion, 4; theft of, 105–6

Burdwan, 165. *See also* India

burkandazes, 52, 192, 198–99, 201

Burke, Edmund, 17, 177

Burnett, Lieutenant John, 200, 205, 215–16

Bysacks, 38, 39

Calcutta, 37–53, 65–73, 80, 84, 95, 99, 105, 117–20, 128, 134, 137, 168, 192, 211, 215, 222; development of civic structures of, 41; eighteenth-century routes for riverine and coastal travel between Patna and, 69*map*; Marine Registry office in, 226–27; Mayor's Court and the Court of Oyer and Terminer and Gaol Delivery of, 9, 205, 259n138; Perrins Garden in, 125; police and magistrates of, 220, 223–24, 229; residential complexes in, 41; route between Dhaka and, 206; sailors as transient members of white,

Calcutta *(continued)*
    219; as significant colonial settlement, 219; silk reeler families from, 165; straggling of sailors around, 140, 228; Supreme Court of, 205; wealthy native families in, 40; weavers as early settlers of, 126. *See also* India
capital: and class struggle on workers, 251n57; emergence of capitalist labor relations and accumulation of, 149, 238; globalizing urges of, 2; mobility of artisans unconstrained by mercantile, 161; modern accumulation of, 17; unbridled extractive rule of the EIC by monopoly, 187. *See also* economy; mercantilism
capital punishment, 12, 49, 227. *See also* law
Carnatic wars (1743–64), 142–43
carpenters, 5, 71–72, 133, 220
cartmen, 5
caste/castes: and capitalist relations of wage labor, 251n57; Dhībar (fisherman), 30–31; fear of crossing the sea (*kālāpāni*) on account of, 164; and hired workers, 22, 30, 237, 247n13; indigenous occupations involving the participation of multiple, 6, 82; and the lives of boatmen at work, 84, 92, 237; patron saints of the laboring or menial, 100; and the regulation of agrarian hired work, 31; rejection in the lower orders of society of, 90; ritual purity of the, 83; slavery as enabling mobility of, 5; untouchable, 100; as widespread irrespective of religion, 86; woodcutting as never an occupation of, 59. *See also* boatmen; India; labor
Central Asia, 32
Ceylon, 164, 166. *See also* Jafnapatam
Chaitanya, 20–21, 90
Chakrabarty, Dipesh, 2
Chakravarti, Ramakanta, 90
Chakwars, 50, 53, 115, 260n147
Chandernagore, 118, 124–25, 129, 141. *See also* French East India Company; India
Charles II (king), 35
chattas, 170
Chatterjee, Kumkum, 24–25, 249n39

Chatterjee, Partha, 3
Chatterjee, Ratnabali, 93, 271n129
Child, Sir Josiah, 130
Chinsurah, 41, 43, 48, 64–73, 79–80, 101, 105, 110–12, 118, 123–24, 129, 135, 158; capital punishment carried out by the VOC at, 121; Dutch village in, 130; factory at, 120; prison escapes from, 122; procurement of raw silk and silk reeling by the VOC and EIC in the region of, 162; public readings of the VOC statutes against desertion in, 132. *See also* India
Chittagong, 141, 207. *See also* Bengal
chowkey, 207; salt, 213, 238
Christianity, 136
Clavel, Walter, 124
Clive, Robert, 12, 111, 142–46, 168, 173, 217
coal, 238
colonialism, 1–3; British magistracy of, 1, 186–94; as co-constitutive of Eurocentric capitalism, 239; free and unfree labor in British, 15, 240; and Indian workers, 2, 21; low-ranking Europeans as the third face of, 108; political and social consequences of, 88; standardized procedures of policing and prosecution of, 187–88; state building of, 6. *See also* Bengal; British empire; British India
Colquhoun, Patrick, 231–32, 235, 239
commercialization, 13; and global trade, 56; and mobility of workers, 22, 187. *See also* mercantilism
Contract Act (1874), 211
contracts, 158, 163, 167, 188; active intervention of the state under the guise of protecting the sanctity of, 188; contract of indenture for a private in the EIC army (1770), 218*fig.*; criminalization of breach of, 188, 239; as holding the head boatman responsible for the desertion of any oarsmen, 211; legal mechanisms to enforce regulations criminalizing breach of, 225, 232; as pro-employer for boatmen, 208–9; template for boatmen's contract (1805), 209*fig.*, 210*fig.*, 211. *See also* labor; law
coolies, 2, 33, 60, 197, 238, 255n67; recruitment of, 202; settlements with, 103; *sirdar*, 211. *See also* labor; workers

Cornwallis, Governor General Lord, 13–14, 190, 198, 204–6, 213–15, 217, 289n16
corvee workers, 15
cowherds, 100
Craven, Paul, 188
crocodiles, 122
crop failure, 29. *See also* agriculture
Crowley, Ambrose: *Law Book*, 149
Curbs, Richard Roger, 221
Curley, David, 25, 61
cuttanies, 177, 180, 183. *See also* silk reelers

Dakṣin Rai, 24, 86
dandies, 71, 78, 105, 195–96, 206–8. *See also* boatmen
darogahs, 69, 90, 96, 192–99; networks of cooperation between magistrates and, 194–205, 209, 214–215, 235
Dasarājā, 100
dastar, 28
Datta, Rajat, 249n39
Dbija Bansidās: *Padmapurān*, 28
Deccan, 131
Defoe, Daniel, 58, 234
de Leeuw, Ewout, 97
de L'Estra, Sieur, 37
Delhi, 131, 203. *See also* India; Mughal state
deportation, 120–21. *See also* desertion
de Reus, Klerk, 168
De Roos (ship), 140
desāi, 46
desertion, 19, 54–55; alternative sociability critical to acts of, 115–18; of boatmen, 67, 103–5, 113, 115, 206, 211; crime and indebtedness as important motives for, 122; criminalizing of, 46–47, 104, 147; as criminal offense in the VOC state, 46, 119–23, 124; death as ultimate punishment for, 121–22, 124, 130, 145; and forced impressments of European sailors and soldiers, 124, 128, 218–20, 224; indebtedness and, 122–23, 123*fig*.; to indigenous armies, 120, 124, 131–35, 137, 139, 163; Indo-Portuguese communities throughout South Asia as the result of, 133; and intercompany rivalry, 123–30, 219; mass silk reeler, 16, 175, 185; as means of EIC recruitment, 112, 119, 123–24, 126, 128–30, 142–43, 147; as means of retaining control over time and wages by sailors and soldiers, 126–27, 230; problem for the European companies of, 116–30, 141, 146, 216; stalling of desertion in the EIC state among soldiers through restructuring the army and revamping military discipline, 109, 142; strategy of desertion to maintain a high wage rate of European sailors and soldiers, 108–9, 126, 141, 147; as treason, 128; treaties among competing companies for extraditing those charged with, 129. *See also* boatmen; deportation; mobility; piracy; robbery; sailors; silk reelers; soldiers
deśmukh, 31
De Stadt Grave (ship), 141
Dewāna Bhābnā, 28. *See also* ballads
de Wind, Christoffel, 97–98
Dhaka, 11, 83, 135, 141, 192; route between Calcutta and, 206. *See also* Bengal
Dharma, 24
Dharmamaṅgals, 32, 59
dharmasūtras, 54–55
Dimock, Edward C., 25
Dīna Chaṅdīdāsa, 89
Dinajepur, 181–82. *See also* India
dingelaar, 76–77, 79
Dirks, Nicholas, 17, 230
di Varthema, Ludovico, 133
Dīwān, 11–12, 131, 159–60, 163, 165. *See also* indigenous peoples
Dīwāni rights (1765), 165, 176, 186
dīwān-i khāliṣa, 43
drought, 163
Dupleix, Joseph Francois, 129
dustoree, 80–81
Dutch East India Company (VOC), 4–5, 8–12, 15–19, 33–53, 81, 104, 142, 229, 232; Batavia council of the, 167; Bengal directorate of the, 35–36, 48, 120–24, 172; cashiers of the, 65, 73; Chinsurah council of the, 123–24, 143; as commercial and state entity, 34–38, 63; company archives of the, 21, 66; deployment of the European rank and file for military or shipping labor by the, 109; directorate

Dutch East India Company (VOC) *(continued)*
of the, 36, 36*fig.*, 37*fig.*, 156–58, 164; fortifications and militaries of the, 42–43, 48, 50–51, 67; governor general of the, 167; graph of average number of deserters from 1680 to 1760, 132*fig.*; hiring boats by distance by the, 76; houses and warehouses of the, 34; Hugli council of the, 48, 60, 94–96, 119–21, 139, 143, 164, 169; jurisdictional authority of the, 48, 50–51, 55; Kassimbazar council of the, 98, 103, 158; Kassimbazar factory of the, 73; landholding rights from the Mughal government for the, 36, 38; officials of the, 60, 66, 79, 94–96, 106, 110, 172, 203–4; Patna fleet of the, 50, 65–74, 84, 94–98, 103–5, 109, 115; porterage of the, 33; production in the VOC's silk re-reeling unit at Kalikapur, 157, 157*tab.*; recruitment of European sailors and soldiers by the, 111–12, 116; recruitment of indigenous soldiers by the, 110; recruitment of Indo-Portuguese soldiers as cheap source of armed labor by the, 110–11; restriction of the mobility of sailors within the *zamīndāri* of the, 119; revenue collection by the, 37–38, 41–42; settlement in Hugli of the, 36–37; silk re-reeling unit (1650–1760) of the, 154–66; States General of the, 45, 48; statutes of the, 46, 121; as *zamīndār-fiscaal*, 36, 38. *See also* Batavia; Dutch Republic; *fiscaal*; police; recruitment; states; *zamīndārs*

Dutch Republic, 34, 128; creditors in the, 127; law of the, 121. *See also* Dutch East India Company (VOC)

Dutch war of independence, 34

Dwija Ramdev: *Abhayāmaṅgal*, 102, 136

economy: eighteenth-century peasant, 5; political, 66. *See also* capital

Elizabeth I (queen), 1

Ely (ship), 219

England: anti-combination laws (1798) in, 227; Articles of War of, 12; centralized state-initiated strategy to control the mobility of peasants in late medieval, 44, 236; crown of, 128; High Court of the Admiralty in, 121; "Hollanders" recruiting soldiers from, 109; Justices of the Peace in late medieval, 44; legislations putting liabilities upon the poorer classes of, 1; need to capture labor in the post-Black Death era of, 44, 236; Parliament of, 144, 186, 189; "pastoral power" of the state in Elizabethan, 44–45. *See also* Britain; English East India Company (EIC); London

English East India Company (EIC), 2–19, 22, 33–45, 48–53, 81, 104; Board of Customs, Salt and Opium of the, 213; Calcutta council of the, 146; cashiers of the, 80; centralized police administration of the, 19, 189–94, 234–35; as commercial and state entity, 34–41, 63, 188; company archives of the, 21, 66; control increased over the market of sailors and soldiers during the eighteenth century by the, 108–9; Court of Directors (London) of the, 178, 217, 222–23; courts set up by the, 49; Dīwāni rights of the, 165, 176; "enlightened despotism" of the, 215; expansion in Indian lands of the military in the early eighteenth century of the, 107; fortifications and militaries of the, 12–13, 42–43, 48, 50–51, 67, 107–47; Fort William council of the, 40–41, 49–50, 79, 126, 165, 173, 193, 260n147; foundation of a colonial state in India by the, 186, 190–91; hiring boats by distance by the, 76; Judicial Department of the, 191; jurisdictional authority of the, 48, 50–51, 55, 187–88, 194–205, 213–14; Kassimbazar council of the, 78, 176; Kassimbazar factory of the, 72; landholding rights from the Mughal government for the, 36, 38; loss of revenue from raw silk production in India after 1765 for the, 177; Madras council of the, 146; Marine Board of the, 222–23, 227; mass resignation of officers of the, 146; mercantilist competition on foreign grounds of the, 109; Military Board of

the, 190–91, 194–96, 205, 209; military
reforms of the, 109, 142–47; as nineteenth-century state, 9, 11–14, 17, 187–94; officials of the, 66, 96, 98, 106, 179; Patna fleet of the, 65–74, 94–95, 99–100, 109, 190, 195, 265n35; protective tariffs against American products by the, 219; "public works" policy of the, 206, 216; recruitment of European soldiers by the, 112; recruitment of Indian soldiers in the late eighteenth century by the, 111; revenue collection by the, 37–38, 41–42, 212; Revenue Department of the, 220; stamping out strategies of negotiation of boatmen by the, 209–10; system of recruitment based on intermediary recruiters for the, 80, 105–6; trade in Bengal of the, 4–5, 65, 183; transition into a landholding power in the early eighteenth century of the, 107, 126. *See also* Britain; England; Fort William; military; police; recruitment; states; *zamīndārs*
English Ordinance of Laborers (1349), 234
English Revolution (1689), 144
Enlightenment, 187, 251n60
Eurocentrism, 149

Factory Laws (late 1880s), 2
Falta, 118–19, 122, 128, 139, 196. *See also* India
famine, 175, 181, 212
Fanon, Frantz, 229
farmān, 46–47, 232
Farrukh Siyar, 131–32, 134, 163
Fatawa-i-'Alamgiri, 47
faujdārs, 43, 47–53, 63, 81, 98–99, 119, 131, 133, 135; dependence on the *zamīndārs* for police and military personnel of the, 48
firingī, 136
fiscaal, 117, 119, 121–22, 143. *See also* Dutch East India Company (VOC)
Fischer-Tiné, Harald, 219
fishermen/fishing, 31, 100
Fletcher, Sir Robert, 146
flight. *See* desertion
floods, 27, 31

florette, 155
Forbes (ship), 218
forest: as autonomous territory, 59; clearance of, 26–27. *See also* labor
Fort William, 193, 201–2, 207, 228. *See also* English East India Company (EIC)
fouzdari jail, 208
Fouzdary Adalat, 198, 200, 215
French East India Company, 124–25, 129–30, 141–42, 172. *See also* Chandernagore

Gadgil, Madhav, 271n146
Gājī Saheb, 86–87
Gangaprasad, 101
Ganga river, 64–67, 72, 81–95, 133, 151, 175, 202–3, 207, 236–37; composite cultural and spiritual world of the lower reaches of the, 86; goddess of the, 85
Gautama Dharmasūtra, 81
Gazette (Calcutta newspaper), 224
Geldzak, Captain Jan, 64–65, 71, 86, 99, 101, 103, 264n16
geographers, 65
Germany, 109
Gerrit de Groot, Michiel, 122
ghats, 195–96
Ghoṣāl, Raja Kriṣṇachandra, 212–13
Ghulam Husain Tabatabai, 53
girdwars, 192
Godinho, Padre, 133
goldaars, 175
goleah, 200, 291n64
gomastahs, 52, 174–76, 179, 182
Gopal, Madan, 180
gouvernament, 35
Gracedieus (ship), 140
Gramsci, Antonio, 22
grhastha, 56
Guha, Ramachandra, 271n146
Guha, Ranajit, 188
Guha, Sumit, 237
Gujarāt, 27, 31, 136
guru, 90–92

Habibullah Khan, 135
hālyā, 30
Hamilton, Captain Alexander, 9, 134

Hamilton, Francis Buchanan, 58–59
Harriet (gunboat), 207
Harriott, John, 231–32, 238–39
Hastings, Governor General Warren, 17, 175, 181
Hay, Douglas, 188
Hayes, Commodore, 224
Hayes, Thomas, 193
H. C. *Cruizers* (ship), 224
H. C. *Indiamen* (ship), 224
H. C. S. *Broxburnebury* (ship), 224
Hercules (ship), 164
Hervet, Gentian (translator): *Oeconomicus*, 57–58, 236
hierarchy: British global, 231; in the creation of a multi-tier security system, 211; of mechanism for mass recruitment of workers, 211, 230; multiple layers of societal, 10; relationship between head boatmen and rowers of, 238
Hinduism, 20–21; conflict of competing deities in, 26. *See also* Brahmins; Manasā; Shiva
Hindus, 85–86, 90, 164; religious figures of, 212; silk reelers as, 284n71
historiography, 6; of labor regulations in the early nineteenth century, 14; the term "custom" in South Asian, 17; of the use of colonial archives, 21. *See also* history
history: of Bengal and the English East India Company, 107; of crime and justice in early colonial Bengal, 215; debunking labor, 7; decolonizing of labor, 21; Indian economic, 8; noncolonial indigenous archive for, 21–22; overreliance on colonial archives for, 21–22; Persianate *tarikh* tradition of the writing of, 25; waged work as an evolving form of social relations in, 5, 8–11, 21. *See also* historiography; India; labor
Hoffmeester, Pieter, 162–63
Hogerwerf, Captain, 71
Holcombe, Captain William, 99–101
Holland, Major John, 112
honey collectors, 25
Hoofmeester, Pieter, 60
Hugli (Bazar Mirzapore), 36–42, 51–53, 64, 79–83, 99–100, 113, 117, 120, 174–75, 196; English factory at, 124; magistrate of, 191; port of, 131; seventeenth-century riverine route from Patna to, 68*map*. *See also* Bengal
Hugli river, 67, 73, 101, 151
Hume, Lieutenant, 201, 205, 207
Hunt, Captain Richard, 50
Hutkova, Karolina, 179

identities: caste, 6; imperial differentiating, 7; liminal, 6; uncertainty of religious, 90
Inden, Ronald, 25
India: contractual relationships of worker-employer in colonial, 94; high levels of commercialization of precolonial society of, 5–6; as hinterland for slaves, 8; indigent Europeans in, 222–23; petitioning practices of subalterns in early colonial, 214; precolonial society of, 21; relative lack of servility in hired work in precolonial, 6–8; timeline for the colonial transition in, 249n33; trade union federations in, 1. *See also* Allahabad; Balasore; Berhampore; Bhagalpur; Bihar; British India; Burdwan; Calcutta; caste/castes; Chandernagore; Chinsurah; Delhi; Dinajepur; Falta; history; Laskarpur; Madras; Malabar; Midnapore; Mughal state; Murshidabad; Paddapar; politics; working class
Indian courts, 133
Indian Ocean, 7–8; maritime travel of the, 68; world of the, 216
Indian Penal Code (1860), 16
indigenous peoples: armies of, 108, 120, 124, 131–35, 137, 139; as boatmen, 2–5, 7, 14; Calcutta's low-income, 41; inaccurate understandings of, 85; manufactories with workers who are, 4, 151; noncolonial archive of, 21–22; rulers and authorities of, 141; as silk reelers, 2, 151; transfer of debt across generations as well-known practice in society of, 160; as travelers, 70; as workers, 2–7, 9, 14, 41–42, 80. *See also* boatmen; Dīwān; labor; workers

infrastructure: embankments, 190–91; inland transport routes, 190; public ferries, 190–92; railway, 189; riverine, 189–90
ironsmiths, 60, 62
Islam, 135–36; conversions to, 140
Islamization, as *pīr* worship, 85

Jacobz, Jacob, 122
Jafnapatam, 164. *See also* Ceylon
Jagadhātrī, 137
Jagajjiban Ghoṣal: *Manasāmaṅgal*, 56, 62
jāgīrdars, 53
Jahāndār Shāh, 131
Jalangi, 72, 80, 86, 97
Jalangi river, 64–65, 67–68, 72–73, 84, 95–96
jalkar, 80
jamadar, 192
James II (king), 144
Jayaraddi, account of Manik Pīr of, 85
jewelry, 62
jogandars, 182
Jones, William, 213
Joshi, N. M., 1–2, 17, 45

Kahalgaon, 101
kahars, 73
kālāpāni, 164
kangani, 18
Kanthi, 60
kārikar, 61
karindas, 43
karkhanas, 148, 161. *See also* manufactories
karmakār/kāmār caste status, 61
Kassimbazar, 4, 11–12, 42–43, 60, 65–67, 73, 78–81, 95–97, 103, 110, 125, 129, 134, 168–69, 211; factory at, 130; privately owned silk filatures in the region of, 179; procurement of raw silk and silk reeling by the VOC (first) and EIC (later) in the region of, 4, 11, 151, 154, 160–76, 178–79; as theater of violent competition to capture the labor market of silk reelers of the EIC, VOC, and other Asian merchants, 167–76. *See also* Bengal
Kayastha, 23, 31

Ketakadās Kṣhemananda: *Manasāmaṅgal*, 29–30, 57, 59, 80
Khan, Nawab Nazim Alivardi, 95, 203
Kharagpur, 50. *See also* Bengal
khalasie, 200
Kherimarie, 96
Kolff, Dirk, 108
Kolkata. *See* Calcutta
Kondecatta, 64. *See also* Bengal
kotwāl, 47, 54
Kṛṣṇa, 20, 88–90, 100
Kṛṣṇadās Kabirāj, 91
Kṛṣṇaram Das, 86; *Rāimaṅgal*, 24–25, 61
Khwaja Khizr, 86
Kolff, Dirk, 204
Kolsky, Elizabeth, 222

labor: access to forested lands as mitigating the dependence of the landless poor on hired, 58; agricultural, 26; Asian world of, 7, 151; child silk filature, 182; competitive settlement of peasants for agricultural, 43–44; controlling and curtailing the mobility of, 2–3, 7, 12–14, 18, 55, 238, 240; convict, 14–15, 236; critique of "free" waged, 7, 236–37; demiurgic, 32; despotic control by the EIC state over labor in the early 1800s, 187, 228; European, 2–4, 7–8; flight and the culture of, 15–19, 142, 189; indentured, 1, 14, 222–23; indigenous, 2, 5–7, 42; intergenerational norms of repaying debt through manual, 55; jurisdictional control over, 47, 187; limits to the commodification of, 60–61; military, 12–13, 47, 54, 108, 131, 188; official termination of forced, 204; polysemy in wage relationship in Indian relations of, 56; power of the state in coercing, 54, 187–88, 240; precolonial forms of, 5–6, 21, 261n171; scarcity of New World, 127; and the state, 10–19, 220, 240. *See also* artisanal work; *begār*; boatmen; caste/castes; contracts; coolies; forest; history; indigenous peoples; migrant workers; mobility; recruitment; silk reelers; slavery/servility; spatial boundaries; workers; working class

Lady Carrington (ship), 224
Lakshmikanta Mazumdar, 37
language: Bengali, 88, 90; rustic language of heterodox sects, 91
Larkins (ship), 224
Laskarpur, 170. *See also* India
Laudani, Raffaele, 16
Lausen, 32–33
law: colonial labor, 1–2, 14, 16–17, 211, 245n4; creating in Bengal a company rule of, 14; law courts in Bengal set up by the VOC and EIC, 49. *See also* capital punishment; contracts; states
Le Goff, Jacques, 23
Les Freres Unis (ship), 219
Lodewijk Vernet, George, 9, 168–70, 172, 174–75
London, 48, 113, 176–80, 238; centralized state regulating labor in, 231–32, 234; "counterterror" of silk weavers in defense of their wages and customary practices in, 180. *See also* England; Thames river

Macaulay, Thomas Babington, 14, 16, 187
Macnamara, Michael, 83–84
Madan Mohan, 20–21
Madras, 121, 143, 207, 221, 224. *See also* India
Magra, 102
Mahiṣadal, 32. *See also* Bengal
Mahiśal bandhu, 55. *See also* ballads
Mainā, 32–33. *See also* Bengal
Maine, Henry, 16, 250n54, 271n128
majhis, 71–78, 83–84, 88, 96, 100, 104–5, 191–200, 206, 208, 214–15; compensatory money for accidents or payments made to, 101; demands of customary wages by the, 212; fighting with, 200, 205; as intermediary gang-labor leader, 211, 235; *ghat*, 78–79, 95, 99, 105–6, 195–97, 211, 235; pilotage work of, 101. *See also* boatmen; boats
Maksudabad-Kassimbazar-Murshidabad transshipment point, 11
Maksus Khan, 11
Malabar, 233. *See also* India
Malda, 72. *See also* Mirdadpur

Malik Barkhordar, 135
Malik Qasim, 134
Manasā, 24, 29–31. *See also* Hinduism
maṅdal, 29
maṅgalkābyas, 10, 23–35, 56–60, 66, 253n17, 253n19; common form of bonded labor discussed in the, 54; and company archives, 26; didactic nature of the, 25; distribution of wages paid by patrons to the artisan after receiving the finished article in the, 60; incorporation of historical commentaries on subcontinental politics in, 25; masters of hired workers in the, 57–58; performance and, 25; as "realistic ideal" of Bengali society, 25, 56; variety of hired work in the, 27, 57–58; wages of artisans in the, 101–2. *See also* poetry
mangroves, 84
Manik Tārā, 31. *See also* ballads
manufactories: agricultural bounties in the form of raw material to augment British, 232; commercial, 148; labor for, 19; local Mughal, 148; rise of seventeenth-century Bengal silk reeling, 149; silk reeling, 149–54, 161–66, 173–74, 181–84; synchronization of work under the system of, 216. *See also karkhanas*; silk reelers
Marathas: raiders of the, 50, 72, 78–79, 110, 125, 134–35, 168, 173; territories of the, 47
Marwar, 21. *See also* Bengal
Marx, Karl, 5–6, 14, 66; Asiatic model of, 246n11; emergence of capitalist labor relations in manufactories like silk reeling units according to, 149–50; mercantilism in the understanding of, 148
Mary I (queen), 235
masons, 33–34, 40, 237
Master and Servant Acts (1880s), 3, 22, 188, 211, 240
Mbembe, Achille, 205
McLane, John, 199
mechanics, 71
mercantilism, 109, 130, 132, 148, 161, 166–67. *See also* capital; commercialization
merchants, 27, 29, 34, 63, 72, 83; Armenian,

38, 73, 100, 171, 173; Asian, 172; British, 169; buying into settlements belonging to European companies by, 38; Christian, Muslim, Hindu, Greek, Dutch, Portuguese, and Armenian, 38, 184; Dutch, 38, 171; European companies obligated to act strictly in their capacity as, 55, 62–63; Gujarati, 171–72; indigenous, 41, 66, 73, 95, 97, 159, 162, 169, 179, 184; as *mahājans*, 83; renegade, 125; securing of *zamīndāri* rights by, 35; salt, 96–97; tobacco, 199. See also *paikars*; trade

Middle Ages, 108

Midnapore, 166, 178. See also India

migrant workers, 40–41, 61; artisans as, 32; provision of shelter/settlement by *zamīndāris* to, 21, 32–33, 193; as silk reelers, 158. See also *berun*; labor; migration; mobility; workers

migration: intraregional, 82; of peasants and artisans to new villages or *zamīndāris*, 193. See also migrant workers

military: coercive recruitment by the, 210; corporeal punishment in the EIC, 280n190; impressment of the native population by the, 202, 207, 216; police recruitment of boatmen and other workers for the, 204–8, 211; subaltern European population (Calcutta or Chinsurah) as part of the, 41–42; transport of equipment for the, 103, 197. See also English East India Company (EIC); police; sailors; soldiers

Minerva (ship), 219–20

mirās, 193

Mircha, 72, 79, 86, 93–95, 97, 99, 103

Mircha-Badderpourgola-Jalangi transshipment point, 79–80

Mirdadpur, 72. See also Malda

Mir Jumla, 42, 54, 81, 133

Mirza Nathan, 133

mobility: of artisans, 161; and the Bengal state, 20–63, 193, 238; of boatmen, 66, 186, 190, 193–94, 216, 230; control of peasants (failed) under *zamīndāri* authorities regarding, 43; control of subjects of EIC government regarding, 46, 55, 187; control of subjects of VOC government regarding, 45–46, 55, 234; as cutting across gender and caste for the destitute, 30, 59, 233; of hired workers, 5, 26–34, 45–46, 59, 63, 238; illegitimate, 45; of non-European dwellers under VOC monitoring, 45–46; practices of physical, 31; representations of, 21; of sailors and soldiers, 130, 186–87; of silk reelers, 161–66, 177, 185; uncontrolled, 233–34. See also desertion; labor; migrant workers; poverty; workers

Mohammad Adraseer, 50, 52

money. See wages

monsoons, 92, 95; season of the, 113, 115; winds of the, 68

Monarch (ship), 220

Montgomery, Captain James, 140

moral dilemmas, medieval Bengali, 25

muchlekhas, 80

Mughal state: Assam expedition (1662–63) of the, 10, 42, 54, 133; authorities of the, 10–12, 34; decline of the, 13; fiscal apparatus of the, 27–28, 34–35, 63; forced recruitment of labor by the, 203; gifting of ceremonial silk robes (*khil'at*) in the, 61–62, 263n204; imperial directives regarding itinerancy by the, 46–47; imperial power of the, 12, 34, 42, 46–47, 51, 85; jurisprudence of the, 234; monopoly trading rights in salt to certain traders conferred by the, 99; officials of the, 16, 28, 34–35, 46–47, 54–55; political geography of the, 10, 85, 186, 203; provincial governors of the, 42; share in revenue of the, 258n114; spread of Islam under the, 23. See also Bihar; Delhi; Gujarat; India; Mughal emperors; Nawabi state; states

Mughal emperors, 10, 26, 28, 37, 43, 46–47, 62. See also Mughal state

Muhammad, 85

Muhammad Hashim, 46

Muhammad Shāh, 10

Mukunda Kabichandra: *Biśallocanīr Gīt*, 61–62

Mukundaram Chakraborty: *Chandīmaṅgal*, 25, 27, 30–31, 40, 54–55, 59, 61

Mungeer, 65, 71. *See also* Bengal
Murphy, Archibald, 195
Murshidabad, 81, 95, 163, 181, 212; courts at, 93, 98; magistrate of, 197, 205–6. *See also* India
Murshid Quli Khan, 11, 51, 53, 131, 163, 257n104
Murvell, Captain James, 140
Muslims, 85–86, 90; religious figures of, 212
mutchlekha, 170
Mutiny Acts (1717, 1753), 3–4, 13, 121, 142–47, 216–17, 227
mysticism, 87; multidimensional world of Bengali, 87, 93; subaltern milieu of heterodox Bengal, 92–93. *See also sarī*

nacaudkhana, 153, 176, 180, 182
nacauds, 153, 177–78, 180–83. *See also* silk reelers
Nadia, 20, 64, 100. *See also* Bengal
nafar, 31
nāibqāzī, 48
naik, 192
Napoleonic Wars, 218, 228
Nimāi, 90
Narayan Deb, 60; *Padmapurān*, 61
nastaliq style, 32
naukā vilās motif, 88, 89*fig.*
Navigation Acts, 217–18
Nawab. *See* Nawabi state
Nawabi state, 10–11, 43, 47, 63, 72, 229; concessions to boatmen on conditions of settlement and service of the, 100; courts of the, 98; fiscal apparatus of the, 35, 63; forced recruitment of labor by the, 203; imperial directives regarding itinerancy by the, 46–47; imperial power of the, 51–52; officials of the, 16, 35, 47, 54–55; political geography of the, 186; Portuguese and Dutch gunners in the army of the, 133. *See also* Mughal state; states
Nawab Nazim Alivardi Khan, 81
Nāẓim of Bengal, 62
Nityananda Datta, 40, 126
Nizamat Adalat, 192, 200, 215

opium, 65, 73, 97; transport of, 103
Ordinance of July 14, 1817, 226–27
Ordinance of Laborers (1349), 44, 236
organzine, 155
orientalism, 213
Orissa, 12, 49, 53, 100, 134, 142. *See also* Bengal
Orme, Robert, 110
Ostend Company, 118–19, 125–26, 128–29
Overgekomen Brieven en Papieren (OBP), 9

Paddapar, 173–74. *See also* India
Padma/Padda river, 82, 151, 163, 168, 173
paik, 198
paikars, 152–54, 156–57, 173. *See also* merchants
Pallas (ship), 139
pān, 61; gifting of, 61–62
Pānch Pīr, 85–87
pargana, 12, 83, 165, 170, 179–81, 191
Parthasarathi, Prasannan, 21, 97–98
parwānās, 46–47, 51, 99, 135, 159, 232
patellas, 72–73, 76, 77*fig.*, 78, 94, 101, 266n40. *See also* boats
Patna, 11, 42–43, 50, 53, 64–68, 72–82, 85, 93–96, 101, 129, 203; boatmen from, 86, 96; eighteenth-century routes for riverine and coastal travel between Calcutta and, 69*map*; native salt traders from, 94–95; seventeenth-century riverine route to Hugli from, 68*map*. *See also* Bengal
pāttā lease documents, 38, 39*fig.*
Patton, William, 221–22
Pavilioen, Anthonij, 164
peasantization, 85
peasants: eighteenth-century economy of, 5; individual farming in Mughal India creating a vast chasm between wealthy and poor, 28; *khudkāstha*, 28; Mughal imperial state not claiming any exclusive control over the labor power of the, 47; *pāhīkāstha*, 28; protection from the excesses of the *zamīndārs* of, 186; small, 28, 30; of various means, 27, 63; violence used against, 46; wealthy, 30, 34. *See also* working class; workers
Pegu, 125
peons, 5, 41, 52, 64, 73, 79–80, 120, 174, 201. *See also* workers

Perlin, Frank, 149–50
Petty, William, 66, 107, 109, 166
Philip II (king), 235
Phoenix (ship), 219
Pielat, Captain, 50, 71
Pieterzoon Coen, Jan, 167
pilotage, 100–101; as emergency work, 101
Pintij, 64. *See also* Bihar
piracy, 141; Arakanese, 207. *See also* desertion
Pīr Badar, 85–87; shrines of, 85
piriti, 89
Pir Khan, 99
pīrs, 85–87; eclecticism in the deification of the, 93; worship of, 86–87, 93
Plassey Revolution (1757), 176
poetry: didactic religious, 10, 23; stylized court, 24; traditions of Sanskrit, 24, 253n16. *See also* ballads; *maṅgalkābyas*
police: coercive recruitment by the, 187, 196–205, 210–11; colonial, 186–230; criminalization of breach of contract propped up by a centralized, 188; divisive nature of jurisdictions of the, 51; of the EIC state, 19, 46, 50–53, 189–205, 207, 217, 230; as final arbiter of wages, 203–4, 216, 230; increase in the use of boats in Bengal by the, 192; magistracy of the, 15, 186, 190–94; metropolitan English, 3, 231–32, 238; superintendence over vagrant sailors of the, 225–26; of the VOC state, 50–53. *See also* military; recruitment; surveillance
politics: of organized labor, 1; relations between the European companies and lower-level political powers in regional Bengal, 50; of sailors on American ships in view of the divide between the EIC state and the USA, 219. *See also* Bengal; India
polwars, 71–72, 76, 77fig., 79, 99. *See also* boats
porsia, 158
porters/porterage, 5, 33, 60, 65, 72
Portuguese empire, 6, 133; settlements of the, 37
postcolonialism, 88

poverty: diversification of labor by those in, 31; itinerant, 20–21, 26, 31; possibilities for both downward or upward social mobility for those in mobile working, 31; of sailors and soldiers, 113–14; working, 26, 31. *See also* mobility
prasād basan, 62
Prasad Sahai, Nandita, 21
Prakash, Gyan, 251n60
Prakash, Om, 56
Printz, Lodevick, 228–29, 235
public works projects, 15, 216
Puranic pantheon, 24; Chandi, 24, 27; Shib, 24
Pūrbabaṅga Gītikā, 10, 25–26. *See also* ballads
Pyle, Captain John, 219

qasids, 73–74
qāzī, 20, 48, 51

race, 7, 239; nineteenth-century hardening of distinctions between Europeans and natives regarding, 189, 217. *See also* racism
racism: legal, 3; as privileges of European soldiers and sailors, 229; as privileges of European soldiers committing acts of violence, 227; separation of the social trajectories of indigenous boatmen and European sailors and soldiers through system of, 217. *See also* race
Radermacher, Samuel, 9
Radha, 88–90
Rai Bal Chand, 159
Rāimaṅgal, 86
Raja Prannanth, 49
Rajmahal, 81, 98, 193, 201
Ram Bhadra, 52
Rameśwar Bhattacharya: *Shibāyan*, 28–29
Ram Singh, 96
Rangpur, 176, 179–83, 192, 197. *See also* Bengal
Ranst, Constantijn, 157–58
rasik, 89
Ray, Aniruddha, 25, 136, 256n104
Raychaudhuri, Tapan, 25

recruitment: of boatmen, 14, 19, 40–42, 66, 83, 100, 105, 187, 205–6, 224; of boats, 74–80; of European soldiers and sailors, 14, 19, 109, 140, 187, 216–17, 220, 228–29; *ghat majhi-majhi*, 78, 80; *lascar-ghat serang*, 78, 267n52; rage of civilian population plagued by forced, 202–4; *sardar-coolie*, 78, 80; of silk reelers, 162–63; of soldiers for the EIC directly from England, 144; of workers for the state, 14, 78, 194–205. *See also* boatmen; labor; police; silk reelers; violence; workers
Rediker, Marcus, 127
Regulation VI of 1819, 192, 196
Regulation VI of 1825, 204
Regulation X of 1819, 213
Regulation XI of 1806, 211–12, 225, 230, 235
Regulation XIX of 1816, 191
Regulation XXII of 1793, 191
Regulation of April 13, 1816, 225, 230
Rennell, James, 65–67
reward: for bounty-hunters of deserters, 120; as customary, 64; as extra-monetary and always adjacent to wages, 63; of indigenous men of means to *majhis*, 212; payments made for emergency pilotage work as, 101; silk garments as, 62; of silk reelers, 158. *See also* wages
riaya, 43
rice, 30–31. *See also* agriculture
robbery, 49, 141, 191, 198–99. *See also* desertion
rowannah, 213
Rowe, Captain Nicholas, 52
Rupram Chakraborty: *Dharmamaṅgal*, 54, 136, 193
ryots, 181, 212

Sahai, Nandita, 62, 98, 237
Sahajiyism, 23, 90–91
sailors: Asian, 109, 217, 219, 225, 227, 294n150; British, 219; the crimp, the spirit, or the soul salesman resorting to extreme violence in the recruitment of, 127; debauching of, 127–28; English, 10; European, 2–7, 14, 16, 18–19, 63, 107–47, 186–230; impressment of, 169; indebtedness endemic among, 122–23, 139–40; Indian, 7; mercantilist disdain for the lack of discipline among European, 132–33; mobility of, 130, 234; proscribing the mobility of, 45–46, 216, 220; sickness of, 126; strikes of European, 139. *See also* desertion; military; soldiers
Salim, Ghulam Hussain, 58
Salimullah, 53
salt, 18; boatmen clinging to the trade in, 99–100, 102, 238; boatmen hired by merchants in, 96; eating of, 60; illegal trade in, 94, 99–100, 102, 213, 216; makers of, 25, 60, 165; monopoly of the EIC over the manufacture and trade in, 207, 213; monopoly trading rights in, 99; native traders in, 94–95; as "security" for boatmen, 100, 106, 213. *See also* boatmen
saltpeter, 65, 73, 78, 172; large saltpeter boats, 95; missing bags of, 105; small saltpeter boats, 96
Sanyal, Hiteshranjan, 82
Sanyasi rebellion, 181
Sarfaraz Khan, 103
sarī, 69–70, 87–93, 270n107; rhythm (*tāl*) of rowing of the *sāri* songs as the boatmen's contribution to the Vaishnava literary world, 89; as rooted in the social and cultural world of late medieval Bengal, 70, 92–93; various exploits of Kṛiṣna as the predominant theme of, 88. *See also* mysticism
sarkār, 46, 50, 53
Sarkar, Jadunath, 81
satire, 234
Scammell, G. V., 133
Scheurs, Ensign, 65, 72
Schonamille, Francois, 125
Scotland, 109
Seif Khan, 53
Sen, Bijayrām, 212–13
Sen, Sudipta, 56, 249n39
sepoys, 143, 196
Seths, 38, 39
settlers, 40, 63
Seven Years War, 12
Shah Jahan (emperor), 26, 28, 37, 43
Shah Machhandali (popular *pīr*), 86
Shah Shuja, 3, 81

Shaista Khan, 42, 135
Shaivism, 87
Shaktaism, 87
shipbuilding, 61, 133–34
ships: capsized, 10; inland fleets of, 4–5, 64–66; intercontinental, 4; intra-Asiatic, 109; merchant, 65–66, 72; private captains of, 19, 65; wreck of, 133, 140. *See also* boats
Shiva, 24; worship of, 29. *See also* Hinduism
Shore, Frederick, 204
Shuja Khan, 99
Shuja-ud-Daulah, 223
Shujauddin Khan, 10
Sichterman, Jan, 49
silk: *adhapanji*, 158, 174; Bengal production of raw, 11, 19, 148, 154, 165, 178–79, 185; contracts of the EIC with *zamīndārs* to increase cultivation of, 165; enormous power of the EIC in fixing the price of raw, 175–76; Italian method of throwing of, 155; *matkā*, 155–56, 174; *naaij*, 155; *pattani/patti*, 152–53, 156, 158, 169–72, 175, 177–78, 183; rearing of, 151–53, 179; soaps for washing raw, 73; *stik*, 155; *tanna banna*, 152–53; *tanny*, 152–53, 155, 157, 170; trade in raw, 4, 11, 148, 154, 177–79. *See also* silk reelers
silk reelers, 2–5, 19, 63, 148–85, 239–40; conversion by the EIC of sections of the peasant population into working as, 184–85; customary labor practices of, 237; as early form of capitalist labor relations on factory floors, 150–51, 157, 160–61, 170–71, 184; family ties of, 164–66; filature system for the reeling of, 12, 148–55, 166–67, 170, 177–79, 184–85, 240; impressment of, 168–69, 174, 176; indebtedness endemic among, 55, 159–62; industrial aspirations of the European companies regarding, 149–50, 185; and the intercompany rivalry between the VOC and EIC, 42, 148, 150, 155, 162, 167–76; loss of power for artisan-waged worker-reelers, 148, 150; mass desertion of the, 16, 163, 167–76; migrant workers as, 158, 162, 168–69; mobility of, 161–77, 185;

monopolistic control over labor in the industry of, 12, 161–76, 180, 184–85, 232; order of the EIC collector of revenues to stop the *zamīndārs* in the Rangpur region from exacting levies from the, 180; Piedmontese filature technology for the work of, 152, 154–55, 164–66, 174, 176–80, 183–85; position in Bengali society of, 13, 149–50; re-reeling in the work of, 149–54, 161–66, 177–79, 182, 184–85; techniques of local, 12, 149–52; theft of silk by the, 183–85; working from home by, 169–71. *See also cuttanies*; desertion; Dutch East India Company (VOC); labor; manufactories; *nacauds*; recruitment; silk; trade; wages; workers
Singh, Devi, 182
Singha, Radhika, 187
Sinha, Nitin, 187, 288n13, 288n15
Siṅhala, 102
sipahis, 13, 111, 144–46, 196, 201, 217
Siraj ud-Daulah, 111, 135, 168
sirdars, 18, 172, 182, 211
Sitakund, 50, 64, 71, 101. *See also* Bengal
Sītala, 24
slavery/servility, 1–2, 5–8, 15; British imperial abolition of, 14; and caste mobility, 5; caste relations for Marx as, 5; and caste servility, 233; debt, 55; household, 8, 57; trade in, 221; various relations of, 2, 7–8, 18, 236. *See also* labor
Slot Aldegonde (ship), 139
Smith, Edward, 179
smiths, 5, 32–33, 72, 100
Sobha Singh, 42, 67
soldiers: artisanal backgrounds of, 108; death and desertion among, 115; debauching of, 127–28; Eastern, 110–11; European, 2–7, 16, 18–19, 63, 107–47, 186–230, 275n28; indebtedness endemic among, 122–23; Indian, 7; mercantilist disdain for the lack of discipline among European, 132–33; mestizo, 110–11; mobility of, 130; Mughal state holding their officers personally liable for errant, 54; proscribing the mobility of, 45; recruitment of, 14, 217; sickness of, 126. *See also* desertion; military; sailors

Sourbuts, Captain, 52
South Asia: identifying vessels in, 266n36; "proto-capitalism" in eighteenth-century, 150; silk reelers as the earliest documented contract workers of, 158–59. *See also* Asia
spatial boundaries, 45–46. *See also* labor
Stanziani, Alessandro, 7
states: garrison, 290n40; and labor, 10–19, 211; lack of centralized authority of the, 56; limits of European companies as, 22, 63; mobile hired work and the Bengal, 20–63. *See also* Dutch East India Company (VOC); English East India Company (EIC); Mughal state; Nawabi state; law
Statute of Laborers and Artificers (1565), 95, 233
Stern, Philip, 11, 35, 252n7
storms, 104
straggling, 140; as nuisance for the VOC and the EIC, 140. *See also* time
Strutton, Captain, 140
subahdar, 10
subahs, 43
subalterns, 22, 214
Subrahmanyam, Sanjay, 136
Sufism, 23, 87, 90; Sufic preachers, 85
Sunderbans, 65, 72–73, 98, 101, 207; desertion of rowers in the leg of the journey through the, 104, 206. *See also* Bengal
Sunderman, Isaac, 112–13
surveillance, 3, 14; of boatmen, 205, 235; machinery of, 186, 191, 206, 216, 239; measures of, 223–24, 226, 228. *See also* police
Swarnalatha, Potukuchi, 214
Swift, Jonathan, 234

ta'alluqdārs, 16, 27–29, 43, 54; as land settlers, 27–28; small, 61. *See also zamīndārs*
tageedars, 182
Taillefert, Louis, 36, 49
tanners, 231
taverns, 117–18
taxation, 81. *See also* wages
teleology, 149

terracotta panels on temples, 89, 89*fig.*, 115, 116*fig.* *See also* art
Ter Schelling (ship), 10, 133–35, 137
textiles, 8, 11, 73, 178
thakurdālān, 137
Thames river, 236–38. *See also* London
thāna, 48, 192, 201; Cātoā, 50; nineteenth-century *thana*-magistrate coordination in recruitment, 194
thanadar, 204
Thomas, Gardiner, 221
Thompson, E. P., 98
tigers, 86
time: conditions of work including wages and, 12; reclaiming by sailors of, 140; "right," 16. *See also* straggling
Tombelle, John, 193, 200
trade: from Asia to Europe, 8, 34; in Bengal, 4, 8; EIC branch involved in China, 189; global textile, 11; high levels of commercialization through global, 56; overseas/overland silk markets for long-distance, 151, 184; regional politics of overseas, 100, 220; sailors and soldiers as the "pillars of any commonwealth" for flourishing through, 107; whole world of, 166. *See also* merchants; silk reelers
transport brieven, 126–27
tughra style, 32

ulak boats, 65, 73–74, 76, 76*fig.*, 117. *See also* boats
untouchables, 55, 61
Ure, Andrew, 185
Utilitarians, 17, 214

Vaishnava *pada*, 88–89
Vaishnavism: Bengal, 20, 23, 87–90, 92; Gaudiya, 20; Gauṛiya, 90; intersection of Islam and, 270n112; Kartābhajā sect of, 90; popular movements of, 100; terracotta motifs on primarily Vaishnavite brick temples, 89, 89*fig.*; theologies of orthodox Gauṛiya, 87, 89–90
van Bevenage, Christaan, 97, 103
van Dam, Pieter, 152–53
van den Broecke, Matheus, 155
van den Brouk, Mattheus, 148

van den Burg, Leendert, 117
van der Helling, Commander, 50, 72
van der Huis, Jan Janszen, 33
van Mollen, Daniel, 155, 164
van Rheede, Hendrik Adriaan, 155–56, 159
van Schyulenburgh, Hendrik: "A picture of the VOC's trading post or the headquarters in Bengal in the city Hugli" (painting), 36, 36*fig*.
Vansittart, George, 9, 165–66, 178
vereering, 101. *See also* wages
Verpoorten, Johan, 162
violence: European colonial, 3, 205; of labor discipline by the police and military, 14, 187–205, 228–30, 239; language of, 174, 230; as perpetrated by the EIC army, 187, 200–205, 207; police and magistrate criticism of army, 202–3, 207; as rule of terror of the *darogahs* as the magistrates' recruiters on the ground, 197–99. *See also* recruitment
Vishnu, 100
Visnupala: *Manasāmaṅgal*, 29
Vreem, Jacob, 122

wages, 98, 188; advance payment to boatmen of full, 212; creating a controlled market for labor to bring down, 197, 216; customs with political significance surrounding, 99–106, 212–13, 237; of European sailors and soldiers in the service of the VOC or EIC, 112, 133–34, 140–41; and food money for boatmen, 212; medieval nonwage/share system applying only to fishermen, whalemen, privateersmen, and pirates by the early eighteenth century, 112; as revenue exemptions for silk reelers, 179–82, 240; rise for European company officials in the eighteenth century of, 111; of silk reelers in the service of the VOC or EIC, 168, 173, 175–76, 178–85; as site of customary rights, 98, 216, 237; stalling desertion through better, 210. See also *bakśiś*; boatmen; *porsia*; reward; silk reelers; taxation; *vereering*; workers
wakīls, 134, 158, 163
Walī Beg, 131

Washbrook, David, 6, 56
wealth: agrarian, 28; employment of servants as index of, 28; formalization of leases and agrarian, 28–29; inequality of, 22, 26
weavers, 8, 13; as settlers in Calcutta, 40
Weber, Max, 32
Wilder, James, 176
Wilkinson, John, 183–84
William III (king), 121
Williamson, George, 151
Wintle, James, 14, 201–3, 207–9
Wiss, James, 178, 182
women: free Christian, 39; as household workers, 8, 236–37; molestation of, 84; sexual labor of, 236; as workers on construction sites, 5
woodcutting, 59, 82
workers: advance payment system as condition for hire of, 104–5, 159; commercialization and mobility of, 22, 187; hired, 63; notions of customary rights and privileges in the premodern or precolonial period among, 98, 230, 237; patron-client relationship with their employers of, 62–63; transport, 103; *zamīndārs* as the primary force for settling and regulating, mobilizing and immobilizing, the lives of, 63. See also *banians*; boatmen; coolies; indigenous peoples; labor; migrant workers; mobility; peasants; peons; recruitment; silk reelers; wages; working class
working class, as political force in nationalist and anticolonial struggle, 1; as working class the interests of workers often at odds with the interests of the state, 108. *See also* India; labor; peasants; workers
Workman's Breach of Contract Act (1859), 1, 16

Xenophon: *Oeconomicus*, 57, 236

Yamuna river, 202
yogic practices, 90

zamīndārs, 10–22, 27–35, 43, 47–52, 63, 81, 229; as absolute proprietors of their land

zamīndārs (continued)
holdings, 14, 36; Burdwan, 35; Calcutta, 106; Dinajpur, 49; diplomatic relations among the, 50; East India companies like other *zamīndārs* in the region regularly solicited for manpower, 134–35; erosion of the power of the Bengal, 186, 194, 234; European companies (VOC and EIC) as, 21–22, 34–43, 62–63, 109, 134; jurisdiction of the, 50, 73, 188, 194, 213–14, 234; as land settlers, 27–28, 55; Laskarpur, 170; levies from the silk reelers exacted by local, 180–82, 212; local system of Mughal, 35, 47–52, 63, 80–93, 100, 186, 199, 203, 234; markets as extensions of the patrimonies of, 56; military power of the, 51; of Muhammad Aminpur, 50; *peshkashi*, 58; rebellion by native, 42, 47–48, 67, 119, 133; rights for merchants as, 35; share in revenue of the, 258n114; small, 61; as solicited for recruitment of labor, 204; untrustworthy nature of, 81. *See also* Dutch East India Company (VOC); English East India Company (EIC); *ta'alluqdārs*

Ẓiā-ud-dīn Khān, 131

Founded in 1893,
UNIVERSITY OF CALIFORNIA PRESS
publishes bold, progressive books and journals
on topics in the arts, humanities, social sciences,
and natural sciences—with a focus on social
justice issues—that inspire thought and action
among readers worldwide.

The UC PRESS FOUNDATION
raises funds to uphold the press's vital role
as an independent, nonprofit publisher, and
receives philanthropic support from a wide
range of individuals and institutions—and from
committed readers like you. To learn more, visit
ucpress.edu/supportus.

www.ingramcontent.com/pod-product-compliance
Lightning Source LLC
Chambersburg PA
CBHW021336230426
43666CB00006B/312